BARBARA KETCHAM WHEATON

SAVOURING

THE PAST

The French Kitchen and Table from 1300 to 1789

CHATTO & WINDUS

THE HOGARTH PRESS

LONDON

Published by
Chatto & Windus: The Hogarth Press
40 William IV Street
London WC2N 4DF

First published in Great Britain 1983 by Chatto & Windus Ltd.

First published in the United States 1983 by the University of Pennsylvania Press.

Copyright © 1983 by the University of Pennsylvania Press

ISBN 0 7011 3920 X

Printed in the United States of America

TO
ROBERT WHEATON

Contents

List of Illustrations

Acknowledgments

In twenty years of studying culinary history I have incurred many debts which it is a pleasure to acknowledge. The director of the Schlesinger Library, Patricia M. King, its curator of printed books, Barbara Haber, and the entire staff have made using it a continuing pleasure. I have also been greatly helped by the staffs of many other parts of the Harvard College Libraries, especially the Houghton Library, Widener Library, the Fogg Museum Library, the Harvard Theatre Collection, and the Kress Library; their riches are legendary, and I could not have written this book without them. I am also deeply grateful to the Bibliothèque nationale in Paris for two years spent with its incomparable collection of French cookbooks. The Special Collections Department of the Iowa State University Library in Ames, Iowa, provided me with material I have found nowhere else. Eleanor Sayre and her staff in the Print Room of the Museum of Fine Arts, Boston, were endlessly helpful in guiding me through the museum's astonishing holdings. I am glad to thank the photographic services departments of the Fogg Museum, the Museum of Fine Arts, Boston, and the Iowa State University Library.

I also want to express my gratitude to the many people who have helped and encouraged me. Among them are Jean Benton, Narcissa Chamberlain and the late Samuel Chamberlain, Jeanette Cheek, Julia Child, Natalie Zemon Davis, Ruth and Jonathon Liebowitz, David R. Miller, Steven Raichlen, David Segal, Pauline Shannon, and Joyce Toomre. I am deeply indebted to the Culinary Historians of Boston who took part in an eighteenth-century-style dinner based largely on recipes from this book, and to my family and friends who are, even now, willing to taste—and comment on—my experiments. At the University of Pennsylvania Press Ingalill Hjelm and Jo Mugnolo have been patient and unfailingly helpful; Trudie Calvert's keen copyeditor's eye has been a great asset.

From the very beginning I have enjoyed the interest and support of my mother, Ruth V. S. Lauer. Above all, I am profoundly grateful to Robert Wheaton, without whom I would never have set out to write this book, could not have continued, and most certainly would never have finished.

Introduction

What! one may perhaps say, yet another work on cookery?
For some years now the public has been inundated by a flood
of writings of this kind.

Le Manuel des officiers de bouche, 1759

THE AUTHOR of the *Manuel* was presenting his book to orient organizers of fine meals in the extensive territory of eighteenth-century French cookery. This present book is intended to help the cook, the historian, and the student of French civilization orient themselves in the largely uncharted terrain of France's culinary history from the end of the thirteenth century to the outbreak of the Revolution in 1789. I also hope to encourage others to read the cookbooks and try the recipes so as to discover the place of cooking and gastronomy in the nation's culture. Ironically, very little serious study has been made of the history of one of the finest culinary traditions in the world.

EARLY WORKS IN FRENCH CULINARY HISTORY

The first extensive history of French cooking was written in 1782 by Pierre Jean Baptiste Le Grand d'Aussy as part of a projected treatise on the private life of the French.[1] His antiquarian interests led him to focus on the distant past rather than his own time, about which he could have told us much, but he did amass a substantial body of information and misinformation that has been mined by other writers ever since. The nineteenth century saw the publication of several culinary guides, beginning with C. Verdot's alphabetically arranged *Historiographie de la table* (1833) and the marquis de Cussy's little essay, "L'Art culinaire" (1844), both of which contain a good bit of chaff. Louis Nicolardot's *Histoire de la table* (1886) is little better. The most widely circulated nineteenth-century work containing information about the cooking of the past was undoubtedly Alexandre Dumas's *Grand dictionnaire de cuisine*, published posthumously in 1873. Fact and fancy alike are embraced in its pages, including the widely believed myths about Catherine de Medici's influential cooks and Sir Francis Drake's equally suppositious introduction of the potato into the Old World, along with a wealth of infor-

mation drawn from Dumas's experiences. Alfred Franklin's long series under the general title *La Vie privée d'autrefois* includes volumes of great interest
to the culinary historian.[2] He rarely allowed himself to generalize but assiduously published extracts from manuscripts and rare books. These compi-
lations and essays make available information that is otherwise very hard to
come by. Collectors and philologists turned their attention to cookbooks as
well. In 1846 Baron Jérôme Pichon published the key to medieval cookery,
the *Ménagier de Paris*, of which he had a copy in his fabled collection. In
collaboration with Georges Vicaire, Pichon also gave the *Viandier* the thoroughly edited publication its multiple versions deserved.[3] Students of the
language, such as Louis Douët d'Arcq, also published cookbooks because
they were a source of little-known words.[4] The most extensive history of
cooking is Armand Lebault's *La Table et le repas à travers les siècles* (1910),
which takes the reader from ancient Egyptian times through to the Romans
and then narrows the focus to France, a pattern that has been followed often
since. Lebault drew heavily on Le Grand's work but corrected old errors,
such as those about the origins of the turkey and the dating of the *Viandier*.

Among the cooks and restaurateurs who have attempted to write the
history of their craft the most valuable contributions have been made by
Bertrand Guégan, Raymond Oliver, and Anne Willan.[5] In the first volume
of his two-volume *La Fleur de la cuisine française* (1920–21) Guégan gives
extracts from important cookbooks and related works from the Middle Ages
to 1800. But Guégan's most important contribution is "Notes sur l'histoire
de la cuisine française," which appeared in his *Le Cuisinier français* (1934). He
brought to his subject a cook's understanding, which enabled him to see it
with a new precision. His evaluations of the classics of French cooking often
differ sharply with accepted judgments. The craft had not previously been
studied by a practitioner, and therefore its mechanisms had been ignored.
Similarly, Raymond Oliver, in *Gastronomy of France* (1967) drew on his own
practical experiences, the traditions of a great restaurant, and familiarity with
his notable collection of cookbooks. The best recent study by a practicing
cook is Anne Willan's *Great Cooks and Their Recipes* (1977), which has chapters on Taillevent, François Pierre de La Varenne, and Menon. Although she
does not give a systematic survey of the development of French cooking,
her awareness of the limits and potentialities of the craft makes her observations valuable. Finally, the periodical *Petits Propos Culinaires* regularly pub-

lishes articles on culinary history; it has appeared since 1979 under the editorship of Alan Davidson and Elizabeth David.[6]

A genre of anecdotal histories of cooking focusing on the personalities of the French court have as their underlying assumption the idea that most famous dishes were invented by famous people.[7] My favorite example is the story that puff pastry was invented by the painter Claude Lorrain.[8] Born in the province of Lorraine in 1600, he was apprenticed to a pastrycook and in this capacity went to Rome at the age of twelve. Shortly after his arrival in Italy his artistic talents became so conspicuous that he left his original trade for the artist's studio, never to return. The mere fact of his brief stint in the craft, combined with the long-held belief that pastrycooks from Lorraine were especially gifted, were enough to suggest to imaginative writers that puff pastry ought to be the invention of a great artist from that country.[9]

I shall pass in silence over many such legends that are both implausible and unprovable. The question of the forms taken by court meals is a different matter. They are considered here when they have some significance for the further history of the table. The reader wishing specific details about the service and menus of meals at the courts of most of France's rulers will find them in the volumes of the Hachette series, *La Vie quotidienne*.[10] This series is also a good source for descriptions of the lives of ordinary people; it covers most periods of French history, as well as many other places at significant moments, and many of the volumes have been translated into English.

THE REVIVAL OF CULINARY HISTORY

The history of cooking and dining have begun to achieve marginal recognition in the last two decades as legitimate aspects of social history and consequently as suitable for serious scholarly investigation. Curiosity about the food of the past has developed partly out of increased interest in food preparation among the affluent consumer-oriented societies of postwar Europe and America. Cultural exchange programs familiarized academicians with exotic cuisines. The enormously influential historical school associated with the French journal *Annales: Economies, Sociétés, Civilisations* stimulated academic research into both the material and cultural conditions of everyday life. Beginning before World War II, the founders of the *Annales*, Marc Bloch and Lucien Febvre, published articles recommending the study of diet, ingredients, and food habits.[11] The sources used by the Annalistes are generally archival documents, such as wills, inventories, and the household accounts of individuals and institutions. These documents supply information about how much of what ingredients were eaten by members of different classes at various times and places. They rarely tell about how foods were prepared or how cooked dishes were combined in menus, though this information is needed to assess the nutritional levels of populations.

Among the notable examples of the use of information about diet are Emmanuel Le Roy Ladurie's *Les Paysans de Languedoc*, various sections of *Histoire économique et sociale de la France* by Ernest Labrousse, Pierre Léon, et al., and Fernand Braudel's *La Méditerranée*. Many important articles on food from the *Annales* have been collected by Jean-Jacques Hémardinquer, a major researcher in the field, in a Cahiers des Annales volume, *Pour une histoire de l'alimentation*. A selection of these has been translated into English as *Food and Drink in History*.[12] A series of essays directed to the general reader has appeared in *L'Histoire*; most of them have been written by another Annaliste historian, J.-L. Flandrin, under the pen name Platine.[13]

In a parallel but largely independent development, historians have increasingly been influenced by the approach of cultural anthropologists to the study of society. Cultural anthropology has long recognized the social importance of food and dining as a means of exchange and communication and as a means of expressing both social stratification and social solidarity.[14] Crises in higher education in America have led academicians in the humanities to seek subjects with a direct appeal to students in what came to be known, alas, as "the hands-on experience." The French saying, *il faut mettre le main à la pâte*, is singularly appropriate to the practice of culinary history.

As historians have turned to the history of the family, especially the role of women, it has become increasingly useful to know something about women's work. The preservation and preparation of food has made up a substantial part of most women's lives, and meals are a focal point for the interplay of relationships within the family. Whatever a woman's cooking ability, her cookery flavored her family's life.

Although the vogue for cooking in the French manner has ebbed somewhat as women have sought work outside the home, a considerable number of people, both male and female, have set themselves exacting standards for the practice of their craft. This is true both of people cooking professionally and of those cooking for their own delight. They also are curious about the history of food. Information is hard to come by because few libraries, especially outside of France, have prerevolutionary French-language cookbooks.[15] Recipes have to be studied in the double context of the techniques of the craft and the cultural circumstances of their time of origin. I am convinced that the kitchen and the table must be studied together. The meal is better understood if we understand the food served; the cookery is of interest only to cooks and gastronomes (and in some instances masochists) until we know the setting in which it is eaten and its significance to the diners.

The character of this book has been shaped by the diversity and unevenness of the sources. In the five-hundred-year span considered here, few or no cookbooks appeared during some periods and an abundance appeared in others.[16] There is little helpful literary material before the sixteenth century, and few journals or diaries mention food. Still-life painting with useful culinary subject matter was not produced until the seventeenth century, but by the eighteenth visual representations were, if anything, overabundant.

Cookbooks, necessarily the principal source, are curious documents. It is remarkable that any were written in the earlier centuries, because so few cooks were able to write or to read them. The question of who wrote, read, and used cookbooks will repeatedly arise in the following pages. As the repertory of dishes grew, from the mid-seventeenth century onward, the utility of a written support to the cook's memory increased, just as having the ability to fix formulas in print gave the imaginative cook a chance at wider fame.

A recipe artificially isolates the actions and ingredients needed to prepare a single dish. In a real kitchen many dishes are being prepared at the same time, and work processes and ingredients for them overlap. A recipe is a cross-section of a portion of the work going forward in a kitchen. From it one can begin to get a sense of how cooking was done. By using many recipes from a particular time and place one can acquire an idea of work patterns and of the resultant character of the style of cooking. Such specific analysis provides the foundation for broader comparisons.

The study of regional styles of cooking is not yet sufficiently advanced to make possible a survey of their history. The best work, most of which has appeared in the *Annales*, has dealt with geographically restricted areas, often drawing on a few local sources. Archives and published documents with references to food are rare, and meaningful descriptions of food preparation processes carried on by and for the less affluent classes are almost nonexistent. Culinary history is the history of ephemeral social events. This difficulty is compounded because for most of the centuries under consideration here both the practitioners and the consumers were largely illiterate. Some work has been done by folklorists, but they often find it hard to uncover detailed information that unambiguously dates from before the nineteenth century. There is a tendency to invoke a time called "autrefois" which, when specified, is often octogenarians' memories of their childhoods. Though fascinating, these seldom go back to the eighteenth century. The best of the folklorists, such as Per Jakez Hélias, in *The Horse of Pride* (French edition, 1975), do not try.[17] The engrossing question, "What were the regional cuisines of prerevolutionary France?" is often asked with the anachronistic expectation that one will learn about succulent delicacies like the ones we can enjoy today. I fear that the true picture will prove to be very different. R.-J. Bernard's "Peasant Diet in Eighteenth-century Gévaudan" documents endemic malnutrition interrupted occasionally by richly enjoyed feasts and death-dealing famine.[18] A study of the use of different kinds of cooking fats in the provinces of France which appeared in the *Annales* in 1961 shows a substantial difference between ideal and practice.[19] Waverley Root, in *The Food of France* (1958), described a nation divided into the realms of butter, cream, olive oil, goose fat, and others.[20] The *Annales* maps, which are based on responses to surveys of actual usages in 1914, 1936, and 1952, show that regional differences are not sharply defined but that economic necessity, rather than traditional preferences, often dictates the use of margarine and the cheaper vegetable oils.[21] Even the legendary peasant pig has faded away (like the Cheshire cat?) in the light of research. J.-J. Hémardinquer demolishes the idea that most peasant families were able to keep pigs.[22] Inventories show that livestock was in short supply, especially pigs. The scarcity of regional *charcuterie* recipes in the cookbooks thus reflects a lack of opportunity to practice with the ingredients.

The history of diet in the regions of France can be written before the history of styles of cooking. Meanwhile, the materials are at hand with which to follow the histories of *haute cuisine* and *cuisine bourgeoise*, twin aspects of a single tradition.

Four Centuries of Fine French Cooking

The chronology followed below is based on the cookbooks because they are the only source detailed enough to supply much necessary information, but the precision implied by their dates of publication is misleading. Cookery, like many crafts, is very conservative; cookbooks take (or should take) years of practice and experimentation to write. Once they are written they may remain in print for years and in use for yet more. Outright plagiarism is a permanent feature of cookbooks, with the result that individual recipes often have life spans reaching across the publishing histories of more than one writer's books. It is the aim of this study to bring some order to the field, to suggest areas for future research, and to encourage cook and historian alike to explore these rich materials. Indeed, anyone who pursues the bibliographical references in this introduction will be well on the way to writing a better history.

In the late Middle Ages the French cookery for which records have survived was similar to that of other western European countries. It was essentially an international cuisine centered around courts. Diners were more interested in the overall effect of a meal than in specific dishes, and the cooking methods usually were simple. By the end of the sixteenth century changes began to take place, particularly in the technically more demanding fields of confectionary and baking. Only by the middle of the seventeenth century did records become sufficiently abundant and clear that the development of classic French cuisine, both for aristocratic tables and for those of the bourgeoisie and prosperous country dwellers, can be traced. While cooks were refining their skills, diners' attitudes were changing. An interest in health was a permanent theme from the sixteenth century onward, replacing earlier concerns about the sin of gluttony. Writers used references to food to signal character traits, social class, and mood. In the seventeenth century technique began to crystallize in a modular way of combining work and ingredients to permit the use of both to provide efficiently executed and infinitely variable dishes and meals. This mental attitude was congruous with other aspects of seventeenth- and eighteenth-century French thought. By the eighteenth century France enjoyed the reputation for having the finest cooks and the best food in Europe. Many of the recipes developed by then have continued to be a part of the national traditions: omelets, bouillon, soups, sauces, pastries. But the great achievement of *ancien régime* cooks was the development of a systematic procedure and a multiplicity of basic mixtures such as stocks and flavoring mixtures that could be used to build meals without reference to written recipes. In the following pages, this complex and irregular development will be traced.

CHAPTER ONE

The Middle Ages

VERY PERIOD of French history has a characteristic meal type. In the Middle Ages it was the feast; in the sixteenth century, the collation; in the seventeenth century, the fête; and in the eighteenth, the intimate supper. The medieval banquet, the flavors of which are least acceptable to modern taste, has appealed most vividly to the modern imagination and has been the most frequently revived. It is exotic and spectacular, and its underlying principles are radically different from those of meals. Seduced by the medieval idea that if something is beautiful it must be good to eat, adventurous cooks and diners believe that if the art of the Middle Ages is attractive, its food will be similarly charming. In fact, the sharp sensation of difference is a reminder of how long ago the fourteenth century was and how very alien are its sensations.

Medieval banquets were exceptional events, the realizations of aesthetic and social ideals. Contemporary chroniclers do not speak of individual dishes; they do not even give menus. They describe appearances, not flavors, the sequence of events, not the dishes. Olivier de La Marche, for example, helped plan two of the most notable *festins* of the fifteenth century: the Feast of the Pheasant in 1453 and the festivities accompanying the marriage of Charles the Bold, duke of Burgundy, to Margaret of York in 1468. Fortunately, his accounts of these events have survived.[1] He describes the clothes, jousts, music, and decorations, but he does not say what was eaten. Even the pheasant at the Feast of the Pheasant did not figure in the menu: that celebrated bird, on which courtiers swore Crusaders' oaths, was alive and surely very much puzzled. About the food, Olivier says that it was "rich and copious," "very richly served," "rich and stately . . . with a multiplicity of dishes and of foods."[2] He does not describe the meal as an occasion for enjoying sequences of flavors; neither the ingredients nor their preparation attracted his attention. Rather, the occasion is seen as the core around which revolve other activities.

Just as church sacraments were enriched with music, visual display, and ritual, so the banquet, the secular counterpart of the Eucharist, took place at the center of a multitude of related activities: spectacles of costume, tapestry, and precious materials and the performance of dance, music, and theater, often incorporating elaborate allegorical meanings. In the excitement, confusion, and din of the hall, no one had much attention to spare for nuances in the flavoring of the food. Even the quantities may not have been so enormous as is generally believed, if one may judge from the consistently sparse amounts of food on tables in manuscript illuminations. The large amounts of food that account books record were bought for banquets must be adjusted to take into consideration not only the often unstated number of diners but also reuse and pilferage.

Such feasts were the outcome of long and careful preparation. Work began months in advance on the wedding festivities for Charles and Margaret. Major renovations undertaken on the ducal palace in Bruges included extensive improvements to the kitchen and related offices.[3] New work tables were installed in the main kitchen and its floor was entirely repaved with stone blocks, a durable, foot-punishing surface that was to remain the standard in most prosperous kitchens through the eighteenth century. Down an adjacent spiral stone stairway, two brick cellars were made for storing staples and jellied dishes. Another set of wooden stairs led to the cooks' room above. Nearby, the butchers' workplace was tiled to serve as an extra storeroom. There was no time to build a permanent roof over the four big ovens that, as was the custom, were set apart from the main building because of fear of fire.

The great hall in which most of the dinners and suppers were held had been prefabricated earlier in the year in Brussels and brought by water to Bruges to be used for a meeting of the Order of the Golden Fleece.[4] The hall alone measured 140 by 70 feet. The head table stood on a dais at one end of the hall; two other tables ran lengthwise down the room. In the center was a buffet decorated with tapestry. Four "unicorn horns" (in truth, from narwhales), greatly valued in the Middle Ages for their rareness and magical properties, stood at the corners of the buffet. It supported a dazzling display of gem-studded gold and silver work, a dramatic reminder of the great wealth of the Valois dukes of Burgundy. Along one side of the hall was a gallery, hung with tapestries, from which ladies could watch the proceedings. The sexes were often segregated at medieval banquets; women were more often the spectators than men.

Every day for a week there was a sumptuous midday dinner, followed by an afternoon of jousting.[5] Each night there was a banquet, though some of the guests still ached from the events of the afternoon. After the banquet ended the tables were dismantled and there was dancing, except on Friday (a fast day), and one other night, when the diners did not rise from table until three o'clock in the morning. Perhaps only then were they sober enough to stand up.

These festivities, albeit of exceptional splendor, reflect many of the characteristics of fourteenth-century aristocratic dining. The fourteenth-century hall was sparsely furnished; the functional specialization of rooms in European domestic architecture came about only gradually between the thirteenth and the nineteenth centuries. The hall's chief piece of furniture was the buffet, where *objets de luxe* were conspicuously displayed and wine and water were dispensed. Rather than a permanent dinner table, for each meal, boards were set on trestles and covered with white damask cloths. The highest-ranking diners sat at a special table, occupying individual chairs. Everyone else sat on benches, in order of precedence. There was a general preference for seating people along one side only. Service was facilitated but, more important, all the diners could observe the spectacle that unfolded during the meal, and, as part of that spectacle themselves, be observed by those in the galleries. A principal reason for going to the expense and trouble of giving feasts was to demonstrate the wealth and power of the host. John Paston was in the crowd that watched the events at Charles's wedding, and he wrote to his mother in England comparing the duke's court to King Arthur's—just what Charles the Bold would have hoped for.[6] The long-term goal of the Valois dukes of Burgundy (already recognized as the "Great Dukes of the West") was the elevation of the duchy to the rank of kingdom. Their lavish entertainments were part of a scheme that included military, diplomatic, and economic efforts.

By modern standards the table was sparsely set. Instead of a plate, each diner had a bread trencher at his place. Trencher bread was baked from whole wheat flour several days before it was to be used. It was sliced with a broad-bladed knife (*tranchoir* in French, hence trencher), then trimmed to a rectangular shape. A high-ranking diner was given four slices; three were arranged in a close triangle, and the fourth was set on top. Exceptionally, the dukes of Burgundy had trenchers made of silver-gilt. The diner put on his trencher the slices of meat he had cut from a large piece, as well as dabs of sauce and

Dives and Lazarus, woodcut, from *Heures a lusaige de Romme* (Paris, 1497). This late fifteenth-century table is set much as a fourteenth-century one would have been. Although the surroundings are opulent, with a heavily laden sideboard in the background, the table itself is sparse. Note the rectangular trenchers. (By permission of the Houghton Library, Harvard University.)

anything of a fairly dry consistency. More liquid foods went into the *écuelle*, a shallow bowl, which was normally shared by two diners. This bowl was the unit of measure used to express the number of diners present; thus a dinner described as being for twenty *écuelles* would be for forty diners. People used knives and spoons but normally not forks, though a few gold ones appear in the royal French inventories of the fourteenth and fifteenth centuries and in similar inventories of the dukes of Burgundy, where they are described as being for mulberries.[7] Presumably ducal fingers could be greasy but not stained. An elegant feature on royal tables was knives and spoons keyed to the church calendar. Lent was marked by ebony-handled utensils, Easter by ivory, and Pentecost by a combination of the two.[8] As a rule, though, tables were not laid with much attention to regularity or symmetry. Drinking vessels were not set at individuals' places. Instead, the thirsty diner summoned a page from the buffet and indicated to him the desired proportion of wine and water. It was uncommon and even incorrect to take wine undiluted. If the diner had sopped his bread in the wine, etiquette required that he either drink the whole amount or pour the unwanted liquid onto the floor.[9] The page then returned the container to the buffet and rinsed it for reuse. Linen napkins were plentifully supplied so that diners could keep their hands and mouths reasonably tidy. Salt cellars of pewter, glass, silver, or gold, according to the wealth of the host, were supplied but were not yet accompanied by pepper pots. The concept of sitting "below the salt" was not in force: usually several salts were set at intervals along the table. If a particularly magnificent salt cellar was in use, it would be set before the highest-ranking diner as a recognition of his or her status.

The glory of the medieval table was the *nef*—a ship made of silver or silver-gilt. It sometimes included a salt cellar or even held a great personage's knife, spoon, and napkin, but its primary function was to indicate by its magnificence the eminence of the diner by whose place it stood.[10]

The setting for the medieval feast, then, consisted of a great hall, hung with tapestry, diners sitting at trestle tables on benches, with little at their places save bread, a bowl, a knife, and a spoon, and spectators and musicians standing by to observe and enliven the proceedings. As soon as the meal was announced, a lavish sequence of events began.[11]

The feast opened with a trumpet fanfare. The guests entered and took part in a handwashing ceremony. As they held their hands over a basin, herb-scented water was poured over them by a page who then proffered a linen napkin. When the diners were all in place, a Latin benediction was said by the chaplain and the dinner was brought in, though the food was probably none too warm, even if the dishes had been covered. The kitchens were at a distance because of the danger of fire. No one ate until the king or duke had begun, and a person of such rank neither ate nor drank anything until everything had been assayed for the presence of poison. Covering the dishes when they came from the kitchen and accompanying them with a guard gave some protection. Testing the food with substances having magic sensitivities to poison gave more. Unicorn horn, which was thought to bleed in the presence of impurity, was much favored. Agate was in more frequent use, being easier to obtain, as were various objects alleged to be toadstone—that (nonexistent) precious jewel believed to be hidden in the head of the toad. Salt was tested with serpent's tongue, known more prosaically now to be the tooth of a shark.[12]

Medieval etiquette was founded on the idea that, in principle, everyone had a rank relative to everyone else in society and that if that rank were properly observed he or she would not impinge on the rights and sensibilities of others or be impinged upon. Although a diner was permitted to partake of anything within reach, food, like people, had its social gradations, and at table a person of high position would find choicer viands—more partridge and less porridge—within reach than would a person of lower rank. Etiquette books written for the guidance of youth advise modesty, temperance, and respect.[13]

An examination of the medieval menus in the *Ménagier de Paris* shows no obvious organizing principles, and the menus always include some items not in any of the cookbooks. Nonetheless, a characteristic meat-day dinner menu is as follows:

For the first course: fish-liver turnovers; a meat stew with a sharp cinnamon sauce; ox-marrow fritters; eel stew; loach [a freshwater fish of the carp family] in broth with a green sage sauce; a large piece of meat; and ocean fish.

For the second course: roast, the best available, and freshwater fish; a piece of meat, larded and boiled; a spiced chopped meat dish garnished with crayfish tails; capon pasties and crisp pancakes; bream [another freshwater fish] pasties; eels; and blancmange.

For the third course: frumenty [wheat berries boiled in broth]; venison; lamprey with a hot sauce; *lechefrites* [no recipe is available, but presumably they were cooked in the dripping pan, or *lechefrite*, under the roast]; roast breams and turnovers; sturgeon in aspic.[14]

Some meals ended with the *issue de table*, a course corresponding to the modern dessert (from the French *desservir*, meaning to clear the table at the end of the meal). Usually offered after the cloth had been removed, it consisted chiefly of hypocras (a spiced wine) and wafers, sometimes with raisins, nuts, and a little fruit. As a special luxury there might be comfits; aniseeds coated with sugar were well regarded. Apart from this final course, which was not a regular feature of meals, the allocation of particular dishes among courses seems to have been nearly random.

The mechanics of dining were fairly simple.[15] A typical main dish consisted of several kinds of meat tumbled together on a platter—a form of presentation later called *service en confusion*. The diner cut off slices of moderate size, taking them with thumb and two fingers, not with a greasy fist. One was not supposed to return unwanted pieces to the common dish or to dip meat directly into the salt cellar. Sauces were pungent and thick; mustards were used heavily. The diner put a spoonful of sauce on his trencher and then dabbed the meat in it. Pies were an important part of the meal, with the crust serving more as a container than as a food. As any baker of freestanding pies knows, tenderness must often be sacrificed for structural strength. For venison pies, which were expected to make repeated trips to the table over several weeks, a rye pastry was used. In serving a pie, the carver cut straight down around the top crust, just inside the pie's vertical wall. Either the entire lid was removed or sections of it were cut or broken away. The diners could then reach in with hand, spoon, or knife, depending upon the consistency of the filling. Rummaging with the hand would have helped distinguish meat from bone, which was commonly not removed from meat, poultry, or even fish. The more liquid foods, such as soups and hashes, went into the bowl to be eaten with a spoon. The sources do not tell how a pair of diners decided what to put into the bowl or how they shared it.

While the diners ate, they observed the spectacle that was performed between courses. The course was called a *met*; the activities between courses were therefore the entremets. The contemporary English term was "soteltie." The subjects, however, were not always subtle, as when a woman in childbirth was depicted as a soteltie for a wedding. There were two basic types: the plainer was a set piece, made of anything from pastry or butter to wood and canvas; the more elaborate ones (the entremets *mouvants*) included automatons or live participants. They were amalgams of song, theater, mechanics, and carpentry, combined to convey an allegorical fantasy or even a political message. The execution of a series of entremets for important festivities occupied large numbers of people. The preparations for the entertainments at the wedding of Charles the Bold brought craftsmen to Bruges for weeks at a time—painters, sculptors, carpenters, and wax modelers by the dozens. The banquet entremets displayed the ducal wealth; their imaginativeness revealed the mentality of a culture. At the Feast of the Pheasant, for example, Philip the Fair was trying, at least ostensibly, to induce his guests to join him on a crusade to rescue Constantinople from the infidel. Assuming leadership of a crusade, traditionally the role of the Holy Roman emperor, would have enhanced Burgundy's claims to higher political status. A programmatic entremet was enacted to stimulate enthusiasm. A giant Saracen entered, leading an elephant (the chronicle unfortunately does not tell how it was contrived). Seated on the elephant was that excellent knight, co-organizer, and later chronicler of the feast, Olivier de La Marche, playing the role of the captive Eastern church. He wore a long white gown and sang, in a falsetto voice, a moving plea to Duke Philip.[16]

The line between entremets made to be eaten and for allegorical purposes was not strictly observed. At Charles the Bold's festivities a course at one meal consisted of some thirty pies, each enclosed in a silk pavilion and each bearing the name of a walled town under Charles's rule.[17] The visual effect was that of a military encampment; the message was clearly a statement of Charles's military strength. A more pastoral, poetic conception appeared at the last of these wedding feasts.[18] Thirty platters were made up to look like gardens, each with a golden hedge surrounding a different kind of fruit tree; each tree bore the name of a ducal abbey. Around the trees were figures of peasants harvesting the fruit while others held baskets with candied spices and fruit for the guests to eat. Other entremets at these festivities were more fantastic: a court dwarf rode in on the back of a lion and was given to the bride, Margaret of York, to whom it sang a song and presented a daisy (in French, *marguerite*); they were followed by a dromedary ridden by Indians who released live birds to fly around the hall. There were also automatons and a whale containing musicians.

How are we to understand these festivities? Johann Huizinga, usually sensitive to the nuances of late medieval expression, wrote that it is "difficult to regard these entertainments as something more than exhibitions of almost incredible bad taste," and he describes the feast as a "barbarous manifestation."[19] I would suggest instead that the medieval banquet be regarded as would an illuminated manuscript page of the same period. The manuscript page is composed of several elements. The written text, the content of which gives rise to the illuminations, is likely to be plain or only moderately embellished; an elaborate initial letter is followed by legible, uniform script. The framed illustration puts the significance vividly before the reader, who, in the fourteenth century, may well have given more attention to the picture than to the written word. Smaller images elsewhere on the page may represent other ideas associated more or less appropriately with the principal subject. Further fantastic ornaments and drolleries seem to reflect free—often very free—associations in the illuminator's mind.

The medieval feast contains similar components. Food is analogous to the manuscript text: eating the meal was the occasion for the events that went on around it. As the lettering of the text was of subsidiary importance on the page to the beholder, so the dishes on the tables were only a modest part of the elaborate spectacle. The major entremets *mouvants*, such as the allegorical conquest of Jerusalem, are comparable to the formal framed scene on the vellum page. The lesser entremets—the fantastic creatures, the singing lions, the griffons spewing forth live birds—are similar to the more loosely related ornaments on the manuscript page. The plausibility of this analogy is supported by the fact that the same artists who were called upon to produce paintings and manuscripts also worked on the feasts. Among the artists who helped create the spectacles for Charles the Bold's wedding were Jacques Daret, who had been a student of Robert Campin, and Hugo van der Goes.[20] Medieval manuscripts are a feast for the eye; medieval banquets addressed the other senses as well.

INGREDIENTS AND SUPPLY

Medieval meals were influenced by the difficulties of supply and storage, by seasonal fluctuations in the availability of ingredients, by the dictates of the church calendar, and by the manner in which the food was eaten. The seasons determined to a large degree what was available for the cook to work with. Late spring, summer, and fall were times of abundance; in winter feast and frugality alternated. In late winter and early spring food materials were most limited in quantity and in the poorest condition. A feast in the depths of winter therefore demonstrated wealth. Throughout the centuries discussed in this book this seasonal pattern holds true and may be observed in the many depictions of labors (or activities) of the months, from the *Très Riches Heures* of the duc de Berry to the series of engravings that were made in the eighteenth century.[21] Although the subject matter is stylized, similar rounds of activities are described in countless books on farm management and horticulture and are reflected in the seasonal food lists in cookbooks. January is represented by banqueting, centered around the twelve days of Christmas ending with Epiphany on 6 January, the feast of the magi, when the king of the feast is determined by who gets the bean in the special *galette des rois*. The following months are generally illustrated by scenes of agricultural labor: plowing, sowing, and pruning fill the days, until May brings a respite, with maying, falconry, and marriages. The remainder of the country year is largely expressed by the harvesting successively of hay, wheat, and grapes, and the year ends with the fattening of pigs and their slaughter in November and December.

Livestock were killed at the beginning of winter because farmers could not feed large numbers of animals through the winter. Breeding stock were kept; the more expendable animals were killed and their meat preserved. Beef was usually salted; pork was salted and often smoked. Fats from both were rendered in glazed earthenware crocks. Slabs of bacon and sausages were hung to smoke in the kitchen chimney for several days, and hams and tongues often received the same treatment after emerging from their bath of spices and brine. These meats were then taken to a dry attic to hang from rafters away from the rats and mice until wanted. Greens were also preserved, packed in crocks in layers interspersed with salt; cucumbers were pickled in brine. Fruit, nuts, and sometimes root vegetables were boiled with honey (sugar was too expensive to use lavishly) or stored in a cool, dark cellar. Herbs and mushrooms were dried, as were orchard fruits.

Even in a metropolis like Paris, with a population of more than one hundred thousand by 1500, the seasons imposed strict limits on the kitchen. Truck gardens in and around the city supplied produce in season, and saltwater fish and foreign delicacies came up the Seine from the ocean. The supply of ocean fish and shellfish was subject to winter storms and summer spoilage and not to be depended upon, and a long spell of wet weather sometimes slowed road traffic. The crucial importance of the food supply is

January, woodcut, from *Le Grand calendier et compost des bergers* (Troyes, 1541). The menu for this snug winter meal consists of a small bird and a neat little pie that could have come from the bakeshop on page 25. It is a hand-raised pie (thus requiring no special pie dish); the round hole in the top allows steam to escape, thus preventing the pie from breaking up as it cooks. The covered pot probably contains mustard and the tankard ale, beer, or watered wine. The only implement is a knife, and there is no discernible pattern to the table setting. (By permission of the Houghton Library, Harvard University.)

reflected by the fact that prior access to it was often a royal prerogative. The sovereign's household had the right to the best of the fish caught in the Seine.[22] A vestige of this practice may be seen in England today, where the monarch still has the right to all sturgeon caught in English rivers.

Other limits on eating patterns were imposed by the fasts and abstinences of the Christian year.[23] Abstinence meant refraining from eating foods of animal origin—not only meat but usually milk, butter, cheese, and eggs as well. Whale, dolphin, and porpoise were considered to be fish: their salted flesh was esteemed as a Lenten delicacy, and the salted fat meat was called the bacon of the poor. When the popes resided at Avignon, whale, originally taken in the Bay of Biscay and salted, was bought for the court there by the hundredweight.[24] With peculiarly medieval logic, the beaver's tail and the barnacle goose were exempt from the Lenten meat taboo: it was believed that the beaver's tail never left the water and that the barnacle goose lived its entire life at sea, so both qualified as fish. At least one skeptical diner found the barnacle goose fishy in the wrong sense. When it was served to him in England in the 1460s, he wrote that "we had to eat it as fish, but in my mouth it turned to meat."[25] Widgeon enjoyed a similar reputation until the early eighteenth century.

Fasting meant reducing the intake of all foods. Fast days included all days before important feasts and all of Advent and Lent. The basic rules had many local variations, with dispensations given to the very young and old as well as to the sick and to pregnant women.[26]

The cookbooks indicate that the fast was strictly observed. Meat-day and fish-day recipes are not segregated in the medieval cookbooks as rigorously as they were in the later, better-organized volumes, but most basic dishes were given in fast-day versions. A thin split-pea purée, sometimes enriched with fish stock or almond milk (produced by simmering ground almonds in water), replaced meat broths. Almond milk was an expensive substitute for cow's milk, and on occasion it was curdled, pressed, drained, and presented as a substitute for cream cheese. Imitations were a feature of medieval cooking, and it pleased both cook and diner to pretend to break the fast, with "eggs" fabricated from fish roe or curdled almond milk, or with the grandest hoax, a "ham" or "bacon" slices made with salmon for the pink meat and pike for the fat. Recipes for such imitations were still being published in France in the eighteenth century.[27]

Lent presented the most severe problems: the salt meat of the previous fall was old, hard, and rancid; green vegetables were in very short supply; root vegetables were growing wrinkled and fruit withered—just when medieval diners were obliged to abstain from eggs and cheese, which would have been a great nutritional boon. Meals in February and March were dreary. Shrove Tuesday, when the last of the pre-Lenten milk and eggs went to make pancakes, heralded the coming of the season when most people were hungry much of the time. The monotony of their diet probably caused less trouble than its insufficiency. Even the well-to-do went to bed hungry when crops failed or supply routes were disrupted. They, however, had more opportunity to buy provisions (especially grain) in times of plenty as a protection against rising prices. Moreover, when shortages came they could sell their surplus at a considerable profit. Variety in the diet came only with the changing seasons. How welcome the early spring must have been, when the year's first fresh greens and herbs appeared and Easter ended the Lenten fast, returning dairy products to the kitchen.

Many staples of the European diet in the nineteenth and twentieth centuries were unknown in the Middle Ages: all the New World foods—potatoes and sweet potatoes, corn, tomatoes, sweet and hot peppers (including cayenne and paprika), allspice, all the beans of the *Phaseolus* family, including green beans, navy, and pea beans, vanilla, chocolate, and turkeys. Nor did medieval European diners have coffee or tea, coconuts, pineapples, or bananas. There were probably no guinea fowl until the second half of the fifteenth century and very few then.

The diet of the prosperous classes was not without variety; indeed, they enjoyed such items as peafowl that are now not generally available. Chickens ran in the elite medieval poultry yard, and there were ducks in the river or moat. Carefully managed artificial freshwater ponds, called stews, produced carp, pike, tench, bream, eels, and other fish. Dovecotes supplied pigeons and squabs to the privileged classes: the right to keep a dovecote, like the right to hunt game, was often a noble prerogative. From the kitchen gardens came herbs for flavor and for medicines; flowers were gathered to ornament food. Herbs esteemed in the Middle Ages but now little used were tansy, rue, pennyroyal, and hyssop. From the fields and forests came furred and feathered game: venison, wild boar, hares, and rabbits, and birds, including many songbirds and others not now generally eaten. Blackbirds, for example, were baked in pies.[28] They could be bought by the dozen in Paris: four and twenty baked in a pie would have served about six, which was a rather standard size for a medieval pie. Live birds were served in pies. The pie was cooked with a filling of bran to prevent caving in; just before presenting the dish, the cook let the bran out through a hole in the bottom of the pie and slipped the birds in through the hole. Obviously, it would have been prudent to alert the carver before trying this trick. The sources neglect to mention how the birds were removed from the hall after the feast.

FLAVORS AND RECIPES

A broad range of flavors was available to the medieval cook, who combined them in ways different from modern custom. In the use of spices and of sharp-flavored fruits mixed with hashed-up meats, medieval dishes might be compared to some aspects of Indian and Near Eastern cookery. The basic distinction in modern French cooking between sweet and salt was not routinely made, nor were pepper and salt automatically used in combination. Some medieval sauces for meat and fish dishes contained sugar, and fruit was commonly combined with meats. Sour and bitter flavors were used extensively. Vinegar, for example, was much used, both in the cooking of meats, where the acid would break down tough muscle fibers, and as one of the principal liquids in sauces. Today, vinegar-based sauces are primarily salad dressings and mustards, though it is sometimes used sparingly to accent soups and stews. Verjuice, a pungent acid liquid, was extensively used in the Middle Ages. It was usually made from the juice of unripe grapes, which was sometimes fermented and sometimes not, but it was also made from crabapples. The flavor of both kinds faded with age. One author wrote that in July the old crop of verjuice was too weak and the new crop too green, so that they must be mixed in equal parts.[29] Sorrel purée was sometimes added, for color and flavor, to make *verjus vert*.

Medieval recipes are difficult to interpret because measurements, proportions, and timings are rarely given. It is therefore nearly impossible to know either how strongly flavored or how moist or dry the resulting dishes were. No pie pastry recipes have been found in French cooking manuscripts. Spices were not very fresh and were often adulterated, so that even when a measurement is given it does not tell accurately how strong the flavor was. I believe that the sauces were strongly flavored but that they accompanied bland foods—roast and boiled meats, poultry, and fish especially. Of the four basic flavors, sweet, salt, sour, and bitter, the last was most differently used in medieval times. Now it is chiefly encountered in ingredients unknown then: tea, coffee, chocolate, and hops (which gives beer its bitter tang) were not yet used. But bitter-flavored herbs, such as hyssop, were used extensively. Probably the most esteemed of such flavors was cinnamon, combining its bitterness with aromatic overtones and vivid color. It was called for constantly in the recipes, and account books confirm that among those who could afford it, it was second in popularity only to pepper.[30]

Aromatic and pungently flavored herbs were highly regarded. Some were supplied by the home garden: saffron, valued for color and flavor, the mints, some kinds of ginger, seeds like caraway, mustard, cardamom, coriander, and cumin, as well as all the onion tribe—the scallion, leek, chive, garlic, and shallot. Most spices came from eastern lands, called vaguely and collectively the Indies. These spices were prized and expensive. Their long-lasting flavor suited them to the slow pace of medieval transportation. Such common modern spices as pepper, cinnamon, cloves, nutmeg, and mace were known, but there were less familiar ones, too: cubebs, grains of paradise, galengale, and long pepper.[31] Cubebs and long pepper come from vines related to black pepper (*Piper cubeba* or *Cubeba officinalis* and *Piper longum*, respectively) and are similar to it in flavor. Grains of paradise have sometimes been identified by modern scholars as cardamom, but more likely they were the seeds of a West African plant of the ginger family, *Ammomum melegueta*.[32]

Visual effects were as important to the medieval diner as flavor—or more so. Relatively few special dishes were served, and their importance derived primarily from their appearance. Vivid colors were highly prized and were often achieved at the expense of flavor. Green, the brighter the better, was a favorite; it came from the juice of spinach or the green part of leeks. Yellow was provided by egg yolk or an infusion of saffron. Red, not very reliably, came from sunflower (helianthus); a purplish color was made from *Crozophora tinctoria* or *Heliotropium europaeum*. These colors were used most in jellies, which improved the effect by adding sparkle. The grandest effects were achieved with gold and silver leaf, both still used to garnish festive dishes in India. They are harmless, at least in the quantities people were likely to have eaten, and flavorless. The sheets of metal leaf were laid on surfaces brushed with egg whites. Typically, gold leaf was used to decorate pastry. The *tourte parmerienne*, for example, made in the shape of a crenelated castle, with chicken-drumstick turrets, had gilded coats of arms.

The paramount showpieces of the medieval banquet were roast swans and peacocks served sewn back into their skins complete with feathers. This feat is more time-consuming than difficult, and the results look better than they taste, at least in the case of peacock (I have not attempted a swan).[33] Nothing more vividly demonstrates the differences between the medieval and modern attitudes toward foods. The modern diner may well be shocked by the appearance of this large, resplendent, alive-looking animal when it is set down on the table. There are so many steps between living creatures and dining that we are not prepared for so vivid a reminder that our meat is slaughtered. The fourteenth-century diner, on the other hand, hunted and hawked and carried his prey back to the kitchen to be prepared and served. A peacock was served with fitting ceremony, perched upright on a platter, its beak and feet gilded. To serve it correctly was considered the test of a good carver. The ranking diner enjoyed the dubious privilege of receiving the head and neck; the carver then sliced enough meat off the bird so that everyone present got a piece.

A well-nourished peafowl has about as much meat on it as a capon, but it is dry, fibrous, and, in my opinion, not well-flavored. Small tastes can be served to a great many people; even in the fourteenth century there were sometimes leftovers. There was a curious belief, going back to the days of Saint Augustine, that the flesh of the peacock was incorruptible. In the *City of God* he describes an experiment that he performed to test this notion.[34] When served peacock one day at a banquet, he instructed his servant to set a slice aside for "as many days as make any other flesh stinking." Inspecting it at the end of this period, he saw that it had not spoiled; even at the end of a year it was shriveled but not decayed, although he does not say that he tried eating it. He uses the incident to introduce a discussion of immortality. The meat may not have spoiled in the dry air of Carthage, but it is unfortunate that a thousand years later good Christian cooks in Europe respected the saint's authority in the matter. Faced with more immediate evidence to the contrary, one cookbook writer remarks on the bird's incorruptibility, saying, "And it will keep well for a month after it is cooked, . . . take off the mold, and you will find it white, good, and pleasant underneath[!]"[35]

The fear of poisoning haunted the great through all the centuries considered in this book, though probably many of the deaths that were ascribed to poison had other causes. The transmission of disease was not understood. Unhealthy meat, contaminated produce, and polluted water were all capable of killing the people who ingested them, without help from poisoners. Night soil was regularly used to fertilize vegetables, and herds of pigs foraged in the refuse on the streets of Paris. Nature provided other opportunities for food poisoning. The widespread use of mushrooms held an element of risk, and even normally wholesome foods can be harmful in special circumstances. Fungus-infested rye, for example, causes ergotism, an alkaloid poisoning; and migrating European quail sometimes become toxic, causing a potentially deadly illness called coturnism.[36] Meats were displayed for sale hanging outside shops, exposed to dust and flies, and game was customarily hung until it was very high. The Paris water supply was bad; wells were scarce and often contaminated; public fountains were inadequate. Many households depended on itinerant water carriers for a daily supply of water. It was usually taken from the Seine on the upstream side of Paris because downstream the river was contaminated (even to the medieval eye and nose) for miles. Some of the pollutants came from a tributary stream that carried off liquid waste from the slaughterhouses and tanneries. Certain medicines were a cause of sickness because harmful ingredients were used: dung and urine, mercury and arsenic were in common use. Many herbs that were then considered medicinal are now known to cause allergic reactions. Even those with medically useful effects, such as foxglove, vary so much in potency that their unmeasured use is chancy.

Much harm was done in kitchens. Without refrigeration, much spoiled food went to the table. Sick cooks transmitted their diseases. Typhoid Mary plied her deadly trade in the nineteenth century, but she must have had many undetected predecessors. Cookbooks often recommended personal cleanliness and even handwashing, but the cook was also instructed to taste frequently, and I wonder how regularly the spoon or finger was washed. Eggshells were emptied (to be refilled with flavorings and spit-roasted) by blowing.

Kitchen equipment did its share of harm, too. The growing use of tinned copper utensils, especially from the sixteenth century onward, was accompanied by warnings that the lining must be in good condition because the dangers of verdigris poisoning were well known. But lazy cooks and improvident housekeepers sometimes failed to get their pots retinned soon enough. Can it be a coincidence that tinned copper utensils were first widely used in sixteenth-century Italy, where reputed poisonings were rife? Lead was also used in glazes for earthenware and in making pewter; leached out of either by acids, such as the vinegar in sauces and salad dressings, it can be lethal.

COOKBOOKS AND COOKING METHODS

Several interrelated French-language cookbooks survive from the fourteenth and fifteenth centuries. These books provide evidence of some development in the cuisine over this span.

The two earliest collections date from about 1300. The simpler, usually known as "The Little Treatise of 1306,"[37] uses a relatively limited repertory; among herbs and vegetables, only onions, garlic, parsley, hyssop, and sage are called for; no fruit, honey, or sugar is used. The second was discovered relatively recently, in the Cantonal Library in Sion, Switzerland.[38] Its recipes formed the core of the cookbook known as the *Viandier* by Taillevent, otherwise Guillaume Tirel, a cook in various royal kitchens in the fourteenth century. He first appears in account books as a kitchen boy in 1326, so was probably not born when the Sion manuscript was written. Paul Aebischer, the modern editor of the Sion manuscript, places it, on the basis of handwriting and orthography, at the end of the thirteenth or the beginning of the fourteenth century. It would be inappropriate to reproach the historical Taillevent with plagiarism. Even today, cooks draw heavily on the work of their predecessors, often without acknowledgment. Moreover, in Taillevent's day the techniques of cooking were transmitted mainly by eye and hand. Cookbooks, ubiquitous today, were exceptional until the nineteenth century. Most cooks were illiterate, holding their knowledge in their heads, hands, and palates. When the rare literate cook wrote down—or the illiterate cook dictated—what he knew, he drew on traditional knowledge.

The Sion manuscript, the "Taillevent before Taillevent" as its discoverer calls it, is more complete than the "Little Treatise" but both are very brief. Neither contains much information about pies, and the "Little Treatise" says little about the stews and hashes that are numerous in the Sion *Viandier*. Sugar is not used at all in the "Little Treatise" and appears only a few times in the Sion manuscript. Honey is absent from both. Hence, the flavor combinations of sweet, pungent, and aromatic that characterize the late fourteenth-century style are not seen in these collections. Not even the sauce cameline (a mixture of toast crumbs, vinegar, and cinnamon, with the consistency of mustard) is sweetened.

The Sion manuscript does use sugar in making frumenty—a porridge of hulled wheat berries, long boiled in broth, milk, or almond milk, that was a favorite all over western Europe. Sugar appears also in a fish pie and twice in recipes for the sick. Through the eighteenth century, sugar was believed to have healing properties. The German scholar Günter Wiegelmann describes some of the characteristic routes that new foods follow when they enter the diet.[39] Scarce or expensive ingredients are often introduced as medicines. Sugar came this way, first as a medicine, later as an ingredient in invalid foods, and then as a luxury food, with aphrodisiac overtones, an association still exploited by the candy industry on Saint Valentine's Day. Although sugar had been known and used, very sparingly, in ancient times, chiefly for medical purposes, it was rare in northern Europe until commercial contact with Islamic culture in the Mediterranean world increased in the eleventh century. The Arabs had planted sugarcane along the northern coast of Africa and, with the spread of Islamic power, in Sicily and Spain. The Normans in Sicily were refining sugar even before the Near Eastern refineries were taken over by the Francs in the twelfth century.[40] As cane growing and sugar refining came closer to French soil, the supply grew and the price fell, though it remained a luxury food into the eighteenth century. Only then, when the supply of cane sugar was greatly augmented from Caribbean sugar plantations and to a lesser extent by beet sugar, was it widely used.

Islamic Mediterranean influence on northern European cuisine was not confined to the increased use of sugar. The Crusades in the twelfth and thirteenth centuries had resulted in the establishment of western European colonies in Greece and the Near East, one of which was the Frankish kingdom of Jerusalem. In the Near East Frenchmen encountered appetizing new fruits such as oranges (probably the bitter orange we call Seville), lemons, dates, bananas, and figs.[41] By the end of the fourteenth century Near Eastern names were being applied rather indiscriminately to many dishes in European cookbooks. They appear not only in France but in England, Germany, and Italy: "Saracen brouet" (a heavily spiced eel stew with cheese); "viande de cipre" (sugared chicken with rice flour and almond milk); a pungent "Saracen sauce" of spiced almonds and raisins with vinegar; "Greek chicken" (spiced and boiled); and "infidel eggs" (hard-boiled and stuffed with cheese).[42]

Fortunately, an Arab cookbook dating from 1226 and originating in Baghdad has survived and has been translated into English.[43] Its author is Muhammad ibn al-Hasan ibn Muhammad ibn al-Karim al-Katib al-Baghdadi. The work reveals a highly developed cuisine with features recognizable in

French cookery as it developed in the course of the fourteenth century. Compared to the two earliest French cookbooks, the Baghdad cookbook employs a much more varied array of spices, herbs, and especially vegetables, although fewer varieties of meat. Mutton is most common, though lamb appears occasionally; the abundant game enjoyed in France is lacking. The recipes often sound far more appetizing than medieval French ones. They are arranged in categories such as "sour dishes" (with vinegar or other tart flavorings), "fried and dry dishes," "sweet dishes," and so forth. Resemblances to foods of the contemporary eastern Mediterranean are striking. Lamb and eggplant are layered and baked with spices; meats are stewed with herbs, spices, rice, lentils, and chick peas; there is a mint and vinegar sauce.[44] Claudia Roden points out that ingredients as well as flavor combinations and cooking methods are often the same as modern ones. Among the most interesting recipes are the sweet mixtures of almonds, dates, pistachios, sugar, and rosewater. This group is important because it reveals the earliest stages of the confectioner's art that subsequently arose in France. The development of confectionary and the related craft of pastrycooking require above average skill and precision and thus serve as an index of technical proficiency, and the plastic qualities of their products supply an outlet for the imaginations of cooks and patrons.

Two examples demonstrate the skills of Arab confectioners.[45] The first recipe is for a taffy; sugar and water are boiled, pistachios added, and the mixture worked with a stick (the translator says poker) until the mixture whitens, when it is cut, like modern taffy, into strips and triangles. The second recipe is for the ancestor of marzipans. Sugar, honey, almonds, musk, rosewater, and starch are cooked, pounded into a smooth paste which is kneaded and cooled, then pressed into wooden molds shaped like loaves and fishes.

Skill and imagination, along with increased use of sugar, become more evident in French cooking in the second half of the fourteenth century, as shown in the versions of the *Viandier* that date from the lifetime of the historical Taillevent. Guillaume Tirel (nicknamed Taillevent) is the only medieval cook whose life can be documented. He first appeared on the culinary scene as a kitchen boy in a royal household in 1326; by midcentury he was in the service of Philip VI and a few years later of the dauphin, whose father was John II. The dauphin ascended the throne as Charles V in 1364, and by 1373 Taillevent is described as chief cook (*premier queu du roi*). He is last mentioned in 1392, when the royal chefs were issued new pairs of knives. His documented career thus spanned some sixty-six years. When he died, around 1395, he was buried between his two (successive) wives, beneath a splendid tombstone, depicted wearing armor, as befitted a man who had received land and a title from his king, and holding a shield that bore three marmites.[46]

The earliest manuscript known to bear his name dates from before 1392, so he could have been directly connected with it.[47] Among the recipes added since the Sion version is one for *taillés*, which would not have been out of place in the Baghdad cookbook. It is a confection of figs, raisins, almond milk, bread crumbs, sugar, and saffron, boiled until thick and served in slices.[48] Sugar is used in other recipes, even in combination with meat and poultry. Many recipes that at first glance appear to be expanded versions of the Sion recipes turn out upon closer examination merely to be saying the same thing with more words.

Another manuscript of the *Viandier*, now in the Vatican Library, is dated by Pichon and Vicaire in the first half of the fifteenth century.[49] The inclusion of some elaborate new recipes led the editors to suggest that they may have been added when Taillevent became the king's chief cook. One is for a pie decorated with fleurs de lis, heraldic emblem of the French monarchy, "and with the coats of arms of the seigneurs who are in the royal presence."[50] Several dishes are exceptionally opulent. Suggested as "an entremet for a prince's meal" is a stuffed chicken, parboiled and roasted, served with meatballs that have been brushed with egg white and wrapped in gold or silver leaf—a feat that requires considerable dexterity. Imagine a roast suckling pig served with a chicken (also roasted) riding on its back, wearing a paper helmet covered with silver leaf and carrying a silvered paper lance. There are also instructions for serving roast swans and peacocks in their plumage. Less picturesque but perhaps more succulent are recipes for pancakes (*crespes*). In one variation they are rolled up around sticks of cheese as thick as a finger and set in a hot place to get dry and crisp.[51] The second part of the Vatican *Viandier* concludes with instructions for making entremets out of tin, wood, cloth, and parchment. These include a tower with Saracens, Moors, and a wild man; Saint George and the Dragon; and Saint Martha.[52]

Of all the medieval cookbooks, the one compiled by the unidentified author of the treatise known as the *Ménagier de Paris* about 1392 or 1393 is undoubtedly the most entertaining and helpful to the modern reader.[53] Scholars believe that he was a prosperous member of the Parisian legal world, associated either with the court of Parlement or with its members. Evidence within the book suggests that he knew people in the circle around the duc de Berry, and a copy of the *Ménagier*, as well as of the *Viandier*, are known to have been in that duke's library. The cookbook is part of a larger, though unfinished, treatise on the duties of the housewife and is addressed to the author's young bride. In his introduction, the author says that he is writing for her because she has begged him for instruction, which she would rather receive in private. He is elderly; she is but fifteen. His extraordinary motive for writing is, he says, a desire that when she remarries after his death, his memory should not be disgraced by her ignorance.[54]

The author of the *Ménagier* was not a cook; he was an employer. But he wanted his wife to know how to manage their household. He searched out copies of the *Viandier* and of other sources which are now lost and sat down with them to compose his own treatise.[55] Indeed, his paraphrases are the chief evidence that the recipes originated in the fourteenth century rather than the sixteenth. One can visualize him at work on his treatise, turning with puzzlement from one garbled manuscript to another, and evidently writing his own impressions as well as copying recipes. Thus, finding a recipe for a vinaigrette of pork which concludes with the statement that it should be brown, the critical householder writes: "Brown. How can it be brown if there is no toast in it. Note: I believe it should be thick, because I found it in the thick soup chapter before, and for these reasons I think there should be toast in it, to thicken it and to make it brown."[56] Precisely because he was not a cook, he described aspects of cooking which any working cook would have taken for granted. The first part of the Vatican *Viandier* concludes with a list of items not discussed in the book because "women and their mistresses and everyone know how to cook them; among these are puréed beet greens, cabbages, turnips, leeks, veal with a saffron and pepper sauce, scallion soup, peas, . . . pork stew, a soup of pork innards."[57] The author of the *Ménagier* describes everyday food, but he touches only lightly on the more elaborate presentations, and some of the recipes he gives were evidently not a part of his regular diet. After a recipe for larded suckling pig, for example, he writes: "Note, that I have indeed seen larded suckling pig, and it is very good."[58]

Because the author of the *Ménagier* takes care to explain processes, his book provides an especially good view of how the cook worked in a fourteenth-century kitchen. This information can be supplemented by useful hints in the *Viandier*'s various versions. The cook's activities centered around the fireplace, which was set against a wall, usually of the main room of a dwelling, for which this hearth was the principal source of heat. A hooded chimney above drew the smoke away. The most notable feature was the pothook, or *cremaillière*, a substantial wrought-iron support, usually adjustable, from which cooking pots could be hung above the fire. The pothook, with its big cooking pot, appeared, with variations in size and adjustability, in kitchens through the eighteenth century and, in rural areas, even later.[59] Andirons, holding the burning logs, stood below the pot; the prudent cook kept a good supply of glowing coals to arrange as needed. The big iron caldron (*chaudière*, hence "chowder") is the ancestor of the stockpot. Into it went anything to be boiled. The medieval cook combined flavors in this pot—meats, poultry, game, vegetables, and sometimes even fish jostled each other in a manner that would horrify the modern classic cook. To boil something, the pot was swung above the hottest part of the fire. Control over the rapidity of boiling was achieved by moving the pot toward or away from the heat or by moving the burning logs and glowing coals.

Other foods were cooked at hearth level. The simplest method was cooking foods in the ashes, truffles, for example, and eggs. One recipe for the latter, appropriately called *oeufs perdus*, describes breaking the shell and dropping the naked egg into the hot embers; when cooked it is removed and the ash cleaned off before serving.[60] Iron and earthenware pots were set on three-legged rings (more stable than four-legged ones) above the hot coals, or the pots had the legs molded into their bodies. Wrought-iron grills with feet were used to cook meats and fish and to make toast. According to the *Golden Legend* Saint Lawrence was martyred by being roasted on a grill, which, by one of those strange turns of the medieval imagination, led him to be made the patron saint of cooks.[61] Some cooking pots had flat or concave lids that overhung their edges; on these lids glowing coals were placed to provide more even heat. Pots with cooking oil for fritters were also set in the coals.

The author of the *Ménagier* observes that soups and stews boil over until salt and fat are added (though adding salt to a boiling liquid causes it to foam up briefly); more in keeping with modern practice, he advises constant stirring to prevent sticking. Both he and the *Viandier* give hints for dealing with burned food.[62] As soon as the catastrophe occurs, the cook should take the pot off the fire and transfer the contents to a clean pot, or hang a bag of yeast in the latter, or cover it with a clean cloth and turn the cloth repeatedly. One manuscript of the *Viandier* recommends breaking up walnuts and boiling them with the scorched food. Putting a piece of pork rind in the bottom of the pot is a preventive measure that has stood the test of time and still serves today. A baking surface is supplied by tile placed in front of the fire, and frying pans were used similarly, either set on a tripod, or, according to the manuscripts, patiently held out over the fire by the cook. Aching muscles have long been a cook's occupational complaint. Fortunately, wool and linen, the most common clothing fabrics, smolder rather than bursting into flame, thus presenting less danger than might be expected.

A third cooking locale was before the hearth. Some andirons had iron baskets at the top in which food could be warmed. Hooks on the andirons or separate supports in front of them held the spits for roasting. The dripping pan (*lechefrite*) stood beneath it to catch the juices and basting liquids as they fell from the turning roast. From it they could be spooned up and poured over the roast again or brushed on with feathers. The *lechefrite* was also used as a place to heat delicate foods gently, oysters, for example. Finally, the chimney was used for smoking fish and meat.

Only the largest households had ovens in their kitchens; people who lived on a smaller scale took food to the neighborhood baker's oven to be baked. In grander houses an oven was built into the masonry of the fireplace. A fire was made in the oven; when the oven walls and floor were thoroughly hot and the fire had died down, the coals and ashes were raked out. Items requiring a hot oven, such as little pies, went in first, and when they were done, and as the temperature of the oven gradually fell, larger, slower-cooking foods went in, such as big pieces of pastry. But much medieval cooking ingeniously avoided the need for an oven. Starches were made into porridges, fritters, or pancakes. Bread was usually purchased. Pies could be baked on the hearth, in a pot set on a tripod with coals under it and on its lid. The French did not at this time make either the pastas of Italy or the dumplings of central Europe, though both already existed in their native lands.

The *Ménagier de Paris* gives us information about preserving, which was in its early stages. It includes a recipe for orange rind preserved in honey and describes a monumental conserve or *composte* of green walnuts, cooked with mustard and horseradish, spices, honey, and root vegetables, including car-

February, woodcut, from *Le Grand calendier et compost des bergers* (Troyes, 1541). This well-equipped bakeshop has two ovens, one of which is being used for bread and the other for pies. Note the hatchet ready to chop kindling, the faggots drying on the rack over the oven's mouth, and part of a balance scale visible just beyond the right-hand oven, above the massive butcher's block. The pie and bread loaves are sitting on the floor. (By permission of the Houghton Library, Harvard University.)

rots.[63] Carrots evidently were a novelty, for he referred to them as red roots, sold by the handful at Les Halles.

There is little resemblance between medieval French cookery and the exquisitely subtle and adaptable craft that developed in the course of the seventeenth and eighteenth centuries. It ranged from the banal to the gaudy; the most necessary skill was management of the fire. Herbs and spices were important, but there are few clues as to how proportions were managed. Visual effects, which could be remarkable, were confined to special dishes for special occasions. It is not easy to get a sense of how the cook managed work and material from day to day, but certainly there was considerable opportunity for improvisation. In the late medieval cookbooks one can discern some influence from the eastern Mediterranean: a readiness to use the increasing supply of sugar and a willingness to labor over details of presentation. The repeated cookings to which many ingredients were subjected may have helped break down the tough fibers of meats but would also have eradicated any sense of freshness. Undoubtedly, the remains of large roasts that were returned from the table to the kitchen after a meal were cut up for pies or chopped up in hashes. Meats emerging from the stockpot fared similarly, especially if they had cooked for a long time. Pies were often sent to the table again and again. Repetition implied a descent on the social scale. The highest-ranking people got the freshest food—the roast as it came from the spit, the pie with its lid untouched. Kitchen and other servants got what was on the dishes that returned to the kitchens. Trencher bread and other table scraps were gathered up in an alms basin to be distributed to the poor. There was probably little waste.

There is little that would be recognized as specifically French in this style of cooking, save some of the ingredients. The combinations were different, and most of the dishes familiar today were absent. The great array of stocks, other basic mixtures, and sauces that underlie modern French cuisine did not appear until much later. Most important, the organization of kitchen and staff that produced them had not yet developed. The slow growth of rational working methods began in the seventeenth century; the sixteenth was, in most respects, a continuation of the medieval style of cooking.

CHAPTER TWO

Cookbooks and Cooking in the Sixteenth Century

RENCH COOKING did not begin to take on its present character until the end of the seventeenth century. Three developments between the middle of the fifteenth and the middle of the seventeenth centuries, however, led to alterations in styles and practices that refined the art of cooking. These were the introduction of printing into France, the beginning of an interest in diet by the educated classes, and the elaboration of dining as a part of court ceremonies.

The first printed cookbooks were recipe collections dating from the Middle Ages, often miscopied from old manuscripts. Advice on diet still adhered to antique doctrine, and the dishes served at festivities received little more attention than Olivier de La Marche had paid to his dinners. By the time Henry III came to the throne in 1574, attitudes were discernibly different than they had been a hundred years earlier. The chronology is roughly as follows. Books containing medieval recipes began appearing in the last decade of the fifteenth century and continued to be reprinted down to the first decade of the seventeenth.[1] In the early sixteenth century advice on eating sensibly and well found its way into print, and writers used references to foods in their work as a means of evoking specific aesthetic responses in their readers.[2] At this stage and for a long time to come most cooks were illiterate, but a number of literary genres were developing that inspired their employers to raise the standards of kitchen and table. The literature of antiquity began to appear in print, giving wider access to the agricultural and culinary writers of Greece and Rome.[3] Contemporary horticulturists contributed increasingly practical advice on the raising of plants and animals for the table.[4] Physicians and apothecaries published recipes that were less practical, but they sometimes included confectionary recipes, and preceptors supplied books on table etiquette for the young and the newly respectable.[5] Finally, in the second half of the century changes made by Catherine de Medici in the organization of court festivities led to the enhancement of the role of eating in that milieu. The increasing supply of sugar available for making preserves and other sweets encouraged the development of sugar-cooking techniques; these delights became the favored offerings on such occasions.

This chronology suggests an answer to the question of whether it was cooks or diners who led the way toward an increasing refinement in French cuisine. Before any significant changes in cooking methods occurred, doctors and diners were reading books about ingredients and diet and discussing these subjects among themselves. These discussions appear to have preceded an interest in gastronomy as such—an interest, that is, in delicious food agreeably presented. The growing belief in the importance of diet in establishing and maintaining health led the French upper classes to give serious attention to their food and the manner in which it was eaten. Diarists, themselves a new phenomenon, were recording what they ate and occasionally how they felt about it. Food began to be a fit subject for literature.

The First Century of Printed Cookbooks

The invention of printing with movable type had a powerful but not an immediate effect upon the craft of cooking. Apart from collections of recipes for confectionary, preserving, and distillation (generally joined with medical and cosmetic recipes), there apparently were no new French cookbooks in the entire sixteenth century. Why, indeed, should there have been any? Who would have written them, and for whom? When literate people began to use written recipes, they did so to prepare medicines and luxury foods and to preserve the produce of their gardens. Cooks learned their craft from other cooks, not from the written word. Those who bought cookbooks were apparently satisfied with defective editions of the same collections the author of the *Ménagier* had turned to a century and more before. In the 150-year period before the introduction of printing into France only three recipe collections had been in circulation: the "Little Treatise of 1306," the various versions of the *Viandier*, and the (now vanished) suppositious ancestors of the *Liure fort excellent de cuysine* family. (The *Ménagier de Paris*, for all its historical interest, is not an original recipe collection.) In the next century and a half there were few additions. If at first glance the number of titles in the bibliographies suggests otherwise, it is because this initial period of printing saw repeated editions of a few cookbooks.

The first printing presses in France were set up in Paris in 1470.[6] About twenty years later the first printed French cookbook appeared—appropriately, the *Viandier*. The first edition reflects little change in the style of cooking since the fourteenth century. Some of the recipes are from the earlier surviving manuscripts, either printed verbatim or paraphrased. It was the first of more than a dozen editions.[7] Those believed to be the earliest bear neither date nor place; those dated from the early sixteenth century are Parisian, and from the 1540s onward they originated chiefly in Lyons. The last edition is dated 1604, some three centuries after the Sion manuscript.

An average printing in the sixteenth century probably ran to between five hundred and two thousand copies.[8] During that century at least ten known editions or printings of the *Viandier* appeared, so thousands of copies of it must have been in circulation during much of the century. Unfortunately, it is not at all clear who, in the absence of literate cooks, was buying, reading, and perhaps cooking from these books.[9] The defective character of the printed books suggests that no one who knew the craft was involved in producing them.

We have already seen how the content of the *Viandier* changed in the age of manuscripts. The printed version is a direct descendant of those manuscripts. The printer used the fourteenth-century introduction verbatim, boldly announcing, "Here begins the viandier for dressing all kinds of dishes which Taillevent cook of the king our lord made," giving rise to an enduring belief that Taillevent was a late fifteenth-century or even a sixteenth-century cook.[10] The contents of the first printed *Viandier* include recipes from all three principal manuscripts, those of Sion, the Bibliothèque nationale, and the Vatican Library. Oddly enough, some fifty come from the earliest, the Sion manuscript. About forty are drawn from each of the other two. There is some overlapping material, of course, and some recipes appear twice in the printed volume. A small group is common to all three manuscript versions: these recipes must hold a record for longevity, having remained in circulation for three centuries.[11]

In thinking about the cuisine of a given period one must always remember that the printed record and actual practice are not identical. Some kitchens will be turning out traditional dishes that originated far back in time, while others are producing an endless flow of new inventions, some of which may be cooked but not recorded for years, if at all. In the New England town where I live today, some cooks specialize in baked beans and chowders, while their neighbors experiment with *la nouvelle cuisine*. Nonetheless, I suggest that the extreme longevity of the *Viandier* recipes attests to a stagnant, or at least a very static, period in the history of French cooking.

The printed *Viandier* was probably drawn from yet another collection, now lost, for it contains many recipes that are not found in the known manuscripts—notably several pie recipes.[12] Moreover, the order in which recipes appear is only intermittently similar to that of any predecessors. In the absence of this hypothetical manuscript source, there is no way of knowing which, if any, of the unfamiliar recipes were added during the fifteenth century.

A comparison can be made, however, between the late fourteenth-century menus in the Vatican Library's manuscript of the *Viandier* and those dating from mid-fifteenth century and therefore already forty years old at their appearance in the first printed edition. A few changes have crept in, most notably in the increased number of sweet dishes in every part of the meal. This growing emphasis on sweetness was probably the most important single development in sixteenth-century cooking. The trend is already present in the mid-fifteenth-century version of the *Viandier*, where sweets appear in most courses. Its menus also show a modest increase in the number of milk and cream dishes. A typical assortment consists of "*lait lardé* [milk curdled, drained under a weight, then sliced and fried], sugared junkets, sugared white cream, sugared strawberries, and candied prunes stewed in rosewater."[13]

A baker's dozen of recipes were added to the edition of the *Viandier* printed by Pierre Gaudoul, who was active as a publisher in Paris between 1514 and 1534.[14] Among these, recipes using grains predominate; the most interesting is for a meat-broth-based oatmeal porridge, thickened with egg yolks. All of the recipes added by Gaudoul were taken from the *Platine en francoys* published in 1505. Only one of these reflects the new direction that French cooking had begun to take. It is for a *potaige appelé verseuse*, which gives quantities and therefore can be prepared in the modern kitchen.[15] A foamy mixture of egg yolks, sugar, cinnamon, orange juice, and rosewater is beaten over heat until thick. The texture is much like a zabaglione, but it is heavy with cinnamon and excruciatingly sweet.

The *Liure fort excellent de cuysine* (Lyons, 1555) is typical of mid-sixteenth-century cookbooks. Most of its recipes could have come from the manuscript *Viandiers*. It still features roast peacock in its feathers, sweet spiced sauces thickened with toast crumbs for meat dishes, and bright colors. At the same time, there are three harbingers of the future. The volume opens with a list of the recipes, alphabetized by their first letter only, and there is an increase in the proportion of recipes for vegetables such as cucumbers, pumpkins, and squash, where, in earlier times, root vegetables had predominated. Finally, as we shall see in chapter 10, there are advances in the art of cooking and baking with sugar.

Not until the very end of the period did a cookbook appear—published in French although not in France—that reflects a new culinary influence, that of Italy. Lancelot de Casteau's *Ovverture de cvisine* (Liège, 1604) is a volume with an exceptional history. It is the first cookbook in French that is not a reworking of medieval recipes; it contains an international collection of recipes both for cookery and for confectionary. What is, to the best of my knowledge, the only extant copy, was acquired in 1958 by the Bibliothèque Royale Albert Ier in Brussels. The only other recorded copy was destroyed in a fire during the Napoleonic wars.[16] Its owner had published a partial and faulty description of the volume before its destruction.

Why, one may ask, should any attention be given to an obscure book that was neither written by a Frenchman nor published in France? Lancelot provides the best available information about what might have been cooked in the second half of the sixteenth century. In the light of French gastronomical chauvinism, it may be ironical that the first original French-language cookbook should have appeared outside of France, but it is not surprising. The development of French cooking had lagged behind that of England, Germany, and Italy during much of the century; these other countries had already begun to produce a steady stream of cookbooks, though after the sixteenth century the Italian production fell off. During Lancelot's tenure in the Liège kitchens, another court cook, Marx Rumpolt, published a handsome volume, *Ein new Kochbuch* (Frankfurt, 1581), which also has a broad geographic range and is much more comprehensive than Lancelot's. Lancelot may well have been aware of the illustrious example set by Marx Rumpolt, who, when the *Kochbuch* was published, was cook at Mainz, another imperial episcopal state relatively near Liège.

Liège was a meeting place of international cultural influences. Lying between ducal Burgundy and the Flemish provinces, it had been strongly influenced by the predominantly French culture of the Burgundian court in the fifteenth century. Its location on the Maas River, however, placed it in the center of the complex cultural and political movements along an east-west axis between France and the Germanies, a north-south axis between Italy and the Low Countries, and across the Channel to England. Although French in language, politically Liège was (at least in principle) under the authority of the Holy Roman emperor. Lancelot's internationalism, like Marx Rumpolt's, may reflect on a culinary level the multinational territorial agglomeration assembled by the Habsburg dynasty in the later fifteenth and sixteenth centuries.

Liège was the seat of a territorial prince-bishopric of the empire. In 1557 a new prince-bishop made his "joyous entry," which had been postponed for some months while the countryside recovered from the effects of a disastrous famine. Lancelot de Casteau, who describes himself as a native of Mons, near Liège, printed in his book the menu of the banquet served on this occasion. Recipes for many of the items listed also appear, so it is reasonable to suppose that he had already taken up his position as head of the episcopal kitchens. He must have given satisfaction, for he remained as master cook to three successive prince-bishops, publishing his *Ovverture* nearly half a century after his first employer's inaugural banquet. In 1562 he became a member of the bakers' guild, five years later of the mercers' guild, and in 1571 a *bourgeois* of the city of Liège. A document dated 28 June 1613 mentions that he is dead.[17]

The menu for the prince-bishop's banquet in 1557 combines such up-to-date items as turkey, molded multicolored gelatins, and an elaborate confectionary course with such medieval favorites as roast swan, peacock pies, and bustards.[18] There are in addition Italian specialties: raviolis, Bologna sausage, and a Parmesan cheese.[19] I would conjecture that Lancelot had some training in Italian kitchens.[20]

To approach Lancelot de Casteau's recipes after those in the *Viandier* and the *Liure fort excellent de cuysine* is like coming into bright sunlight from a dimly lit room. The *Ovverture de cvisine* shares a defect with the latter: its table of contents appears to offer more organization than is really there. Recipes are listed that are not included, and all those that begin "pour faire" appear under the letter "p." Moreover, like the *Liure fort excellent de cuysine*, the alphabetization considers only the initial letter of each title, and recipes lacking titles may or may not be in the table of contents. Such defects persisted into the seventeenth and eighteenth centuries: rational organization came very slowly to cookbooks.

In the *Ovverture de cvisine* the recipes are sorted into three groups, according to the kinds of meals in which they are used. The first is a "petite ordinaire de cuisine," recipes for daily fare, particularly addressed, Lancelot tells us, to ladies who like to cook, as well as to all kinds of *cuisiniers*.[21] It includes some of the earliest pastry recipes in French, a cream-puff recipe (*pâte à choux*) used for fritters, and one for what are basically cinnamon buns. There follow lists of vegetables and herbs, and the section concludes with a generous selection of pie recipes.[22] The first part of Book Two is of special interest because it hints at the way work was to be organized in French kitchens in the seventeenth century. Its recipes may appear at first glance an unlikely combination: sausages, meat and fish jellies, pastries, and confections. I think they are grouped together because the dishes were all prepared in one place, the *office*, or cool kitchen, whose modern counterpart in a large establishment is the *garde manger*. This organization of the work space is not reflected in earlier French-language cookbooks. The remainder of Book Two contains more pastry recipes and additional soups and stews, which reflect the international character of the region: olla-podrida and an *adobado* of sturgeon, a capon stew "in the Hungarian manner," that archetypical Netherlandish specialty, the *hutspot*, or as Lancelot calls it, *heusepot* (a veal stew), partridge "in the Catalan manner," and a leg of mutton "roasted in the Irish way."[23] Book Three "treats of several sorts of meats, and of arranging a grand banquet for princes and princesses," concluding with the menu for the dinner of 1557.

This volume differs from earlier cookbooks in the clarity with which the recipes are written. One feels that the distance between the cook and the printed page has been greatly reduced and that the cook is in the habit of talking and even writing about his craft. As a court cook, Lancelot was not obliged to belong to a guild and therefore would not have been bound by oath to withhold its secrets from the public. He was in Liège for some years before joining a guild.

Lancelot's individual recipes are expressed with a coherence new to the literature. He specifies measures of weight, cuts of meat, and proportions. The order in which work is done is generally reflected in the phrasing of the recipe, a virtue not universal even today. The modern reader may be frustrated by the writer's assumption that the reader is familiar with the dish being prepared, but the recipes are coherent even when they are not easily intelligible, and many of them are more appealing than the average medieval recipe.

Sugar continues to be prominent; cinnamon is still the dominant spice. But there are fewer of the substitutions medieval cooking took for granted, such as pea purée to replace meat stock. There is an increase in the quantity and variety of vegetables, including some stuffed root vegetables, which continued as a popular garnish through the eighteenth century.[24] All in all, this obscure little volume deserves to be better known. Even if cookbooks of the period were plentiful the *Ovverture de cvisine* would hold its own.

NEW ATTITUDES ABOUT DIET

Not long after the printing press began to supply the kitchen with recipes a century or two old, it also began to produce newly written books dealing with the relationship between food and health. These were addressed to medical men, apothecaries, and other educated individuals with an interest in their own health and in that of their households. In the field of medicine, there were books on health in general, on the wholesomeness or harmfulness of various foods, and collections of recipes for medicines and foods for the sick. For the private individual there were treatises on the arts of gardening and farming and on etiquette. Finally, all over Europe, printed editions of classical Greek and Roman works on food appeared. The writings of Apicius were available (in Latin) from 1498 onward, and in 1514 the Aldine Press published the Greek text of the *Deipnosophists* by Athenaeus.

The first important book published in France showing this new concern with diet was a translation of Bartolomeo Platina's *De Honeste Voluptate*, a composite work consisting of a cookbook dating from about 1450 embedded in a lengthy discussion of how to live in an agreeable and healthful manner. Platina, a humanist scholar and the first papal librarian, was the author of a monumental history of the popes.[25] *De Honeste Voluptate* was translated into French as *Platine en françoys* by Desdier Christol, prior of Saint Maurice near Montpellier, which was the site of France's preeminent medical school in the sixteenth century. The first edition was printed in Lyons in 1505. The work achieved wide distribution in time and space. It had been the first cookbook to be printed, in 1474, and was also translated into German. It was reprinted more than a dozen times in Italy and nearly as often in France.[26]

Platina was more generous than many borrowers of recipes, acknowledging his debt to the man who supplied the recipes: "Ye immortal gods, what cook can surpass my Martino of Como, from whom I have taken nearly all of what I write."[27] Martino of Como was in charge of the kitchens of the Cardinal Ludovico Trevisan, patriarch of Aquilaea, whose table was famous in Rome for its excellence. The recipes, of which there are about one hundred, are not profoundly different from the earlier French ones, though some pasta recipes are included. Platina translated these recipes from Italian into Latin and inserted them in the later parts of his treatise.[28] His ideas of what constituted a healthy life were based on the writings of the late classical physician Galen and of the medieval school of Salerno, which followed Galen's teachings. Two aspects of Galen's thought affected sixteenth-century diet. First, he believed that eating fruit caused fevers. As a modern writer has pointed out, "the summer was a time when there was a high incidence of infections, and it is not surprising that the popular fancy saw a relation between the diarrhoeas and dysenteries of the hot months and the laxative effect of a liberal diet of fruit. . . . There can be no doubt that this widespread belief greatly increased the likelihood of a scorbutic condition."[29] Second, Galen's doctrine of humors still governed dietetic theory in sixteenth-century Europe. According to this theory, everyone has one of four dominant "complexions": sanguine, phlegmatic, choleric, or melancholic. Each of these is moist or dry and hot or cold; each is the result of a "humor" or bodily fluid. The sanguine person's humor is blood, his quality hot and moist; the phlegmatic is cold and moist; the choleric is hot and dry; and the melancholic is cold and dry. Moreover, plants and animals have similar characteristics, and therefore the foods that derive from them must be chosen appropriately.

Platina's book is largely devoted to cataloging all the foods people were likely to eat according to this system. He quotes Socrates as saying we should eat to live and not live to eat.[30] In the summer the choleric should eat cold meats, purslane, melons, squashes, lemons, plums, cherries, and "all other foods which cool"; the melancholic should avoid eating fruit in the autumn, "for it will engender fevers"; the phlegmatic are to be sustained with goose, game, and other hot meats.[31] The qualities of foods also determine the order in which they appear on the table.[32] First come laxative foods: fruit, leafy vegetables, and anything eaten raw with oil and vinegar, but also sweets. (In the twentieth century, in many places people have returned to eating salads at the beginning of the meal.) The second course is to be of soup and roast and boiled meat or fish, and the final course consists of cheese, nuts, and more sweet preserves. Some foods require special placement: peas should be eaten in the middle of a meal, for if eaten at the end "they will engender bad dreams and melancholy." Lettuce is recommended as a soporific.[33]

What gives this book a special cross-grained piquancy is the occasional disharmony between its recipes and the dietary theory that surrounds them. Beef is cold and dry, nourishing but difficult to digest, and often the cook must add spices, herbs, and sauces "to amend their malice," although sometimes the malice remains unamended.[34] The author is then torn between theory and practice. For example, Platina copies several of Martino's suggestions for serving pike, with blancmange, or with garlic sauce, orange juice, or mustard, but he concludes his recommendations by saying that "this fish is the most unwholesome and harmful of all."[35]

Platina's observations about the natural history of plants and animals and their health-giving (or destroying) qualities draw heavily on classical and Arabic writers: Pliny, Columella, and Avicenna, among others, including some information that is fairly recherché. Hedgehogs were, to my knowledge, little eaten in Renaissance Italy, but, perhaps because Pliny wrote about them, Platina includes them among the foods he evaluates: his praise for hedgehog was then translated into French, though the demand for information about its digestibility cannot have been great.[36]

Is there any evidence that *Platine en françoys* influenced the French table? I believe that there is, though not at the level of recipes. Platina served as a model of the educated gentleman who took food seriously. His extensive use of classical sources helped to legitimize the table as a subject of literate conversation. Food at medieval banquets was little discussed in contemporary writings, and early sixteenth-century descriptions are not much more informative. Two minor literary genres, however, appeared during the century: the learned discourse on diet, often concentrating on a single ingredient, and the rhymed celebration of food and drink. Jacques Pons's *Sommaire traitté des melons* (Lyons, 1583) is a good example of the first type. Pons was dean of the medical faculty at Lyons and later became a physician to Henry

IV. He opens with a discussion of the relationship between the melons of the ancients and those of his day and considers such eternal questions as to how to grow good melons and how to select a ripe and well-flavored one.[37] Like Platina, he gives a selection of recipes and follows them with discussions of the good and bad effects of eating melons. Among the effects to be feared are cholera and excess: he enumerates celebrated people who died of surfeits of melon. Against this he balances what he describes as Henry IV's passionate fondness for them.[38] In sum, this treatise is a model of how a liking for good food could be combined with an interest in health, antiquity, and pleasure. This attitude, not specific recipes, is what the French learned from Platina and other Italian writers. Talking about the pleasures and dangers of the table continued unabated from this time onward, illustrating a constant ambivalence in people's attitudes toward food as a source of both nourishment and pleasure. People could argue about the life-preserving benefits of the temperate life, they could display a familiarity with the literature of antiquity, and they could evince their *joie de vivre* with drinking songs.

During the first half of the seventeenth century, physicians continued to write books advising the diner to eat moderately, and cooks persisted in writing no books at all, though they were no doubt refining their skills. When La Varenne published the *Cvisinier françois* in 1651 he wrote that he had been practicing his craft for three decades. Books on maintaining good health continued to attempt to undermine diners' confidence in their diets. A good example is Gui Patin's *Traité de la conservation de santé par un bon régime et legitime usage des choses requises pour bien et sainement vivre*, whose second edition appeared in 1632. He was still following the dictates of Galen and the school of Salerno; pastries all have some bad qualities, except for *biscuits* and macaroons; he cites a number of people who died from eating melons. (Some authors vary this theme, mentioning victims who died of eating ice and snow.) Mushrooms should never be eaten, and truffles are distinctly evil and would be better used to fatten pigs.[39] Fortunately, his advice and that of similar writers seems, then as now, to have gone largely unheeded.

It was François Rabelais whose capacious and well-furnished mind united the multiple strands of early sixteenth-century gastronomy. Trained in medicine at Montpellier, he made three trips to Rome and read widely in ancient literature. He knew the dietary theories of antiquity (his annotated copy of

Galen is in a Scottish library today), and he wrote a poem about garum (the ancient Roman counterpart of soy sauce, based on fermented fish), in which he spoke of its qualities as an aid to digestion.[40] Another of his interests was horticulture, and during a trip to Italy he obliged his patron by sending back seeds of salad greens, including cress and romaine lettuce.[41]

The table-related parts of Rabelais's *Gargantua et Pantagruel* were drawn out of this rich background and his own experiences.[42] In Book Four, Pantagruel's travels take him to the island of Messer Gaster, "first master of arts in this world. For if you believe that Mercury was the prime inventor of the arts, as our ancient Druids thought, you are greatly in error. The satirist is correct when he says that Messer Gaster—Sir Belly—is the true master of all the arts."[43] He then explains at length that all the rest of the body is dependent upon Messer Gaster and will perish unless it obeys his commands immediately. The inhabitants of this land are the Gastrolators, and their religious practices consist of making offerings of food to their god, Manduce. The list of these offerings goes on for pages and shows how faithful to the medieval kitchen France was as late as 1547, when this book appeared.[44] There are cold roast loins of veal spiced with powdered sugar, salmagundi, blood puddings, pork chops with onion sauce, pasties, tarts, comfits, and clotted creams. Among charcuterie, he speaks of chitterlings, saveloys, and salamis; among salads, various cultivated and wild greens, asparagus, and fava beans; there are seventy kinds of candied fruits and spiced comfits. A few exotic foods are mentioned, notably couscous, which Rabelais may have enjoyed in Rome; the dish then enjoyed a degree of popularity in Italy. There is a recipe for it in Bartolomeo Scappi's cookbook of 1570, as well as one for caviar, which Rabelais also mentions.[45] Sturgeon still swam in many of Europe's rivers, and the roe as well as the fish itself was widely eaten. Roe was served hot, on slices of bread, with pepper and the juice of sour oranges, or cold, with spices. After this period of popularity, caviar sank into obscurity until the eighteenth century when it again came into fashion.

The celebration of the pleasures of food and drink in prose and verse has continued down to the present. For every writer with the stature of a Brillat-Savarin there have been dozens of pedants, riders of hobbyhorses, and third-rate versifiers. The battle between Carnival and Lent was a favorite topic.[46] As we shall see in chapter 12, in the eighteenth century there was intense debate about the relationship between diet and behavior. Versifiers celebrated onions, cheese, and herring; they summarized the teachings of the school of Salerno; and they exhorted readers to either temperance or intemperance.[47] Writers of prose engaged in controversy, the display of erudition, and on occasion took the kitchen and table as a point of departure for more serious literary endeavor.[48] The long history of these genres has yet to be written; it will require stamina of the scholar who attempts it.

SIXTEENTH-CENTURY CONFECTIONARY

If no similar burst of loquacity was recorded in the kitchens, the specialized workshops of apothecaries and physicians did contribute to the written records of developing technique. In the sixteenth century the sugar-refining industry grew substantially over much of Europe.[49] Although sugar remained expensive, it was produced in sufficient quantities to be available as a medicine and as a luxury item. The industry had long been operating in Italy, where techniques for cooking with sugar had been developed earlier. The association between medicine and confectionary was to last for a long time. From the Middle Ages to the nineteenth century sugar was sold by apothecaries. According to contemporary dietary theory, sweets, especially sugar-based, were warming and laxative. The action of the bowels was the subject of considerable medical attention, perhaps because it was often one of the few bodily functions on which physicians could have some predictable effect with their treatment. Apothecaries and physicians were the first to gain experience in dealing with this technically demanding ingredient. Since literacy was normal in this class, the first really new recipes to be printed were for confectionary.[50]

The *Secreti del reverendo Donno Alessio Piemontese* (Venice, 1555) was translated into French and published in Antwerp in 1557 and Paris in 1558; the astrologer-alchemist Michel de Nostradamus produced a volume first published in 1555 in which he makes observations about sugar refining and cooking based on what he had learned in his Italian travels. The loquacious title pages of both works reflect the medical context in which sugared foods existed at the time: *The Secrets of the reverend Seigneur Alexis, of Piedmont, containing excellent remedies against various diseases, wounds and other accidents, with the manner of distillation, perfumes, confitures, etc. . . .*; the *Bastiment de Recepts containing three little parts; the first treats of the different virtues and properties of things; the second is on different kinds of scents and the composition of them; the third embraces some medical secrets suitable for safeguarding health . . .* ; and Nostradamus's *Excellent and very useful little work, necessary for all who wish to have knowledge of various exquisite receipts, divided into two parts; the first treats of different ways of [making] cosmetics and scents to brighten and embellish the face. The second shows us the way and manner of making preserves of several kinds, as much with honey as with sugar, and must* [boiled-down unfermented grape juice].[51]

Nostradamus, like Rabelais, received his medical training at Montpellier, where Platina's work had been translated. In addition to the section on cosmetics, his *Opuscule* contains recipes for preserved fruit and for jellies and other sweets. They were separated into two categories—liquid and dry—a division that remained in use through the eighteenth century. Liquid preserves include all the fruit-based jams, jellies, and preserves in syrups that are familiar today, as well as similar preparations made with nuts, flowers, and vegetables. Dry preserves included candied fruit, nuts, seeds, and vegetables—anything that can be conveniently eaten in the hand. This group blends into confectionary, especially in the case of nut and seed preparations.

Nostradamus uses both sugar and honey as sweetenings. The latter was then more economical and easier to obtain, though only the former could be used for dry preserves. Drawing on his knowledge of Italian sugar refining, he gives detailed instructions for clarifying sugar and for making various confections. The experienced sugar cook's sensitivity to hot and humid weather is observed here for the first time, as is repeated insistence on working only with the best quality of sugar, requirements that are as important today as they were then. "From good wares good products are made, and from ugly or bad, bad work."[52] Mixtures of sugar and water have significantly different properties depending upon small changes in proportion, therefore a considerable degree of control is needed. Alexis of Piedmont's widely circulated *Secretes* contains a small but significant collection of confectionary recipes. The remainder of the book deals with everything from hangover remedies and directions for making soap to the treatment of paralysis. Some of the preserving recipes are for old favorites—a quince paste called *cotignac*, for example, was a regular feature of fourteenth-century menus—but new ingredients and recipes predominate. Sun-dried peaches are boiled in a sugar syrup and then dried again, to be stored for winter, "for it is a lordly thing."[53] Melon slices are marinated in vinegar, then boiled in honey with spices, a recipe Jacques Pons was to rework; orange rind is similarly treated.[54] A sweet spiced Italian biscuit also appears: *morselets a la Neapolitaine.* The recipe is more lucid than many of his others, "an exquisite thing, for they are very savorous, fortifying the stomach and sweetening the breath."[55] To the modern taste they are harsh in flavor and tough. The sweet pastries and confections would have been a welcome change from the usual mixtures, and the combination of expense and pleasure virtually guaranteed acceptability.

The number of manuscript recipe collections circulating in the Middle Ages can never have been large, so the quantity of sixteenth-century printed cookbooks that was produced represented a very substantial increase in the number of recipes available to the literate cook (or supervisor of cooks). From the mid-seventeenth century onward the numbers of books and of recipes were to grow yet more dramatically. But even though cookbooks still played a very modest role in the gastronomic life of France, the social exchange and consumption of good food came to occupy a more important place in people's lives, and this change in the social attitude toward food was a force that encouraged subsequent innovation in its preparation.

Festivals, Dining, and Diners in the Sixteenth Century

N THE COURSE of the sixteenth century meals at Valois court festivals changed. It has been suggested that these changes were the result of Italian influence.

Festivities at the court of Francis I resembled those of the Burgundian dukes more than they did those of Renaissance Italy. At the Field of Cloth of Gold in 1520, diplomacy, splendor, and quasi-military competition mingled in a way that would have been entirely familiar to a medieval courtier. The chroniclers of this event describe much the same range of activities in much the same way as Olivier de La Marche had done.[1] Unfortunately, this similarity extends to a continuing silence on the details of the banquet menus. Surviving records of expenses indicate that the same ingredients were purchased as in the previous two centuries: there are few vegetables but many varieties of birds, including those old ceremonial standbys, stork, bittern, and peacock.

Italian Renaissance artifacts appeared on sixteenth-century French tables as elsewhere in aristocratic French life, but their use was superficial. They ornamented the table without changing the basic structures of dining. Consequently, the overall effect remained more late medieval than Renaissance. A notable example is the great salt made by Benvenuto Cellini for Francis I.[2] It is purely Italian. Its form departs dramatically from the ship-shaped *nefs* of the Middle Ages. Instead, Neptune, god of the sea in classical mythology, reclines, facing a similarly recumbent Earth goddess. Since most salt was then obtained by evaporation from seawater, the use of Neptune was as appropriate as the use of ships had been. In Cellini's piece, the salt was contained in the open dish, while pepper is said to have been kept (inconveniently) in the small classical temple at the sea god's elbow. But this superb piece of metalwork did not inspire emulation, nor did its example lead to any important changes in the way the royal table was set. Indeed, after the death of Francis I it does not seem to have been used, and in the reign of Charles IX it was given away.[3]

Charles VIII's invasion of Italy in 1494 initiated six decades of intense French military involvement in Italy. Although the influence of Italian culture had been felt in France before 1494 and would persist long after the Peace of Cateau-Cambrésis in 1559 (which formally concluded the Italian wars), Italian influence was strengthened by the constant diplomatic and military intercourse of this period. In the course of the fourteenth and fifteenth centuries Italy had been the focal point of the cultural movement known as the Renaissance. The Italians of the period claimed that this revival constituted nothing less than a rebirth of civilization—particularly in the high arts and in the comportment of cultivated persons. As Italian influence spread north of the Alps, so too did the idea of a rebirth; in historical writing, particularly from the time of Voltaire onward, the Renaissance came to be identified with a broad range of changes in elite culture, in particular with a greater refinement in tastes and manners.[4]

This very simplified view of the Italian Renaissance and its influence on northern Europe has been greatly modified by historical research in the past hundred years: the influence of Italian humanism is now regarded as much narrower in scope, and the elements of continuity between medieval and early modern civilizations have received greater emphasis. Nevertheless, the earlier view has left its mark on the history of cooking in the widely believed notion that the refined techniques characteristic of modern French cuisine were introduced by Italian cooks who traveled to France with Catherine de Medici, Florentine bride of the future Henry II.[5] This theory is wrong on two counts: French *haute cuisine* did not appear until a century later and then showed little Italian influence; and there is no evidence that Catherine's cooks had any impact on French cooking in the early sixteenth century. Indeed, French sixteenth-century cooking was very conservative and in general continued the medieval traditions.

Because the myth of Catherine de Medici's cooks has been so persistent, I would like to consider it briefly. The scenario runs thus: Catherine, born in Florence and raised in a convent there and in Rome, where her uncle, Giulio de Medici, was Pope Clement VII, was affianced to Henry, the second son of Francis I, king of France. When she came to France in 1533 she was accompanied by a train of attendants and servants—perfumers, fireworks manufacturers, embroiderers, and also cooks, pastrycooks, confectioners, and distillers. Her pack animals are said to have carried to France for the first time parsley, artichokes, lettuces, forks, and glazed earthenware plates. When the court tasted the food and drink prepared by these skilled craftsmen, a revolution in fashion is said to have occurred, and no one wanted to eat the spicy old medieval hashes. In some variations of the story the Italian cuisine thus transported was in the direct tradition of ancient Rome. Thus, under the inspiring glow of the Italian Renaissance, true French cuisine was born.

The known facts are somewhat at variance with the legend. When Catherine de Medici arrived in France, she was just over fourteen years old, and there was little expectation that she would become queen because her husband's older brother was still alive. Henry was deeply involved in his long-lasting liaison with Diane de Poitiers, who set fashion at the court. Catherine's position was further weakened because for the first fourteen years of her marriage she bore no children, and there were frequent rumors of divorce. Thus she was hardly in a position in those early years to bring about a revolution in taste.[6] The interchange of ideas and people between France and Italy had begun before she was born and continued after her death. In the four decades following Charles VIII's invasion of Italy many members of the French aristocracy had taken part in a series of military campaigns there. In addition, there was a steady stream of traffic between the French church and the Vatican. Catherine's mother, Madeleine de la Tour d'Auvergne, was French, though she died very shortly after Catherine's birth. Francis I's cousin Renée was duchess of Ferrara, and his daughter Marguerite was married to Emmanuel Philibert of Savoy. During the 1530s and 1540s Rabelais made three trips to Italy, and in the 1550s Montaigne traveled there extensively. A Frenchman did not have to travel to Italy to see the work of Italian artists. Francis I had invited Leonardo da Vinci to his court when Catherine was an infant; Francesco Primaticcio and Il Rosso Fiorentino were already painting at Fontainebleau when she arrived. And Benvenuto Cellini had worked for Francis I in the 1540s. Indeed, the king had arranged the marriage between Henry and Catherine, and she might be considered one of his imports. Since the fifteenth century Lyons had been the center of a large and influential Italian community that was active in trade, banking, and, more recently, printing. This community had representatives at court. Many of Catherine's Italian associates there—most notably the Gondis—were already living in France.

Among the stream of ecclesiastics and diplomats traveling to France from various parts of Italy was one who may inadvertently have been responsible

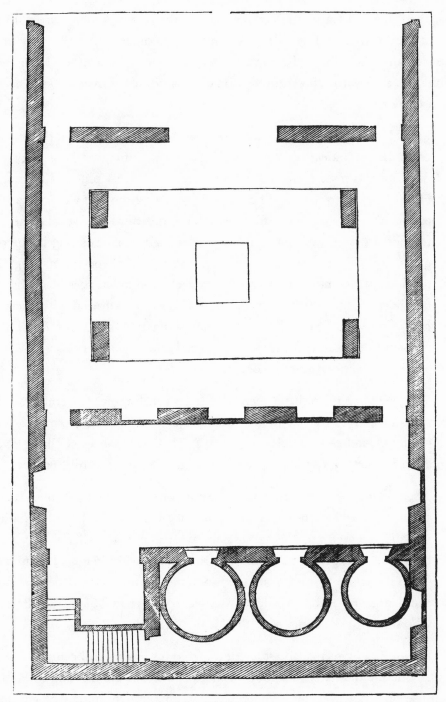

Plan of a kitchen, woodcut, from Philibert de l'Orme, *Le Premier tome de l'architectvre* (Paris, 1567). De l'Orme states that he brought this design back from Italy "because of the convenience of its ovens for cooking bread and pastry." The rectangular central space is raised for cooking and roasting, but there are still no masonry *potagers* for cooking over charcoal. An effort has been made to rationalize the work space. The kitchen is no longer a place for sociable gatherings. (By permission of the Houghton Library, Harvard University.)

for the legend of Catherine's cooks. This was the Neapolitan Cardinal Caraffa, the brother of Pope Paul IV, a papal diplomat often in France and, incidentally, the only cardinal ever beheaded for crimes. Among his household was a steward who amused Montaigne with his conversation. The essayist reports:

> I asked him about his job, and he replied with a discourse on the science of guzzling [*la science de la gueule*], delivered with magisterial gravity and demeanor as if he had been expounding some great point of theology. He spelled out to me the differences in appetites: the one we have before eating, the one we have after the second and third course; the means, now of simply gratifying it, now of arousing and stimulating it; the organization of his sauces, first in general, and then particularizing the qualities of the ingredients and their effects; the differences in salads according to the season, which one should be warmed up and which served cold, the way of adorning and embellishing them to make them also pleasant to the sight. After that he entered upon the order of serving, full of beautiful and important considerations.[7]

The legend seems to have been born from this fragment of conversation that was picked up by one of the collaborators on Denis Diderot and Jean Le Rond d'Alembert's *Encyclopédie* in 1754. There it was used to illustrate an unfavorable account of the progress of cooking in the sixteenth century:

> The Italians were the principal inheritors of the debris of Roman cookery, so it was they who made the French acquainted with the art of dining well [*la bonne chère*], the excesses of which so many of our kings attempted to suppress, but finally it triumphed in the reign of Henry II, when the cooks from beyond the mountains came and settled in France, and that is one of the least debts we owe to that crowd of corrupt Italians who served at the court of Catherine de Medici.[8]

Like so many myths, the story of these cooks has a small central core of truth. She undoubtedly had cooks in her suite when she traveled to France because virtually everyone who traveled with the expectation of comfort took cooks along to assure eating reasonably well. Unfortunately, however, there is no evidence that cooking in France improved in the 1530s and 1540s or that the cooking of these decades had any identifiably Italian character. What evidence there is suggests the opposite. Visible changes in this general

D d d ij

Cross-section of a kitchen, woodcut, from Philibert de l'Orme, *Le Premier tome de l'archi-tectvre* (Paris, 1567). The high windows and the lantern surmounting the work space serve to carry away heat and fumes.

period occurred in the attitudes of the diners, not in the performance of the cooks. Catherine's influence on dining in France came later, after the death of Henry II, and involved court festivals, not actual cookery.

Henry II, like his father, Francis I, favored quasi-military events as the focus of court festivities. In 1559 he died of injuries suffered in a tournament, leaving Catherine de Medici a widow. Three of her sons reigned in turn, but each of their reigns was preceded by periods when she was regent, and she exercised considerable influence while her sons were on the throne. These three decades of her life, until her death in 1589, were marked by a series of destructive civil wars. France was divided, in religion between Catholics and Protestants and in politics between groups of nobles vying for control of the government. In sixteenth-century politics the religion of the ruler determined the religion of those in his territories. Henry IV, the heir to the French throne after Catherine's Catholic but childless sons, was a Protestant. Strong Protestant movements, mostly following the teachings of John Calvin, had sprung up among skilled tradesmen such as printers and in some areas, such as the southwest, where the queen of Navarre and many members of the nobility were Protestant. There was also a strong Calvinist (Huguenot) party at court, though its size varied. The situation was at best unstable, and in the second half of the century there were eight successive periods of civil war, in which both sides were led by heads of noble families. The monarchy was very weak and could maneuver only by shifting back and forth among the other parties. The French Protestant and Catholic nobility spent forty years killing each other, with some assistance from the crown, before rebuilding began under Henry IV.

The duc de Guise was the leader of the Ultra-Catholics, and his wife was a daughter of Catherine and Henry II. Another daughter, Marguerite, later married the king of Navarre, the Huguenot leader who ruled as Henry IV. The Catholic duke's father had been assassinated by Protestants; Henry IV's father was killed in battle against the Catholics. The stain of the Saint Bartholomew's Massacre colored all of late sixteenth-century French life. A contemporary, Pierre de l'Estoile, wrote in his journal: "The disease of the century . . . is passion and partisanship."[9] The expenses and disruptions of civil and foreign war left France in a desperate economic situation. Even the bankers in Lyons and Antwerp who lived by lending money to warring kings had gone bankrupt. The public festival became a weak government's way of expressing aspirations, of urging courses of action, of demonstrating wealth and power, and, above all, of concentrating attention on the head of state and his family.

There were three basic types of festival.[10] The first was the ceremonial entry, in which, in carefully negotiated order of precedence, the court, nobility, army, church, and local dignitaries would process, magnificently accoutered, through allegorical arches, past nymphs and shepherds declaiming verse, into the city. Some of the greatest artists of the day worked on these events, which were the most public of the three types. The second was the military festival, featuring displays of horsemanship and mock combat, in a nostalgic look backward to medieval chivalry. After the death of Henry II these events were less emphasized. Finally, there were festivals, called masquerades by Roy Strong, which combined drama, dance, and the serving of food. These last were Catherine de Medici's specialties.

Her festivals took place both indoors and out, though gardens were the preferred setting.[11] Boats were disguised as whales (with musicians inside— an echo from the Burgundian court) and horses as elephants. Spectators were sometimes included in the activities, as at Bayonne on 24 June 1565, when they floated along a river in boats, past a series of allegorical happenings, to an octagonal banqueting pavilion set among trees on an island. Catherine's daughter, Marguerite de Valois, was only a child at the time, but years later, writing her memoirs, she remembered that enchanted midsummer's day on the river as "a superb festival given by the queen, my mother, on the island, with a ballet, and the shape of the room, which seemed to have been adapted for this purpose by nature, having hollowed out a great oval meadow surrounded by tall trees in the middle of the island. There the queen, my mother, arranged large alcoves all around the sides, and in each a round table seating twelve persons; their majesties' table alone was raised at the end of the room on a tall dais four steps above the lawn. All these tables were served by troops of diverse shepherdesses, dressed in cloth of gold and satin, according to the various costumes of all the provinces of France."[12] They performed dances of their provinces while the banquet went on. Afterward there was a concert, followed by dancing by nymphs in artificial light. "But envious fortune could not bear the glory, and brought on a strange tempestuous rainstorm." Everyone rushed, drenched, for the boats, abruptly ending the day's festivities. The whale was blown off course by the wind and beached.

The organizers of the festival improved upon reality by commissioning artists to produce visual evidence of what should have been. The pictures that have come down to us of this and other *ancien régime* festivals were not drawn on the spot. They were made, sometimes years later, using, at best, the records of those who executed the events and the recollections of those who attended.[13] The Valois tapestries, for example, show the whale as it was meant to be, untroubled by contrary winds. In the background of the tapestry the diners enjoy themselves under a clear sky.

Catherine de Medici's contribution to the development and refinement of French dining was in the planning and execution of these festivals. Modern scholars regard her as having been one of the most imaginative producers of court festivals in a period characterized by such displays.[14] In this medium her gifts for planning and invention had full play. If she could not keep armies in the field or form lasting alliances with her neighbors or argue sense and stability into her children, she could and did bring the leaders of hostile factions together at court. There, where the rules of etiquette were maintained between assassinations and massacres, she could oblige all factions to sit down and break bread together and to join in ceremonies of order, as when high-ranking ladies performed a ballet of the fourteen provinces of France, much at variance with the chaos actually prevailing in the provinces.

In 1564, as a part of her effort to knit together the divided kingdom, Catherine embarked on an epic journey with her second son, Charles IX, who was then just fourteen. The tour of his realm lasted more than two years and cost, people complained, as much as a military campaign. The object of this Grand Voyage de France was to secure the loyalty of the people by showing their monarch to them.[15] It is hard for us today to grasp how powerfully people were affected by belief in the person of the monarch, how meaningful were direct acts of homage. The queen regent and the young king went, with his court, to both Catholic and Protestant strongholds, visiting the Ultra-Catholic duc de Guise in his duchy of Lorraine and the Huguenot Constable de Bourbon, Louis, prince de Condé, at Chateaubriant. In bringing Charles before all these parts of the population, the queen mother was trying to compel their obedience to him.

The queen's motive in making this trip was political, not gastronomic, but it probably showed more people how the court dined than a lifetime of giving banquets. The king had a master chef in his entourage, one Guillaume Verger, who was assisted by a staff of five cooks and an unknown number of kitchen boys. They must have worked under a great variety of conditions because the royal party sometimes stayed in castles and other times in inns or simple farmhouses. The complications of supply and the endless work that had to be done must have taxed their skills to the utmost. Some eight thousand horses were required to move this peaceful army.[16] As it slowly circled France, people in the regions it passed through saw how and what the court ate. Local cooks must have had temporary jobs in the kitchens that were set up along the way, thus the opportunity to observe the techniques used by court cooks. Many at that time considered court style to be Italian style, and if they learned to make a sauce from a court cook's recipe, they may have thought that they had learned an Italian sauce.

THE COLLATION

The archetypical medieval court meal was the banquet, ornamented with exotic birds in plumage and punctuated by entremets *mouvants*. The characteristic sixteenth-century court meal was the collation, at which most or all of the food was cold and the emphasis was on sweets. Allegorical themes were still prominent, but the programs drew more consistently on classical mythology.

Such a meal was offered to the court by the high officials of the city of Paris in the spring of 1571.[17] The guest of honor was Elizabeth of Austria, bride of four months to Charles IX. The royal couple, the queen mother, and the court were present. The young queen entered a tapestry-hung room to the sound of a trumpet fanfare, which, according to the official description, "testified to the incredible joy everyone felt at her arrival." The iconographic theme of the day was the healing of division by a wise leader. The tapestries offered to the queen's view told the legend of Cadmus and the dragon's teeth, as interpreted by Niccolo dell'Abbate, with emphasis on Cadmus's marriage to Harmonia, daughter of the Olympian gods, and on the founding of Thebes. Roy Strong has described the culminating scene, "in which Cadmus and his bride . . . rode in a great ship with four other smaller ships, representing Religion, Justice, Nobility and Merchandize, chained to it. In other words, the vision was of the royal couple guiding the four estates of the realm, to a happy haven of peace and imperial greatness."[18] Probably most of those present would have recognized the story, for educated people were familiar with classical mythology. To elucidate the meaning of the allegory there were twenty Latin couplets. The official description goes on to tell how Elizabeth and the princesses in her suite took part in a ceremonial handwashing, as was done in the Middle Ages, and then everyone sat down to dinner. They were served "with all the rarest and most exquisite fishes in season, both freshwater and from the ocean."[19] (It was a fast day.) The queen was served by the provost of merchants, from covered dishes, which were carried by the gentlemen and officers of her household, presumably as a safety precaution in an age that was nervous about poisonings. The arrival of each dish was announced by trumpets, "and the service was so well organized, above and beyond the excellence and diversity of dishes and good wines, that several of the . . . gentlemen testified that they had never in their lives seen the equal."[20] The qualities of the food praised were rarity and refinement, whereas in the fifteenth century abundance had been the most desired characteristic.

On this occasion, dinner was followed by dancing, and dancing by a collation, which was attended by the king, his brothers, and high-ranking noblemen. These guests are said to have admired the novelty of the collation, the description of which reads like a candy-store inventory. There were preserves, both dry and liquid, a variety of sugared nuts, fruit pastes, marzipans, sweet biscuits, "every kind of fruit in the world" (no mean feat in May!), and a sugar paste dish representing several kinds of meat and fish.[21] Alexis of Piedmont would have been delighted. The principal table decorations were six large reliefs sculptured in sugar, which set before the young queen the story of Minerva and how she brought peace to Athens. The day's events ended with the gift to the queen of a large and valuable silver-gilt buffet service from the provost and aldermen. She was suitably grateful and graciously volunteered that she would always speak on behalf of the city to the king, her lord and husband.[22] Parisian governments had long known the most direct route to their rulers' affections, though they did not always take it.

DINING AT THE COURT OF HENRY III

Around 1600 Thomas Artus, sieur d'Embry, who was a member of the court of Henry IV, wrote *Description de l'Isle des Hermaphrodites*, a satiric account of life at the court of Henry III. Its dominant theme is that nothing is what it appears to be, a reference to Henry III's sexual ambiguity. Artus's sometimes heavy-handed satire includes a lengthy account of the conduct and contents of a late sixteenth-century court meal.

Cooks and diners have long argued over whether the best cooking makes food "taste of itself" or transmutes ingredients into something new and unrecognizable. To satisfy its advocates, food that tastes of itself should be locally produced and in season, served at the peak of its natural ripeness; in contrast, transmuted food is a compound of the rare, the exotic, and the difficult, made from ingredients belonging to other places and seasons and produced by techniques that require special skills or equipment. From the sixteenth century onward, both points of view have had persuasive supporters; they are the extremes to which the pendulum swings. In the late sixteenth century, in the early eighteenth, and in the nineteenth the transmutationists usually prevailed; at other times the purists have had the upper hand. At present two parts of our society are pursuing separate paths: traditionalist cooks and diners interested in fine cooking emphasize recognizable ingredients; food technologists and the mass market are more interested in the final combination of flavors. Ironically, today the simpler ingredients are likely to be more expensive. Most of us would not recognize many of the ingredients prominent in processed foods. How many of us can differentiate, with eye, nose, or palate, among hydrolized vegetable protein, guar gum, and BHA? Food technologists claim that they can synthesize the flavors of our familiar foods, transmuting, for example, textured soy protein into bacon. Analogously, the chefs and confectioners who served the sixteenth-century diner contrived to astonish him by clever deceptions. The plates of sugar "fish" at the reception for Elizabeth of Austria exemplify this point of view. Then, as now, the willing suspension of disbelief on the part of the diner is essential.

Artus's narrator, describing the island, explains that "all the dishes had to be disguised, so that no one would recognize their nature. . . . We esteem all kinds of pastries and preserves, both dry and liquid, the more insofar as they are brought from a different climate than our own, and they are esteemed increasingly in proportion to their expense." A diner desiring fish will send away to the ocean for it, and even an omelet must be dusted with powdered musk, ambergris, and pearls, and the smallest must cost at least fifty écus."[23] What a splendid opportunity to cheat!

A new luxury makes its appearance: cold, whether in the form of ice or snow. "In summer they always stored away in suitable places . . . great blocks of ice and heaps of snow, to mix with their drinks, which must certainly have engendered extraordinary diseases. For those who are truly of our company must be fearless in the enjoyment of pleasure, and they must expose themselves to all sorts of dangers for such great good and satisfaction."[24] At the meal the traveler sees ice and snow being served.[25] A substitute for snow—or should we interpret it as an imitation?—is found in the *Ovverture de cvisine*, among the banquet foods for princes and princesses:

> To make snow. Take a pot of new cream, four ounces of sugar, four ounces of rosewater; take a little whisk such as a handful of twigs, and beat the cream for half an hour, then let it rest, and you will see the foam rising on top like snow; then take a skimmer and lift the snow off and put it in a dish with a trencher [bread?] over it, to let the snow drain, and beat the cream again as before, until you have enough snow; then put it in little dishes, with a sprig of rosemary, and serve thus.[26]

Here is an item doubly offensive to the purist: food that is not what it seems and an imitation of an effete luxury at that.

The sumptuous damask tablecloth "was pleated so that it resembled a rippling river that a breeze was gently blowing across." This was done despite the excellence of the cloth itself, "because nothing pleases these people, no matter how good it may be in itself, if it is not disguised [*desguisée*]." The napkins for individual diners were also elaborately folded, a fashion still in force a hundred years later, though Artus's traveler expresses "astonishment at the time they wasted in so trifling an exercise."[27]

The reigning Hermaphrodite has a *nef*-like piece of silver-gilt to hold his napkins and a casket containing his eating utensils: knife, spoon, and, at long last, a fork.[28] The addition of the fork reflects half of an important change that was coming to northern European tables from Italy in the late sixteenth century. The necessary other half was the replacement of the bread trencher by pewter, silver, or glazed ceramic plates, whose firm and impermeable surface made it possible to serve more liquid sauces and to serve preparations most conveniently cut with knife and fork by individual diners. The dukes of Burgundy and assorted royalties had forks that were used for special purposes, but only in Italy were they much used. A Byzantine princess, brought by marriage to Venice in the eleventh century, used one to eat her dinner and because of it was condemned for excessive luxury in a sermon by Peter Damien.[29] Large wrought-iron kitchen forks were known in the sixteenth century, and by then carvers were using more moderately scaled ones in their work at tableside. Italian writers of books on carving expected the carver to balance the article being carved on a fork held in the left hand, while slicing off appropriate pieces with a knife held in the right—a precarious and greasy exercise at best.[30]

But the combination of knife, fork, and spoon which we take for granted did not appear until the sixteenth century. The earliest printed reference where they are grouped together that I know of is in Scappi's cookbook of 1570.[31] The fork is two-tined and therefore not convenient to eat with. The diners on the Island of Hermaphrodites are wearing ruffs, and they tie their napkins over them, "as if they were going to have their beards trimmed. . . . They never touched the food with their hands, but carried it to their mouths with their forks, stretching out the neck and leaning their bodies over their plates."[32] The salad course presented special problems. "They took it with forks, for it is forbidden in this country to touch the food with the hands; preferring to touch their lips with this little forked instrument [*ce petit instrument forchu*] rather than with their fingers. Then they were served some artichokes, asparagus, peas, and shelled fava beans, and it was a delight to see them eating all this with their forks, for those who were not as nimble-fingered as the others dropped as much on their plates, the dishes, and all around as they put in their mouths."[33]

Sweet preserves and confections end the meal; their medicinal and aphrodisiac properties are stressed, as is the degree to which the confectioners and apothecaries have changed the nature of the ingredients. Of the fruit course Artus writes, "It was made up of everything which was least natural, for it was almost all disguised in things like tarts, liquid preserves, and other inventions, for they say it is very bad for the health to eat fruit just as it comes from the tree."[34]

Separating reality from satire, one finds described here the typical sixteenth-century collation, with a profusion of exotic and seasonal delicacies, an emphasis on sweets and pastry, and a more stylized presentation than would have been the case in the Middle Ages. The eating process was to become tidier as people learned to use forks. The expense of individual preparations and the belief that foods affect health for good or ill encouraged the diners to notice and think about what they were eating. When literate diners began to care about what they ate, to think, as Platina had stressed, about the health-giving (or destroying) qualities of individual foods, they became more interested in cookbooks that gave them ways to prepare the foods they wished to eat. Moreover, in the second half of the century individuals began to write down their responses to the pleasures and disappointments of the table.

GENTLEMEN IN THE HINTERLANDS

While the court was learning to use meals as a focus for its ceremonies, less exalted individuals in the hinterlands were recording in their journals the place of foodstuffs in their daily lives. The impressions of two celebrated diarists, Gilles de Gouberville and Felix Platter, an essayist, Michel de Montaigne, and a poet, Pierre de Ronsard, provide excellent insights.

Gilles de Gouberville was a Norman gentleman, a bachelor, who lived on his manor near Cherbourg with his legitimate sister, several illegitimate half-brothers, and more than a dozen servants. For fourteen years, from 1549 to 1563, he recorded in his journal the affairs of his manor, gifts given and received, horses shod, crops planted, and often what he ate.[35] It is the most detailed single source available for rural life during the Wars of Religion.

Normandy is often considered synonymous with apples. Gouberville pressed cider and perry every fall, beginning the fruit harvest in September and sometimes making cider until December. He owned "a vessel to distill eau-de-vie," so he probably turned his cider into Calvados as well. When a new press was put into service during one harvest he stayed home to supervise its initial use.[36] As a good orchardist he kept bees; Thomas Drouet did double duty for him as beekeeper and butcher, coming in to strain honey and to slaughter the pigs and other livestock.[37] Gouberville grew a variety of vegetables: old standbys, such as onions, fava beans, and cabbages (from seed supplied by a neighboring female cousin, to whom he subsequently returned forty bushels of cabbages).[38] He planted turnips, peas, beets, saffron, spinach, and lettuces.[39] The ecclesiastical calendar is reflected in the food preparation. The feast of Epiphany was celebrated on 6 January with a special cake containing the bean that determined the king or queen of the feast; the cake was usually bought in Cherbourg or brought by a guest.[40] Gouberville always recorded who got the bean. Just before Lent began a hog was slaughtered to save forty days of feeding and to provide a ham for Easter.[41] In Lent the journal records modest purchases of figs, dates, raisins, and rice.[42]

Occasionally Gouberville remarks on an especially succulent dish. In December of 1556 he had a cygnet for supper, "the fattest and most tender it

November, engraving, from *The Twelve Months* by Virgil Solis. Cattle are being slaughtered and pigs fattened in an oak wood. In the middle ground a woman uses a long-handled skillet to catch the blood from an ox as it is slaughtered; it will be used to make *boudins* (black puddings). (Courtesy of the Museum of Fine Arts, Boston.)

was possible to see," and on another occasion "a braised carp, very good," which a friend's wife "had prepared in her own way [*à sa fantasie*]."[43] Taste in the country was generally conservative, however. When he mentions a specific dish it is very likely to be something that could equally well have been cooked a hundred years before: a venison pasty, a veal stew, *boudin*, a larded shoulder of veal, a bittern. Culinary disasters are recorded, too: the cod so salty that he was sick the next day, an underdone loin of veal.[44] Fish and shellfish abounded—Gouberville lived two miles from the coast. Sometimes, however, when he sent to Cherbourg for fish, there was none because it had all been sent away to a neighboring market or ocean storms had kept the fishing fleet in harbor.[45]

Food was more than a source of work and pleasure in Gouberville's world. It was an important medium of economic and social exchange. A good portion of his rents were paid in produce. On one occasion he went to collect

December, engraving, from *The Twelve Months* by Virgil Solis. If the landscape were flatter this could be a scene at Gilles de Gouberville's manor house. In the foreground a woman and a young girl are putting hams to soak in a tub of brine. Behind them carcasses are scalded to remove excess bristle. Note the boning and chopping knives in the border.

"nine bushels of wheat, a loaf of bread, and thirty eggs" but was unsuccessful.[46] When his tenants and neighbors were sick or lying-in he supplied honey, cider, white bread, pears, and sometimes meat. If the sick were farther up the social scale he added wine or jelly.[47] When his sister broke her leg he sent cherries and a venison pie.[48] Besides comforting the sick with apple cider, he engaged in a continuous round of exchanges of gifts of large and small food items. When a friend's son was married he sent "a bushel of wheat, a pumpkin, and two dozen pears"; after another local wedding he received a pie, a curlew, and two partridges that were left over.[49] If the guests at weddings had not regularly brought gifts of food with them, marriage celebrations would have been prohibitively expensive. Occasionally Gouberville received a gift—a couple of oranges and lemons, for example—and immediately gave it to someone else. "Francoyse, dam de Couret, had sent me two glasses of meat aspic by her menservants. . . . I sent Pistel at once to Trou-

Four sources of supply for the country kitchen: poultry yard, dovecote, fishpond, and bee-hives, engraving, from Olivier de Serres, *Le Theatre de l'agricvltvre* (Paris, 1600). The wicker cage is to protect and restrain young birds. The man on the right is beating on a pan; the noise was thought to frighten the bees into forming a swarm, thus preventing their loss. (By permission of the Houghton Library, Harvard University.)

ville to carry the said aspic, some chickens, and some pigeons to Guillemette [who is sick]."[50] A modern scholar has observed that Gouberville regularly sent food to women he was interested in.[51]

Gouberville's kitchen was the hub of his indoor activities. He recuperated from a bout of illness there, did the paperwork for his manor's business, and drowsed by the fire.[52] An armoire built under an ogival arch on one wall must have given the room a certain distinction, and he served dinner to guests there. It served other purposes, too: a tenant with a dislocated knee was brought there for medical attention; on one rainy day a pig was slaughtered there.[53] It was an all-purpose room.

In 1552, while Gouberville was living on his domain in Normandy and rarely traveling far, Felix Platter, a young Swiss Protestant, left Basel to study medicine at Montpellier. At his farewell dinner his mother surprised him by serving a quail he had raised as a pet—not, certainly, a modern mother's idea of a heartening send-off.[54] His trip was uncomfortable. For safety, he traveled with a group of merchants as far as Lyons. At one inn people plotted to murder him; at another bad food made him sick. He had the gift of insatiable curiosity. Seeing his first olive trees, with fruit both ripe and unripe, "[he] tried them all, but found them very unpleasant and bitter."[55]

He matriculated at the medical school and entered vigorously into the intellectual and social life of the German student community. As a skilled lutenist he was welcome at evening parties, where his friends bribed him with sugared almonds to play for them. While Gouberville was celebrating the feast of kings with his Norman household, Felix Platter was playing his lute at a "superb banquet" the German students had arranged for themselves. To learn anatomy, he attended public dissections and also clandestine ones, even participating in grave-robbing expeditions. He also developed the medical student's tough-mindedness, recording what he ate before setting out for one such excursion.[56]

During his four years in Montpellier, Platter lodged with a Marrano family, Spanish Jews forcibly converted to Christianity. Both the student and his hosts were defined by their diets as outsiders in the local society. The Marranos continued to abstain from pork.[57] Mutton was the household's usual meat, and beef was eaten more rarely. Cabbage, root vegetables, and salads formed a regular part of the family's meals. The usual beverage was red wine, watered, though Platter became very fond of the local white muscat. As a Protestant who had not grown up observing Lenten taboos, Platter found its abstinences constricting. He took to cooking eggs with melted butter in paper over hot coals. A maid discovered his cache of eggshells, and there was a great rumpus in the household.[58] It was a dangerous act at a time when his coreligionists were regularly being burned at the stake in Montpellier and in a household where his landlord's abstention from pork made his religious loyalties suspect, too.

The diary reflects the changing seasons. Mardi Gras was celebrated by an orange-throwing melee in the Place-Notre-Dame. Platter noted the arrival of the first cherries in the spring, the Saint Bartholomew's onion market on 24 August, and the wine harvest in the fall, which was once marred by the drowning of a harvester in a vat of grapes.[59] Similarly, the ceremonial events of student life were marked by festive meals: the arrival of a new German student and the conferral of a doctor's degree upon an old one were equally occasions for eating. After receiving his degree, one such celebrant and his friends marched in procession through the town, splendidly dressed, carrying stalks of fennel with sugar figures; they concluded with "a splendid collation with all kinds of confectionary," as well as excellent hypocras.[60] Rosemary, marjoram, and thyme grew wild in the fields around the town, and the rosemary grew to such a size that it was used as firewood, which must have been magnificently aromatic.[61]

Just before his departure, his friends engaged in a macabre joke: they

Winter, from *The Four Seasons*, engraving by Crispin de Passe after Martin de Vos. Garlands of sausage, game, waffles, and stacks of pancakes help insulate the diner against winter's wind. Note the pierced skimmer at the top of the border, next to the three-legged earthen pot. Hungry foxes were especially interested in the henhouse in winter. (Courtesy of the Museum of Fine Arts, Boston.)

served him a pie made with cat meat, which he mistook for hare, commenting that when he found out what it really was he did not mind too much.[62] His friends were fortunate that he did not react like a woman of whom Montaigne writes: when told, as a joke, that the meat she had just eaten was cat, she sickened and died of horror.[63]

In 1557 Platter returned home to Basel, where he enjoyed a long and distinguished career as a physician and rector of the university. Curiosities he had sent home during his student days became the nucleus of a widely admired collection. Nearly a quarter century later he was visited by a distinguished nobleman, jurist, and intellectual from Bordeaux then traveling to Italy by way of Germany and Switzerland. Michel de Montaigne had, according to his biographer, Donald M. Frame, "five strong reasons for the trip: health, heartsickness over France, weariness of domesticity, desire to see Venice and Rome, and sheer love of travel."[64] Often when Montaigne arrived in a town the local people of consequence called upon him and his traveling companions and presented them with gifts of food and wine, quince paste, and seasonal and local delicacies, thus putting food in the service of polite intercourse.[65] When he reached Basel in 1580, he recorded seeing "the house of a doctor named Felix Platerus, the most painted and enriched with dainty adornments in the French style that it is possible to see; which the said doctor built very large, ample, and sumptuous." He visited the doctor, admired his herbal, and the next night dined with Platter and other notable people of the town. Montaigne enjoyed German food and remarked that he wished he had brought a cook with him to learn the style of cooking so that he could enjoy it upon his return to Bordeaux.[66] In Rome he encountered forks but did not use them much. He was much taken with glazed earthenware plates, which were "so white and neat that they seem like porcelain, and are so cheap, they really seemed to me more pleasant for eating than the pewter of France, especially when it is dirty, as you find it in the hostelries." When traveling back to France to become the mayor of Bordeaux, he wrote that he knew when he had left Italy because the French olive oil gave him indigestion as the Italian never had.[67] In his essay "On Experience," he describes his eating habits:

> I would feel as uncomfortable . . . without washing when I leave the table or get up in the morning . . . as I would be without really necessary things. I would dine without a tablecloth, but very uncomfortably without a clean napkin German fashion; I soil napkins more than they or the Italians do, and make little use of spoon or fork. . . . We are told of that tough soldier Marius that as he grew old he grew fastidious in his drinking, and drank only out of one particular cup of his. I too indulge my preference for a glass of a certain shape and do not willingly drink from a common glass, any more than I like to be served by a common hand. I dislike all metal compared with a clear and transparent material. Let my eyes also taste, according to their capacity. . . . I am not excessively fond of either salads or fruits, except melons. My father hated all kinds of sauces; I love them all. Eating too much bothers me, but I have as yet no really certain knowledge that any kind of food intrinsically disagrees with

me. . . . Radishes, for example, I first found to agree with me, then to disagree, now to agree again. In several respects I feel my stomach and appetite vary that way; I have changed back from white wine to red, and then from red to white. I am very fond of fish, and have my fat days on the lean days, and my feasts on the fast days. I believe what some say, that it is easier to digest than meat. And as it goes against my conscience to eat meat on fish days, so it goes against my taste to mix fish with meat, the difference between them seems to me too great.

Ever since my youth I have occasionally skipped a meal; either to sharpen my appetite for the next day . . . or to conserve my vigor for the sake of some action of body or mind. . . . I think it is healthier to eat more slowly and less, and to eat more often. But I want to make the most of appetite and hunger; I would take no pleasure in dragging out three or four puny meals a day, regulated as if I were taking medicine. . . . The most usual and common way of living is the best; all peculiarities seem to me things to be avoided; and I should hate as much to see a German putting water in his wine as a Frenchman drinking it pure. . . . It is bad manners, besides being harmful to health and even to pleasure, to eat greedily, as I do. I often bite my tongue and sometimes my fingers, in my haste.[68]

On the ceiling beams of his tower study Montaigne had inscribed quotations from his favorite Greek and Roman writers. The one most often associated with him is Terence's "I am a man; I consider nothing human foreign to me."[69] This passage illustrates the introspective curiosity that guarantees Montaigne an extraordinary place in intellectual history. It is of particular interest, however, because it indicates close attention to diet and dining, an interest perhaps most extensively and finely expressed by Montaigne, but also evident in many contemporary writings.

As Montaigne expressed his lively attitude toward experience in his discussion of dining, so Ronsard, in his poem "La Salade" used the choice of food as an image of a simple, natural life.[70] The poem was addressed to Amadis Jamyn, who had been his friend and secretary for nearly a decade when Jamyn left to take up a position at the court. In his poem Ronsard contrasts the simplicity and healthfulness of country life with the pomp and false pride of the court, a theme that would remind his readers of classical literature—of Horace or of Hesiod. He tells how the two of them will wash their hands and go out into the country and then, along a pure stream, gather good wild plants for a salad, taking into account their therapeutic qualities: burnet for the blood and so forth. All the ingredients will taste of themselves, and they will be dressed with a rosy vinegar and walnut oil. The rustic meal strongly resembles the Zen tea ceremony, infusing an everyday act with spiritual values. Ronsard contrasts the simplicity of this style with that of the court, which is expensive to purse and soul alike and where the tables are laden with everything that looks most delicious, a hundred dishes, and yet all of them tasting alike.

These literary examples from the second half of the sixteenth century illustrate how the attitudes of diners focused on the qualities of individual dishes, thus creating a clientele for an improved cuisine. Foods, whether as raw materials, cooked dishes, or meals given to mark occasions, became an appropriate way of offering friendship, showing concern, and marking relationships among people. Because it occupied a conspicuous place in the lives of individuals, the pleasures and ceremonies of the table could be invoked by writers as recognizable images.

Olivier de Serres

The style of life evoked by Ronsard in "La Salade" found its practical parallel a generation later in Olivier de Serres's *Le Theatre d'agricvltvre et mesnage des champs*, first published in 1600. This is the first French book on agriculture and horticulture in which a working knowledge of the subject predominates over the enumeration of advice cribbed from classical authors. De Serres was as familiar with the writings of Columella, Pliny, Varro, and others as his predecessors had been, but he also drew on his own experiences farming in the Ardèche, west of the Rhone, in the foothills of the Cévennes mountains. A classicist and a Huguenot, he tells of how his flock of peacocks once raised the alarm when hostile Catholic soldiers approached, comparing the birds to the Capolotine geese who saved Rome by their outcry at the invading Gauls.[71] Physicians who depended upon Galen had the advantage that the human body was unchanged, even if the medical advice was faulty. The agricultural writings of classical authorities, however, were not suited to the very different climate, soils, and products of early modern France. De Serres was able to learn from long practical experience in farming his own land, from his lively interest in new plants and new methods, and from his acquaintance with other horticulturists. He was known as an expert in his

Farmyard, engraving, from Olivier de Serres, *Theatre de l'agricvltvre* (Paris, 1600). At the left, the master and mistress survey their domain; in the background, a gardener pushes his wheelbarrow and another workman threshes; the dairymaid churns butter in her dairy; and poultry and pigs scavenge for food. (By permission of the Houghton Library, Harvard University.)

own day; Henry IV's minister Sully called him to court to advise on the raising of silkworms in one of the French government's intermittent efforts to establish a domestic silk industry.[72]

The *Theatre d'agricvltvre* opens with a discourse on the planning of the country house. De Serres considers the placement of the kitchen carefully. He dismisses the two most common locations—the basement of the house, undesirable because of noise, smells, and the danger of fire, and the side of the entrance court, which became the standard location in the next two hundred years. De Serres opts for placing it on the main floor of the house, so the master and mistress "can rebuke the sloth, noise, blasphemy, and thievings of both male and female servants." Even at night, when, under the pretext of finishing their work, the servants are engaged in mischief, if their employers are close at hand these ribaldries will be held in check, whereas, if the kitchen were in the courtyard and the employers up in their bedroom, the servants would be left in utter liberty.[73] Moreover, kitchens situated in basements and near stables are damp, smelly, and unhealthy. Supplies can be better supervised when they are closer at hand. He acknowledges that most people do not follow his advice because privacy is becoming more desirable. Quoting Anne de Montmorency on the deterioration in the quality of cooking when the master ceases to dine in the kitchen, de Serres suggests, as a compromise, an ante-cuisine, as it were, "a little dining room through which everyone would have to pass on his way to the kitchen: by this means [the

The kitchen garden, engraving, from Olivier de Serres, *Theatre de l'agricvltvre* (Paris, 1600). It was in such a setting that de Serres carried out his innovative horticultural experiments. (By permission of the Houghton Library, Harvard University.)

master would be] nobly served his food, without mixing with the dregs of his domestics, and [would keep] them all at their work." [74]

The increase since the Middle Ages in the variety of garden produce reflected in the *Theatre* is remarkable. De Serres sets forth the principles of operating four kinds of garden: the orchard, the kitchen garden (*potager*), the medicinal garden, and the flower garden. For each of these he describes the work of planting, cultivating, and harvesting, according to the season, phase of the moon, and plant variety. Treatments of cabbage make a good example of changing attitudes. The author of the *Ménagier* mentions it briefly; Gouberville grew it. De Serres discusses varieties, uses, diseases, and when and how the heads are to be harvested and stored. He includes instructions for growing the less common kinds, including cauliflower (*cauli-fiori*), "as the Italians call it, which are still rather rare in France; they hold an honorable place in the garden because of their delicacy." [75]

He also grew artichokes, the most esteemed vegetable in sixteenth-century France, and cardoons, various kinds of peas, and all sorts of root vegetables, including horseradish, carrots, turnips, and parsnips, as well as cucumbers, melons, and pumpkins. [76] A modern scholar, Le Roy Ladurie, in his book *Les Paysans de Languedoc*, has documented the spread of the artichoke,

> this blossom of the thistle, improved by the Arabs, passed from Naples to Florence in 1466, carried by Philippo Strozzi. Toward 1480 it is no-

ticed in Venice, as a curiosity. But very soon it veers toward the north-west, towards the usual rustic way stations. . . . Artichoke beds are mentioned in Avignon by the notaries from 1532 onward; from the principal towns they spread into the hinterlands . . . ; [appearing as] *carchofas* at Cavaillon in 1541, at Chateauneuf du Pape in 1553, at Orange in 1554. The local name remains *carchofas*, from the Italian *carciofo*. . . . They are very small, the size of a hen's egg (1618) [as the still-life paintings show] and are still considered a luxury, a vaguely aphrodisiac tidbit which one preserved in sugar syrup.[77]

By 1580 they were being cultivated in Languedoc and were esteemed enough to serve as little presents.

De Serres worked with a wide range of food materials. Though there is little in his great work to suggest that he was interested in culinary innovation, his instructions to the gentleman farmer on how to raise better and more varied produce made future culinary advances possible. A farming gentleman would not have been well pleased to see his beautiful new artichokes botched by an incompetent cook, or wasted, or sold for less than their full value at market. "In vain will you have your fields worked, and their fruits ingeniously locked up in storehouses, if, from there, they are transported as if in a torn bag."[78] The kitchen garden must be as large as possible, not only to provide for the household but also, if there is a fair-sized town nearby, so the produce can be sold at a profit—a real advantage in a society where cash was hard to come by.

Voices of Dissent

As long as there has been fine food there have been people who disapprove of it. Gluttony is one of the seven deadly sins, but its definition was often extended from meaning simple excess to taking excessive pleasure in eating. In 1490 an almanac titled *Le Kalendrier et compost des bergers* (Paris) included a "tree of vices" that set categories of gluttony.[79] This "tree" reads like a program for the development of the arts of kitchen and table in the *ancien régime*. It describes five branches of gluttony. The first comprehends a desire for delicate foods, flavor, and novelty because of expense or unseasonableness, exquisite preparation, or a desire for unnecessary variety. The second branch includes eating voraciously of foods appropriate to people of a higher or lower station than oneself, being too interested in filling one's belly, and not sharing one's food with the poor. The third branch is a desire for singularity: dishes "made, by art, differently from the way others make them," or chosen because they are difficult to make and require much work and effort; dishes that contain many ingredients, are deliciously sweet, and are made without regard to expense. The fourth branch is to eat without regard to schedule, that is, early, late, too often, or without regard to the seasons of the year and the rules of the church. The fifth branch, repetitiously, is to eat too much, too expensively, or too often.

Jean Bodin, in a treatise of 1574 on France's economic problems, considers wastefulness among the nine causes for the drastic increase in the cost of living in the sixteenth century, and he singles out expensive dining as one of those wasteful practices of his day because it causes a general rise in the cost of victuals.[80] Waste occurs, he says, because of a change in eating habits:

> People are not satisfied in an ordinary meal to have three ordinary courses, the first of boiled things, the second of roast, and the third of fruit; it is also necessary for a meat to be served five or six ways, with so many sauces, hashes, pastries, with so many kinds of salmagundis and other varied motley oddities as to make great prodigality. If old-fashioned thrift had continued, if for a banquet they had but five or six kinds of meat, one of each kind, in its natural way, without putting in all these new dainties, they would not make such a waste, and foods would be a better price.[81]

Continuing the long medieval tradition of sumptuary legislation, Michel de l'Hôpital, the chancellor of France for most of the 1560s, attempted to regulate the scale and variety of meals, whether "weddings, banquets, festivities, or at private tables," by restricting the menu to three courses of six platters each and by limiting the amount of food on each platter.[82] In his monograph on the natural history of birds, Pierre Belon digresses to include "a discourse upon the principal delicacies and feasts of divers nations." The French, he writes, are the most magnificent at table, serving "a thousand little preparations [*desguisements*]," on an abundance of silver plate which is more for show than anything else. He describes the order of the meal, now clearly articulated, "which opens usually with everything which is soft and liquid, and which should be served hot, such as *potages*, fricassees, hashes, and salads [sic]." The second course consists of a variety of roast and boiled meats, birds, "and other terrestrial animals," or on fast days, fish. The meal ends with the *issue de table*—"cold things such as fruit and dairy preparations and sweets." The French so delight in variety, he says, that the meal of a simple bourgeois may dirty "two, three, or four dozen plates, enough to keep two men busy all day cleaning them."[83]

The novelist Noël du Fail, in discussing the style of eating among ordinary people, expresses the sense that by 1585 fashions had changed for the worse:

> In the time of the great king Francis I, in many places people still put the cooking pot on the table, on which was simply a big dish filled with beef, mutton, veal, and salt pork and a big bunch of vegetables, cooked and compounded together, so that it made a broth, the true restorative and elixir of life. . . . From this mixture of victuals, thus arranged, everyone could take what seemed good to him, according to his desire, and thus everything went along simply, with goodwill.[84]

Du Fail contrasts this with the modern style practiced by ambitious men who divide up the foods, distributing pieces according to rank, thereby giving rise to jealousy and discontent. The old simplicity has given way to sauces, and the big old platter has been replaced by "little bowls filled with mere empty shows." The bouillon that combined so many meats remained standard through the eighteenth century; it was not lost but became embedded in more elaborated routines.

Food was one of the less expensive luxuries, and then, as always, an increased prosperity was often accompanied by a change in the style of dining. Anne de Montmorency, constable of France under Henry II, was quoted by Olivier de Serres in 1600 as having said that "when a gentleman attains an income of £500, he no longer knows what it is to eat well, because, wishing to eat in the grand style, he eats in his formal room [*salle*], at the mercy of his cook, where previously he had taken his meals in the kitchen, having himself served according to his own tastes."[85] As, one might add, did Gilles de Gouberville.

The many representations of the parable of Dives and Lazarus that were painted, drawn, and printed in the sixteenth and seventeenth centuries suggest that many people of conscience felt uneasy about dining well in a society where others starved.[86] In January 1596, Henry IV and his mistress, Gabrielle d'Estrées, were enjoying a festival at Monceau while famine ravaged the city. The diarist Pierre de l'Estoile wrote, "Meanwhile processions of the

January, engraving, from *The Twelve Months*, by Etienne Delaune (1568). The diner has left the kitchen to put himself at the mercy of his cook. The kitchen and dining room have been separated, but the square of trencher bread has not yet been replaced by pewter or earthen plates, and the cook still works at the hearth, not at a raised masonry stove. (Courtesy of the Museum of Fine Arts, Boston, Horatio G. Curtis Fund.)

poor took place in Paris, in such numbers as were never seen; they cried for hunger while in their mansions the rich gorged themselves with banquets and luxuries, an abominable affront to God, whatever excuse is given."[87]

In spite of the nostalgia for bygone simplicity and the disapproval of extravagance and of its uncharitable displays expressed by these writers, by the early seventeenth century the pleasures and ritual forms of dining had been integrated into the social life of both the aristocracy and the bourgeoisie. The importance of diet to health was accepted by all. Setting a good table was a recognized way of exhibiting one's cultivated tastes. Delicacies were a universal medium of social exchange among individuals. Meals were incorporated into the repertory of court life. Writers could use metaphors of cooking and eating to flavor their ideas. Those who followed fashion had begun to expect innovation and finesse, as well as abundance, from their cooks.

CHAPTER FOUR

Markets, Guilds, Ingredients, and New Foods

THE USE OF NEW INGREDIENTS and flavor combinations and the development of new cooking techniques interacted to give birth to *haute cuisine* in France, and, above all, in Paris. Necessary to development of these stylistic innovations, however, were the institutions in Paris that provided foodstuffs and foods for the public and the new ingredients that became available, as well as the private kitchens and the people who prepared the developing cuisine. In these two chapters I have chosen to deal with the entire period from the late Middle Ages to the end of the *ancien régime*. An expansion, an improvement, and a growing refinement occurred in all these subjects during this period, and I shall subsequently describe how these changes were expressed in the preparation and degustation of food.

THE MARKETS, FOODS, GUILDS, AND DINING PLACES OF PARIS

During the *ancien régime* as today Paris was the central meeting place of France's culinary life, as for so much of the rest of her culture. Paris attracted the most skilled craftspeople, the wealthiest clientele, and the most fashionable novelties. In Paris the highest prices were paid, and recognition came to talent most quickly. The city gained its special character from the interplay between the Paris that was a conglomeration of villages and the Paris that had been since the twelfth century one of the great centers of European civilization.

Paris the metropolis was served by the great specialized markets, such as Les Halles and the poultry and meat market on the quai de la Mégisserie, and by purveyors of luxuries that were available in small quantities at large prices.[1] Concurrently, the inhabitants of the village-oriented Paris shopped in their own neighborhoods, where markets like those on the rue Mouffetard and at the intersection of the rue de Seine and the rue de Buci often persisted for centuries. Coexisting, the metropolitan and local markets were to some extent segregated by geography, by timing (such as the change in midmorning from wholesale to retail at Les Halles), or by guild regulations.

The guild system of production and distribution had developed in the Middle Ages and functioned until it was abolished in 1791 during the Revolution.[2] The guilds operated under the regulation of the city and of the crown (or both) and were subject to the imposition both of regular taxes and of special charges and fines. At times the need of the government for money led to the issuing and revocation of charters at such an excessive and arbitrary rate that certain trades were nearly destroyed, as happened, for example, when Louis XIV put the squeeze on the Paris guild of *distillateurs-limonadiers*.[3] The guild sold, in boutiques and by street vendors, both citrus drinks and distilled beverages. Three times between 1673 and 1707 the central government arbitrarily put up for sale new masterships in the guild; the established masters had either to accept the loss of their monopoly, to purchase the new masterships, or to buy the government off with the payment of a lump sum.

In matters of public health the food guilds were regulated by the city, which enforced the use of accurate weights and measures and the sale of wholesome ingredients. Bread, the dietary staple, was the most closely supervised.[4] Some of the work of enforcing these regulations was delegated to the appropriate guilds. Regulations forbade the sale of meat pies for less than four deniers apiece because it was not possible to make them for less except by using tainted meat, and these cheap pies were bought by the poor and by children, who got sick.[5] A pastrycook who was found to be selling unwholesome food—meat, for example, that had been kept for three days and was declared to be corrupt and stinking—had to pay a substantial fine, and the offending article was publicly burned in front of his shop.[6]

By limiting the number of masterships, the guild statutes assured a monopoly to those who held them. Many guild regulations, however, were written with a view to preventing a single merchant from getting a disproportionate share of the supply of raw materials, of the labor force, or of the market. A cook was allowed to have only one apprentice at a time.[7] Since it was generally believed that the total amount of wealth was finite (an economic idea that has recently resurfaced as "the zero-sum society"), if one person had more trade, another would have less.

In most trades a person could work only within the guild hierarchy, though of course there were also many occupations for which no guilds existed—domestic service, for example. Exceptionally, the guild of cook-caterers, the *cuisiniers*, was matched by a parallel, nonguild hierarchy, that of the court

kitchens. The Paris cooks' guild regulations allowed for the lateral movement of a cook from those kitchens to enter the city guild at his own level
of proficiency, as attested to by letters from the court kitchen.[8] Thus, a scul-
lion or an assistant cook, a full-fledged cook, or a master chef could enjoy
an unusual degree of mobility. Presumably, a certain amount of traffic moved
from town to palace as well; this certainly took place in the eighteenth century, when the cooks in Paris were widely regarded as being superior to
those at Versailles, where they were sometimes summoned to cook for special occasions.

Some two dozen food guilds were in existence by the eighteenth century.
These may be divided roughly into two groups: the suppliers of basic materials, such as the butchers, fishmongers, grain merchants, and gardeners;
and the suppliers of prepared foods, such as bakers, pastrycooks, saucemak-
ers, and caterers. Some merchants supplied foods of both kinds. The *char-
cutiers*, for example, sold pork both raw and in cooked and cured forms. The
roastcooks, the *rôtisseurs*, who supplied pies and cooked dishes, also had a
lively sideline in uncooked meat and poultry, which the butchers and poulterers were constantly trying to suppress. The annals of the guilds echo yet
with their clashes: those same poulterers wanted to sell pies, to the indigna-
tion of those same pastrycooks.[9]

ANCESTORS OF THE RESTAURANT

Restaurants did not become an important part of the Parisian gastronomic scene until after the Revolution. A long history, however, lay behind
them in the form of the services that had been provided by the artisans and
merchants of the food guilds.

In the fourteenth century the author of the *Ménagier de Paris* had described the arrangements made for a wedding, whose organizers drew on
the services of a baker, pastrycook, wine merchant, butcher, waferer, poul-
terer, and an apothecary, as well as an *épicier* for spices, preserved fruit, sugared nuts, loaf sugar, pomegranates, rice flour, and hulled wheat.[10] The organizers also rented linens for half a dozen tables of guests and for kitchen
use, earthenware pots, wooden and metal spoons, iron cooking utensils, and
pewter plates and tankards. Finally, the hall in which the feast took place
was rented, as were the tables and benches.[11] Throughout the years meals
could be ordered served either at a hired hall or in tavernkeepers' facilities.

Most cabarets were chiefly frequented by the lower strata of society, but

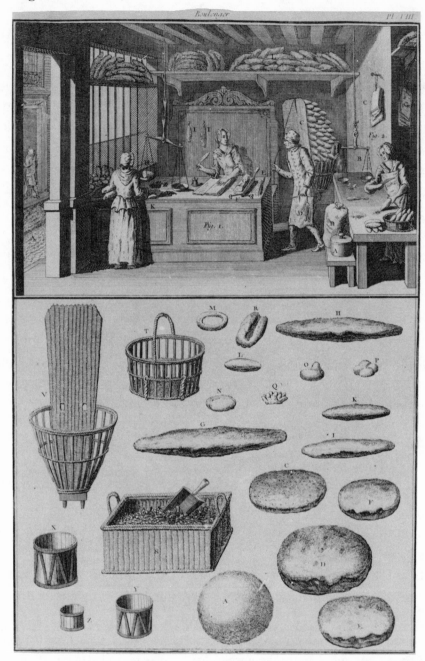

The baker's shop, engraving, from Paul Jacques Malouin, *Description des arts et métiers* (Paris, 1767). The baker's wife behind the counter is working on her accounts; at her left is a bread-cutter similar to those still used in neighborhood restaurants in Paris. The ambulant vendor carried a bunch of talleys in his left hand—sticks that were notched to record customers' indebtedness. The girl at the right is chipping the crusts from rolls; the chippings were sold "to the poor and country people" to put in their soup. Below: rolls and loaves of various shapes; among the small ones are the artichoke roll (Q), a ring-shaped roll (M), and a *pain à la ségovie* (O), which is curiously knobbed on top. (Courtesy of the Department of Special Collections, Iowa State University Library.)

The Pastrycook, engraving, from *The Trades* (1633) by Abraham Bosse. The blazing fire in the back of the oven serves the need of the artist for a light source, not the baker's need for steady, smokeless heat. Among the wares mentioned in the verse below are macaroons, cakes, turnovers, *biscuits*, and cream puffs. To judge from the table leaves stored under the cloth in the foreground, this pastrycook must undertake catering as well as direct sales to the young and old customers in the shop. The pies cooling on wicker racks in the foreground are a proof of his skill. (Courtesy of the Museum of Fine Arts, Boston.)

some catered to the wealthy. Bodin cited a taste for caterers' expensive meals as one form of gastronomic wastefulness: "Everyone today wants to dine at le More's, Sanson's, Innocent's, and Havart's, ministers of voluptuousness and expense, who, in a well ordered and regulated society would be driven out and banished as corruptors of behavior."[12] If these places were not quite restaurants in the modern sense, they had many characteristics in common with them. They served meals to all comers at fixed, and often posted, prices, offered a degree of choice, and sometimes enjoyed a considerable reputation. Competition among the better cabarets for the favor of wealthy patrons encouraged high standards of performance; the importance of novelty to their fashion-conscious customers obliged the caterers to exert their culinary imaginations.

In the late sixteenth century a Venetian ambassador reported on the services available:

> Do you want to buy your provisions all prepared? The roasters and the pastrycooks, in less than an hour, will arrange a dinner for you, or a supper, for ten, twenty, or a hundred people; the roaster will give you the meats, the pastrycook the tarts, the meat pies, the little cooked dishes, and sweets; the cook will give you aspics, sauces, stews. This art is so far advanced in Paris that there are tavernkeepers who will give you something to eat at their places for all prices, for a teston, for an écu, for four, for ten, even for twenty apiece if you wish it, but for twenty écus I hope they will give you manna *en potage* or roast phoenix, or whatever in the world is most precious.[13]

Private dwellings in Paris were often available for hire when their owners were away with the court or residing at their country estates. There were also *hôtels* that were kept as inns, where rooms could be hired to live in or to put on special meals. The person giving the banquet could make all the arrangements or could engage the services of a *traîteur*, a caterer who would either serve a meal at his own premises or in a place of the patron's choosing. These *hôtels* could be superb. For example, in the late seventeenth and early eighteenth centuries, part of the palace on the rue de Seine that had belonged to Henry IV's first wife, Queen Marguerite, was used as an *hôtel meublé*.[14] A book of advice on shopping and services in Paris, *Le Livre commode contenant les adresses de la ville de Paris . . . pour 1692*, classed it at the top of the list of furnished lodgings, among the magnificently decorated apartments for great noblemen.[15] The *Livre commode* catalogs lodging and eating places in order of price and services. Meals at the most expensive tables cost between ten and forty sols. Usually the diners all sat together at the table d'hôte, but there were also "some inns where there are three different tables, at fifteen, twenty, and thirty sols a meal."[16]

Travelers often found in the table d'hôte a practical solution to the problem of eating, and it was also considered a good place to practice speaking French, though the menu was usually dull. One traveler summarized the style current in 1727: "They serve you a *soupe* [broth with bread], some boiled meat or a piece of beef, a veal fricassee or some chops, a few vegetables, some roast, and as dessert, some milk, cheese, biscuits, fruit in season, and so it goes from one end of the year to the next."[17] People of quality, this writer tells us, keep good tables, and sometimes one finds well-flavored dishes at the *rôtisseurs*, but cooking for the table d'hôte is less well done and monotonous. "One would willingly pay a little more for better cooking and more variety." Late in the century Louis Sébastien Mercier, in *Tableau de Paris*, described the inconvenience of eating

> in the midst of a dozen strangers. . . . The center of the table (toward what are called the *pièces de résistance*) is occupied by the regular custom-ers who monopolize these important places. . . . Armed with tireless jaws, they eat up greedily as soon as the signal is given. . . . Unhappy the man who is slow to chew up his share. Seated between these greedy, agile cormorants, he will fast during the meal. In vain will he ask the servant for sustenance; the table will be cleared before he is able to get served.[18]

The word *restaurant* was originally applied to a group of fortifying meat broths. The poet Clement Marot used the word in this sense in the early sixteenth century.[19] François Massialot's *Cuisinier roïal et bourgeois*, first pub-lished in 1691, gives a recipe for a *restaurant* made with beef, mutton, veal, capon, squabs, partridges, onions, root vegetables, and herbs. The ingredi-ents are placed, without any added liquid, in a lidded pot sealed with a flour and water paste. The pot is then set in a bigger one, which is filled with water, brought to a boil, and allowed to simmer for five or six hours. The broth, which is by this time very succulent, is strained off and degreased. A hollowed-out bread loaf is filled with the chopped, seasoned meat from the capon and other tidbits, and the loaf is then simmered in the broth. Before serving, it receives a garnish of cockscombs, sweetbreads, and other delica-cies sautéed with bacon.[20]

The *traîteurs* had a monopoly on the sale of ragouts in eighteenth-century Paris. In 1765 a man named Boulanger who was not a *traîteur* set up a busi-ness that evaded this restriction by offering *restaurants* for sale to the public on his premises. The geographer of culinary Paris, René Héron de Ville-fosse, describes it as having offered "a choice, on little marble tables without a cloth, of poached poultry with coarse salt, fresh eggs, and broth."[21]

THE SPECIALIZED MARKETS

Nowadays we take for granted a considerable array of specialty stores carrying world-renowned brands of luxury foods. We also cynically take for granted the existence of a powerful network of promoters of this merchandise. The praise of a piece of equipment or a particular supplier's mustard, especially if uttered by the right person, can give a notable boost to sales. By the late seventeenth century, when the fashionable world had begun to pay close attention to what was on its table, the first signs of promotional advertising appeared. Nicolas de Blegny was both the seller and the promoter of a line of supplies and equipment for making the new beverages, coffee, tea, and chocolate. He was also a scoundrel. In 1693 he was convicted of swindling and was imprisoned for seven years, after which he retired to live out his years in Avignon.

In his role as entrepreneur, de Blegny presented himself to the public as "adviser and physician-artist to His Majesty the King and to Monsieur [the king's brother]." He wrote one of the earliest treatises on the new beverages, *Le Bon usage du thé, du caffé et du chocolat* (1687). A few years later he published the shopper's guide, *Le Livre commode pour . . . 1692.*[22] Although a treasure trove for the modern student, the latter work seems to have been written to promote de Blegny's and his relations' enterprises. Presumably to conceal his interest, he took the precaution of publishing it pseudonymously, as Abraham du Pradel. Thus he could point out that "an interesting treatise on tea, coffee, and chocolate is sold at the Widow Nion's on the quai de Nesle," not mentioning his own authorship, and recommend his relation's apothecary shop.[23] He did not, however, mention his own place of business, so perhaps by then the venture had failed. A cornucopia of good fare from the provinces spills out of the pages of de Blegny's guide.

The Provençals who lodge in the cul-de-sac by Saint Germain l'Auxerrois sell, wholesale, Roquefort cheeses, olives, anchovies, Saint Laurent wine, figs, raisins, prunes, almonds, and other dried fruits from Provence. . . . Le Sieur Boursin . . . does a special business in *boudin blanc.* . . . There are frequent arrivals of boats at the quai de l'Ecole bringing apples and pears from Normandy. . . . The Dijon stagecoach brings two kinds of exquisite and inimitable preserves [including the prunes that were a favorite of Madame de Sévigné's son-in-law] and barberry jam. . . . [Other merchants] sell fine capers, oranges and lemons from Provence, mandarin oranges, and Portuguese. . . . [Other merchants are] renowned for their fine melons.[24]

The manufacture of Auvergne, or Cantal cheese, engraving, from *Encyclopédie: Recueil de planches . . .* (Paris, 1763–77). In the foreground a workman presses curds in a wooden mold; the whey drains out to be collected in a pan. In the background milk is being heated, and at the right curd is pressed under a board weighted by rocks. The conical article hung from pegs on the wall is a *chausse*, or cheesecloth strainer. (By permission of the Houghton Library, Harvard University.)

Of all the food specialties that came in to the Paris markets, the butters from neighboring villages and the cheeses from more distant regions won the loudest applause. Tobias Smollet called French butter "exquisite."[25] The *Livre commode* enumerates butter specialists.[26] They clustered around the pewterer's guild hall, and around nine o'clock in the morning the peasants who sold little loaves of butter from Vanves, always at a premium price, could be found. Isigny in Normandy, the site of a salt-manufacturing industry, was noted for the quality of its salted butter, which was sold on the rue de la Cassonnerie. Butters from other parts of Normandy and from Brittany could be purchased in other locations.

If I knew the name of a muse of cheesemaking, I would invoke her before launching into a discussion of this quintessentially French food. As early as the 1390s the *Ménagier de Paris* included a little verse warning against buying cheese with too many eyes like Argus, weepy like Mary Magdalene, or pale like Helen. A good cheese, he wrote, is eyeless, not weeping, and white, but firm, heavy, and with a good rind.[27] By 1600 Olivier de Serres could enumerate a long list of cheeses, although one must wonder how much the ones that bore familiar names actually resembled the modern versions.

> As to the cheeses, the cow's is not so delicate as either the goat's or the ewe's, although it is more abundant. It is, nonetheless, much in demand, and, as I have said [elsewhere], it takes its fame from the climate and pasturage. For such a reason are the cheeses of Auvergne [Cantal] known in all parts of France, from one ocean to the other, where they are transported in great quantity. [Platina had referred to them earlier.] In diverse other regions of this kingdom there are also mountains fertile in cows' cheeses because of their exquisite pasturages. Similarly there are byways of mountains, foothills, and plains in the provinces of many regions celebrated for good cheeses of diverse sorts and diverse milks. Brie, among others, is known for its good cheeses called *angelots*, and Lesbaux in Provence, on the border of Languedoc, which, because of the delicacy of their little cheeses, are much prized . . . ; and similarly the province of Brittany. As to the cheeses which are imported into this kingdom . . . , those of Milan [Parmesan] and Turkey [?] hold the first rank, and after them those of Switzerland and finally, in the greatest quantity and the most used, those of the provinces of Holland and Zeeland.[28]

He makes no mention of the blue cheeses, but he does speak of "cheeses from Lombardy the size of millstones."

Fifty years later Nicolas de Bonnefons obliged with simple home recipes for cheesemaking;[29] in the eighteenth century, in *La Cuisinière bourgeoise*, Menon listed many of the same cheeses de Serres had.

> We have the *chevrette* cheeses which are made with goat's milk combined with one-third cow's milk; when they are properly finished they are very good. The most abundant cheese in Paris is Brie, and when carefully chosen it is excellent. We have [cheeses] from Brittany and from Languedoc, Dutch cheese, of which the blue kind [*persillée*] is the best, Gruyère, which should be selected for fatness and big eyes [what would the author of the *Ménagier* have said?]; Parmesan and Roquefort—the most highly esteemed of all, and in consequence the dearest. We also have soft new cheeses, which are served with coarse salt. Little cream cheeses, eaten

with cream and sugar; all these sorts of cheeses are served *au dessert*; it is only Parmesan and Brie which are used in the kitchen.[30]

THE NEW FOODS

Despite the considerable demand for novelty in the France of the *ancien régime*, the many foods from outside Europe that were discovered during the explorations of the sixteenth century and later and were esteemed in world trade were slow to be adopted. Indeed, in the sixteenth century, the only New World food immediately accepted in France was the turkey.

The *coq d'inde* (or Indian rooster—in German, *Indianischer Henn*) was brought from Mexico to Spain early in the century. Its use spread quickly through Europe, replacing peacock as an important roast for banquets, though so far as I know it was never served sewn back into its skin. It resembled the peacock closely enough to give cooks and diners a model in using it. This similarity greatly smoothed the path of acceptance. Turkey was a luxury meat, an exotic item at a time when the givers of banquets desired praise for serving all the kinds of meat that were in season. The earliest French turkeys I have encountered so far in print were the pets of a ten-year-old princess, Jeanne d'Albret. She had six pairs, which were evidently not intended for the table because records indicate that provision was made for their care in November 1528 when she left the Norman residence where she had passed her childhood.[31] Half of the eggs laid by these birds were to be given to a nearby convent. In 1549, the accounts of a banquet given in Paris for Catherine de Medici mention sixty-six turkeys.[32] In 1559 Gilles de Gouberville received a pair as a gift from a neighbor, and he rewarded the servant who brought them with a larger tip than was his custom.[33] By 1565 they were bought in Toulouse for yet another banquet given in honor of the queen and her son, Charles IX, then making the Grand Voyage de France.[34]

Charles Estienne wrote in 1564, with the distaste apparently felt by most growers of turkeys:

Whosoever he was that brought us these birdes from the island of India lately discovered by the Spaniards and Portingales, whether we call them cockes or peacockes of India, hath more fitted and prouided for the tooth than for any profit. For they may rightly be termed coffers to cast oates into, a devouring gulfe of meate, and wherein there is no other pleasure to be taken, but only in their crie and furiousness when they are come to be great ones: or continuall cheaping whiles they be little. . . . It is very true that his [the turkey's] flesh is fine and delicate, but without taste and of hard digestion. . . . And this is the cause why men use to powder them, lard them much, and season them with spices. There is much more pleasure and goodness in the flesh of a peacock.[35]

Olivier de Serres wrote of the turkey as "very frail when young, always greedy, and so stupid and brutish that it has not got the sense to avoid the depredations of men and beasts. . . . Even the mothers kill their own off-spring by walking on them."[36] He advised that, rather than let them rampage about the kitchen garden damaging the plants, a young turkeyherd take them out into the highways and byways to forage for their food. By the seventeenth century, the stupidity of turkeys was so generally recognized that to be duped was to be *dindonné*, corresponding to the English "gulled."[37]

Lancelot de Casteau included turkey in two of the four courses of the banquet celebrating the entry of a prince-bishop of Liège in 1557; for the first course it was boiled (accompanied by oysters and cardoons), and for the third course it was roasted and served cold.[38] By the middle of the next century several recipes had been developed. The size of a turkey made the use of stuffings practical and desirable; usually they were meat-based. The best known is La Varenne's delectable *poulet d'inde à la framboise farçi*.[39] Other recipes used turkeys in pies; the trimmings and giblets went into little ragouts. One sumptuous pie contains a turkey stuffed with squabs, ox palates, mushrooms, truffles, artichoke bottoms, cockscombs, sheep kidneys, and sweetbreads.[40] The bird remained popular from the time of its introduction; the 1767 *Dictionnaire portatif de cuisine* enumerates some forty ways of preparing it, in company with everything from cucumbers to anchovies, and roast, boiled, and fricasseed.[41] By then the paramount luxury dish on opulent tables was the truffled turkey, costing twenty livres or more.[42]

Although the potato eventually became an important part of the French diet, it gained only slow acceptance after its introduction as a food plant in the late sixteenth century.[43] Olivier de Serres described it as

a shrub called *cartoufle*, . . . similar to a truffle, and called such by some people. It came from Switzerland into the Dauphiné recently. Its fruit is stored all winter in sand spread out in a cool cellar, providing it is kept away from the depredations of rats, for they have such a taste for this food that, if they can, they will eat it up in no time at all.

He goes on to say, bewilderingly, that potatoes resemble truffles in taste as well as in appearance and that a cook "so dresses all of them that one can recognize little difference between them."[44]

Negative attitudes delayed acceptance. Elsewhere in Europe it was suggested that if God had intended the potato to be used as food it would have been mentioned in the Bible, and in eighteenth-century Burgundy peasants refused to eat them because they believed that potatoes caused leprosy.[45] The upper classes declined to use the tuber on the grounds that it was coarse, insipid, and caused flatulence. In times of prosperity it served as animal fodder, especially for pigs, and in times of famine as food for the starving—associations that won it no favor. Unlike the turkey, the potato did not resemble any familiar, accepted ingredient that cooks already knew how to prepare or that diners wanted to eat. Comparisons with truffles and chestnuts were often made. Even modern improved varieties of potato would disappoint anyone trying to substitute it for them.

Recurrent bad wheat harvests and the famines that followed encouraged some agronomists to suggest that the potato could be useful as an alternative starch. In the last quarter of the eighteenth century, Antoine-Augustin Parmentier conducted a prolonged campaign to get the potato accepted as a source of nourishment. He grew potatoes successfully on ground believed to be barren; when they blossomed, Louis XVI wore a potato flower in his buttonhole, thus ensuring a brief popularity at court.[46] A meal was served at court under Parmentier's supervision, featuring potatoes served twenty different ways. Unfortunately, however, most of Parmentier's efforts went to trying to substitute potato starch for flour in baking. As any baker knows, potatoes and potato starch are valuable ingredients but are best used in moderation. A typical formula then used a proportion of one-third potato starch to one-third each wheat and rye flour; such results met with acceptance only in times of want.[47] These misdirected efforts may have done more harm than good by creating a distaste for potatoes. Attempts to find other ways to prepare the potato would have been more successful. There is no evidence that its capacity to take on a wide variety of textures was appreciated in eighteenth-century France or that its mild flavor combined well with other ingredients then in use. Its flavor was abused as insipid, while the less versatile Jerusalem artichoke was exploited more extensively than it is today, and indeed potato breeders had not yet produced the improved varieties we know. In France the potato was valued chiefly as a source of starch, as animal fodder, and as a cheap food for the poor long after it had become a popular food elsewhere, most notably in the British Isles and in Germany. Martin Lister, an English traveler in Paris at the end of the seventeenth century, observed that "one scarcely finds any potatoes at market—those wholesome and nourishing roots which make up so great a resource for the people of England."[48] As late as at the end of the next century Le Grand d'Aussy, the first historian of the French table, wrote:

> It was in the reign of Louis XV that some of our provinces adopted it, but at first it gained only a moderate acceptance in France. . . . In time, however, the potato was accepted in the capital, and even, astonishingly, became fashionable. Physicians analyzed its principles; authors wrote to extol its virtues. . . . One even saw it appear with distinction upon the best tables. But this moment of favor, so little deserved, passed quickly. The pasty flavor, the natural insipidity, the unwholesome quality of this food, which like all unleavened starches, is windy and indigestible, brought about its rejection in delicate houses, and sent it back to the common people, whose coarser tastes and more robust stomachs are satisfied by everything which is capable of appeasing hunger.[49]

It must be noted as a failure of eighteenth-century French culinary imagination that cooks did not invent ways of exploiting the potato's good qualities. The preoccupation with finding a product to make wheat go farther distracted from other efforts at invention. Le Grand places potatoes in the cereal and starch section of his book, following a discussion of famine breads and preceding a brief notice about the Jerusalem artichoke, which he incorrectly calls "only a variety of potato."

The origins of both had been forgotten by the time he was writing. The Jerusalem artichoke, *helianthemum tuberosum*, had been found in North America by Samuel de Champlain; it was unknown in South America. A few members of a tribe of Brazilian Indians were brought to France and exhibited at Versailles; the tribe's name was written *taupinambou* in French, and the people called *taupinambours*. The new tuber, recognized as Indian food and arriving at about the same time, received the Indian name that happened to be in peoples' minds.[50] Confusion subsequently arose over the origins of the potato so that when Le Grand wrote in the late eighteenth century, the Peruvian origin of the potato had been forgotten, and he thought that it had come to Europe from North America by way of England.[51]

The verbal confusions that accompanied the arrival of new ingredients in Europe often make it hard to know what foodstuffs are being referred to. Lewis Carroll's Humpty Dumpty, who paid words extra for bearing the burden of special meanings, would have been bankrupted by early modern European practices in naming new foods. Various tubers that had long been eaten in Europe were known as earth apples and earth pears (in German *erdapfel* and *erdbirn*; in French, *pomme de terre* and *poire de terre*). When the new tubers from North and South America arrived (including the sweet potato, which has never become important in the French kitchen), they were designated by the same names.[52] To complicate matters, at least four varieties of "white" potatoes were in circulation, all with different flavors and colors of skin and flesh.[53] Because contemporary authors used the names of plants they already knew for the new tubers and were unreliable in describing the flavor, even when "*pomme de terre*" is used, it is dangerous to make a positive identification unless the context gives clear guidance.

It is hard to imagine a time when there were no beans to make cassoulet in Castelnaudary, Carcassonne, or Toulouse, much less any varieties of bean for cooks to argue the merits of, but until Columbus returned to Spain from his second voyage in 1493 with seeds of *Phaseolus vulgaris*, the only bean known to Europeans was the broad, fava, or horse bean, *Vicia fava*.[54] The New World bean was one of a handful of the newly discovered vegetables to gain general acceptance in much of Europe by the end of the eighteenth century.

Like some other foods, beans may have become popular because a predecessor existed that they could replace and to which they were in some respects superior. The broad bean has a long history. It was described by Pythagoras in the sixth century B.C. as unwholesome. Later writers generally have assumed that this assessment resulted from the vegetable's flatulent quality. Some people of eastern Mediterranean and southern Italian origins suffer from a hereditary enzyme deficiency called favism, the symptoms of which, anemia, jaundice, fever, and diarrhea, can be brought on by eating fava beans.[55] These beans had been grown in Languedoc long before seeds of *Phaseolus* beans were brought there from Spain at the end of the sixteenth century. One may conjecture that the ancestor of cassoulet was made with fava beans. It is instructive to be reminded that a dish whose traditional ingredients cooks and diners debate with passion is, in its modern form, not very old. The earliest known reference to *Phaseolus* beans in France dates from 1594, and Olivier de Serres called them *phasiols*.[56] The English lexicographer Randle Cotgrave, in his dictionary of 1611, defines "Faseols" as "Fasels, long Pesons, Kidney Beanes, Sperage Beanes, French Beanes, Romane beanes, Garden Smilas" and gives a similar definition under "Phaseoles."[57] By the mid-seventeenth century the crop was important enough that its prices at market were recorded.[58] At the same time, recipes for them first appeared in cookbooks.

The green bean was generally referred to as the *haricot*; the mature bean, dried and divested of its pod, was called the *fêverole*.[59] The latter seems to have been less used in polite society, perhaps because of its windy nature, but its resemblance to the fava bean was close enough to guide cooks in preparing it. The *Encyclopédie* recommends the nourishing qualities of the dried bean "to those who have a good stomach, and who are young and robust, or who exercise heartily; but persons who are delicate, . . . and those who lead a sedentary life should abstain from them, for they are windy, heavy on the stomach, and hard to digest."[60] The green beans, on the other hand, were welcome at the best of tables. Their convenient resemblance to asparagus (as in Cotgrave's "sperage beans") gave cooks an idea how to prepare them. Bonnefons, in *Les Delices de la campagne*, says they are good eaten green when young; and in *Le Jardinier françois* he gives directions for sun-drying the beans or preserving them in vinegar or salt with cloves and pepper, to be rinsed thoroughly several months later for use in winter salads.[61] In 1692 Massialot enlarged upon this theme: "You will use them in winter, to mix with your salads of little green pickles (*cornichons*), anchovies, beetroot, capers, and samphire (*passepierre*); arranged in divided dishes it makes a very handsome effect."[62] Certainly any note of green on the midwinter table was most welcome, though their color could not have been very vivid by then.

Louis Liger's *Œconomie générale de la campagne* of 1700 includes an instructive calendar for gardeners, listing by month what is to be planted, the other garden work to be done, and the seasons when the crops are to be harvested. He says beans should be planted in April, risking the dangers of frost in hopes of getting an early crop, and then planted again in May for safety's sake. By June the vines will need supports, and in July the crop can be harvested. He advises that some be plucked to enjoy while they are green and tender.[63] Other writers, of whom Vincent La Chapelle is the first, advise cutting them in thin strips lengthwise, a practice that is also followed in *Les*

Soupers de la cour (1755) and is still called "frenching."[64] The dried beans tardily appear in *La Cuisinière bourgeoise* (1746) as an accompaniment to a leg of mutton, which has remained a classic combination.[65] This useful if unspectacular plant was easily assimilated into the French diet. It made a beneficial addition for all classes, available fresh in summer and both as a preserved green vegetable and as protein-rich dried beans in winter. In time it became so much a part of French cuisine that gastronomes could seriously argue over the relative authenticity of local variations.

CHOCOLATE, TEA, AND COFFEE

Chocolate was the first of the foreign drinks to arrive in Europe. Hernando Cortes wrote to the Holy Roman Emperor Charles V about it and brought some with him when he returned to Spain in 1528, serving it to Charles when they met at Toledo.[66] It would be interesting to know how enthusiastically it was received, for chocolate, as drunk by the Aztecs, was a mixture thickened with cornstarch, spiced with hot peppers, allspice, vanilla, and other native plants, and dyed a reddish color with annato (*achiote*).[67] Despite these ingredients, chocolate drinking became popular in Spain during the sixteenth century. Gradually the recipe was simplified and adapted to the European palate. Sugar or honey sweetened it; vanilla (also now arrived from the New World), cinnamon, and sometimes black pepper were added to enhance the flavor.

To my knowledge the first person to use chocolate in France was Cardinal Richelieu's older brother, who took it for splenetic vapors sometime before 1642. When the daughter of Philip IV of Spain, Maria Theresa, went to France to marry Louis XIV, she was accompanied by a maid who specialized in making chocolate, for which the princess had a particular liking.[68] It was, indeed, one of her few pleasures. Gradually the use of chocolate spread. There are recipes for preparing it in the works of Philippe Sylvestre Dufour (1685) and Nicolas de Blegny (1687), but the earliest recipe using it as an ingredient in cooking is in Massialot's *Cuisinier roïal et bourgeois* (1691). This may be the only published Aztec recipe in seventeenth-century France, using chocolate as a thickener.

Widgeon [*macreuse*] in a ragout with chocolate. Having plucked and cleaned your widgeon, eviscerate it and wash it. Scald it and put it in a pot and season it with salt, pepper, bay leaf, and a bouquet garni; you make a

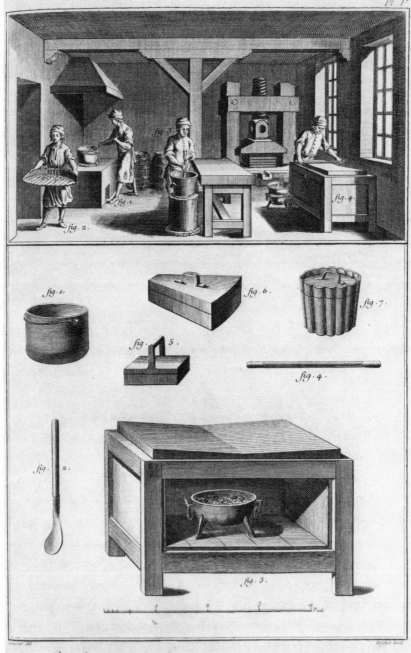

Confiseur. Chocolat et Moules pour les Fromages.

The confectioner's shop, with equipment for making chocolate and ices, engraving, from *Encyclopédie: Recueil de planches . . .* (Paris, 1763–77). In the lower part of the plate is a chocolate-bean grinding stone, with a charcoal brazier set beneath it to keep it warm. The molds with lids are for freezing ices and iced cheeses; the spoonlike tool is a *spadule* for scraping and stirring ice mixtures as they freeze. (By permission of the Houghton Library, Harvard University.)

little chocolate which you throw in. Prepare at the same time a ragout, with the livers, mushrooms, morels, truffles, and a *quarteron* of chestnuts. When your widgeon is cooked and arranged on its dish, you pour your ragout over it, and serve it garnished with whatever you wish.[69]

With the sole exception of the indefatigable plagiarist who gave us the *Dictionnaire portatif de cuisine*, subsequent writers did not take up this recipe.

As a beverage, chocolate was usually prepared with water, though sometimes with milk. It was frothed with a chocolate stick—a stick with a carved knob and often rings, which was moved rapidly up and down in the mixture to produce a rich foam. They are still used in Spanish-speaking parts of the world. Menon's recipe from the *Maître d'hôtel, confiseur* (1750) is typical.

Ordinarily one chocolate tablet is used to a [four-ounce] cup, but the proportion is ten cups to the pound; so you take as many tablets as you wish cups; melt the plain [unsweetened] chocolate in a coffeepot in which you have put water to the amount that you want to make; boil it and let it simmer a little over hot coals; when it is melted . . . mix the yolk of an egg with some [previously prepared] chocolate and put it in your coffeepot. Put it back over a gentle fire and stir well with the chocolate stick. It must not be allowed to boil at all after you have put the egg yolk in; the number of egg yolks must be in proportion to the number of cups you make. You need one for four or five cups.

Chocolat à l'Angloise is made in the same way as the preceding, except that you take the white of an egg and beat it, and take off all the first foam; put the chocolate to melt in it, and finish in the same way. It should be observed that chocolate is better if it is made the day before it is wanted, and ordinarily one leaves a good leaven for those who are in the habit of making it every day.[70]

The alertness and organization of eighteenth-century cooks are testified to by the assimilation of chocolate into the repertory of the *office*, the supplementary cool kitchen where preserving and confectionary were done. Except for Massialot's Aztec recipe, chocolate was adapted to preexisting recipes. In Massialot's *Nouvelle instruction pour les confitures*, written at the end of the seventeenth century, we find sweet biscuits flavored with chocolate and chocolate marzipan.[71] Vincent La Chapelle provided recipes for chocolate ice cream, one made with cream, another custard-based.[72] Menon has similar recipes, but more of them. His *Maître d'hôtel, confiseur* is organized by season but includes a select group of ingredients available all year around, to which chocolate and coffee were most welcome additions. There are also some chocolate candies: the still familiar diablotins—flat disks of bitter chocolate, thickly sprinkled with nonpareils, chocolate "olives" (which we call chocolate truffles), and a conserve of chocolate, which turns out to be very like fudge.[73] Dipped chocolates, however, were not invented until the nineteenth century.

Tea was the least popular of the new beverages in France, but it has always had a certain number of fanciers there. Although Marco Polo had mentioned tea in his account of his travels in Asia in the thirteenth century, it was only in the later part of the sixteenth century that travelers and missionaries in the Far East began to send back accounts of it.[74] The first tea to arrive in Europe came to Holland in 1610; regular shipments began in 1638. By 1652 it was being drunk in London, although Samuel Pepys, who was generally up-to-date, did not drink his first cup until 1660—and then at a coffeehouse.[75]

By the mid-seventeenth century, tea had made its way to France. Mazarin took it as a remedy for gout, and in 1648 a thesis about its medicinal properties had been sustained at the Faculty of Medicine in Paris by one Armand-Jean de Mauvillain.[76] He favored it, though the healthfulness of all three beverages was the subject of interminable debate. From the beginning of their popularity, two camps formed around each drink. The opponents of tea claimed that it was hard to digest and dangerous for anyone to drink, especially if over forty years of age.[77]

By the 1680s books began to appear in France on all the new beverages. Of these, the best are Philippe Sylvestre Dufour's *Traitez nouveaux et curieux du café, du thé et du chocolate, ouvrage egalement necessaire aux medecins et à tous ceux qui aiment leur santé* (1685) and de Blegny's *Le Bon usage du thé, du caffé et du chocolat pour la preservation et pour la guérison des maladies* (1687). Both books include instructions for brewing tea, but the most striking is found in Massialot's *Nouvelle instruction pour les confitures* of 1692. The secondary uses he recommends are omitted in later editions.

The ordinary way to prepare tea is to boil in a suitable vessel as much water as one wishes servings, and when it boils one takes it off the fire to put in the tea leaves in proportion, that is to say a dram [three grams or one teaspoon]. Then you cover the pot and leave your tea thus to infuse for the third part of a quarter of an hour. During this time the leaves sink down to the bottom of your teapot, or coffeepot, and the water will take on their color. You pour it into your cups . . . in which you have put a half spoonful of powdered sugar, and you drink it like coffee. . . . You can smoke tea as you do tobacco, after having lightly moistened the leaves with drops of brandy sprinkled over it; and the sediment of ash which remains in the bottom of the pipe is marvelous for whitening the teeth. Tea leaves may be used for a second infusion, by boiling the liquid a little, which one does not do at all the first time: but this is being too economical if one is taking it for health.[78]

The culinary uses of tea were few, though Vincent La Chapelle (1742) does give one recipe for a tea-flavored custard.[79] Although in France tea never achieved the popularity of coffee, it had its steady drinkers. In 1692, N. Audiger praised its medicinal qualities: "Its properties are to abate the vapors of the brain, to cool and purify the blood. It is usually taken in the morning, to waken the spirit and to give appetite, and after meals, to aid digestion."[80]

If chocolate was the most useful of the new ingredients for cooking, coffee had the strongest impact on French society. The cafés to which it gave rise became the setting for some of the liveliest intellectual and social life in Europe. One enthusiastic historian suggested that these new nonalcoholic drinks were responsible for the Enlightenment because for the first time people gathered in a social setting without getting drunk.[81] Such a notion is frivolous. There had always been alternatives to strong drink, and European civilization had some achievements to its credit in the previous several centuries. But to some extent the cafés did take over the role that taverns had long played as gathering places for dissenters. It might also be argued that they had a share in the making of the modern restaurant, offering a choice of drinks and often of sweets at a fixed price and in a more civilized setting than most taverns provided.

Like tea and chocolate, coffee was first known to Europe from the descriptions of late sixteenth-century travelers.[82] The Dutch initiated its commercial exploitation, as they had for tea, when a shipment of coffee beans arrived in Holland in 1637. By 1660 trade on a large scale had begun. The product arrived in Venice from the Near East, passed through the Fondaco dei Tedeschi (the German commercial community), thence north into the German-speaking areas, or was shipped from Venice to Marseilles, where it had been drunk as early as 1644.[83] Since coffee was very popular in the Moslem world (despite a prohibitionist movement of considerable strength in the seventeenth century), and the border between Turkish and Christian areas was long and unstable, Europeans had the opportunity to encounter coffee. Individuals in France were experimenting with it in the 1660s.[84]

A Turkish ambassador to the court of Louis XIV started the French drinking it in earnest in 1669. Then, in 1672, an Armenian named Hartounian or Pascal sold it at the Foire-Saint-Germain, an annual Left Bank Shrovetide festival. After considerable success there, he opened a permanent shop, but it failed and he moved on to London. Thereafter an increasing number of merchants sold it through shops and ambulant vendors. The vendors were usually dressed in "Armenian" garb—baggy trousers and vests of bright colors. The most prominent of the shopkeepers was Francesco-Procopio dei Coltelli, perhaps from Palermo, who had begun as a waiter in Pascal's shop.[85] Procope, as he was called, joined the guild of *distillateurs-limonadiers* and opened a succession of respectable and even fashionable cafés throughout Paris over a period of years. The most notable was one facing the Théâtre-français, decorated with tapestries, mirrors, crystal chandeliers, and marble-topped tables. In addition to coffee, tea, and chocolate, he sold biscuits, liqueurs, and another new item: ices.

Coffee, too, had its friends and foes, one side praising, the other condemning the fact that the beverage kept people awake.[86] Like the other drinks, it was first taken as a medicine. It was brewed with very finely powdered grounds in the pot, in the Turkish manner, the grounds merely being allowed to settle before the liquid was poured into cups. This same finely powdered coffee was also put directly into ices and sweets, to be chewed up by the coffee enthusiast.

Attempts to grow coffee in Europe were more successful than those made to grow tea. At the end of the seventeenth century the Dutch had brought some shrubs back from their colony of Batavia (Jakarta) in the East Indies. The plants flourished, and in 1714 a descendant of one of these plants was given to Louis XIV; he sent it to the Jardin des Plantes in Paris, where it thrived and produced offspring.[87] Some of these were stolen by an imaginative army officer, Gabriel Mathieu de Clieu, who had conceived the idea that coffee could be grown in the French colonies in the West Indies. After a

Coffee seller, engraving, by the comte de Caylus after Edme Bouchardon, *Etudes prises dans le bas peuple où les cris de Paris* (1746). The bulbous shape of the pot and its high-set spout are intended to prevent the flow of coffee grounds into the cup; the pot stands on a small brazier. The common cup was part of the equipment of all street vendors selling beverages. (Courtesy of the Museum of Fine Arts, Boston, Sargent Collection.)

dramatic ocean voyage, enlivened by the presence of a Dutch spy, pursuit by pirates, and a period of drought during which de Clieu shared his water ration with the seedlings, the latter were established in Martinique. Authorities on coffee say that most of the plants in this hemisphere are descended from these seedlings, and thus from that single plant in Paris.

In the *office* coffee was used in much the same way as chocolate—as a beverage with either water or milk as a base, in ices, and in junkets.[88] Coffee-flavored waffles were in vogue briefly.[89] The inventors and manufacturers of equipment for all these new beverages had a field day. Coffee roasters and grinders proliferated. De Blegny advises the aspiring coffee brewer to prepare it in a pot with a bulbous bottom, whose shape would prevent the grounds from pouring out with the liquid, and with a high-set spout with a grid at the base further to restrain the grounds. He also recommends that it be drunk when freshly brewed. If made in the morning for the day's trade, it should be kept hot because reheating adversely affects the flavor. It is a splendid remedy for drunkenness, headache, and melancholy, it fortifies memory and judgment, and it is also recommended to relieve gout and scurvy.[90]

The dietary and health properties of chocolate, tea, and coffee are still being debated. But there is no disputing that they and the other new ingredients, as well as the broadened range of foodstuffs available to the cook, gradually altered the character of French dining. But the methods by which food was prepared for the table brought about even more radical changes. In the next chapter we turn to the kitchens where this took place and to the men and women who staffed them.

CHAPTER FIVE

Kitchens and Cooks

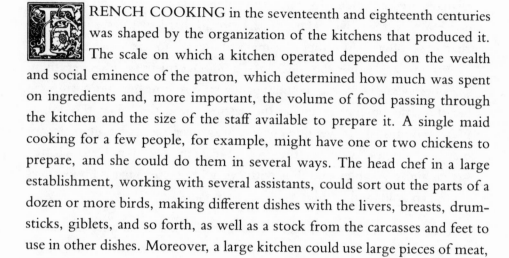RENCH COOKING in the seventeenth and eighteenth centuries
was shaped by the organization of the kitchens that produced it.
The scale on which a kitchen operated depended on the wealth
and social eminence of the patron, which determined how much was spent
on ingredients and, more important, the volume of food passing through
the kitchen and the size of the staff available to prepare it. A single maid
cooking for a few people, for example, might have one or two chickens to
prepare, and she could do them in several ways. The head chef in a large
establishment, working with several assistants, could sort out the parts of a
dozen or more birds, making different dishes with the livers, breasts, drumsticks, giblets, and so forth, as well as a stock from the carcasses and feet to
use in other dishes. Moreover, a large kitchen could use large pieces of meat,
such as hams, whole legs of beef, turtles, and saddles of venison, which the
small kitchen never saw. Finally, the large kitchen had a richer array of leftovers that became ingredients for new dishes.

French *haute cuisine* developed in the seventeenth century in the large
kitchens of the aristocracy and subsequently was chiefly practiced in the
kitchens of wealthy houses, in restaurants and clubs, and on ocean liners. In
those settings, with specialized cooks using specialized ingredients, it was a
practical and efficient system. Out of the kitchens of small establishments
came the cooking we call regional and bourgeois—which is more useful for
most modern cooks.[1]

THE SMALL HOUSEHOLD

Audiger, in *La Maison reglée* (1692), describes in detail how households
of all sizes were organized and operated, what the expenses should be, and
how responsibilities were to be allocated.[2] In a one-servant household that
servant was usually a woman, and she had a great deal of work to do. She
did all the marketing and cooking, the washing up, and the cleaning of the

kitchen. She had to be prompt in doing her errands and must not gossip about her employers, "as do the majority of maids."

> When one sends them to buy something, most of the shopkeepers say "Aha, my girl, so now you're with M. or Mme. So and so." "Yes, madame," answers the servant. "Have you been there long?" says the other. "No, Madame," replies the maid. "Really," continues the other, "they change servants often. So what kind of people are they, what do they do? How do they live? They must be really hard to please, since they change so often." And then the maid plunges into the subject and tells everything she knows about her master and her mistress, and everything she doesn't know. While the merchant's wife is amusing and occupying her thus, the butcher gives her the nastiest meat; the baker, the worst-made and most short-weighted bread; the grocer, the worst oil; the chandler, the runniest wax; and the greengrocer, the oldest and most rotten greens and vegetables; and thus with everything else. That is how everything gets sold, and nothing is left over in Paris.[3]

This same woman was expected to keep track of all the pewter and silver, the kitchen equipment, and everything that was sent out to the laundress. She made the beds and cleaned the rooms, got the children up and dressed and off to school, and fed them and put them to bed at night. She kept their clothes clean, oversaw their prayers, and was supposed to keep them from crying and fighting. Audiger cannily recommends that she give them little treats so they will not complain about her to their parents. On the other hand, she was to refrain from giving manservants the choicest bits of foods and her master's wine. The bad servant cheated on her accounts, squandered her employer's goods, and undermined the morals of other servants and of the children of the family, "and this is what often brings all the disorder of a house."[4]

The good servant, in contrast, put everything "in good order," was prudent, prompt, and uncomplaining; she could expect to enjoy little kindnesses daily. Sometimes maids' employers "even see them married and comfortably settled; in a word, they support them and esteem them always, and act as their protectors in everything that may happen to them."[5] This passage is a veiled reference to the fact that young female servants often became pregnant by the men in their employers' families. The employer then might contribute a dowry sufficient to enable the maid to marry. The gradations of seduction (by either sex), exploitation, and blackmail must have been infinite, and one must wonder that the single servant ever had time to cook.

Some women worked as maids as a lifelong career, whether they married or not; others were the daughters of peasants in the countryside around a town who went into domestic service for a few years to accumulate a dowry, money and possessions which they brought to their own households. Some women returned to service when they were widowed to support themselves and their children.[6] Audiger does not make it clear whether maids were expected to be literate, but literacy was well-nigh nonexistent among this class in his day.

A more prosperous establishment would have a full-time cook, "sometimes a man, but often only a woman," who was expected to have a thorough knowledge of cooking. "She should know how to make a good soup, cook all kinds of meats, make ragouts with them, as well as with fish and eggs, and with all kinds of vegetables for the other days. Also, she should not be ignorant of the ways of making some fruit compotes and a few other bagatelles for the dessert."[7] She was responsible for cleaning the kitchen, dining room, and stairs, and she did the marketing, unless, in a yet larger household, she worked under the direction of a housekeeper.[8] She was required "always to keep her equipment very tidy and very clean, as well as the kitchen itself, and not waste wood or charcoal, or anything else under her management. She should also be prudent and of good conscience in her accounting of expenditures, neither quarrelsome nor a flatterer, devoting herself entirely to satisfying her master and mistress, and serving meals always in the way and at the times which they prescribe."[9]

The servant who did the marketing had a job with substantial fringe benefits. She got out of the house regularly for freedom and a breath of fresh air. Unsupervised, she could buy food at one price, charge her mistress a higher price, and pocket the difference—a practice known as "shoeing the mule." Mules are not normally shod, so a charge for mule shoes is likely to be fictitious. A dialogue has recorded this practice: *La Maletote des cuisinières, ou la manière de bien ferrer la mule* (Paris, 1713), which may be roughly translated as "the cooks' tax, or how to pad your accounts effectively."[10] An old cook by the name of Marie and a young maid meet at market. The young woman complains of strict supervision, and the old one tells her to revenge herself by shoeing the mule or painting the monkey (making a fool of her employer). The maid says that everything she buys is repeatedly weighed, every penny counted, and still she is accused of "pillage and theft." Marie proceeds to give an extensive discourse on the tricks of the marketing trade. Merchants, attorneys, and notaries are the most promising employers. The food-sellers must be given to understand that the maid's word is law in her household; if they want her custom they must pay her a sou for every livre spent and give her an abundance of presents at special holidays. Then she will graciously speak well of them to Madame.

When the maid returns to the house she can pretend to have lost her marketing money. If the footman who keeps the accounts will falsify them for her (making an eight out of a zero, for example), there will be further possibilities for profit. She can juggle supplies, pretend to buy things twice, and resell foods that come back from the table or out of the storeroom. The fat that falls from the roasts into the dripping pan is a legitimate perquisite, but she can greatly augment it by selecting fat-laden meat at market. Similarly, the ashes from the fire are hers to sell so the more fuel she burns the more ashes there will be.[11] Old Marie concludes by asking the young maid to admire her handsomely furnished room. From the profits made by cheating, "in the course of one year I got the table, the armchair and side chairs, and the bed, without once having been caught in the act [*en flagrant délit*]."

Marie's husband does as well with his employer. Every time that nobleman goes from Paris to Versailles the husband makes twenty sols on the horses' fodder and bedding. "Finally, when we both want to retire, we will live happily for the rest of our days. Form yourself, my child, on these splendid examples."[12] The maid goes off, full of gratitude and information, to avenge herself. Hostility and distrust apparently were characteristic of the servant-mistress relationship, as borne out by court records: servants were often accused of theft and even violence against their employers.[13]

The first book to appear in France directed specifically to female cooks was Menon's *Cuisinière bourgeoise*, published in 1746. It is addressed to the cook and to the housewife who cooks. The author of the *Ménagier* had written for his young wife in the late fourteenth century, and Bonnefons dedicated *Les Delices de la campagne* "to Ladies," but both were addressing them in their capacity as managers and did not expect them to do much cooking. Even in 1746 Menon wrote for the mistress as much as for the maid, for the former was more likely to be able to read. One passage, though, is directed specifically to the female cook. In discussing pastry for cold pies, he writes:

Cooks who have the dexterity to dress a pâté four inches high have only to use the same pastry as in the previous recipe [for *tourtes*]. Follow the same method for composing the inside; the cooking of it and the sauces are the same; the satisfaction which she will have from it is the power of being able to vary the look of a table with the same ingredients, and of doing justice to her ability.[14]

This sense of mastery was as much within the grasp of a woman working in the kitchen as of a man. She could not compete with him, though, for jobs in the big houses. Audiger allots her 90 livres, while giving the man who heads the kitchen in a large establishment 300 livres.

Lois Banner raised the question, "Why are women not great chefs?" She concluded that it is because they are not hired for the jobs men do, not because they have inherent defects.[15] In eighteenth-century France, where sex roles were usually very strictly defined, women were not hired for managerial jobs in the kitchens of the wealthy. But gifted women who were trained as cooks could earn substantially more than other women in their class and circumstances and were respected and admired by others exercising these skills. A *cuisinière* could make a domain for herself in the kitchen. Her skills were an important part of the household economy. In an economically unstable society she was relatively secure if she was good at her work. She did not have to supply the tools of her trade so needed no capital. If she lost her job, her skills were portable, and mobility gave a degree of protection. She may have been exploited, but perhaps no more than men of her class.

La Cuisinière bourgeoise could only have been written by someone who believed that the female cook was capable of discriminating judgment. It consists largely of suggestions; there are relatively few formal recipes. The ancient and honorable tradition of French bourgeois cooking is in large part the result of women's work and invention. Different modes of cooking are, however, not the exclusive preserve of either sex. Recipes, ingredients, and techniques are neuter and can be used by men or by women. The sex of a cook cannot be determined by the flavor of the food that comes to the table.

The conditions under which a cook worked limited what she could cook. Many of the ingredients that would have been prepared on the premises of larger establishments were not used in smaller kitchens because their preparation required special equipment or specialist cooks or simply produced

J·B Simeon Chardin *pinxit*.   *Lepicé Sculpsit* 1742.

LA POURVOÏEUSE.

*A vôtre air j'estime et je pense,   Que vous prenez sur la dépense
Ma chere enfant, sans calculer,   Ce qu'il faut pour vous habiller.*
                                                                    Lepicie

*Paris chez L'Auteur au coin de L'Abreuvoir du Quay des Orfèvres
& chez L Surugue graveur du Roi rüé des Noyers vis a vis le mur de S.* Yves J.   *Avec Privilege du Roi.*

The Return from Market, engraving by François Bernard Lepicé after J.B.S. Chardin (1742). The verse cynically surmises that the servant is buying her clothes out of the marketing money. In another engraving after Chardin's painting the accompanying verse is written from the opposite viewpoint: "We spend all our toil keeping food in our mouths / While our spirits cry out and our hearts are in pain; / They too have their needs, / We recognize that; why must they be denied?" Note the large copper water-storage tank in the adjoining room. (Courtesy of the Museum of Fine Arts, Boston.)

more than could be eaten by a few people. Ordinary houses did not usually have ovens. To have fresh bread ready for early meals a baker had to rise in the small hours of the morning. A servant could not do that and also work all day, even in the *ancien régime*. Even wealthy households were supplied by professional *boulangers*. The more luxurious baked goods came from the *pâtissier* (pastrycook), who had an ample array of ovens and special gear. Confectionary and liqueurs were usually bought. Spit-roasted meat could be bought from the roastcooks' shops.

By the beginning of the seventeenth century, however, even the female cook was no longer dependent on her fireplace alone, for with a little luck her kitchen might be fitted with a brick *potager*, "a slightly raised place where one prepares soups, or where there are several little charcoal stoves on which they are simmered."[16] Instead, or in addition, there would be a portable oven to be set by the coals on the hearth (resembling modern versions used by campers). A second supplement to the *potager* and hearth was the chafing dish, a copper brazier standing on legs above a small quantity of charcoal. They are much in evidence in kitchen still lifes by painters who exploited the light and dark effects of glowing coals. With these tools and a reasonable array of pots and pans, the cook would have had the means of preparing simple but palatable food.

But the cook's time was limited, as were her work space and storage facilities. A certain amount of advance preparation was possible, within the limits of the inexorable spoilage timetable. She started her day's cooking by putting the big stockpot on the fire (*mettre le pot au feu* was the phrase used). It could receive leftover vegetables and meat that might not last until another meal, and it would also be used to cook newly purchased meat and poultry. The flavor of the stock, therefore, varied from one day to the next, but it was always a mingling of many meats and vegetables. The cook was obliged to use her time efficiently to get through an ordinary day's work in good order, so she favored recipes that were not too complicated. The result was likely to be dishes in which individual ingredients were readily recognizable—those foods that taste of themselves. But fashion preferred greater complexity, so people had elaborate food when they could afford it. *Cuisine bourgeoise* was often literally *la cuisine de la bourgeoise*—the cooking done by the moderately affluent housewife, either as the principal cook in the household or sharing the work with a maid. A painting by Antoine Raspale, dating from the eighteenth century, in the Musée Réattu at Arles shows such a scene in a Provençale kitchen. Madame froths a pot of chocolate, while the maid deals with the vegetables: social stratification is reflected here in the allocation of tasks.

THE LARGE HOUSEHOLD

In a large establishment with an extensive staff, work was more articulated and subdivided; the staff had specialized training, and more space and equipment were available. There were infinite gradations in the size and complexity of households. Many intermediate-sized households had *specialtiés de la maison* according to the tastes and wealth of the employer. The largest establishments were elaborate. Writing in 1692 after thirty years' experience as a maitre d'hôtel, Audiger gave an extensive description of "the manner of directing a noble household, so that everything is done with economy and without any inconvenience for the nobleman or for his steward." [17] A maître d'hôtel superintended all the food services: supply, storage, safeguarding, and accounting for the silver, linen, and wine and planning, preparation, and serving of meals. After the steward (who was often responsible for managing one or several estates and was often of a higher birth), he was the best-paid domestic in the house and the most powerful, presiding over a pair of kitchens. The larger of those, the *cuisine*, was hot and often steamy; in it the food for the principal part of the meal was cooked. The smaller kitchen was the *office* in which sugar cooking and distillation took place, salads were made, and the final course of the meal was prepared and dressed. The staff for both *cuisine* and *office* were hired and fired by the maître d'hôtel. He also had the potentially lucrative duty of settling the contracts for the supply of food to the household. The opportunities for "shoeing the mule" were, of course, proportionately magnified in such opulent surroundings, and the process could be carried out in decorous privacy.

A story is told by Brillat-Savarin that illustrates the way employers could be managed by their domestics. The Prince de Soubise, intending to give a fête that was to end with a supper, asked his maître d'hôtel to plan a suitable menu. This dignitary brought it to him, and, as Brillat-Savarin writes:

The first thing the prince turned his eyes to was this: "fifty hams." "What's this, Bertrand," he said; "I think you are cheating me. Fifty hams! Do you want to treat my whole regiment?" "No, my prince, only one of them will appear on the table, but the rest is no less necessary to make by *sauce espagnole*, my white stocks, my garnishes, my. . . ." "Bertrand, you are robbing me, and this item will not get by." "Ah! Monseigneur," said the artist, scarcely able to contain his anger, "you do not know our resources! Order these fifty hams, which so offend you, and I will put them into a crystal bottle no bigger than your thumb." What response could be given to so positive an assertion? The prince smiled, bowed his head, and the item got by.[18]

In large households much of the food supply was contracted for on an annual basis—sometimes even triennially—with purveyors who acted as middlemen. A modern scholar, Pierre Couperie, has located and tabulated more than three dozen such purveyorship contracts that were made for the households of various members of the nobility and the royal family, including Louis XIV, dating from between 1602 and 1711.[19] They set the prices at which various ingredients were to be supplied (subject to their availability in the marketplace, which was extremely uncertain). Couperie found that some purveyors, several of whom were women, were operating on a very large scale, undertaking to supply several important establishments at one time. For example, a single family purveyed to the household of Cardinal Mazarin from 1624 until 1640, while also supplying food for the households of Louis XIII and the duc de Chevreuse. Large sums of money were involved; advances of as much as 30,000 livres were paid. Payment usually was due monthly or quarterly. Tracing trends over the century, Couperie found that prices went up, except for foods that went out of fashion. Since this rise was contrary to the declining trend of grain prices in the period, it suggests that there was a strong demand for the foods consumed by the wealthy. The foods listed in specific contracts support the idea, proposed in the next chapter, that French tastes changed in the mid-seventeenth century. From 1650 to 1670 some foods disappeared which had been in favor from the Middle Ages onward: pork, even suckling pig, was used less. After this period the more exotic wild birds, such as egret, bittern, stork, crane, herons, wild goose, peacock, and swan were rarely mentioned. Whale and lamprey disappeared from the lists after 1650. Fashion smiled on other foods: the use of lamb increased, though mutton was still preferred for its stronger flavor; the chickens and capons of Mans and Bruges were especially esteemed, as were heath hens, larks, buntings (*ortolans*), railbirds, and teals; from 1661 on cockscombs (sold by the pound) and foies gras (sold by the half dozen) appeared. Salt cod from the New World and tuna preserved in oil or brine were increasingly used.

Usually the maître d'hôtel was trained first in the *cuisine* or in the *office*. He needed to be experienced in kitchen work and capable of maintaining order there.[20] He hired and fired the staff in kitchen and *office*, spent the money, and kept the accounts. He planned the meals, considering both his master's tastes and his own knowledge of fashionable delicacies. When a special meal was to be given, he did the advance planning. After consulting with his suppliers about what was "newest and best," he planned the menu. This required covering the tabletop with at least three changes of symmetrical arrangements of suitably varied preparations. He then conferred with the cooks and *officiers d'office* about what equipment they needed, checking to be sure that it was on hand or renting it if necessary. A similar survey was made of plate, linen, and glass for setting the table. Finally, if necessary, extra help was hired. In the kitchen the maître d'hôtel's subordinates were the head cook (*écuyer* or *officier de cuisine*), the roastcook (*rôtisseur*), assistant cooks, and kitchen boys (*aides* and *garçons de cuisine*).

Audiger emphasized that the head cook should begin each day's work by seeing that everything was clean and tidy.

> That done, he should start his stockpot and set out his meats, which he should be very familiar with, so that he will be able to prepare them to the *seigneur*'s taste. . . . It is also his duty to know how to prepare all sorts of hot and cold pastries [Audiger may be assuming the presence of an oven], as well as all kinds of ragouts and hot and cold entremets, and he must be careful not to waste any of the materials entrusted to him. He must also know how to allocate things among the master's and domestics' tables in the house, and he should be careful to use the foods left over from midday for the evening, and from the evening for the next midday, so as to benefit the household in using them often to prepare little made dishes [*petites entrées*]. He should also be able to organize the kitchen boys and be obeyed by them, to store and allocate the wood and charcoal, to use bacon well, to successfully dress [*déguiser*] all kinds of fish, eggs, and vegetables, and to be careful always to have supper and dinner ready at the hours decreed by the *seigneur* or his maître d'hôtel.[21]

In return for all this skilled labor he received wages of 300 livres and many fringe benefits. Like the *cuisinière bourgeoise*, he received as legitimate

LE CIGNE ET LE CUISINIER . Fable LIV .

The Swan and the Cook, engraving by Pierre Aveline after J. B. Oudry from Jean de La Fontaine, *Fables* (Paris, 1755–59). The fable tells how a drunken cook (wearing a typical eighteenth-century chef's cap and white jacket and trousers) has killed a goose, which hangs from the rack in the upper left-hand corner; he prepares to kill the swan, though not holding it efficiently. The swan, perceiving its end, bursts into song. The tipsy cook, moved by the beauty of the song, spares the swan's life. The kitchen is handsome, with plenty of space, a squared stone floor, and a solid work table. Note the brioche-shaped loaf on the shelf behind the cook. (By permission of the Houghton Library, Harvard University.)

perquisites the ashes from the fire and drippings from the roasts, which would yield substantial benefits in a large establishment.[22] His assistants did the cleaning up and the time-consuming chores, such as skimming the stockpot, paring, chopping, slicing, boning, washing up, and tending the fire. Neither the kitchen boys nor the scullery maid, at the bottom of the pecking order, appear to have had any perquisites. According to Audiger, their wages were 75 livres a year, but some *marmitons* worked for little or nothing, since these jobs gave them an opportunity to learn a craft and to make invaluable contacts. In these humble situations most young people learned both the basic techniques and the tricks of their trade.

The cooler, smaller kitchen, the *office*, was the domain of the redundantly titled *officier d'office*. Audiger also calls him the sommelier, but his responsibilities included more than the care of the wine cellar. The *officier* combined the roles which in England were filled by the butler and the stillroom maid. It was a situation of trust, marked by the possession of many keys. He had charge of everything the table was set with—gold, silver, glass, and linen, as well as all the equipment in the *office*; he was accountable to the maître d'hôtel. The household's bread and wine were his responsibility. In making the annual contract with the baker, his perquisite was the thirteenth loaf of every dozen furnished—hence the baker's dozen.[23] He was expected to know how to make "all kinds of preserved fruit, both liquid and dry, stewed fruits, creams, sweet cakes, marzipans, syrups, flavored waters, and distilled liqueurs."[24] In a very large establishment he would have had an assistant to help him set the table and to do all the carrying, cleaning, and counting.

Less equipment was needed in the *office* than in the *cuisine*, but it was more specialized, including alembics for distillation, molds for jellied preparations, and elaborate cutters for marzipans, copper candying pans for caramelizing almonds, and sometimes even a chocolate-grinding stone. There would be small charcoal braziers and perhaps a *potager*, but no fireplace. Shelves for storage and a large work table were essential because many preparations called for draining and drying. Sugar readily absorbs water from the air, which is why candymaking is difficult in hot weather and why crisp cookies go limp. The well-equipped *office* had, therefore, an *étuve*, a charcoal-warmed storage space in which preserved fruit and candies could be kept dry for long periods of time. It had room at the bottom for a small charcoal brazier and latticework shelves above, through which the warm, dry air could circulate. A small portable *étuve* could be made from iron sheeting;

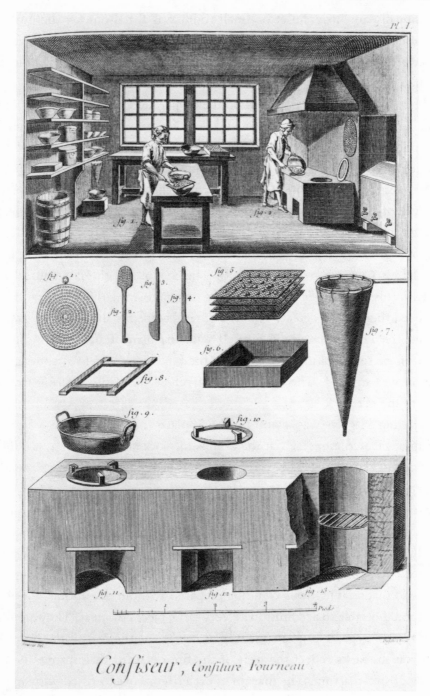

Confifeur, *Confiture Fourneau*

The confectioner's workroom and equipment, engraving, from *Encyclopédie: Recueil des planches* . . . (Paris, 1763–77). The upper half of the plate shows a confectioner's workroom; below are the tools of his trade—the conical cloth strainer for clarified sugar, wire racks, spatulas, and a big copper preserving pan. The principal piece of equipment is the *potager*, the masonry-enclosed charcoal brazier at which most of the cooking was done. (By permission of the Houghton Library, Harvard University.)

occasionally an entire closet or small room was fitted out for the purpose. Because the *office* was drier and better ventilated than the kitchen and because fewer people passed through it, both table linens and silver were kept locked up there.

Here the *officier d'office* supervised the preparation and arrangement of the final course of an important meal and nearly all of a cold collation. During the sixteenth and seventeenth centuries there was little change in the dessert offerings, which consisted mainly of liquid and dry preserves. Around 1700, frozen desserts, little cakes, and coffee and chocolate became fashionable. Because of the distinction between *office* and *cuisine*, the regular cookbooks of the seventeenth and eighteenth centuries give scant attention, if any, to dessert.[25] Often it is not even included in their menus, as, for example, in Massialot's *Cuisinier roïal et bourgeois*. The menus for the last course published in his *Nouvelle instruction pour les confitures* similarly ignore what has preceded them. One detects a source of rivalry in this sharp division. Only the maître d'hôtel concerned himself with the plan of an entire meal, and most of the real cooking took place in the kitchen. In the final course, decoration was stressed. The *officier's* inventiveness went into offering rich variety to the eye.

The big kitchen was a hot and busy place, but, at its best, very well organized. Descriptions hint at the origins of work stations such as are found in large kitchens today. The scale permitted several people to work together as a team, each making his specialties—forcemeats, sauces, stocks, garnishes—which were combined into completed dishes. By the end of the seventeenth century working conditions were better than they had ever been. L.S.R.'s *L'Art de bien traiter* gives a good picture of the well-set-up kitchen in the 1670s: the room should have at least two large wood-burning fireplaces so that sizable meals could be prepared without disruption.[26] At least one should be able to accommodate very large pieces of meat. They are lined with tiles (a hygenic improvement over brick). At the rear of the fireplaces cast-iron firebacks reflect the heat of the fire outward to improve the efficiency of spit-roasting. The margin of each fireplace is fortified with an iron framework that supports hooks and cranes from which to hang pots. It also has a shelflike flat iron bar, four or five inches wide and perhaps six feet long, on which skillets, saucepans, and cooking pots can be set, freeing the cook's hands for other work. There may also be a mechanical turnspit to revolve several spits simultaneously. L.S.R. says that dog-powered spits are

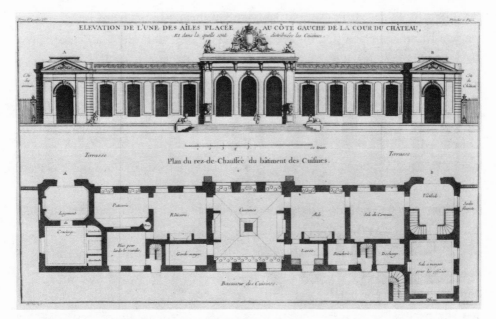

Kitchen wing of the Grand Trianon at Versailles, engraving from J.-F. Blondel, *De la distribution de maisons de plaisance . . .* (Paris, 1737–38). In this building the work spaces have been articulated as thoroughly as the work, with separate rooms for cooking, roasting, and pastrymaking. Charcoal braziers are abundantly available. They are all installed under windows to carry away the carbon monoxide produced by the burning charcoal. (By permission of the Houghton Library, Harvard University.)

more suitable for country use and that when you turn a spit by hand you roast yourself at the same time as the meat. Nonetheless, it was a job often assigned to kitchen boys.

In addition, there would be several charcoal-fired stoves at which the cook would stand to prepare ragouts and other delicate mixtures demanding close supervision. L.S.R. advises that these ranges be set near a window where the light is good. This would also have helped to waft away the carbon monoxide generated by the burning charcoal, which must have been a special menace in kitchens located in basements. The relative comfort and convenience of raised stoves should not be underestimated. It would have been miserable to work for long hours year-round at a blazing hearth. In comparison, the less intense heat and the chance to work standing up in a lighter and less crowded place would have encouraged the cook to pay closer attention to the fine points of his or her art. A big kitchen also boasted a brick oven built into the masonry of the chimney, which allowed the cook to prepare foods otherwise taken to the baker's oven or cooked surrounded by ashes on the hearth.

The *batterie de cuisine*—pots, pans, and skillets—hung from racks and sat on wall-hung shelves and in freestanding dressers. Food was stored in a variety of places: fresh meats in a screened box (to keep out flies) hung in an airy place; spices and staples in a locked cupboard; fruit and vegetables in a dry cellar (regularly inspected for signs of spoilage); hams and other preserved meats hung from the rafters in the kitchen or in a dry attic. In the courtyard, which the kitchen often shared with the stables, chickens and ducks fattened on table scraps and scratched in the dust for oats and hayseed. Rats were a problem everywhere.

The cheapest cooking utensils were of earthenware. For sturdier utensils, tinned copper was the material of choice, but when grandees took their turn at the chafing dishes in the early eighteenth century their greater dignity was reflected in saucepans lined with silver. Stockpots of iron, earthenware, or tinned copper were needed, as well as a big one "which serves as wet-nurse for the others." The list of equipment in *L'Art de bien traiter* reads like the catalog of a modern French restaurant-supply house.[27]

To understand the pressures that the kitchen staff worked under, one must bear in mind the conditions of life for the majority of working-class people in seventeenth- and eighteenth-century France. Because of the high infant mortality rate, average life expectancy at birth was thirty years or less. Chronic undernourishment was the lot of those who survived. Families lived in one or two rooms, owned few possessions, and had little or no savings. Those who survived did so by hard work—when they could find it—and by artful dodging. People who worked in kitchens at least had the near-guarantee of a full stomach, a warm place to sleep, and the opportunity to pilfer food for hungry mouths at home. A clergyman, Claude Fleury, writing on the duties of masters and servants, says that the maître d'hôtel should not let married domestics carry their food rations home without the explicit permission of the master.[28] L.S.R. chillingly recommends the use of guards at the door to keep out "the starving people who are the common plague of kitchens."[29]

Kitchens sometimes had a lively social life of their own, as described by le sieur Crespin in 1641:

> I remember a household where I used to be which was always full of love-affairs, so that everyone from the smallest to the greatest was tainted by this raging disease. And, to tell you the truth, I have never seen people

so quick and charitable to help each other out in pursuing these matters. . . . When Monsieur said that nothing was cooked well, or that the
meat smelt bad, or that everything was too salty, the maître d'hôtel excused the cook, though he knew where all these defects came from, and
did not say that the dishes were badly prepared because the cook was in
love. On the contrary, he made excuses to Monsieur, saying that it was
because of the weather, or that the cook was sick, or the firewood was
green, that by mischance the pot happened to break when the soup
was being dished up. . . . There were so many good excuses he could
find for the cook . . . who reciprocated in excusing the maître d'hôtel's
faults to the *seigneur*, and in not revealing that he went out walking with
his mistress every day, or else that they were giving themselves a good
collation at the *seigneur*'s expense.[30]

With so much activity in the kitchen, it is not surprising that there was
sometimes disruptive rivalry, as illustrated by the story of a celebrated chef
named Moutiers in the reign of Louis XV. "He was a cook for M. de Nev-
ers, hired at considerable wages, and with the remarkable conditions of never
having to cook supper for him more than twice a week, and to have three
suits of clothes a year of his own choosing. The king wanted to take him
on; they tried him out at several suppers. There was a lot of intriguing by
the king's kitchen staff to prevent his being hired, by not furnishing him
with what he needed to cook well."[31] These maneuvers did not succeed.
Moutiers entered and remained in the king's service and was promoted to
serving the famous little suppers in the king's private rooms. He controlled
expenses so well that the sumptuous meals he served cost one-third or one-
quarter what they had previously. No wonder he was unpopular with his
colleagues! Moutiers served the king until he died in 1748 at the age of
forty-two.[32]

There were striking instances of loyalty as well. When the Cardinal de
Retz was in financial difficulties, late in the seventeenth century, his cook
and *officier* elected to stay with him without their customary wages. "It is a
heroic thing," wrote Madame de Sévigné, "such sentiments in those people.
They prefer the honor of not leaving to the better conditions of the court.
One cannot hear of them without admiring their attachment."[33]

Cooking was a difficult but a rewarding métier. The opportunity to experiment with an abundance of ingredients would have had the quality of

fantasy in a society where starvation was an omnipresent threat to most people. When this opportunity was combined with the need for skill and invention by cooks to achieve professional advancement and the need for conspicuous display of wealth by the privileged class through lavish hospitality to maintain status, the craft of cookery flourished.

CHAPTER SIX

The Beginnings of Fine Cookery

THE MIDDLE of the seventeenth century saw the publication for the first time in France of recipes that combined an integrated repertory of techniques, basic mixtures, and raw materials, governed by accepted rules. This was the same period when Descartes was attempting to construct a rationally consistent philosophy and when architects were bringing the design of buildings into conformity with rules governing proportion and the use of ornament.[1] At the same time, etiquette and dress were becoming increasingly governed by elaborate conventions. In the kitchen, French cooks sorted out materials and techniques, making their craft more efficient and receptive to innovation. This new approach to the art of cookery was practiced both in the large and small kitchens described in the previous chapter, though the differences in scale led to different styles of cooking. In all cases the manner of working was strongly marked by the spirit of organization that was to become the hallmark of classic French cuisine.[2] This cuisine resulted in part from the techniques employed, such as the many ways of binding sauces or the use of vegetable mixtures as flavorings and of forcemeats as adjuncts to roasts and ragouts, and in part from the systematic organization of dishes of varying scale and complexity in a patterned array set out on the table.

In the decade of the 1650s the dearth of French cookbooks ended as chefs overcame their longstanding reluctance to commit their ideas to paper. It is not clear why French cooks did not start publishing their recipes earlier or why they began to do so in the mid-seventeenth century. Elizabeth Eisenstein has described the ambivalence felt by the professional and academic elites when formerly secret information was published; a similar mechanism may have been operating in the kitchen.[3] In the culinary crafts as in others, secrets have always been part of the practitioner's stock-in-trade; even today some cooks do not share their recipes. Perhaps the balance shifted, and secrecy became less valuable than fame. When more people could read, the cook gained economically through the fame brought by published recipes.

It may be, too, that the pace of innovation had accelerated, so that dishes were being demanded which cooks trained in the oral tradition had not had an opportunity to learn, thus creating a market for cookbooks. Maîtres d'hôtel, who were more likely than cooks to be literate, also had to bring themselves up-to-date. As soon as some cooks began to publish, others followed. But France had been exceptionally slow in producing original cookbooks before the 1650s, lagging far behind other countries. It is probable that by this decade none of the earlier cookbooks were in use. In Italy, Bartolomeo Scappi had published *Opera . . . in sei libri* in 1570; in Germany, Marx Rumpolt had published his *New Kochbuch* in 1581; and in England, Hugh Platt's *Delightes for Ladies* came out about 1600. The cooking described in all these books had moved beyond the Middle Ages, toward recognizable national cuisines. If, as we have seen, there is little evidence in previous centuries of classic French cooking, the midcentury chefs and publishers could say, in the words of Molière's Sganarelle, "Nous avons changé tout cela."

In his study of the chronology and geography of cookbook publishing in seventeenth- and eighteenth-century France, Alain Girard points out that the launching of the cookbook in 1650–51 "is the work of a very small number of Parisian publishers."[4] By his meticulous enumeration, there were seventy-five editions of cookbooks published in the second half of the seventeenth century, which, he estimates, would have yielded some ninety thousand cookbooks in circulation during that period. The growing number of these volumes was in itself an inducement to literacy for those who cooked.

LA VARENNE AND *Le Pâtissier françois*

La Varenne's *Cvisinier françois*, first published in 1651, was the first of an ever-increasing number of more or less original cookbooks, which were soon joined by volumes of advice on household management and the giving of banquets. Their authors addressed the prosperous classes, both urban and rural, noble and bourgeois. Virtually everyone at court and many people of property (*les gens de bien*) in the cities had country places, so these categories overlapped.

The new era in *haute cuisine* is signaled in the dedication of the *Cvisinier françois* to the marquis d'Uxelles:

Although my humble birth does not make it possible for me to be capable of having a heroic heart, it does nevertheless give me enough true

A Paris Chez Melchior Tauernier Graueur et Imprimeur du Roy pour les Tailles doulces demeurant en lisle du Pallais sur le Quay qui regarde la Megiserie.

Disposition du Festin fait par sa Majesté & Mrs. les Cheualliers apres leurs Creations faite a Fontaine Bleau le 14me. May 1633. Auec Priuilege du Roy

LES CHEVALIERS DU SAINT-ESPRIT. — LE BANQUET.

Banquet of the Order of the Holy Spirit at Fontainebleau, engraving, by Abraham Bosse (1633). Louis XIII sits alone, eating his separate meal. The crowded tabletops are a strong contrast with the sparse medieval counterparts; the broad-rimmed plates add to the effect. Full visibility and ease of service are achieved by seating diners on one side of the tables only. (Courtesy of the Museum of Fine Arts, Boston.)

feeling not to forget my indebtedness. I have discovered in your household, during ten full years' employment, the secrets of preparing foods delicately. I dare to say that I have practiced this profession with the great approbation of princes, marshals of France, and an infinity of persons of consequence. . . . I have thus set down in writing what I have for so long had the honor to practice in your service, and have made of it a little book, which bears the name of your clerk of the kitchen.[5]

La Varenne clearly was a man with ample self-esteem. His cookbook justifies that pride; in it the printed record of French cooking breaks decisively with the Middle Ages. He enjoys the distinction of having published the first great French cookbook and of having set the tone for the *grand siècle* of cooking that followed.

He begins, as have many of the best French cookbooks ever since, with a recipe for bouillon "for the nourishment of all your dishes, whether they be soups, entrées, or entremets."[6] As did medieval cooks, he used just two basic stocks, one for most meat-day dishes and one principal fish stock for fast days. But the basic stock now was an element in a system then in a very early stage of development. This nascent system, which may be called modular, gives the cook an array of basic components on which to draw, while leaving freedom to make adjustments to suit the needs and possibilities of the moment. In the *Cvisinier françois* the basic mixtures include bouillon, liaisons, farces, and herb and spice mixtures. Some are prepared in advance, to be used as needed. His recipe for a roux is the earliest I know of. The flour is cooked in pork fat rather than butter—"Take care that it does not stick to the pan"—then onions are added, which nowadays would be cooked in the fat before adding the flour. This mixture is stored in an earthen pot. When the cook wishes to make a sauce, he or she takes the roux and adds bouillon (another of the reserves), then flavors the mixture with mushrooms and vinegar. There are other possible liaisons: one is made with ground almonds, egg yolks, and lemon juice, another with mushrooms, and a third with truffles.[7] This first stage of the new cookery was sketchy, but within seventy-five years the grand design was essentially complete. It is a method that allows the cook to manage with whatever materials are available and with a minimum of specific recipes—a practical advantage to the illiterate, because only a limited amount of memorizing is needed, and to the cook working in the real world, where very exact specifications can rarely be met.

The *Cvisinier françois* is organized for use by a busy cook or maître d'hôtel. It has two sections: the first is for meat days, the second for fasts. There are lists of what is in season at different times of the year and what dishes are appropriate for each course of a meal. La Varenne recommends entrées suitable for use in the country or the army—both extreme conditions for the Paris-based chef. There is, as well, a list of foods that may be served on Good Friday, the strictest fast day in the Christian calendar.[8]

Favorite dishes from earlier centuries appear: venison pie and blanc-mange, for example, and a larded roast loin of veal, served with a vinegar, verjuice, and bread crumb sauce, which Rabelais would have recognized. As is often the case when culinary change comes about, recipes are not dropped immediately; rather, the repertory is enlarged to accommodate new inventions, while the old favorites linger on less prominently. As new flavor combinations become the accepted norm, the old ones seem incongruous. Finally, when they no longer fit into menus, they are left out of the more carefully assembled cookbooks and are eventually forgotten. In the *Cvisinier françois* the old and new styles coexist. By the mid-eighteenth century the demand for up-to-the-minute recipes drove out many of the survivals or drastically updated them. La Varenne included recipes producing the old flavors and textures, such as pungently spiced sweet and sour combinations and the small-scale roughness of toast crumbs and hashed ingredients. But alongside these old standbys are new recipes that introduce a fresh array of textures and flavors. The replacement of porous bread trenchers by ceramic plates made it possible to serve both more liquid mixtures and firmer ones requiring the use of knife and fork. Many compositions were suitable for serving in individual portions; the egg-size piece of meat or stuffed vegetable became a standard format. Garnishes of cockscombs, artichokes, and truffles surround larger pieces of meat, such as legs of mutton or roast chickens. Although pies of all sizes continued to be standard fare, their smaller relatives—turnovers, pastries, and little fried crusts—were experimented with and would be immensely popular through the eighteenth century. Well-seasoned mixtures of meat, poultry, and fish, either used as farces or formed into meatballs, were very widely used. The custom, still artfully practiced in France, of slipping a well-seasoned forcemeat between the skin and breast of a bird dates from this time, as does the use of shellfish in poultry stuffings. La Varenne roasts a capon until it is partly done, and while it cooks he heats oysters with mushrooms and clove-stuck onions in the dripping pan beneath. Next the partially roasted bird is stuffed with the mushrooms and oysters and then simmered with a seasoning of capers. The sauce is accented with just the touch of the capers' astringency.[9] Similarly, a daube of mutton is made with herbs and orange peel, "but very little, for fear of bitterness."[10] This moderation is characteristic of the new cookery: it is subtle but not bland. The long age of cinnamon and pepper had ended.

La Varenne's recipe for blancmange is midway between medieval and modern.[11] It is based on a stock made from veal, chicken, and milk, flavored with lemon rind and almonds, and sweetened with sugar. The medieval use of sweetened meat broth survived, but the texture was smoothed out; it had become a true jelly.

Because he worked for the marquis d'Uxelles, it is often stated that La Varenne invented the mushroom, shallot, and butter mixture known today as *duxelles*, but although he made abundant use of mushrooms, no such recipe is to be found in his writings. He does give an excellent, simple recipe for *champignons à l'Olivier*:

> Clean them well, cut them in quarters, and wash them in several changes of water to take off the earth. Put them between two dishes [*plats*] with an onion and some salt, then on the chafing dish so they will give off their liquid. When they have been pressed between two plates [*assiettes*], take some good fresh butter, with some parsley and scallions, and fricassee them; after that put them to simmer and when they are well cooked you may add some cream or some blancmange, and serve.[12]

His *potage de profiteolles* is characteristic of a genre that remained in favor through the eighteenth century and deserves to be revived. He devotes an entire chapter to these *potages farçis*.

> It is made thus: you take four or six rolls, you take out all the crumb from them through a little opening made in the top. You take off the lid and you dry it out with the rolls; you cook them in lard or bacon fat, and then you put your rolls in your *potage* to garnish it, and fill them with cockscombs, sweetbreads, forcemeat balls, truffles, and mushrooms. Add broth just until the rolls are soaked; before serving pour the *jus* and what you have over them, then serve.[13]

Well suited to the newly developing modular organization of work and material, such *potages* could be made with whatever the cook wished to use from units already at hand.

Roasts are very simply prepared. They are painstakingly larded, with many patterned rows of fat pork scarcely thicker than a matchstick; painters made effective use of them to enliven the texture of still lifes—Sebastien Stosskopff of Nancy and Paris, for example. In some instances the roastcook left the wing of a bird on, with the head and feet, presumably to verify its identity. Sauces, which are for the most part simple and old-fashioned, appear in the chapter with the roasts. Cauliflower, artichokes, peas, and asparagus are all used; with the latter La Varenne offers a sauce that is close to being a hollandaise. It is made with "good fresh butter, a little vinegar, salt, nutmeg, and an egg yolk to bind the sauce; take care that it does not curdle."[14] Since no measurements or proportions are indicated, the exact character of this sauce cannot be known, but it is very different from medieval ones.

He gives a recipe for making hams in the manner of Mainz (*jambon de Mayence*) in which the ham is rubbed with salt flavored with pepper, cloves, and anise and then smoked.[15] To prepare it for the table the ham is soaked and boiled, then the rind is peeled back and the meat strewn with parsley and pepper and stuck with cloves. The rind is then returned to its original position and the meat kept in a cold place. It is served with a garnish of flowers. The spicing and smoking would have produced a pungently flavored meat, which could play a vigorous part in hashes and garnishes. Such a ham is depicted in *Still Life with Silver* by Alexandre François Desportes in the Metropolitan Museum of Art in New York and in many other still-life paintings.[16]

The recipes for meatless days are enticing, too. Even the Good Friday foods are ingenious and appealing. For other fast days, when dairy products and eggs were allowed (by the seventeenth century), the cook's options were greatly enlarged. In preparing a ragout of oysters, La Varenne sautées them in butter with onions, parsley, capers, and bread crumbs. "Take good fresh ones," he writes, "open them, and take care that they have not begun to spoil at all, striking them against each other, for those which sound hollow . . . are good for nothing but salting." Soles with a sorrel stuffing are brushed with butter and grilled.[17] Significantly, the egg recipes are excellent. Skill and invention in egg cookery indicate the presence of an alert and resourceful cook; egg recipes are prominent in the best French cookbooks from this time onward.

Finally, there is a short section of pastry recipes, including instructions for making puff paste and a hot-water crust. The egg yolk *tourte* looks good; it resembles a modern lemon curd tartlet.[18]

With such an abundance of recipes for all occasions, it is not surprising that the *Cvisinier françois* remained in print well into the eighteenth century.[19] Subsequent cookbooks called for increasingly expensive ingredients and ever more lengthy preparation. La Varenne's useful book moved down the social ladder, a rung or so each decade, but in doing so came within the reach of growing numbers of people.

A second book, on confectionary, bearing La Varenne's name on the title page, appeared first in 1667 as *Le Parfaict confitvrier* and later, somewhat rearranged, as *Le Confiturier françois*.[20] Its contents supplement the *Cvisinier*, and its style is similar—terse, with a strong emphasis on the management of materials and equipment and a variety of basic preparations. The confectioner keeps on hand spice preparations, colorings, flavored syrups, and distillations. The stages of sugar-boiling have been codified. Preserves, jellies, and fruit pastes, though old favorites, are now used in ever-diversified combinations. Like Nostradamus a hundred years before, the author uses musk and ambergris and gives a recipe for quince paste, though the more recent is sweeter. Both have marzipan recipes, but where Nostradamus uses a simple mixture of ground almonds, rosewater, and sugar, La Varenne offers fifteen varieties, beginning with a simple one based on syrup and going on to elaborate combinations using egg whites, glazes, and fruit pastes. Not all of these are new. The innovation lies in the cook's perception of how to combine elements to invent, to improvise, and to work efficiently.

Le Pâtissier françois is traditionally ascribed to La Varenne, though his name does not appear on the title page or in the permission to publish.[21] It is essentially a collection of pastry and egg recipes, beginning with some useful introductory remarks about procedures and, most unusually, definitions of weights and measures. There are pies and tarts, a few cakes, wafers, waffles, and cheesecakes, and a series of chapters on egg cookery, with special emphasis on omelets. Among the basic compositions used in the *Pâtissier* are several kinds of pastry dough, spice mixtures, pastry creams, egg washes to give baked goods a healthy shine, clarified butter, and some cake batters—notably a section of *biscuits*. This is the first appearance of recognizable cakes. *Biscuit* is very much like the modern ladyfinger (*biscuit à la cuillière*).[22] It is made with sugar, flour, and eggs (but no butter) and spiced with anise or coriander. Prolonged beating supplies the air bubbles that raise it.

Like the *Cvisinier françois*, the *Pâtissier* contains a good proportion of recipes that are still attractive and would, in their own day, have been practicable in many a prosperous kitchen. The author, however, does not assume that his reader had an oven built into the fireplace wall: many of the recipes include directions for cooking pies and cakes either in portable metal ovens or in the medieval way in iron pots with hot coals on the lids and under the supporting trivet.

La Varenne's books, and, to a lesser extent, the *Pâtissier*, stand at the beginning of the tradition of *haute cuisine*. In them we see the specialist cook setting up his kitchen and practicing his skills. It is assumed that the cook will have an ample and varied array of ingredients from which to produce a considerable volume of interesting dishes for the dining room. He must work efficiently to serve a large household, and he must be in touch with current fashion.

THE BEGINNINGS OF CLASSIC FRENCH HOME COOKING

In the countryside a different set of forces shaped the cuisine. With fewer shops and markets the householder was obliged to look elsewhere for food-stuffs. A pair of books, *Le Jardinier françois* of 1651 and its companion volume, *Les Delices de la campagne* of 1654, show how this was managed. Their author was Nicolas de Bonnefons, *premier valet du roi* to the adolescent Louis XIV.

For whom in the social spectrum of seventeenth-century France was Bonnefons writing? He was using his prestige and experience gained by association with the court to address an audience that lived on a more mod-est scale in more modest households. This group constituted the patrons and patronesses of what I call, for the sake of convenience, *cuisine bourgeoise*.

France in the seventeenth century—by contrast to the sixteenth—seems to have enjoyed little, if any, general economic growth. Nevertheless, a re-distribution of what wealth there was, was taking place. The growth and extension of the royal bureaucracy and increased military expenditures were supported by increased taxation, which placed an especially heavy burden on the peasant class. Part of these increased taxes found their way, directly or indirectly, into the coffers of certain segments of the propertied classes—the *gens de bien*. The court nobility benefited from lavish pensions provided by the crown. Others who profited were tax collectors and moneylenders to the crown; purveyors to the army and to the court; and, above all, a large class of officeholders who bought their offices from the crown, and, with the offices, access to nobility. These people often invested their increased wealth in agricultural land around the cities. Years of dearth and famine, which were frequent in the seventeenth century, gave those with a reserve of grain and of ready money an opportunity to buy land from the peasants, to acquire local lordships (*seigneuries*) with whatever prestige and feudal dues the latter still entailed, and to establish modest country seats.[23] A part of these rural holdings—usually the land immediately around the landholder's residence—was devoted to raising fruit and vegetables, primarily for the use of the owner and his household both in the country and in the city; any surplus could be sold.

Hence, behind a façade of static social stratification, there was considerable social mobility in seventeenth-century France. The widespread sale of royal offices, which was more widely practiced here than elsewhere in Europe, provided access to nobility to persons of property, although the process often took place over several generations. Alongside (and to some extent intermingled with) the traditional nobility "of the sword," there grew up another nobility, that "of the robe," families whose fortunes often originated in commerce, industry, or the liberal professions. These families, without ever losing sight of their nonnoble (*roturier*) background, were in the process of acquiring the attributes and manner of life of the nobility.

Bonnefons's books are a clear expression of the interest of these classes in expanding their horticultural horizons. Market gardening was widely practiced in and around Paris. There was still considerable space within and just outside the city, where intensive cultivation yielded profitable crops. Bonnefons conducted a seasonal seed trade in Paris. The 1651 edition of the *Jardinier* states that his gardening instructions are intended for the Paris area, and he says that he sells seeds there from April through June. "If you have need of our seeds I will furnish you with all the kinds of plants which you have seen, and I have the others, sent from Italy, which we do not grow."[24]

In the *Jardinier* Bonnefons emphasizes production and preservation; in the *Delices*, preparation and consumption. Each volume is divided into three books; those in the former treat fruit trees, the kitchen garden, and preserving. In the *Delices*, Book One deals with breads, pastry, and wine and other beverages; Book Two with the selection and preparation of vegetables and fruit, nuts, eggs, milk, and cheeses; and Book Three with meat, poultry, game, and fish. The number of recipes is relatively small, but their quality is high. The stress is less on measurement, though rules of thumb are given, than on detailed descriptions of the varieties and conditions of the ingredients suitable for each process and on how these processes are to be carried out. In making a compote of sweet Calville apples, for example, the skin is left on and the apple is merely cored. If the syrup does not jelly enough, peelings of more acid, more pectin-rich reinette or capendu apples (which Cotgrave in his *Dictionarie* says are "more delicious than the pepin") may be boiled in it. Each kind of dried preserved fruit has its special presentation: prunes in individual paper wrappers, grapes in clusters of seven, and small pears in bundles of three or four.[25] The following baked apple recipe is representative of Bonnefons's style:

Apples are cooked whole in front of the fire, after the stem and core have been hollowed out, putting into the hollow of each a piece of sweet butter, which you have rolled in powdered sugar; if their tops have not been taken off, they must be pricked in several places with the point of a knife, because of the steam which would burst the skin and waste the best part of their pulp. One cuts them in half and hollows out the skin a little all around, then one puts them to roast on the coals; and to serve them one takes off all the skin, which leaves the apple like a little hat; then one sugars them.[26]

A medieval recipe would have had more ingredients, and the flavor of the apple would have mattered less. Throughout both his books, Bonnefons is restrained in his use of spices. His recipes require a smaller investment in ingredients and equipment than those of La Varenne and the *Pâtissier*. On the other hand, the variety of produce is impressive. He lists orchard fruit by season.[27] Imagine having the choice of seventy-four kinds of pear ripening in August and September—among them the Amazones, the Merveilles rouges, the Belles et bonnes, and the Sauvages douces.

Both volumes are dedicated to "the Ladies." The reasons given for the dedication shed some light on the role women played in the management of kitchen and table. In the dedicatory epistle of the *Jardinier* he cites the example of ladies of rank who profitably sell the excess produce of their orchards to fruiterers. He has little patience with those literary writers on gardening "who make use of the subject rather to display the strength of their genius than to give some kind of instruction." He says that gardens will please all the senses. The sense of smell "finds its contentment" in both flowers and fruit; sight in colors "so vivid . . . that the finest colors are dimmed by their brilliance." Even the gardener's ears are delighted by hearing the beauty of the garden praised, "and especially the size and variety of your fruit," while the sense of touch is gratified in handling and peeling it. "As to taste, it is enough to say that dainty feeders [*frians et delicats*], after having more than sufficiently gorged themselves on many kinds of good dishes, do not think they have had a really good meal, if they do not finish their feasts with fruit."[28]

Bonnefons says that there are three advantages to having a garden: it gives pleasure to a great variety of people, who will praise you for it; your house will be furnished with its produce; and "you will be able to sell the

Wives When Their Husbands Are Away, engraving, by Abraham Bosse. This is not a bedroom but a magnificently appointed living room, in an age when bedrooms were not separate spaces. The ladies are doing themselves well with turkey, sausage, plenty of wine, and a blazing fire; the maid is offered a bribe not to tell on them. (Courtesy of the Museum of Fine Arts, Boston.)

crop from a quantity of your trees to the fruiterers, who will pay cash in advance which you can depend upon for part of your revenue. I know ladies of lofty station who do so, and avow that this profit makes them even fonder of their gardens, and makes them more liberal in their necessary expenditures." Presumably, the sense of hearing was also delighted by the chink of coin dropping into the family coffers. Bonnefons tells us that the book has been printed in a small format so that ladies can easily carry it with them, "to confront the work of their gardeners with this little volume, . . . to judge their ability or negligence."[29] Plainly, the female surveillance is crucial.

In the kitchen, too, under the watchful eye of the lady of the house, fruits and vegetables are preserved and milk and cream become butter and cheeses, extending the useful life of the farm's products. Bonnefons tells his readers that "Messieurs your husbands will exert themselves in vain to amass wealth if you do not spend it prudently."[30] There are several enticing recipes for fresh cheeses and flavored creams. He begins at the very beginning: "Kill a calf which has never had any food but pure milk," and goes through the preparation of rennet to the actual process of cheesemaking. He assumes that a single dairy may turn out several types of cheese—fresh cream cheeses to be eaten within a day or two and cheeses with a cooked curd to be salted, pressed, and stored in a cool place for weeks or months, for use when milk production is down.[31]

The emphasis throughout is on preparations in which the flavors of individual ingredients will be recognizable. He states this principle most clearly in Book Three of the *Delices de la campagne*, on the cooking of meats, poultry, and fish, which he dedicates to maîtres d'hôtel in the houses of the great. He appeals to them for simplicity and in doing so defines for the first time the difference between the kinds of cookery practiced by La Varenne and himself:

> This Third Book which I present to you has as its subject the real flavor which should be given to each kind of flesh and fish, which the majority of your cooks do not study. So preoccupied are they with the good opinion which people have of their abilities that they imagine that so long as they disguise and garnish their dishes in confusion they [the cooks] will pass for clever men, but that is where they are wrong. . . . I tell you for your instruction that nothing is more pleasing to Man than diversity, and the Frenchman has a special inclination to it. That is why you must try as much as you can to diversify food, by flavor and by the form in which you present it. A *potage de santé* should be a good bourgeois soup, well filled up with good ingredients well chosen, and reduced to a small amount of bouillon, without hashes, mushrooms, and spices, nor other ingredients, for it should be simple because it bears the name of *santé*. A cabbage soup should taste entirely of cabbage; a leek soup of leeks; a turnip soup of turnips; and thus for the others, leaving the *compositions* for bisques, hashes, *panades*, and other made dishes [*deguisemens*] which one should rather taste than fill up on. . . . (Let us leave to foreigners many of the depraved ragouts; they never enjoy good fare except when they have cooks from France.)[32]

To judge from the ever-growing complexity of court cookery in the following decades, his advice was not taken. But his books sold well, probably because they appealed to a broader audience. The *Jardinier françois* was reprinted as late as 1737, with few changes; the last edition of the *Delices de la campagne* appeared in 1741, just five years before the first edition of its spiritual descendant, Menon's *Cuisinière bourgeoise.*

Bonnefons had a successor at court, Jean de la Quintinie, whose skill as a gardener earned him the opportunity to design kitchen gardens and orchards for Nicolas Fouquet at Vaux-le-Vicomte, the prince de Condé at Chantilly, and Jean Baptiste Colbert at Sceaux.[33] This work in turn earned him the patronage of Louis XIV. The superb establishments de la Quintinie directed at Versailles inspired gardeners all over Europe. He addressed himself to solving horticultural problems and is credited with innovations in techniques of transplanting, soil improvement, and the production of out-of-season fruit, vegetables, and flowers. He began work on the famous kitchen garden at Versailles in 1678; it included espaliered fruit trees, asparagus beds, and a multitude of other fruits and vegetables. Subsequently, he started the great orchard there. By interesting the most fashionable people in high-quality garden fare, he did much to enlarge the range of cooks' materials. When the king of France took pride in offering his guests the finest asparagus, the earliest peaches, the newest variety of carrot, all Europe followed his example. The cook as well as the gardener was obliged to develop new skills, and many of the newly developed recipes from this time are designed to use an increasing variety of garden stuff.

Another sign of the value assigned to produce during the seventeenth century is its appearance in still-life paintings, especially French ones, alongside or in place of flowers. These pictures display a hierarchy of fruit and vegetables that remained consistent throughout the seventeenth and eighteenth centuries. At the top of the scale are what might be called landowners' produce: peaches, grapes, asparagus, and citrus and other tree fruits, all of which require a substantial investment of skilled labor, space, time, and equipment. They enjoy, at the painter's hand, a suitably dignified presentation and are displayed in porcelain or silver bowls. The setting may be out of doors on a stone ledge, or indoors on a handsome table; there is likely to be a suggestion of coolness to the atmosphere. Humbler produce generally is found in a kitchen setting. Root vegetables, copper pots, and legs of lamb crowd each other in succulent profusion, and there are often some glowing coals to add interest. A few items are welcome anywhere: hams, artichokes, and pies, as well as leafy greens with which the artist could lighten the otherwise solid subjects.

FOLLOWERS OF LA VARENNE

Developments in the art of cooking after La Varenne and Bonnefons published their books can be followed in two lesser-known works: Pierre de Lune's *Le Cvisinier* (1656) and the anonymous *Le Cvisinier méthodiqve* (1662), later published as *Le Cuisinier françois ov l'école des ragouts*.[34] De Lune describes himself as the former *escuyer de cuisine* to the late duc de Rohan. In both volumes old recipes mingle incongruously with new ones; both contain additions to the ranks of basic combinations and classic dishes. Among the survivals is de Lune's recipe for a *popeton à l'Angloise*, a purely medieval mixture of fish, pike livers, dates, prunes, and raisins, with macaroons. Elsewhere there is a Lenten "squab" pie. The imitation squabs are made of ground raw fish, appropriately shaped, with pike livers tucked inside; they are cooked in butter and then baked in a crust with imitation cockscombs made from the same fish composition, along with mushrooms, morels, and soft fish roes. The *Cvisinier méthodiqve* has a large number of more or less revised old favorites, including *galimaufrée*, blancmange, and *civé*. The recipe for *civé* might be called flexible—or merely vague; it begins: "Take whatever kind of meat pleases you, for example, a piece of fresh pork, or veal, or better still half a hare, and add to it more meat if you need to," and continues in this haphazard manner.[35] In a cheese soup, meat stock, eggs, and aged Italian cheese are finished off with cinnamon sugar.[36]

Innovations are prominent in both books. De Lune begins with a preface describing ingredients one should have on hand; they include a number of the new subunits cooks were learning to work with. His basic seasoning packet is a bundle of bacon, scallion, thyme, cloves, chervil, and parsley, all tied up with a string. On fast days the bacon is replaced by a peeled lemon. The garnishes his cook is expected to have ready include peeled, chopped pistachios, sliced lemons, waiting in cold water, cut-up oranges, pomegranate seeds, olives, capers, fried parsley, bread in an egg batter (our french toast), and a roux of bacon fat and flour. An important basic component that is used in the new way for the first time in the *Cvisinier méthodiqve* is *coulis*: it is a rich meat or fish flavoring, thickened with flour or ground almonds and often mushrooms. These early *coulis* recipes seem sometimes to have had the hashed meat left in and would therefore have been sandy-textured.[37] In later decades it became customary to strain them. In either case the *coulis* is used to reinforce sauces and can be poured over roasts and made dishes and into pies after baking.

An enduring favorite that appears in the *Cvisinier méthodiqve* is bisque, a rich soup made from squabs or other choice poultry, game, or fish.[38] It is so characteristic of mid-seventeenth-century cooking techniques that it must be described in detail. A stock is made with beef, mutton, veal, and chicken. The squabs are cooked separately, in their own broth. The meat stock is simmered in a deep serving dish with slices of bread until the stock has reduced and the bread has begun to stick to the bottom of the dish. The squabs are then arranged on the bread and garnished with mushrooms, sweetbreads, cockscombs, and artichoke bottoms. At the last minute a few final tidbits are added: pistachios, the meaty juice from a roast, and a little lemon juice. Finally, sliced lemons are arranged around the edge of the dish. Several features of this recipe are characteristically mid-seventeenth-century. First, the stock is made with a multiplicity of meats (astonishing to the modern cook and certainly not in conformity with Bonnefons's requirement that foods should taste of themselves). The result is a full-flavored, if anonymous, broth, and the method is not necessarily wasteful because all the meats used to make it would themselves be used again elsewhere. Second is the cooking down of bread, meats, and vegetables in a much-reduced broth or in fat until they begin to brown, which became a favorite technique at this time and remained a standard practice in the eighteenth century. Close supervision was required to bring the browning to the correct point and no further. This browned material—the gratin—has served ever since to enrich savory dishes. Finally, garnishes are used and superimposed to the point of absurdity. There was a tendency to use the same ones over and over again, with few attempts to adapt them to the dishes they adorned. The general belief seems to have been that more garnish meant more magnificence. The effect, of course, was to make everything look alike—and sometimes taste alike.

In the next chapters, I shall describe the sometimes parallel, sometimes divergent courses of *haute cuisine* and *cuisine bourgeoise*. In actual practice, the two styles were never entirely separate. The wealthiest aristocrats did not eat all their meals at court feasts, and some prosperous members of the middle class could afford to pay the wages of the most skilled cooks and to buy the costliest ingredients.

CHAPTER SEVEN

Court Festivals of Louis XIV

A VARENNE AND BONNEFONS had published their cook-books when Louis XIV was an adolescent. From 1648 until 1653 the young king's hold on the throne was threatened by the Fronde, a complex of civil wars that pitted first Paris and the high courts (parlements) of Paris and Bordeaux and then much of the high nobility against the royal government. With the end of the Fronde, the monarchy stabilized, and, after the death in 1661 of Cardinal Mazarin, who had dominated the government, Louis undertook the direction of government. He gave close attention to small as well as large matters, and he adapted court ceremonies and festivities to meet both his personal requirements and government policies. Sixteenth-century ceremony had been largely public, with solemn entries and similar processions predominating, though some functions were restricted to the court, such as dances and masques in which courtiers both played roles and formed the audience. During the second half of the seventeenth century the emphasis came increasingly to be on events in the semi-restricted world of the court.[1]

Louis XIV did not like Paris, probably because he associated it with childhood memories of the Fronde. As the years passed he spent less time there and more at Versailles, Fontainebleau, and Marly. In these settings the service of food was incorporated into the proliferating formalities of court life. Louis's court combined an insistence on a classicizing adherence to rules with a demand for novelty, ideal circumstances for La Varenne's modular approach to luxurious, large-scale cooking.

Court Festivals

Catherine de Medici had used court entertainments to urge her political programs upon a divided and even hostile court. The Sun King drew his courtiers to Versailles and kept them there, dependent upon him for favors. The entertainments he gave served to display his magnificence to the French nobility and representatives of foreign governments, to attract people to the court, and to evince royal favor to the fortunate.[2] It was the king's good fortune to have his staff unwittingly assembled for him by Nicolas Fouquet, who was, early in the reign, his superintendent of finances. Like other government officials of his time, Fouquet diverted a substantial portion of the royal tax revenues into his own coffers. Some of this money he put into the creation of a great estate, Vaux-le-Vicomte. He had a gift for finding skilled artists, many of whom were just beginning their careers. The house was commissioned in 1657; its architect was Louis Le Vau. The gardens were laid out by André Le Nôtre, who had been hired away from the garden staff at the Tuileries, and Jean de la Quintinie was in charge of the horticultural aspect of the landscape. Charles Le Brun oversaw the sumptuous decoration of the interior. While building Vaux-le-Vicomte, Fouquet was spending yet larger amounts of money on strengthening his fortified castle of Belle-Isle, off the coast of Britanny, and hiring his own private army. But Louis remembered the Fronde, when noblemen with private armies had driven him out of Paris, and he was not inclined to let such a situation arise again. Plans were made to arrest Fouquet as soon as royal troops could be moved to the vicinity of Belle-Isle.[3]

Meanwhile Fouquet enjoyed a brief, brilliant triumph: in August of 1661 he invited the king and court to Vaux for a spectacular festival. Molière wrote a comedy-ballet for it (*Les Facheux*) with stage sets by Le Brun and music by Jean Baptiste Lully.[4] Afterward the event was commemorated in verse by Jean de La Fontaine.[5] The man in charge of supper, as well as of all the other arrangements, was Vatel. Everyone pronounced the food delicious, though unfortunately no one wrote down the menu. When Fouquet was arrested three weeks later, the king moved artists, designers, gardeners, and even the orange trees to Versailles and began his lifelong program of building and landscaping. Only Vatel went elsewhere—to serve the Prince de Condé at Chantilly.

The banquets and festivals, so notable in the annals of the reign of Louis XIV, took place in the midst of ongoing building construction and new planting. Contemporary prints show a high proportion of trellis to tree in the gardens. Although trees of great size were brought in (this being one of de la Quintinie's specialties), everything was raw and new except for the core of the palace, which had been Louis XIII's modest brick and stone hunting lodge. The entrance courtyard of this old building, modified in Louis XIV's time, was the setting for performances of many of Molière's plays and for some notable collations. To amuse the court, to honor his mistresses, and to dazzle all Europe, the king put on the series of entertainments that began with a festival called the Pleasures of the Enchanted Isle in May 1664.[6] The theme for the festival, which occupied several days, was taken from a tale of Lodovico Ariosto: Versailles was declared to be an island, put under a three-day enchantment by the sorceress Alcina. Roger and his knights were held prisoners by her beauty, and its spell was eventually broken by the use of a magic ring supplied to Roger by one Melissa, disguised, the narrator tells us, as Atlas. According to André Félibien, who wrote the descriptions, there were six hundred guests, "besides an infinity of people necessary for the ballet and the theater, and artisans of all kinds who came out from Paris."[7]

It opened with a parade, led by d'Artagnan, of the Musketeers, on horseback. He was richly dressed in the king's fire-red livery and carried a lance and shield, on which shone a sun bearing the words: "Nec cesso, nec erro [I neither yield nor err]," an allusion "to the devotion of His Majesty to the affairs of his state and the manner in which he would act."[8] D'Artagnan was followed by a chariot bearing Apollo and then by allegorically costumed people who represented the four ages of man, the twelve [sic] hours of the day, and the twelve signs of the zodiac. Displays of horsemanship followed. As night fell, torches were lit in the gardens, and musicians performed a concert. As they played, figures representing the four seasons entered, carrying great platters of delicious food. Next the twelve signs of the zodiac danced with the seasons in "one of the most beautiful ballets that anyone had ever seen." There followed forty-eight more people carrying broad trays on their heads containing the collation. "The first twelve were dressed as gardeners, with baskets painted green and silver, with a good number of porcelain bowls filled with preserved fruit and other good seasonal things; then came twelve grain harvesters with red baskets, twelve wine harvesters with baskets the color of dead leaves, and finally twelve old men in furs, their baskets imitating ice." Each of these groups carried seasonally appropriate food.[9] Others came bringing meat (presumably game) "from Pan's menagerie." Félibien writes that "the sumptuousness of the collation surpassed anything that can be described, as much in the abundance as in the delicacy of the things that were served there; it was also the most beautiful sight that the senses could behold; because, in the night, against the verdure of these tall trellises, an infinity of tall chandeliers, painted green and silver, each bearing twenty-four candles, and two hundred torches of white wax,

Banquet of the King and the Queens, engraving, by Israel Sylvestre, from André Félibien, *Les Plaisirs de l'Isle enchantée* (1664). Supper on the first evening of the festival of the Pleasures of the Enchanted Isle was held in the new garden at Versailles. Louis XIV sits in the center of the table with his brother, wife, mother, and a selection of court ladies. Spectators stand behind guards in the foreground. (By permission of the Theatre Collection, Harvard University.)

held by as many people wearing masks, gave a clarity almost as bright and pleasant as day."[10] The Sun King had no need of nature's sun. Félibien records, however, that on the second day of the fête the king grew tired of so much verse and ordered Molière and his troop to finish quickly and in prose.[11]

The diners at the collation on the first day sat along one side of a semicircular table; the king, his wife, and his mother were in the center, flanked by ladies, including two of his mistresses, and his brother and sister-in-law. On some occasions the king was seated on the main axis of the building, which ran through the royal bedchamber and was continued in the gardens. The publicly acknowledged guests of honor were the two queens; it was understood that the one who ruled his heart at that moment was his new mistress, Louise de La Vallière.[12] It was the custom at these banquets to seat the most beautiful as well as the highest-ranking ladies at the king's table. The queen might be there, or she might instead be obliged to preside over an all-female table in another room or *allée*—there was no question of her selecting a few favorite gentlemen. The remaining male courtiers were then relegated to a third table in yet another place. On some occasions this segregation was enforced even before the meal began, with the diners being allocated to a series of more or less exclusive antechambers. It may be remembered that in the Middle Ages the two standard forms had been either for all the men and women to sit together in order of precedence or, more usually at banquets, for the men to dine while the women watched from a secluded position such as a balcony. But by the end of the seventeenth century the table was becoming a place where culinary pleasure was spiced with flirtation.

On the second evening of the festival celebrating the conquest of the Franche Comté the *officiers* of the *office* built a collation which was a triumph of their art. It was an immense confectionary structure that occupied nearly all of a sizable table,

> leaving only a wide border around the edge, for the place settings and the platters of food. It [was composed of] all kinds of fruits ingeniously arranged in one hundred dozen little porcelain dishes, which served as the solid body of the agreeable building. It was divided by sixteen arcades, and each arcade had two pairs of serpentine columns which carried the cornice. These columns were gilded and garnished with flowers, as were the bases and capitals. In the middle of the arcades hung double garlands, and above the columns were chandeliers illuminated with candles. One hundred little vases of tuberoses and orange flowers were set on the cornice, completing the decoration of the upper part of the building. But the almost incredible quantity of porcelain basins and dishes filled with fruit, and the large number of crystal vases used for the ices [*les glaces*] and liqueurs, made this table a sumptuous one, on which the foods were served with an extraordinary magnificence.[13]

In July of 1678 Colbert organized a fête in the park at Versailles featuring splendid food structures. Fifteen tables were arranged as buffets, laden with all the components of a superb meal.

> One of the tables represented a mountain, with several caves in which were various sorts of cold meats; another [table] was like the façade of a palace built with marzipan and sugar paste. There was one filled with pyramids of preserved fruits, and another with an infinity of glasses filled

Banquet in the small park at Versailles, engraving, by Jean Le Pautre, from André Félibien, *Relation de la feste de Versailles . . .* (Paris, 1679). Each of the massive pyramids on the table was built up with layers of porcelain dishes and preserved fruit; around the base of the centerpiece were fruit pastes, preserves, greenery, and sugared fruit. Louis XIV stands at the left, indicating the display to his guests, while spectators watch from the archways. When the royal party is through with its collation the bystanders are allowed to enter and eat the remains. (By permission of the Theatre Collection, Harvard University.)

with all kinds of liqueurs, and the last was composed of caramels. Between the tables were orange trees bearing preserved fruit; on either side stood two other trees with similar fruit of different species.[14]

In the middle of this circle of tables and trees was a fountain thirty feet high, to add its agreeable sound to the night air. Let us hope that the mist of the fountain kept away from the confectionary.

Distinctions of position were clearly marked at these court festivities. For many courtiers participation meant merely forming part of the eager audience, watching the more favored from behind a barrier of guards. But at the end of such meals, roles were reversed, and the spectators performed for the people they had been watching. Accounts repeatedly conclude with a phrase such as, "after the king and queen had eaten, all the tables were abandoned to pillage, as is the custom on these occasions."[15] Again, "the destruction of so handsome an arrangement served to give another agreeable entertainment to all the court, by the alacrity and disorder of those who demolished these castles of marzipan, and these mountains of preserved fruit."[16] This moment of planned disorder in the midst of such rigorously planned order is reminiscent of comic low-life scenes in serious theater. But real disorder was not wanted, and part of the skill in being a courtier lay in recognizing the rare moment when spontaneity was required.

The king was the most conspicuous diner at Versailles. His meals came from kitchens located about a quarter of a mile away from where he ate. The kitchens at Versailles were in a vast building designed by Jules Hardouin Mansart and completed about 1685. The building they occupied was constructed around a four-sided courtyard and contained about a thousand rooms; above the kitchens lived some fifteen hundred people. Many of the principal officers served in rotation, a quarter of a year at a time. There were two divisions to the kitchens: the commons, which cooked for most of the palace personnel, and *la cuisine du roi*, which served the household of the king.[17] Once the royal dinner had been prepared, it was carried in procession to the king's table under an armed escort.

> [First came two of the king's own guard,] then the doorkeeper of the hall, the maître d'hôtel with his baton, the king's waiter, the pantler, the comptroller general, the comptroller of the *office*, and others, who carry the food, the head cook and the keeper of the silver plate. And behind them two more of His Majesty's guards, who allow no one to approach the food.[18]

As this parade passed, men stood still, removed their hats, bowed as if in the royal presence, and said, "C'est la viande du roi."[19] It may be assumed that finishing touches were administered by the cooks from the kitchen and *office* when the food reached its destination.

The king ate in two modes. On special occasions he supped in public with members of the royal family, *au grand couvert*. Midday dinner was a private meal, *au petit couvert*, eaten in his own room, sometimes attended by his brother and, in later years, his son. Louis was a hearty eater. His sister-in-law, the Princess Palatine, has described him at table: "I have often seen the king eating four full plates of soup, a whole pheasant, a partridge, a big dish of salad, two big slices of ham, some mutton with *jus* and garlic, a plate of pastry, and then fruit and some hard-boiled eggs."[20] The duc de Saint-

Simon stated that the king damaged his health by excessive eating, though he lived to be seventy-seven, despite assiduous medical care. His doctor required him to eat quantities of fruit, and Louis loved sweets and salads as well. His soups [*potages*], of which he ate several for supper and dinner, "were full of *jus*, and extremely strong, and everything that was served to him was heavily spiced, at least twice as much as was usual for any ordinary dish. . . . That, and the sweets, were not by the advice of Fagon [his doctor]."[21]

The Princess Palatine was no mean eater herself. Her main outdoor activity was hunting; indoors she wrote letters, in which she often wrote about food. She missed the good German beer soups. After forty years at the French court, she wrote to her sister back in Germany:

> I am all German when it comes to drinking and eating, and I have been all my life: nobody here can fry things properly; the milk and butter are not as good as at home [*chez nous*]; they have no flavor, they taste like water; the cabbages aren't good any more, because the land they are grown in isn't fat [she sent to Germany for her cabbage seeds], but light and sandy, so the vegetables don't have any strength, and the dairy herd doesn't give good milk. Good God! How I wish I could eat the good dishes your *cuisinière* makes for you![22]

And again writing to her sister:

> No one is surprised if I eat blood pudding with pleasure. I have also made Westphalian type raw hams fashionable here. Everyone eats them now, and they also eat many of our German foods—sauerkraut, and sugared cabbages [sweet and sour?], as well as cabbage with fat bacon, but it is hard to get it of good quality. They never used to eat game before—I put all that in fashion, as well as kippered herring; I taught the king how to eat them, and he found them very much to his taste. I have so accustomed my German belly to German dishes that I cannot bear to eat a single French ragout.[23]

Of course game always had been eaten, and no surge of Bavarian recipes appeared in the cookbooks after this princess arrived at the French court, but certainly Westphalian and Mainz hams were highly regarded, for which she may or may not have been responsible.

In the circumscribed world of the court, very small events were seized upon as pretexts for excitement. There was, for example, an endemic tendency to hysteria over green peas. In 1660 Audiger was returning to France from Italy, where he had studied the art of distilling liqueurs. He had a grandiose scheme for getting the monopoly to sell the specialty liqueurs of Italy in France, and he needed a device to bring himself to the king's notice. As he traveled north in early January, he found some excellent green peas growing near Genoa. He had them packed up with rosebuds and greenery. Arriving in Paris a fortnight later, he contrived to be introduced into the royal presence. Several courtiers were also there, and according to Audiger's account, the comte de Soissons "himself took a fistful of peas, which he shelled in His Majesty's presence, and which were found to be as fresh as if they had just been picked."[24] The king had them taken to the comptroller of his kitchen to be cooked for himself, his mother, and Cardinal Mazarin. Like so many clever stratagems, this one was not entirely successful. Audiger did not get his liqueur monopoly, but he did establish early peas as a fashionable luxury at court.

When de la Quintinie's kitchen garden at Versailles began to produce out-of-season vegetables, none was in greater demand than peas. They even found their way into humorous fiction. *Le Mercure Galant* was a monthly publication, often running to three or four hundred pages, that reported on fashion and society as well as on French and international news. Its contents varied with the decades. For a while it ran a monthly competition; the names of the winners were published and indicate a circulation that reached all over Europe. Its June 1679 issue contains a comic story about two suitors attempting to purchase the affections of a lady with extravagant gifts. She indicates a taste for peas. After a series of maneuvers, including an attempt by one suitor to avoid so expensive a tribute, the story ends with a plethora of peas; the lady's mother uses the excess to pay an overdue debt to her lawyer, and the parsimonious lover is punished by being present at the exchange.[25]

A popular story of the time tells of a miser who was obliged to offer an expensive dinner. Symmetry demanded a dish of peas for each end of the table, and he tried to economize by using chopped asparagus for one of the dishes. He arranged with the servants beforehand that the dish with the imitation peas was to be dropped "accidentally" before it got to the table. Inevitably, the peas fell and the asparagus survived to betray the host.[26] Such stories are still current, and there is probably a medieval roast peacock version derived from a Roman dormouse original. In fact, the dish of asparagus disguised as peas appears in several cookbooks of the period, but it was probably intended to surprise and amuse rather than to deceive; it is quite tasty. Massialot mentions *asperges en petits pois*, "with a green purée of pea-pods or something else, a croûte in the center, and a garnish of *pains de jambon*"[27] (toasted rolls hollowed out and rolled with braised ham slices in a meaty sauce)—hardly a cheap substitute.

By the end of the century the king and his court were aging; tedious formality took the place of youthful zest. But if Madame de Maintenon is to be believed, peas could still be depended upon for excitement. She wrote to the Cardinal de Noailles in May 1696:

> At court, the chapter of peas continues. The impatience to eat them, the pleasures of eating them, and the joy of eating them again are the three points which our princes have been discussing these last four days. There are ladies who, after having supped with the king, and supped well, find peas at home to eat before going to bed, at the risk of indigestion. It is a fashion, a furor.[28]

Arrangement of the Table and Service of the Food

In the minutely patterned society of the seventeenth-century French court and of those who followed its fashions, there was, ideally, a place for everything, and this required a fully elaborated pattern. Gradations of privilege marked every courtier's position in the hierarchy. A modern scholar has worked out a diagram indicating who was allowed to sit on what kind of chair, bench, or stool in whose presence, and similar rules governed the putting on and taking off of hats.[29]

It is therefore not surprising that the setting of a table and the serving of a meal were also closely regulated. The manner in which it was done was known all over Europe as *service à la française*, and it remained the standard form until it was replaced by *service à la russe*, beginning in the 1860s.[30] A typical meal consisted of three courses; the first and second were prepared in the *cuisine* and the third in the *office*. For each course the foods served were ranked by size and arranged symmetrically on the table. Just as the cooks in the kitchen combined their basic mixtures, raw materials, and garnishes into finished platters, so the maître d'hôtel composed these platters into a pattern for the table. Typically, a small but luxurious supper might be set out on a square table, with a large tureen of soup in the center. The corners of the table would be occupied by four medium-sized platters, each with a different delicacy; four small plates would be placed between the large ones. The pattern would be completed with eight small dishes set round the outside of the main body of the course—these are the hors d'oeuvre (in this first phase of development, spatially, not temporally, outside the main body of the meal).[31] The diners' places were set around the edge of the table. When the first course was eaten the dishes were removed, though not more than four at a time according to Bonnefons, to preserve the pattern.[32] The arrangement of dishes for the second course closely followed the pattern of the first. For the third course, a similar repetition took place, but variations were permitted.

As it was a simple matter for the cook to vary his recipes, working within the framework of culinary practice, so it was simple for the maître d'hôtel to adjust his menu to fit tables of all sizes. Diagrams with appended menus are a regular feature of cookbooks from the end of the seventeenth century onward. The early editions of Massialot's *Cuisinier roïal et bourgeois* have woodcuts illustrating meals for small numbers of people. By the time the second French-language edition of Vincent La Chapelle's *Cuisinier moderne* appeared in 1742, it contained (along with more modest menus) a foldout plan for setting a horseshoe-shaped table for one hundred people, with nearly five hundred items in two courses, the courses being subdivided by the replacement of the first batch of foods with another. These supplementary offerings were called the *relevées*—that is, they replaced the ones that had been removed.[33]

The most important dish in each course of a seventeenth-century French dinner was the biggest. The handsome silver tureens and their eighteenth-century ceramic counterparts that can still be seen in museums formed a principal part of the decoration of any banquets.[34] The soup that went into them was the focus of the first course and contained expensive ingredients. In the second course it was replaced by a substantial, elaborately garnished piece of meat or fish. This was called the roast, but it could, in fact, be cooked by other methods. The lesser dishes ranged around it were expected to display the generosity of the host and the skill of his cooks. Unless the table was very large, every plate contained something different. As in the Middle Ages, the diners ate primarily what they could reach, but (with the exception of royalty, who were often served special dishes) the practice of arranging food in declining order of social rank down the table had ceased.

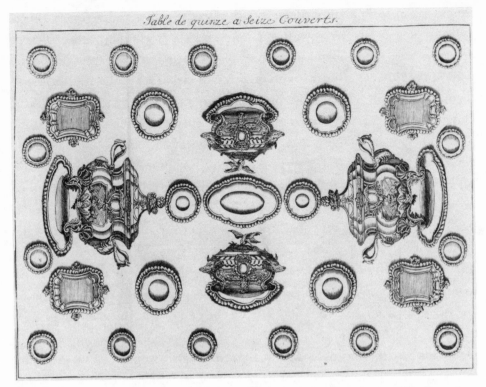

Table de quinze a Seize Couverts.

Table setting plan for a supper, engraving, from Vincent La Chapelle, *Le Cuisinier moderne* (The Hague, 1742). The tureens and dishes are all silver; three decades later they would be porcelain. La Chapelle supplies the first two courses of a menu for this meal. The third would be supplied by the *office* and therefore would be the responsibility of another craftsman. The meal opens with a pair of soups in the tureens, flanking a quarter of veal; the four entrées are poultry, and the hors d'oeuvres are delicate little made dishes, such as mutton chops with chicory, glazed eels with an Italian sauce, and a dish of chicken breasts; while the first course is still on the table the soups are replaced by a turbot and a salmon. The second course repeats the pattern of the first with new dishes, including a ham for the center and cakes to replace the turbot and salmon. Among the new hors d'oeuvres are sweetbreads, artichokes, duck tongues, and eggs with a meat sauce. (By permission of the Schlesinger Library, Radcliffe College.)

If a diner wished for something out of reach, a servant was summoned to fetch it, though it was not good manners to do this too often.

The rules for eating a meal politely were set down in 1695 by Antoine de Courtin in his *Nouveau traité de la civilité qui se pratique en France parmi les honnestes gens.* The verbose Courtin provides a rich store of useful information. The medieval custom of offering water and a towel for certain handwashing survived, but it was practiced only by the highest-ranking people; the polite minor guest did not intrude himself into the ritual. Gentlemen removed their hats while grace was being said but put them back on when they sat down and wore them throughout the meal, except during toasts. They also kept their swords and short capes on. Only the king ate bare-headed. The diner sat up straight, keeping his or her elbows off the table, and generally refrained from impinging on the other guests. He was to be neither too eager nor too fussy and was never to be the first to put his spoon in a dish, except to serve others. Courtin takes forks for granted. Louis XIV is said to have eaten with his fingers all his life, but the fork had long since become a standard part of bourgeois and aristocratic table settings. Among Courtin's rules are the following:

> One must . . . not gnaw on bones, or break them and suck out the marrow. You should cut the meat on your plate, and then carry it to the mouth with the fork. I say with the fork, because it is . . . very indecent to touch something greasy, or with a sauce, or in a syrup, etc., with the fingers; and furthermore, it obliges you to commit two or three other indecencies. One is to wipe your hands frequently on your napkin, and to dirty it like a kitchen towel, so that everyone who sees you wipe your mouth with it feels sick. The other is to wipe them on your bread, which is very indecent, and the third is to lick your fingers, which is the ultimate impropriety.[35]

He shows a similar delicacy with soups. Each diner uses his own spoon to help himself from the tureen. The polite person who wants a second helping wipes his spoon with a piece of bread before putting it back into the tureen, and the especially sensitive diner will send it to the sideboard to be washed.

He itemizes the choicest morsels of popular dishes, so that the considerate guest may offer them to people he is serving. Dining required participation. *Service à la française* covered the table with dishes; everyone could reach some things and not others and could expect to be called upon for assistance. These interactions were regularly marked by acknowledgments of relative social position. When a man served a higher-ranking woman he tipped his hat, while both the right to carve and priority in taking food from a dish were also indicators of rank.

Traps awaited the unwary. Olives were to be taken with a spoon, never with a fork, but walnuts were taken from their dish with the bare hand. Oranges served with the roast were cut crosswise; fish must never be touched with a knife unless it was in a pie. If a truffle came in with some of the ash in which it was baked still clinging to the surface, the ash must be scraped away with a knife, not blown, for "the breath is sometimes disgusting to people, besides which it will get ashes on the table."[36] Most of the behavior required of a diner was a mixture of common sense and consideration, which would facilitate the service and enjoyment of the meal. There were also seemingly arbitrary rules—signals, in effect, that the diner was a member of a social elite. In addition, the participants, through the use of reiterated gestures, articulated their social relationships. Then as now, "table manners" served not only practical but symbolic functions.

The serving of an elaborate meal required very careful planning. The *Mercure Galant* remarks regularly on devices used in the managing of such meals. For example, at one banquet held in the great hall of a château, four staircases were built leading from the parterre below up to the windows of the hall. Food was brought from the kitchen to the foot of the stairs and handed over to the king's own Swiss guard, who marched up the stairs and handed the platters through the windows to the domestic officers and pages of the king, who then set them in place. Meanwhile, the reverse process was being followed in removing the first-course dishes. The gazette observes that this organization permitted the meal to be served in just two hours, though it consisted of more than six hundred dishes in three courses.[37] On another occasion the maître d'hôtel avoided confusion by lining up his footmen in two rows along the length of the table. At a signal, the front row stepped forward and cleared the table. As they stepped back, the footmen in the back row, who had the dishes for the second course, stepped between them to place the new platters on the table, "without any disorder" the *Mercure Galant* commented, quoting an observer who said that "one would think oneself seeing an exercise of military men."[38] Later the system was improved by putting distinguishing marks on the dishes so the Swiss guard could be more easily directed to where the dishes belonged.[39] It is probably just as well that at this stage in the development of table setting the services for great banquets were usually made of good solid silver, not porcelain.

What effect was aimed for by the givers of banquets? A description from the *Mercure Galant* for October 1677 of a collation given by the king at Fontainebleau suggests an answer: "The collation of the first ball was superb. France grows in magnificence daily, and it may be that nothing like it has ever been seen."[40] The editors of the *Mercure Galant* were so impressed that they included a foldout diagram of the table setting. It is indeed impressive and shows a concern for vertical as well as horizontal scale—a new feature. Large, square, tiered pyramids are set diagonally down the long table, introducing an element of geometric variety into the composition, which is otherwise made up, on the horizontal plane, entirely of circular shapes. The vertical accents are the great pyramids and the candlesticks and candelabra that alternate down the length of the table. There are also shallow crystal bowls holding glass goblets filled with water ices and porcelain hors d'oeuvre dishes filled with fruit compotes. The area around the table was enclosed by a balustrade. The elect supped within; lesser courtiers watched from outside and refreshed themselves from strategically placed buffets.

> The spectacle [writes the observer] enchanted my eyes, and I do not know if they could have borne it very long. Picture to yourself this dazzling mass of lights which abetted each other, so that, when the lights of the candlesticks shone on the crystal of the candelabra, and those of the candelabra on the gold of the candlesticks, they were all augmented by the reflection from the luster of the caramels, themselves already brilliant, and from the crystallized sugar of the glistening preserved fruit. Add to this what the variously colored fruit, the ribbons on the baskets, and the crystal of basins could do, and to all that add the effect produced by Their Majesties' jewels and those of the forty ladies who were at the table. . . . It is impossible to imagine anything that has ever been seen that could be more brilliant.[41]

The reporter of that meal adds that "credit must be given to M. Bigot, comptroller of the king's household. There is certainly no man more intelligent, nor one who knows better how to order all these kinds of things."[42] Managing the logistics of these entertainments was a difficult business, and since 1671 the shadow of Vatel's death hung over everyone who undertook them.

Out of the wreckage of Fouquet's establishment at Vaux-le-Vicomte much of the key personnel had been recruited to work at Versailles. But Vatel, the maître d'hôtel, was not among them. It is believed that he left the country for a while. In 1669 he reappeared in the service of the prince de Condé as comptroller of the household at Chantilly.[43] The following year, as part of an effort by Condé to reinstate himself in the royal favor after some conspiratorial maneuvering, that prince invited the king and all the court to visit

DESSEIN DE LA COLATION QUI FUT DONNE A MONSEIGNEUR PAR MONS. LE PRINCE,
DANS LE MILIEU DU LABIRINTE A CHANTILLY. *le 29 Aoust 1688.*

Collation at Chantilly, given by the prince de Condé in the Labyrinth, on 29 August 1688, engraving by Jean Berain. One can imagine that Vatel's ghost haunted this scene, which is heavily dependent on abundance and symmetry for its effect. Bonnefons would have been delighted by the prominence given fresh and preserved fruit. (Courtesy of the Museum of Fine Arts, Boston, Ellen Page Hall Fund.)

Chantilly for a three-day festival. Nine years had passed since Fouquet's ill-starred festival at Vaux. Was Vatel still haunted by the memory of it?

Our only extensive account of the tragedy that took place comes from a pair of letters written by Madame de Sévigné to her daughter.

Here is what I learned on coming home, which I cannot get out of my head, and which I hardly know how to tell you: it is that Vatel, the great Vatel, maître d'hôtel of M. Fouquet, who was at present with M. le Prince [de Condé], this man of an ability which distinguished him above all others, whose good head was capable of sustaining all the cares of a state—this man, whom I know, seeing at eight o'clock this morning that the shipment of seafood [*la marée*] had not arrived, was not able to bear

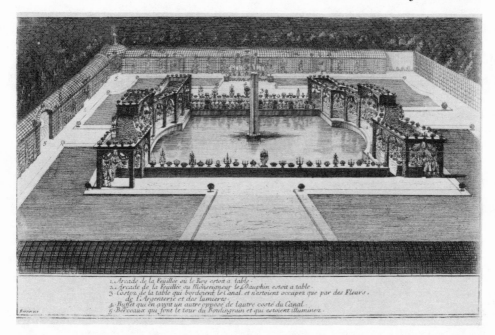

Louis XIV and the dauphin at supper by a canal, engraving by Jean Berain. This must have been one of the *ancien régime*'s most spectacular meals. The king dined in the arcade at the right, his son opposite. The long tables joining the two pavilions held flowers and candelabra. In the background is a richly decorated buffet, echoing the displays of precious metalwork at medieval banquets. (By permission of the Houghton Library, Harvard University.)

the blow which he saw was going to fall on him, and, in a word, killed himself with his sword. You may imagine the horrible disorder which such a terrible misfortune caused to the fête. Imagine that the fish arrived, perhaps just as he died. I know nothing more at present; I think you will find this enough. I do not doubt but that the confusion must have been great; it is a grievous thing at a fête costing 50,000 écus. . . .

26 April . . . But this is not a letter, it is the account which Moreuil . . . has given me of what happened at Chantilly, regarding Vatel. . . . The king arrived Thursday evening, the hunt, the lanterns, the moonlight, the promenade, the collation in a place carpeted with jonquils, everything was as desired. They supped: there were some tables where the roast was lacking, because there were a number of diners who had been by no means expected. This dumbfounded Vatel; he said several times, "I have lost my honor. This is a blow which I cannot bear." He said to Gourville, [his assistant and successor], "My head is spinning; I haven't slept for a dozen nights; help me give the orders." Gourville reassured him as best he could. The roasts which had been lacking, not at

the king's table, but at the twenty-fifth, kept haunting him. Gourville told M. le Prince. M. le Prince went right to his room and said to him, "Vatel, everything is going well; nothing was so handsome as the king's supper." And he replied, "Monseigneur, your goodness overwhelms me; I know that the roast was lacking at two tables." "Not at all," said M. le Prince. "Don't trouble yourself about it; everything is going well." The night passed: the fireworks did not succeed; they were obscured by a cloud; they had cost 16,000 francs.

At four o'clock in the morning Vatel was roaming all over the place. He found everyone asleep. He met a little purveyor who brought him just two loads of seafood; he asked him, "Is that all there is?" He answered him, "Yes, sir." He did not know that Vatel had sent to all the seaports. He waited a while; the other supplies did not come at all; his mind grew feverish, he believed that there would not be any more seafood at all; he found Gourville and said to him, "Monsieur, I cannot survive this blow. I have honor and reputation to lose." Gourville laughed at him. Vatel went up to his room, set his sword against the door, and ran it into his heart. . . . At last he fell dead. The seafood, however, was arriving from all directions; they looked for Vatel to oversee its distribution; they went to his room; they knocked, they broke down the door; they found him drowned in his own blood; they ran to M. le Prince, who was in despair. . . . Nevertheless, Gourville tried to make up for the loss of Vatel . . . ; they dined very well, they had a collation, they supped, they strolled, they gambled, they hunted; everything was perfumed with jonquils, everything was enchanted. Yesterday, which was Saturday, they did the same, and in the evening the king went on to Liancourt . . . for his next visit.[44]

Because there was a tradition that the king did not stay where there was death in the house, the poor comptroller's body was spirited away and buried after a hasty and obscure funeral, arranged by the resourceful Jean Hérault de Gourville.[45] Madame de Sévigné says that he was "praised and blamed"—the latter presumably for bringing "horrible disorder" upon the fête by his suicide; praise and blame have been conferred upon Vatel ever since. There are those who say that if he had been a cook he would have been able to improvise; given the requirements of table setting that were in force at the time it would have been merely difficult to invent supplemental roasts; but there was absolutely no way he could have served a fast-day dinner to several hundred people at short notice without fish. Later writers criticized him for not having ordered his provisions extravagantly enough, but they were not considering the limitations of seventeenth-century supply; Vatel's contemporaries certainly never accused him of parsimony. Antonin Carême praised him for his sense of honor, seeing in Vatel a man who could not bear to live under the shadow of professional failure.[46] But it seems clear from Madame de Sévigné's letter that the unfortunate man was in the grips of a nervous crisis. The practical difficulties may have triggered his suicide, but his behavior had already begun to show an excess of anxiety before the late arrival of the fish.

Anyone undertaking a really important banquet could hope or fear that the *Mercure Galant* would report the event to its subscribers all over fashionable Europe. In January 1677 it remarked of a ball given at the house of M. Rainchain that "never had neatness, good order, and magnificence appeared thus together."[47] In that same year, when the king and queen visited Colbert at Sceaux, it reported of the supper that one could not sufficiently emphasize "the extreme neatness; furthermore, the dishes were seasoned as well as they possibly could be to achieve delicacy."[48] Some years later at the annual banquet given by ecclesiastics for the Parlement in Paris, we read that "the meal was magnificent, delicate, and well-considered, and there was none of that confusion which usually reigns on this sort of occasion."[49]

Murphy's Law (if anything can go wrong it will) gave great anxiety to the organizers of banquets and balls. For example, a maître d'hôtel was expected to be ready to deal with uncertain numbers of guests, even though the serving of a meal required rigid symmetries in its presentation. Guests frequently came uninvited. At a supper given by the duke of Alba in 1705 some thirty or forty people were expected. When the time came to sit down, it was discovered that there were in fact eighty guests. The *Mercure Galant* reports with an admiration we may well share that everything was so well managed that there was only a fifteen-minute delay.[50] A month later, however, when the dauphin gave a masked ball, the service of refreshments was a fiasco—and this, too, was recorded by the *Mercure* for the amusement of polite Europe: "The collation consisted of sixty large baskets [elaborate gilded affairs, containing complicated arrangements of fresh and preserved fruits and perhaps confections] which would have required more than sixty men to carry them, if they had been able to get through to all the places where they were supposed to have been taken."[51] The manager of the affair suffered double mortification—first the night itself and then the continentwide publicity. Who would wish to be a maître d'hôtel under such circumstances?

CHAPTER EIGHT

Massialot and the Regency

A VARENNE was a great cook in his day, but eventually his recipes became dated. The fashionable world of Paris and the court deserted him, though elsewhere his influence continued to be felt. Translations appeared in England and Italy, and cheap editions of the *Cvisinier françois* were published well into the eighteenth century in provincial towns for sale by colporteurs.[1]

The first attempt to supplant La Varenne was made by Pierre de Lune, with his *Cvisinier*, in 1656. Although the list of foods by season from the *Cvisinier françois* is reproduced without credit, showing some acquaintance with contemporary practice, de Lune has a lamentable medieval habit of binding sauces with crushed macaroons, to which, on fast days, he adds puréed pike livers.[2] The work is largely original. The first part of the book gives recipes arranged by season; in the second part there are recipes for egg cookery, salads, pastrymaking, and preserving—much of the art of the *office*.

A plagiarist followed in 1662, the suitably anonymous author of *L'Eschole parfaite des officiers de bouche*. It describes itself all too correctly as "one book which contains several," presumably a reference to its subdivisions such as the "cuisinier royal," the "grand écuyer tranchant," the "confiturier royale," and others. The cookbook section chiefly consists of substantial chunks of de Lune's *Cvisinier*, along with borrowings from the *Liure fort excellent de cuysine*, which had been published way back in 1555. The other sections include virtually all of La Varenne's *Confiturier françois* (first published in 1660, and, as *Le Parfaict confiturier françois*, in 1667), filled out with some paraphrases of the *Pâtissier françois*. This anthology must have met a need, for the work was revised and reprinted as late as 1742. The 1708 version included what may be the worst recipe for toothpaste ever published.[3] It is made of half a pound of finely sifted ground brick, four ounces of similarly treated porcelain, and one ounce of coral, moistened with essence of clove and cinnamon. The volume also contains a substantial number of new recipes that are quite good. It can be argued that this work served chiefly to give a broader distribution to the recipes of La Varenne and de Lune.

Cookbooks of the *ancien régime* displayed a substantial amount of still-traceable plagiarism. One result was that individual recipes had a longevity greater than the books in which they initially appeared. A second result was that the actual number of recipes in circulation at a given time was less than it appears to be. This situation also prevailed in seventeenth- and eighteenth-century England, where it was complicated by the fact that a fair number of French recipes were translated into English and then replagiarized. Similar borrowings could no doubt be found in other countries. To be sure, no cook invents his or her repertory. All practitioners of the craft learn it from other practitioners, whether by working at their sides, by reading their writings, or, nowadays, by observing electronic images. But the purveying of recipes, in the *ancien régime* as today, was marked by plagiarism, sometimes lightly concealed by paraphrase. This is a permanent and disagreeable feature of the craft of cooking.

The next challenge to La Varenne came from one "L.S.R." in his book *L'Art de bien traiter.*[4] The author avows that he is "right to reform this antique and disgusting manner of preparing things and of serving them, the inconvenience and rusticity of which produce only useless expenses without discretion, an excess of profusion without order, and finally, only awkward superfluities, without advantage and without honor." He states, at length, that good food depends on choice and delicate seasoning, not on a profusion that exhausts art and nature. The vigor of L.S.R.'s attack on La Varenne for the "absurdities and the disgusting lessons" with which "he has long deluded and lulled the stupid and ignorant populace" suggests that La Varenne must still have been influential. L.S.R. ridicules some of his predecessor's recipes: "Do you not begin to tremble immediately at the account of teals in hypocras, larks in a sweet sauce? . . . This fried calf's head, doesn't it make you laugh, or rather weep with pity? [for the calf, the diner, or La Varenne?] . . . and an infinity of other rubbish which one would tolerate more willingly among the Arabs . . . than in a temperate climate like ours."[5]

He obviously expected to replace La Varenne; he did not succeed. His recipes do not measure up to his invective, and the book soon went out of print. It has, however, some specialized information. We learn, for example, that if one's napkin-folding is not up to the mark there is a specialist in Paris named Vaultier who will do it for hire.[6] The most interesting part of the book describes how to stage various kinds of meals: dinners, collations, and suppers. Evening meals are preferred because the light of candles adds to the sense of luxury. After a ball one could serve a collation, or one might offer an *ambigu*, at which everything was served simultaneously—hot and cold dishes, sweet and savory. It had the advantage, in crowded rooms, of requiring little service, since it was all set up at once; we would call it a buffet. L.S.R. also gives general instructions for organizing banquets by a river (with boats and woodwind music), in gardens (with plenty of flowers, candles, and cool drinks), or in a grotto, where there should be a combination buffet and fountain.[7] After the guests are served and seated, jets of water rise from between the roast meats and pyramids of fruit. It sounds potentially a little soggy.

MASSIALOT

It was the destiny, however, of François Massialot, not of Pierre de Lune or L.S.R., to take La Varenne's place. His prudently titled book, *Le Cuisinier roïal et bourgeois*, appeared in 1691, in the later part of the reign of Louis XIV, after the great festivals and four decades after La Varenne's books.[8] Virtually nothing is known about Massialot himself, but the *Cuisinier roïal et bourgeois* contains evidence about the milieu in which he worked. He describes himself as "a cook who dares to qualify himself royal, and it is not without cause, for the meals which he describes . . . have all been served at court or in the houses of princes, and of people of the first rank."[9] The earliest editions contain menus of meals that were served during 1690 to the highest circles of the court, including the dauphin, the king's brother (the duc d'Orléans), his sister-in-law (the sauerkraut-loving Princess Palatine), and the king's nephew (the duc de Chartres, the future regent).[10] These banquets were given at a variety of places, including Sceaux, Meudon, and Versailles.

There was a persistent, though shadowy, group of people who were referred to in the seventeenth and eighteenth centuries as "the best cooks in Paris" [*les meilleurs cuisiniers de Paris*], men at the top of their profession who did not habitually work for a single employer but were engaged at premium wages to cook or to superintend the cooking of meals for special occasions.[11] The diarist Edmond Barbier describes how the meals at Choisy, where Louis XV regularly visited Madame de Pompadour, were prepared by such people. The king's regular household officers did not accompany him, which Barbier found deplorable. Instead he was served by cooks and *officiers* from Paris who are chosen by the governor of Choisy, and whom they give a hundred écus or more a year to be present on these trips, which is thought to be bad for two reasons: the first, that these special affairs [*extraordinaires*] are infinitely expensive, having no order at all; neither maîtres d'hôtel, nor comptrollers, nor regular suppliers, and consequently there is much pillage; the second is that it is not seemly that the king should be fed other than by the hand of the officers in charge of his household; but this way is more convenient and less embarrassing. Moreover, the official cooks are not too skilled; the others, for the special affairs, are the finest in Paris.[12]

Massialot's descriptions of the meals he catered and his advice for equipment needed for special meals imply that he worked primarily as a freelance cook. Moreover, his books bear no dedication, which is unusual for the time and suggests that he was not associated with a single household. He may well have been a member of that elite guild of *queux, cuisiniers, porte-chappes* [master cooks and feast-furnishers], who would have been, I believe, that group referred to as "the best cooks in Paris."[13] At the end of the sixteenth century they had won the exclusive right, against the intense opposition of the caterers, pastrycooks, and roasters, to cater for all weddings and banquets. This monopoly limited the range of activities available to cooks in other guilds, though presumably they were free to supply those caterers with their own specialties.

  By the end of the seventeenth century, the freelance cook, operating independently of a specialized food guild or of a great household, had come to play an important role in the development of Parisian *haute cuisine*. Many domestic posts were temporary; a cook or supplementary cooks were hired for the winter and dismissed when the family went to its country estate where less entertaining was done. There was, therefore, a continuous but ever-changing supply of cooks available for special occasions. Working in different houses and with a series of different colleagues gave these men a wide range of contact with what was going on in their craft. Such circumstances were ideal for a rapid spread of information and innovation. In addition, the preparation method of combining standardized elements was perfectly suited to a changing staff. A well-trained cook, new to a post, could be told to make up a farce, a *coulis*, a stock, and both he and his chef would know what was meant. The kitchen required teamwork; at the same time, the short-term nature of much employment fed the fires of competition. A cook had to get along with the rest of the staff, but he might have to compete with them for future jobs. Exquisite food was valued by the aristocracy, therefore, one of the ways nonnoble or newly noble families could advance their social ambitions was by offering meals that were too good to refuse. The aristocracy grumbled, but if the host was rich and powerful and the entertainment was splendid enough, they accepted the invitations.[14] Freelance cooks, available to anyone who could afford them, assisted in the process.

How these cooks managed the logistics of catering may be seen in a note appended by Massialot to his menu for the *grand repas* presented at Sceaux by the marquis de Seignelay (Colbert's son):

> For such a meal one must begin the day before: in the evening put three or four large stockpots on the fire, with a quantity of meats, bunches of fines herbes, and some whole onions. At the same time cook a quantity of large and small chickens, with some roast partridges, which, with blanched fat bacon and some fat will be used for the forcemeats on the day of the meal, and the broths from them will be used to make the *jus* of beef and veal, *petit-jus* and *coulis* and ham essence. For the soups, the *jus* and *coulis* must be made separately, and the same for the entrées and entremets. There must also be a lot of chopped scallions and parsley, and a number of bunches of fines herbes, to put in the ragouts. One makes a large amount of *coulis*, of partridges, squabs, and chickens, all separately. . . . The kitchen equipment used at Sceaux consisted of sixty little hand-held saucepans, twenty round saucepans, as many large as small; twenty stockpots, as many large as small; thirty spits; and to make this meal there were thirty-six *officiers de cuisine*, as many chefs [sic] as assistants.[15]

Massialot's is the first cookbook in which the recipes are arranged by alphabetical headings—a step toward the first culinary dictionary. The recipes are preceded by a section of menus and lists of seasonal food, intended to assist maîtres d'hôtel and purveyors in purchasing food and organizing meals. Recipes are usually listed by their main ingredients or by their place in the menu (entrée, entremets, hors d'oeuvre), but some entries are devoted to food types and to basic mixtures. The arrangement of the recipes and the cross-referenced index show a considerable advance over the organization of the *Cvisinier françois*. Massialot tends to develop recipes in pairs—a fast-day and a meat-day version—for many categories of foods. For example, a newly important basic mixture, the marinade, forms an entry.[16] There are two main types: those used for poultry and feathered game and those used for fish and shellfish. This is a typical pair, the fast-day version mirroring the poultry recipes.

Massialot gives few quantities. He is addressing trained cooks, who would know by the scale on which they worked what amounts would be appropriate, and maîtres d'hôtel, who had no need to be so specific. This makes difficulties for the modern interpreter, but some of the recipes are still so appetizing that they reward the effort of reconstruction. There is, for example, a recipe for a hot *sauce Ramolade* composed of anchovies, chopped capers, parsley, and scallions, cooked with *jus*, a drop of oil, a clove of garlic, and seasoning.[17] It may be served hot on hot lambs' tails, or with cold, crumbed grilled poultry.

Basic mixtures are emphasized, and in this respect the book is perhaps better suited to the large or royal household than to the small or bourgeois one, though many of the individual recipes are practicable in a modest kitchen. Massialot's recipes for *coulis* produce thick, meaty purées, with an emphasis on the flavor of browned meat, heightened with aromatic herbs.[18] Fast-day *coulis* are made with root vegetables. His *jus de champignons* is smoother than a *coulis*, and the recipe ends on a practical note:

> After you have cleaned the mushrooms well, put them in a pan with a piece of bacon, or of butter if it is a fast day: sauté them over the charcoal fire, just until they begin to stick to the bottom of the pan. When they are well browned, add to them a little flour, and fry it again with the mushrooms. After this, add to it some good bouillon, and take it off the fire, putting this juice in a separate pot, seasoned with a piece of lemon and salt. You can use the mushrooms chopped fine or whole for your soups, or for the entrée or entremet dishes.[19]

There is no waste of material or effort here.

The cook is beginning to borrow from the vocabulary of chemistry: essences are a new entry into the ranks of *fonds de cuisine*, and in the next century they would be of importance.[20] Massialot's recipe for an *essence de jambon* is made with browned ham to which is added a *jus*, enhanced with additional herbs and garlic, truffles, and further thickening; he recommends adding it to anything containing ham (to augment the flavor). Elsewhere he puts an essence of garlic into a rice, mushroom, and cockscomb dish, and on another occasion roast turkey is accompanied by an essence of onions.[21]

The rapid development of new recipes is seen in the successive versions of the *Cuisinier roïal et bourgeois*. The first important changes come with the edition of 1703. Definitions are added and some refinements introduced, such as a glass of white wine in the fish stock. Among the new recipes are a "ham" made of mutton, a "new omelet" with an elaborate filling, and spit-roasted carp.[22] The latter was one of the principal luxury items in the fast-day menu and was served in increasingly elaborate presentations into the nineteenth century; Carême made a specialty of *carpe à la Chambord*. Important changes in Massialot's book came with the edition of 1712, when, under the title *Le Nouveau cuisinier royal et bourgeois*, it was refurbished and expanded to two volumes. The additional space was used to add recipes, to amplify the style of writing, which had been terse, and to add helpful advice. Engraved plans of tabletops replace the old woodcut views of tables. The menus are new. Many of the dishes listed are unchanged, but the balance between large and small dishes has shifted: there are more small and medium-sized ones, and there is now a third course served from the kitchen, with lighter meat dishes, more vegetables, and a few sweets. These call upon the cook for the greatest skill and imagination. The ragout, that well-spiced stew or sauté often used as a garnish, receives its own entry in 1712, where it occupies the longest section in the book.[23] A typical menu in 1691 serves a course of fifteen dishes, only four of them hors d'oeuvres. By 1734, out of a course of thirteen dishes, six are hors d'oeuvres.[24] Revision continued. As late as 1705 a ragout of larks is finished with a decorous garnish of truffles, mushrooms, and foies gras, moistened with meat stock and bound with eggs and cream.[25] The old-fashioned flavor combinations have become incongruous; their replacement takes the form of basic components: stock, liaison, and garnish.

Before another revision appeared, a storm arose, in the form of Vincent La Chapelle's work, which appeared in English in 1733 as *The Modern Cook* and two years later, published in *The Hague* but written in French, as *Le Cuisinier moderne*. Its many virtues will be discussed in the next chapter, but its great defect is that La Chapelle took large amounts of text from Massialot's book. The plagiarisms from Massialot have been meticulously described by Philip and Mary Hyman.[26] In the first English edition fully one-

third of the recipes were taken from the *Nouveau cuisinier royale et bourgeois*.
It is not surprising, then, that the next edition of the latter work contained
a generous helping of recipes (fifty-four by the Hymans' count) from the
Cuisinier moderne. Was this in fact Massialot's doing, or had he retired or
died? We do not know. In any event, the violent reaction in La Chapelle's
edition of 1742 blew them off the pages of the two final editions of the
Nouveau cuisinier royal et bourgeois in 1742 and 1748–50.[27] His illustrious shade
may have found some comfort in the fact that his own book had stayed in
print after his rival's.

This tempest in a stockpot should not be allowed to obscure Massialot's
great achievements. He advanced the codification of technique; by presenting his material in dictionary form he put it at the cook's fingertips, anticipating the methods of the eighteenth-century dictionary makers. He lived
up to the claim made by his book's title. Although his menus were served
to royalty and were too expensive for any but the wealthiest hosts, many of
his individual recipes were within the reach of the smaller household. By
publishing these freshly devised recipes he made it possible for people far
from the court to partake of the same kind of food. By increasing the range
of practitioners of a modernized cuisine he helped to accelerate its development.

THE REGENT

One of those who had eaten Massialot's meals as a youth was the most
famous diner—and erstwhile cook—of the early eighteenth century, Philippe, duc d'Orléans. The duke, who became regent for the young Louis
XV in 1715 when Louis XIV died, preferred Paris to Versailles. Like his
German mother, the Mainz ham and sauerkraut enthusiast, he was endowed
with a prodigious appetite. While on a diplomatic mission to Spain he had
learned to cook and did so at his notorious supper parties in the Palais-
Royale, his residence.[28] The duc de Saint-Simon, who was often present,
has described "the exquisite fare, prepared in a place especially set up for it,
on the ground floor, where all the utensils were of silver; they [the cour-
tiers], led by the regent, often turning their hand to the work with the cooks."[29]
The duke's entertainments were an early version of the rococo *souper intime*,
the archetypal eighteenth-century meal. His guests must have enjoyed a sen-

sation that was rare at court: hot, freshly cooked food. It ought to have been an encouraging atmosphere for a cook to work in, but the suppers often degenerated into orgies. There was heavy drinking; guests were expected to end the evening on the floor in a stupor.[30] There was little opportunity for the exercise or recognition of culinary genius in the midst of diversions so strenuous that Peter the Great of Russia, not otherwise remembered for his fastidiousness, declined to return for a second evening "because he found the behavior too free."[31]

A certain amount of cooking undoubtedly took place. It is my belief that many of the noble chefs of the period were as dependent on ghostcooks as modern politicians are on ghostwriters. Vincent La Chapelle offers a recipe for partridges *à la bourgeoise*, "which one may prepare at the table, without having dressed them in the kitchen."[32] The partridges have been cut up, and a plate containing minced shallots, parsley, and fine bread crumbs waits at the side of a spirit lamp. A deep dish with a glass of champagne is brought to a boil with salt, pepper, a piece of butter, and the shallots. The partridges are added and then the crumbs, to bind the sauce. It cooks briefly, is covered with another plate to cook a little longer, and is served after a final seasoning of lemon or orange juice and perhaps a truffle or mushroom. Such a dish would be suitably expensive but does not require a very long period of concentration. The vogue for playing at lower-class activities that was characteristic of eighteenth-century aristocratic life should not deceive us into thinking that these people contributed substantially to the advancement of the activities involved. No one credits Marie Antoinette with advancing the science of sheeprearing. If the regent knew what good, up-to-date food was, it was because he had eaten it at least since his adolescence. He and his friends probably did not invent, but they certainly evoked invention and by encouraging inventive cooks helped to legitimize their craft.

The alliance between food and love, or at least dalliance, was very strong throughout the eighteenth century. There was lively interest in aphrodisiacs. Certainly the combination of luxury, intimacy, and the pleasures of the table is very powerful. A tasty (but not heavy) meal was regularly included in programs of seduction.[33] Thus, the French ambassador at Venice in the mid-eighteenth century, the abbé (later cardinal) de Bernis, had a cook by the name of Durosier, who prepared meals for the ambassador's assignations with his mistress, M.M., in his Venetian *casino*. Giacomo Casanova, who

The Exquisite Supper, engraving by J. B. Moreau, from *Le Monument du costume* (Paris, 1783).
Restif de la Bretonne described this scene in a brief anecdote, as having "the most elegant
table, innumerable comforts scattered around a very small space, and a centerpiece representing the three Graces; everything breathed an air of the most exquisite sensual pleasure.
[The marquis] gave a signal; the servants disappeared" (*Tableaux de la vie* . . . [Neuwied,
1789], 1:102–7). (By permission of the Houghton Library, Harvard University.)

claims to have had a share in the pleasures to be found there, has left us a description of a supper for two:

> The service was made of Sèvres porcelain. Eight made dishes composed the supper; they were set on silver boxes filled with hot water which kept the food always hot. It was a choice and delicious supper. I exclaimed that the cook must be French, and she [M.M.] said that I was right. We drank only Burgundy, and we emptied a bottle of "oeil de perdrix" champagne and another of some sparkling wine for gaiety. It was she who dressed the salad; her appetite was equal to mine. She rang only to have the dessert brought, together with all the ingredients for making punch. In everything she did I could not but admire her knowledge, her skill, and her grace.[34]

Plainly, the process of eating the meal was part of the seduction. Casanova had an abiding faith in the stimulating properties of drink, truffles, oysters (especially when dropped down the front of a dress and then retrieved), ices, and egg whites, but ambience mattered a good deal more. The atmosphere of privacy, pleasure for all the senses, more or less acknowledged wickedness, and expectation were the real aphrodisiacs of the eighteenth-century seducer. The regent may well have provided society with a conspicuous example. It might be as a memorial to him that ever since his death in 1723 the Palais Royale has remained one of the most celebrated locales in Paris for both food and prostitution.

CHAPTER NINE

French Cooks Abroad

HE CULTURE OF PARIS and of the French court set the style for much of aristocratic Europe in the seventeenth and eighteenth centuries. French was the language of the upper class and of those who modeled themselves on it. When the elector of Hanover became George I of England he was no more comfortable with English than his new courtiers were with German, but they could converse with each other in French. The Venetian-born Casanova, dwelling, at the end of his life, in a castle in Bohemia, wrote his memoirs in French. Similarly, France was the fountainhead of fashion in matters of cooking.

Frenchmen have consistently been less willing to emigrate than other Europeans. But in 1685 the Protestant community in France received unwelcome encouragement when Louis XIV revoked the Edict of Nantes, which since 1598 had allowed a degree of toleration to the Huguenots. Obliged to choose between conversion to Catholicism or emigration, some fifty thousand families left their native land to settle in England, the North Netherlands, the Protestant parts of Germany, and elsewhere. Among them were skilled artisans, including workers in the food trades. The Huguenots are often hard to trace after their arrival in Protestant lands, where they sometimes mixed with local Protestant congregations. Nevertheless, J. Jean Hecht has established that there were cooks among the parishioners of the Huguenot churches of London.[1]

In addition to those who were exiled for their beliefs, many artisans left France simply to earn a better living. For those whose skills were in demand among the fashionable, travel could be rewarding. For the cook, service abroad sometimes meant dealing with an employer who was more interested in the prestige of having an expensive French cook than in savoring that cook's food. But the work was well paid, and the cook was often conspicuously placed; hence more is known today about the cooks who left France than about those who remained.

The style of cooking they practiced was that characteristic of the large

French aristocratic household. There is little evidence that they introduced either French recipes or French techniques permanently into the everyday cookery of the countries where they worked; if they had been preparing dishes that were practical in smaller kitchens, their influence would probably have been wider. There have been Frenchmen in the best kitchens all over the world ever since. Ironically, they have probably had more influence on the ordinary cooking of France than of other countries, for the more tactful of them have introduced into France a variety of dishes from abroad—sweet baked goods, puddings, and improvements in roasting techniques, for example.

In Germany the influence of French cookery was slight before the seventeenth century. In his study of the development of German cooking from 1500 to the present, the culinary historian Günter Wiegelmann has observed changes in the patterns of word borrowing and recipes.[2] In the sixteenth century, when trade with eastern Europe brought food and other goods to market in Germany, Slavic food words were taken into the German language. After the Thirty Years' War, when the Peace of Westphalia (1648) established France as a power in internal German politics, the pattern changed. Instead of Slavic borrowings, such French words as *fricassee* and *ragout* entered the language. French recipes were translated into German. La Varenne's *Cvisinier françois* appeared as *Der französische Koch* in 1665. Anna Weckerin, Maria Schellhammer, and other German writers began to include French recipes, if not methods, in their cookbooks. As early as 1687 a commentator complained that "nowadays everything has to be French with us. French clothes, French dishes, French furniture . . . to such an extent that even French diseases are exclusively in fashion."[3]

Where there was French food, there were also French cooks and maîtres d'hôtel. In the seventeenth century they served at the courts of Prussia and Hanover, and in the eighteenth century French chefs cooked in the kitchens of Hanover, Prussia, Saxony, and many smaller courts.[4] There were also in these places Spanish and Italian bakers and confectioners; the latter enjoyed a special renown. Occasionally Englishmen and Netherlanders appear. The French were, however, far and away the most numerous and the most highly paid.

The most famous Frenchman in German kitchens was Noël, the son of a Périgord pastrycook. Casanova, who visited him in Berlin in 1764, described him as "a very cheerful man . . . the greatly cherished cook of Fred-

erick the Great, the King of Prussia."[5] Casanova claims, inaccurately, that
Noël did all the king's cooking with the sole assistance of one kitchen boy.
He was, in fact, the maître d'hôtel, overseeing a staff of a dozen people of
several different nationalities, who prepared their countries' specialties. Each
day a proposed dinner menu was submitted to the king, with each cook's
suggestions; Frederick would mark the items that pleased him, strike out
those that did not, and add his own orders. One such menu testifies to the
discordant coexistence of two styles of cooking on his table. The two German cooks, Pfund and Voigt, offered boiled beef with parsnips and carrots,
salmon "in the style of Dessau," and peas, herring, and sour pickles. The
king noted his satisfaction with all of these. For the same meal the Frenchmen, Henaut [Hénault?] and Blesson, suggested a cabbage soup *à la Fouquet*,
small pies *à la Romaine*, and chicken breast fillets *à la Pompadour* garnished
with ox tongue and croquettes; among these the king praised only the soup.[6]

At the end of his life Frederick ate a meal that included polenta made
with an abundance of Parmesan cheese and with garlic squeezed over it, a
piece of beef *à la russienne* (meaning here, stewed in brandy); this was followed by an eel pie so highly spiced that a bystander remarked that "it must
have been baked in hell." The king then had convulsions and died a few days
later.[7]

French cooks working abroad had to adapt to such incongruous circumstances. The necessity of combining French cookery with that of the employer's country was persistent, and we will observe it again in England and
the Low Countries. Some cooks added to their repertories in these circumstances, but for many the necessary professional compromises added to their
ongoing reluctance to leave Paris.

In Italy, too, French cooks were part of the entourage of the fashionable.
Sir Horace Mann described English visitors to Florence setting up households there with Frenchmen in their kitchens.[8] Probably the most celebrated
French table in Italy was that of the Cardinal de Bernis, who was the French
ambassador to the Vatican in the late eighteenth century. The abundance and
excellence of the cardinal-ambassador's table was the more welcome because
Rome was notorious for the sparseness of its hospitality.[9] By this time, the
cardinal had become a vegetarian—a diet that enjoyed a certain vogue in the
late eighteenth century.

J. Jean Hecht has observed that because foreign domestics in the English
household commanded higher wages than native servants, their employ-

ment added to the employer's prestige, just as their foreignness lent a cosmopolitan air to his establishment. There was also a general feeling that English servants did not have the capacity for servility that could be expected of citizens of a despotically governed land like France. The French servant, moreover, was expected to bring with him from Paris—none ever seemed to come from other parts of the country—a knowledge of the best and most recent ("alamode") fashions, whether in dressing hair, making clothes, or preparing food. Hecht has located a number of French ladies' maids, but no *cuisinières* have turned up.[10] This pattern of sex-role allocation was characteristic of French kitchens. The only women present in the kitchens of large houses in France were likely to be washing dishes and scrubbing vegetables, and the *office* was equally the province of men. In England, on the other hand, although large kitchens were the territory of men, women were usually in charge of the English equivalents of the *office*—the dairy and stillroom. The role of the housekeeper in a large establishment in England had no French equivalent.

As early as 1577 William Harrison, in his *Description of England*, had complained of the excessively various and abundant diet of "the nobility of England (whose cooks are for the most part musical-headed Frenchmen and strangers)."[11] French influence on English life became pronounced, however, with the Restoration of the Stuart monarchy. Charles II and James II, and their followers, had spent much of their exile in France. After their return to England, the styles of the French court became the required fashion for all who wished to be up-to-date. Samuel Pepys's diary reflects the process as it was taking place. Immediately upon Charles II's return, Pepys's patrons, the earl and countess of Sandwich, embraced the continental styles. After dining with them, Pepys quoted the elated earl as "very high how he would have a French cooke and a Master of his Horse, and his lady and child to wear black paches [sic]; which methought was strange, but he is become a perfect Courtier."[12] A few months later Pepys exchanged the English style of dress, with cloak and rapier, for the French fashion, with coat and sword; he learned the French manner of drinking healths; he ate "a fine French dinner"; and on another occasion his wife (who was from a Huguenot family) served him "a pleasant French fricasse [sic] of Veale for dinner."[13]

After the Restoration no great establishment was complete without a Frenchman presiding over its kitchen. The most famous was Clouet, who even achieved the distinction of a society nickname. As "Chloe" he appears in the letters of Horace Walpole, Lady Mary Wortley Montagu, and the earl of Chesterfield. Clouet's employer was Thomas Pelham-Holles, the duke of Newcastle, who, with his brother Henry Pelham, was prominent in Whig governments in the 1740s and early 1750s. The duke lived in great style. His country house, Claremont, in Surrey, was designed by Sir John Vanbrugh, with gardens laid out by William Kent.[14] For Newcastle, as for other great lords, hospitality was a political tool: he gathered people around his superb table to consolidate his party's strength. In 1745 we find the earl of Chesterfield asking Newcastle to invite to one of "Chloe's" meals a young Dutchman who is visiting London, because "his father is the ruling man of Amsterdam; he had a French tendency in politics, but I have been pulling at him ever since I have been here [at the Hague] and with some success."[15] Chesterfield sent his son to dine there, too, as a part of the education of that disappointing youth, warning him at the same time against the heavy drinking he would encounter.[16]

Clouet was endowed with a full measure of self-respect, reflected in contemporary stories about him. On one occasion he came into conflict with a member of English society. A miserly diner-out who decided to stage a dinner borrowed Clouet from the duke "to prepare and superintend" the meal. The host was unwilling to pay as much as such an entertainment cost, and Clouet "left the house in a passion."[17]

Clouet was working for the duke as early as 1738, when Lady Mary Wortley Montagu referred to him, and he seems to have remained in Newcastle's service through much of the 1740s.[18] By 1753 he had left England and was back in Paris, working as maître d'hôtel for William Keppel, earl of Albermarle, the British ambassador. Newcastle needed a new cook; his correspondence on this subject with the earl and with Clouet has survived, and some of it has been published by Romney Sedgwick.[19] Newcastle asked Albermarle and his maître d'hôtel to find him a good cook in Paris. The assignment proved difficult; cooks were, as usual, reluctant to leave the city. When one Hervé, a highly recommended practitioner, was persuaded to travel to London, his cooking did not please Newcastle or his guests. The English had become accustomed to the earlier stage of *la nouvelle cuisine*, which Clouet had been practicing a few years before. Back in Paris Clouet must have brought himself up-to-date, for we find him putting Newcastle firmly in his place. The duke had complained that Hervé's

soups are generally too strong, and his entrées and entremets are so heavily disguised and made up that it is impossible to guess what they are
made of. He never serves little hors d'oeuvres or light entrées, and he
has no idea of plain, simple dishes such as you used to make me, and
which are so much in fashion here—for instance, tendons of veal, fillets
of young rabbit, pigs' and calves' ears, and little dishes of that sort. As
for roasts, he understands nothing of them. Nor has he any notion of
\grosses pièces. In a word, he bears no resemblance whatever to your style
and your cuisine, or to what I require.[20]

Clouet's reply rings a note of professional solidarity:

> Masters who do not like these made-up dishes ought to have the good-
> ness to announce their desire, or to make them known, so that the cook
> may demonstrate his ability by conforming to them. It is also extremely
> unfortunate for a cook when his master cannot judge for himself, so that
> he is all too often judged by critics who have no knowledge. . . . It is
> indeed very rare to find one who is both a good cook and a good *rotisseur*
> [sic]. In most of the best houses in France a cook never makes the roast.
> Kitchens are staffed by chefs, assistants, pastrycooks, *rotisseurs* and scul-
> lions. The whole team, when it is well managed and well supplied, turns
> out excellent things for those who like them.[21]

The unfortunate duke must have felt thoroughly chastised. Eventually a
suitable man was found, one Fontenelle. But shortly after, Albermarle died
suddenly. Clouet, who had signed the purveyorship contracts for the impe-
cunious Albermarle's magnificent establishment, was left responsible for debts
of £36,000. What happened next is not clear; he may have reentered Newcastle's service. Horace Walpole speaks of him as being at Claremont in 1758,
but the next year a former colleague wrote that the cook was in Paris "with
his new master, marshal Richlieu [sic] (for there I am informed he now lives
as steward or *maître d'hôtel*) [sic]."[22] In 1759 this colleague, William Verral,
published *A Complete System of Cookery*, in which he writes with admiration
of Clouet's cuisine. Denying allegations of extravagance against Clouet, Verral
describes how the chef

> completed a table of twenty-one dishes at a course, with such things as
> used to serve only for garnish round a lump of great heavy dishes before

he came here. . . . The second or third great dinner he drest for my Lord
Duke, he ordered five calves' heads to be brought in, which made us
think some extravagant thing was on foot, but we soon saw it was just
the reverse of it; he made five very handsome and good dishes of what
he took, and the heads not worth a groat less each. The tongues, pallets,
eyes, brains, and ears. The story of his *assiette* of popes-eyes, the quintessence of a ham for sauce, and the gravy of twenty-two partridges for
sauce for a brace, was always beyond the credit of any sensible person. . . . I am afraid I shall launch out too far in encomiums on my
friend Clouet; but beg to be excused by all my readers. . . . He was of a
temper so affable and agreeable, as to make every body happy about him.
He would converse about indifferent matters with me or his kitchen boy,
and the next moment, by a sweet turn in his discourse, give pleasure by
his good behaviour and genteel deportment, to the first steward in the
family. His conversation is always modest enough; and having read a
little he never wanted something to say, let the topick be what it would.[23]

Verral describes a style of cooking more French than English. He was
accurate in calling his book *A Complete System of Cookery*, for he realized
that the special character of French cooking comes from the systematic use
of specified techniques and rules for combining basic ingredients. He begins,
for example, in the true French style, with a detailed recipe for bouillon,
emphasizing the importance of using root vegetables, and goes on to include
all the basic mixtures of the French kitchen: *coulis* of meat and of fish, forcemeats, braising mixtures, and liaisons of egg yolks and of *beurre manié*.[24] The
way he uses his materials supports Verral's defense against accusations of
extravagance. From two chickens, for example, he gets two attractive hors
d'oeuvres and still has the wings and giblets to use elsewhere. The first recipe is for "breast of fowls a la Binjamele" (by which Verral means béchamel),
which consists of roasted, skinned, sliced chicken breast, served in a rich
cream sauce flavored with scallions, parsley, and the juice of an orange. "This
sauce may serve for any sort of white meat," he tells us, "and is now very
much in fashion." The pendant to it is for "balons of fowls." The second
joints, legs, and feet of the birds are left in one piece, and the thigh and leg
bones are removed. The skin is left intact. After marinating briefly in a ten-
derizing mixture of white wine and vinegar, they are stuffed with a well-
flavored forcemeat, carefully sewn up, and braised. When tender they are

drained and tidied up, to be served with a sauce made of *coulis*, gravy, and the juice of either an orange or a lemon.[25]

One can understand why the duke of Newcastle wished for someone to cook for him as Clouet had done and why Horace Walpole wrote that New-castle "was governed by his cook."[26] Eventually this assertive craftsman was fired "at the instance of the Duke of Grafton for whom he was to dress a dinner for Marshall Belleisle, but he sent word he had tired himself with playing at bowls."[27] Clouet obviously did not fulfill the English stereotype of the servile Frenchman.

Vincent La Chapelle

Of all the cooks who took part in France's culinary diaspora, Vincent La Chapelle, by writing down his recipes, left the most enduring monument. His *Modern Cook* appeared in several editions; the first was in two volumes of highly idiosyncratic English and was published in London in 1733; he is described as head cook to Newcastle's correspondent, the earl of Chester-field, who is best known today for the letters he wrote to his son.[28] In 1728 Chesterfield was made ambassador to the Netherlands, and he lived at The Hague until 1732. The purpose of his embassy there was to arrange the marriage between William IV, Prince of Orange, and Anne, the daughter of George II. La Chapelle may have entered Chesterfield's service during the earl's stay in The Hague. In October 1728, Chesterfield wrote to a friend in Paris, the duke of Richmond (noted for keeping an excellent table), as follows:

> Dear Duke,
>
> I believe you will easier pardon the trouble I am going to give you, than you would the excuses that I ought to make you for it. So I'll pro-ceed directly to the business.
>
> You must know then, that I have a cook that was sent me about six months agone from Paris; who though he is not a bad one, yet is not of the first rate; and as I have a mind *de faire une chère exquise* [to serve exquisite fare], I should be glad to have a *Maître Cuisinier d'un génie supér-ieur*, who should be able not only to execute but to invent *des morceaux friands et parfaits* [delectable and perfectly executed tidbits]: in short such a one as may be worthy to entertain your distinguishing palate, if you should come to The Hague. If you can find such a one, I beg of you to

make the best bargain you can for me, and send him to me here. But unless you can find one who is allowed by all Paris to be at the top of his profession, don't send me any; those I have already being tolerable ones. Though this may be a very troublesome employment for you, yet you will allow it would have been wronging your taste, if while you were at Paris, I had addressed myself to anybody but you *en fait de cuisine*. . . . You need not be in haste to send me this cook, because if I have him any time this two months it will be soon enough, so that you have time to choose upon trial and deliberation.[29]

The earl was acquainted with men who cooked. Elsewhere he writes: "There is hardly a French cook that is not better bred than most Englishmen of quality, and that cannot present himself with more ease, and a better address, in any mixed company."[30] One is reminded of Verral's description of Clouet.

A little information about La Chapelle's career is available. When his *Modern Cook* appeared in London in 1733, the year Chesterfield's embassy to The Hague ended, La Chapelle described himself as head of the earl's kitchens. Two years later an expanded edition in French was published in The Hague, and its author is described as chef de cuisine to the same Prince of Orange whose marriage the earl had negotiated. Chesterfield had added a large banqueting room to his house in The Hague and inaugurated it with a banquet on the prince's birthday; it may have been here that La Chapelle's talents came to the prince's attention.

To judge from the evidence in the *Cuisinier moderne*, La Chapelle must have had experience in the kitchens of Paris; he demonstrates familiarity with what ingredients were and were not available there. He gives a recipe for a strong meat broth that a duc de Bouillon took for gout, though without saying he cooked in that household.[31] His English and Dutch recipes testify to his readiness to learn, even outside France, a rare quality in a French chef and one that he shared with Carême.[32] There is evidence that he was exceptionally well traveled. An entire chapter is devoted to the problem of preserving and serving palatable food on a long sea voyage. He also assists the traveler by giving recipes for pocket soup, the boiled-down, dried broth tablets recommended by Casanova, which could be reconstituted with boiling water.[33] In describing the use of red peppers in a leg-of-mutton and rice dish *à l'indienne*, he speaks of "the little red *piment* [capsicum pepper], which they call *Piment enragé*, because of its strength. Since in Europe it is likely that some cooks and other people will not know this kind . . . of *piment*, unless they have been in Portugal, or in the Indies, as I have . . . as a substitute one may add two or three chopped cloves of garlic."[34] The reference is ambiguous, since it does not specify East or West Indies, but a little later he says that "although I call it mutton, it is really only goat; for mutton is very scarce in the Indies, as well as beef and veal; one sees more water buffaloes there than beeves." The buffaloes suggest that he traveled east, not west, but the New World pepper suggests west; I do not know when it arrived in the East Indies.

Unfortunately, the work of La Chapelle is built around a substantial core of plagiarism from Massialot's *Cuisinier roïal et bourgeois*. *Le Cuisinier moderne* appeared first in English, published in London in two volumes in 1733 as *The Modern Cook*, and then in French two years later in a three-volume edition published in *The Hague*; the final revision was in five volumes and was also published in *The Hague*, in 1742. The English edition contains the highest proportion of plagiarisms. In an article in *Petits Propos Culinaires* Philip and Mary Hyman enumerate the percentage of plagiarized recipes, which comprise 28 percent of the English edition, falling to lower percentages in the French editions; the diminution results in part from the elimination of some of Massialot's recipes and in part from the introduction of new material.[35] Of course, as the Hymans observe, it is hard to be sure that the new recipes are La Chapelle's own.

The organization of *Le Cuisinier moderne* is by type of dish: soup, entrée, entremet, hors d'oeuvre. He plagiarizes himself as well as Massialot, for he repeats numerous recipes, changing only the principal ingredients. For example, four-fifths of the turkey recipes also appear in his chicken chapter. Elsewhere he uses recipes that seem to have been acquired in a batch, inserting them without any attempt to smooth out inconsistencies, as in his chapter on cooking perch, which contains eleven recipes, six of them with unassimilated Dutch names.[36] Nonetheless, the *Cuisinier moderne* is well named: much of the repertory of classic French cuisine is present in recognizable form: even the last editions of Massialot seem old-fashioned by comparison. Among the classic recipes are *poularde au riz, gigot de mouton au chevreuil*, a *chartreuse* of partridge and cabbage, galantines of chicken, chicken fricassee, *blanquette de veau*, veal chops *en papillotte*, a soufflé mixture, *pièce de boeuf à l'écarlate, crème brulée*, and *oeufs au beurre noir*. The names, however, are not

always the same as those used today, and sometimes there are basic differences in preparation. In the recipe for *blanquette de veau*, for example, he calls
for meat that has already been roasted, and this continued to be the practice
throughout the eighteenth century. But the techniques resemble those used
in fine cooking today. Vegetables are cooked in a *blanc* (a boiled mixture of
flour, water, butter, and salt) to keep them from discoloring; later in the
century cooks would add lemon or vinegar to make the technique even more
effective. Puff pastry is used extensively, and there are many ice creams and
"frozen cheeses." Stiffly beaten egg whites are folded into pastry cream to
make a *crème Saint Honoré* for filling cakes and pastries. The same mixture is
baked in a puff paste shell until it rises and is served hot; it is the first soufflé.
He also uses the new flavors: coffee and chocolate appear in custards and ice
creams.

The twentieth-century cook finds dozens of recipes worth experimenting with, although important adjustments must be made. The *pièce de boeuf
à l'ancienne* in Julia Child's *Mastering the Art of French Cooking* descends recognizably from La Chapelle's *piece de boeuf en surprise*.[37] In the original recipe
a solid piece of beef is braised and, when cool, hollowed out. The shell is
brushed with a mixture of Parmesan cheese and bread crumbs and then with
butter. Baked in an oven until crisp and gilded, it is then filled with a luxurious mixture of creamed squabs. Squabs are not so easily found today; and
the modern recipe substitutes ham, mushrooms, and the beef obtained by
hollowing out the shell. The two main problems posed by La Chapelle's
recipes for a modern cook are time and expense. Otherwise any experienced
cook can find pleasing ideas and even recipes worth bringing into the
twentieth-century repertory. One is for his spit-roasted chickens with a sauce
of blanched green walnuts and ham essence. Lacking a walnut tree, one
would have to substitute ordinary walnuts, but it is still a very tasty dish.
His *génoises* (unrelated to the modern cake) are delicious little fried turnovers
of crisp pastry with a button-sized filling of pistachio pastry cream. Why
did we stop making them?

The recipes that cannot easily be executed now are the very elaborate
ones, which require expensive ingredients, lengthy preparation, or both. We
would not be likely to prepare his hot entremet with fifty duck or goose
tongues, even if we could get them.[38] On the other hand, the *entrée de pigeons
à la lune* sounds delectable: medium-sized squabs are split and skewered open,
then braised for fifteen minutes with slices of veal, ham, and bacon. They

are arranged a little distance apart on a serving dish, and each is surrounded by a band of well-seasoned forcemeat. Each squab is then covered by a *salpicon* of diced sweetbreads, truffles, and mushrooms; this in turn is topped with a heart-shaped piece of puff paste. The whole is baked in the oven until nicely browned. After the juices are drained off, the edges of the dish are cleaned and a ragout of slivered sweetbreads, mushrooms, truffles, foies gras (in season), cockscombs, and crayfish tails is placed in the spaces between the walled-in squabs. This is, however, no ordinary ragout: it is prepared half white and creamy, with a *coulis* of chicken breasts, egg yolks, and cream, and half dark and meaty, with *jus* and a good ham *coulis*.[39] One is reminded of the intricately worked gold and enamel snuffboxes of the period, in the making of which an infinity of work was lavished on every surface, and the use of precious materials sometimes became an end in itself. If there are few recipes that would be almost unperformable today, the menus that are composed from them are absolutely impossible to execute. I doubt that even the most ambitious modern cook or the wealthiest host could present an authentic aristocratic eighteenth-century meal. If the partridges, truffles, hams, and other meats were not prohibitively expensive, cockscombs and cows' udders would be hard to come by, and there would have to be as many skilled cooks in the kitchens as diners at the table.

The entrée of *pommes d'amour* may not be impossible, but it is certainly unusual. Usually served two to a dish, the "apples" are warm, breast-shaped mounds of white meats, rather like galantines in composition, with nipples and veins of ham showing faintly under a layer of chicken skin, or, "if you want to go to the expense," the skin of a suckling pig.[40] These were very popular; there are fast-day versions using fish as well. Both appear regularly on menus, though so vivid a reminder of the martyrdom of Saint Agatha might not appeal to everyone.

The last volume of the final, 1742 edition of his book is especially rich in recipes of foreign origin. La Chapelle's tin ear for language has changed some spellings. Earlier he had made the English "marigold" into "marygools," and now macaroni appears as "macarollis." There are several pasta recipes, for which there was a vogue in France from about this time that continued through the rest of the century. There are also beer soups, *escabeches*, liver *à la Hessoise* (with Rhine wine and raisins), and a considerable number of sauerkraut recipes. The readiness to use other cooks' recipes made him an exceptionally receptive traveler. Although not all of these recipes became established as a part of the French cuisine, he was, I think, responding to a problem that arose after the foundations of French cookery had been laid. With the establishment of the basic repertory of mixtures and techniques came the danger that the changes on them would be rung off mechanically—as, indeed, La Chapelle did himself. Reaching out to other culinary traditions offered freshness and innovation.

La Chapelle responded to the inclusion of recipes from the *Cuisinier moderne* in the 1739 edition of the *Nouveau cuisinier royal et bourgeois* with a vituperative attack in volume 4 and an extensive critique at the end of volume 5 of the 1742 edition.[41] He reprints there a baker's dozen of Massialot's recipes, following each with his own angry remarks. For example, after a recipe for a knuckle of salt pork with a purée of green vegetables, La Chapelle says, "To make this entrée you don't have to be a cook," and of an ox tongue recipe he writes, "It wasn't necessary to put this entrée down as new, because as long as I have been cooking, I have seen it served and I have served it. This would-be author was not even born yet. When a man wants to criticize he should not take things from the ancients in order to pass them off as something new."[42] He also catches Massialot leaving out the flour in a cake recipe—a mistake everyone who writes recipes dreads. La Chapelle tells us that if he were going to plagiarize he would choose a better book than Massialot's, though, as has been clearly demonstrated, his position on this point is exceptionally weak.

Despite his flaws, La Chapelle's contribution was important. He published coherent recipes for dishes that have been classics ever since; he had a fluent if sometimes unthinking familiarity with the interplay of techniques and mixtures that underlies *haute cuisine*. In his writings and wanderings, we see both the outward flow of French culinary ideas and the ingathering of foreign recipes for French tables. Carême, who studied old cookbooks closely, refers to *Le Cuisinier moderne* more frequently than to any other book of the eighteenth century. He often expresses disapproval of what he calls *la cuisine ancienne* but is proud to belong to its tradition. La Chapelle, who traveled widely and learned from his travels, served as a model. Each could claim to be "the modern cook" of his own day.

CHAPTER TEN

Pastry, Baking, Confectionary, and Table Ornament

BAKING AND CONFECTIONARY are the most plastically exploitable food preparations. Doughs and sugar mixtures can be modeled, cut, imprinted, cast, and colored. They can feed the eye as well as—indeed often better than—the stomach. Since confectionary is not eaten until the later part of the meal, when hunger has moderated, it is less urgently needed for nourishment, and the cook is therefore freer to indulge decorative imagination. The basic decorative forms used for foods generally imitate those found in the more enduring and familiar arts of a given period. Confectionary came, therefore, to form an important part of the decoration of an elaborately set-out table. Because of these distinctive characteristics, developments in the arts of the pastrycook and confectioner are best treated as a separate subject over the entire time covered by this volume.

Preparation of these foods requires special technical skills. The cook who works with doughs and with sugar must pay close attention to fluctuations in temperature and humidity. No cook would try twice to spin sugar on a rainy day. Some flours absorb more liquid than others; differences in gluten content produce elastic or crumbly doughs, either of which may be right or wrong in a given situation. Bakers, pastrycooks, and confectioners work with less forgiving materials than their counterparts in home kitchens. But, because they cater to a luxury market, a high level of skill is expected of them.

PASTRY AND BAKING

Although it is popularly assumed that pies were an important part of the repertory of medieval cooks, in fact the manuscript cookbooks contain no recipes for pie pastries, and the variety of other baked goods is not great. Recipes may be missing because most baking was carried on by members of the pastrycooks' guilds in their own kitchens, presumably without the assistance of written advice. But there are enough recipes to suggest the range of baked goods and how it changed over time.

The ever-helpful *Ménagier* offers the largest assortment of pies, as well as a small selection of fritters and a few rissoles and pancakes, or *crespes*. It is not clear whether the author's kitchen had an oven, but the presence of many flour-based dishes that do not require one suggests that his cook worked with alternative methods. Rissoles, for example, are made by enclosing mixtures in a crust and frying them in fat. In a recipe for *pastés norrois*, which are little pies "the size of a three denier piece" filled with chopped cod livers and spices, he says that if, when the pastrycook brings them, they have not been cooked, they may be fried in oil. He describes the making of a filling for beef marrow pies, which is then carried to the pastrycook to be put into a crust; alternatively, he writes, they may be fried in lard.[1] Imagine the greasiness of fried marrow or fish liver pies! Unadulterated fat was much more welcome on the table at that time than now.

Despite the lack of crust recipes, there are some clues to the mystery of how pastrycooks worked. Pies were usually made with savory fillings; fruit fillings were exceptional. The pies seem to have been predominantly hand-shaped; the *pâté en pot* is generally designated separately and was later usually called a *tourte*, and the metal or earthenware container it baked in was a *tourtière*. One may guess that for freestanding pies some sort of hot water and melted lard crust was used, as has been done in more recent centuries. I know from experience that such a crust can be used with the medieval fillings. Pies that were to be kept for any length of time (even for some weeks) were made with a whole wheat crust combined usually with rye flour. Otherwise the preference was for using as fine a wheat flour as was possible economically and technically. On occasion the crust was colored with saffron, a practice that lasted into the second half of the eighteenth century; the coloring of breads with saffron survives in England today. The tougher doughs used for venison pies served more as containers than as part of the food. The fillings were generally dry, consisting, for example, of unboned birds, often with slices of more or less fat bacon on top. A moister pie would be more likely to collapse in the baking, even if supported by a band of paper. The recipes do not always make clear whether a pie was to be covered. In at least one instance a pie is baked uncovered, then partway through cooking a mixture of milk, saffron, and spices is added. Meanwhile, a top crust is baked separately to be set in place after cooking. This technique would produce a less desiccated result. Moisture was more usually added in the form of a sauce, typically cameline, poured in through a steam vent after baking, just as we do today with aspic for a *pâté en croûte*.

A cook needs no oven to bake a pie. The author of the *Ménagier* describes the process of cooking an herb and custard pie in a metal skillet. The lower crust is baked first, then the filling is poured in and the upper crust set in place. A second skillet, filled with glowing coals, is set over the top of the pie to complete the cooking process.[2]

The remaining baking recipes in the *Ménagier de Paris* all use varieties of batter. Flour, salt, white wine, and eggs are combined in unspecified proportions to produce liquids ranging from "as thick as pap [*bouillie*]" to "as thin as fresh cream." Typically, the products, whether crêpes or fritters, are served sprinkled with sugar. Favored kinds of wafer included cheese, of unspecified type, either grated and mixed directly into the batter (which would probably have stuck to the wafer iron) or sliced and sandwiched between two layers of dough.

The medieval versions of the *Viandier* have few recipes. The first printed editions have many pies but no fritters, rissoles, or wafers, perhaps reflecting an origin in a kitchen with an oven and therefore no need for substitute pastries. The recipes resemble the *Ménagier*'s but contain fewer helpful asides. There are two fruit pies: an apple pie with figs, raisins, fried onions, wine, and spices and a pear pie in which the hollows of the pears are filled with sugar.[3] Both pies have top crusts gilded either with saffron (presumably infused in cream) or with eggs; then as now the pastrycooks' term for the gilding mixture was *dorure*.

The *talemouse* was a popular pastry; it appears on medieval menus, though recipes for it appear only in the seventeenth century; they have remained in the repertory down to the present day.[4] Indeed, most of the pastry eaten in the Middle Ages has remained in use, with the principal changes being in the flavorings used. Pies of ham, of game, or of eels can be found in menus from subsequent centuries. The pastry recipes in the *Liure fort excellent de cuysine* of 1555 differ only in a few particulars from earlier recipes, which is hardly surprising since this is the volume that is known to have originated in a now-lost earlier manuscript. Two recipes, however, are portents of things to come: both are fancifully named, and both mark an increasing level of skill in working with eggs. The first is "imitation snow," made of milk, egg whites, rice flour, and sugar, beaten "like butter" to a froth—the snow—

which is skimmed off and served on a dish.[5] The use of stiffly beaten egg whites was to lead in the following century to the invention of meringues. Some of the dishes of snow in the *Isle des Hermaphrodites* may have come from such a source. The second recipe is for a pastry called *brides à veaux*, which literally means "calves' halters" and figuratively, according to Randle Cotgrave, "fopperies, gulleries, grosse tricks, or lyes; vnlikely tales, or things"—the point being that calves do not wear halters. The pastry version, says Cotgrave, is "hollow, round, and wreathed cracknels of fine flower, sugar, salt, and yoalkes of egs, incorporated together with water, and white wine."[6] The *Liure fort excellent* recipe adds rosewater and a little white cheese; the mixture is to be firmer. They are baked in a gentle oven [*four doulx*] on a piece of buttered paper and served cut into lozenges, with butter and sugar over them. Crisp and ornamental, they must have combined agreeably with the creamy dairy mixtures and sticky preserves of the sixteenth-century collation.

Lancelot de Casteau's *Ovverture de Cvisine* has a remarkable assortment of pastry recipes including two for a pastry that resembles strudel. In the first, a dough of flour, eggs, and water is kneaded for fifteen minutes and then rolled out into thin sheets. One sheet is used to line a *tourtière* and then is spread with butter and topped with a second sheet. A blancmange filling is added, and the *tourte* is topped off with four more buttery layers. This is the first instance I know of in French cookery in which an effort is made to achieve a layered crust. Elsewhere Lancelot uses sheets of dough brushed with lard and formed into a log, then rolled again and cut into pieces which are used to make covered meat pies. In yet another recipe, this time using a yeast dough, spread with cinnamon sugar and raisins, rolled, and cut crosswise, then baked with the pieces standing on a cut side, he comes very close to producing cinnamon buns.[7]

Further advances in pastry cooking are seen in a gnocchi mixture (he calls it *agnoilen*), poached in broth, which is similar to the panada used in modern quenelles. A similar dough is used in a quartet of fritter recipes.[8] The tidy sequence in which these recipes are presented as much as the recipes themselves indicates a substantial advance in the pastrycook's expertise. The first recipe lists the ingredients, with measurements, and gives detailed instructions about forming and frying the dough (again, it is much like a *pâte à choux*) in butter, turning the pastries as they cook. They are done, he tells us, when the crust has split and does not shrink when withdrawn from the hot fat. In the second version the dough is extruded through a nozzle, and in the third it is spread out on a board and cut into sticks before frying. Finally, instead of being made into fritters, a sweetened version of the dough, with added butter, is spread on a sheet of greased paper and baked in the oven.

These are impressive gains. By the end of the sixteenth century, the beginnings of layered pastries, the exploitation of *pâte à choux* for baking, frying, and poaching, and the tentative beginnings of using air whisked into egg whites and into cream were evident. It is, though, only with the *Pâtissier françois* of 1654 that all the basic flour mixtures of the pastrycooks' art are at hand: doughs such as *pâte feuilletée*, the white-flour and rye-flour crusts for raised pies, cream-puff pastry, and even the egg-and-sugar-foam-based batters from which sweet cakes developed. Moreover, the book begins with these basic mixtures, just as the cookbooks used in ordinary kitchens were beginning to do at this time. Next come recipes for a spice mixture, for pastry creams, gilding, and a simple royal icing. The introductory section concludes with the earliest description I know of in a French cookbook of weights and measures.[9] The repertory includes a substantial proportion of those pies, fritters, rissoles, and wafers which had been on the scene for more than a century, along with new cakes, small cakes, near-cookies, and even a few puddings. The deceptively named *tourte d'oeufs aux pommes* is a crustless baked mixture of apple pulp, sugar, flour, and eggs, baked in a buttered *tourtière* until firm and served garnished with sugar, rosewater, and preserved lemon peel—an attractive and practical recipe.[10] The author remarks that in place of apples one may use melon or pumpkin; made with pumpkin it would be close to the modern pumpkin pie filling.

The *Pâtissier françois* is the first extended account of the art of the professional pastrycook. Its contemporary, *Les Delices de la campagne* by Nicolas Bonnefons, demonstrates the degree to which the cook in the kitchen of a prosperous small household was expected to produce fine pastry. Bonnefons offers a modest selection of sweet, rather small-scale pastries, such as wafers, rissoles, darioles, flans, and *talemouses*. His recipe for the latter is sufficiently precise to give an idea what it looked like:

> You roll out some *pâte feuilletée* into a circle with a rolling pin and in the middle of it you put a cheese farce and then close your pastry on top (pinching it together) to make three horns, which is the shape of the *talemouse*; you allow just a little of the filling to show in the center, not

enclosing it, so that in the oven the filling will puff out and take color as it cooks.[11]

The filling is made with two kinds of cheese, eggs, additional yolks, butter, flour, and water.

In his recipe for *biscuit de roy* Bonnefons makes a remark that serves as a reminder of how imperfect the written record is for the history of this craft. The *biscuit* is made from a foamy batter, rich in eggs, and it continued to be the standard type of cake up to the Revolution, though there are no recipes for it earlier than the decade of the 1650s. After describing how to make the batter and "dress it in tinned *tourtières*, or paper, of whatever shape you wish, which must be buttered so the crust does not stick," he continues: "From this same dough is [made], a little firmer, a loaf three inches high, like one of those big Rheims gingerbreads, which after cooling a little, is cut into slices, to serve at table. This was the fashion forty years ago, before *biscuit de Savoye* was invented, and they called it a pastrycook's loaf [*pain des pâtissiers*]."[12] Here is a recipe surfacing only after it had been in use for nearly half a century. There is no way of knowing how often this happens because we are entirely dependent upon the unreliable written record.

Massialot's writings on cooking and confectionary include a wide range of baked goods. He carries forward the trend toward greater systematization, an increase in the proportion of sweet flavors, and an emphasis on skill and delicacy. Coffee and chocolate are used as flavorings. *Biscuit*-batter-based cakes continue to proliferate: there are now two dozen varieties. The use of beaten egg whites is better understood, impelled, perhaps, by the fact that the pastry creams and *pâtes à biscuit* often call for extra egg yolks, leaving a surplus to be used up. Thus meringues and macaroons now appear. Massialot describes meringues as "a little sugar-work, very pretty and very easy . . . , also very convenient in the *office*, since it can be made in a moment." For *meringues jumelles* a pair of walnut-sized meringues is stuck together with a dab of fruit preserves.[13] In another case he felicitously adds pistachios, which continued to be an ingredient favored by pastrycooks and confectioners up to the Revolution and beyond. One is reminded of the pistachio confections in the Baghdad cookbook from centuries before.

Just how many past practices remained in use is seen in Vincent La Chapelle's *Cuisinier moderne*, where more than a hundred pie recipes and nearly two dozen fritters are to be found, many of them recognizably close to those

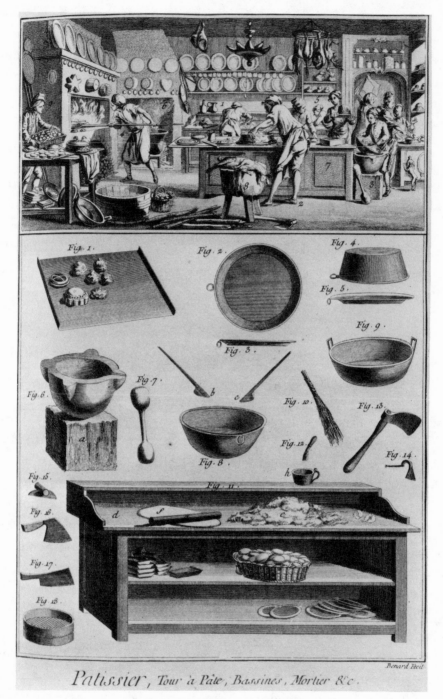

The pastrycook's workshop, engraving, from *Encyclopédie: Recueil de planches* . . . (Paris, 1763–77), shows a busy, well-arranged room. Below is illustrated the *tour à pâte*, the pastry-cook's work station, with storage shelves and an ample working surface. The raised wall around it protects the pastry from excessive heat and cold. Figures 4 and 5 show a *tourtière*, the pie plate with its raised lid. (By permission of the Houghton Library, Harvard University.)

of previous centuries. What is new is the freedom with which the cook manipulates ingredients, using well-developed techniques and combinations. Moreover, this way of working is easily communicated from one cook to another because the concepts are standardized. For example, the chapter on hot fish pies opens with a carp pie that is used as a model to which the subsequent recipes refer. This model draws on basic recipes elsewhere for its crust and *coulis* and in turn gives instructions for a fish forcemeat that may be used "for little fast-day [dishes], all kinds of pies and *tourtes* of fish." [14]

Subsequent eighteenth-century cookbooks reveal little more innovation. Sweets continue to increase their share of space, reflecting the increasing supply of sugar. The 1790 edition of Menon's *Cuisinière bourgeoise* contains a wider range of sweet baked goods than any cookbook since La Chapelle published the *Cuisinier moderne* half a century before, reflecting the wider availability and lower cost of sugar.

BREAD

Although there are two bread recipes in the *Pâtissier françois*, the first important·collection is in Nicolas Bonnefons's *Delices de la campagne*, which gives bread recipes for country dwellers who were not satisfied with the products of a village's communal bake-oven. He begins with several bread recipes; the various types are defined in large part by what kind, or kinds, of flour are used, ranging from all whole wheat to all white. Other cereals, such as rye, oats, barley, and fava beans, he tells us, are used only by the poor. He stresses the importance of using the best possible water. Citing the excellence of bread from Gonesse, he states that the same recipe made elsewhere, even using the same wheat, is much less beautiful and good; the difference is the water. He offers a curious rule for choosing among alternatives for those who do not live in Gonesse. One takes a pint each of the water from river, spring, well, and rain and weighs each pint; the lightest in weight will be the best—a pretty puzzle for the physicist. A preliminary sponge is made by mixing a portion of the flour with beer yeast, for a slow rising, after which the remaining flour is kneaded in. After a second rising, loaves of about sixteen pounds are formed, and when they have risen they go into the oven for about four hours of baking. Small loaves, of course, require less time. Only in the recipe for *pain du Montauron* is salt called for; this is a milk bread made with "the whitest flour you can get." Bonnefons speaks of brioche; his recipe calls for butter and a soft cheese, which would probably have been like our cream cheese, but his brioche contains no eggs, and the shape is not described. The loaf is gilded with beaten eggs, to which some people, "for economy," add diluted honey.[15]

By the end of the seventeenth century, the array of baked goods available in the shops of Paris was impressive. In reading de Blegny's descriptions in the *Livre commode* one can almost smell the bread baking in the ovens: rye bread and milk rolls, fine bread and coarse bread, soup breads, a variety of little rolls, and "the rusks one eats with liqueurs." Some of these breads were leavened with brewer's yeast (*pain de levure*), others with a sourdough starter (*pain de levain*).[16]

An eighteenth-century tome on the starchy arts by P. Malouin includes a handsome series of plates illustrating the techniques, equipment, and products of milling, baking, and noodlemaking. Fortunately, the plates are annotated beyond the needs of common sense (we can recognize a doorway, even now, without assistance). As a consequence, they show us what many loaves and rolls looked like which we would know otherwise only by name. Malouin tells us that the queen's baker, M. Bouillard, was famous for his little light rolls known as *pain à caffé*. They were made with white flour, yeast, salt, and creamy milk. The mixture was allowed to stand for some hours, which gave a richness of flavor that was believed by those not privy to his secret to be due to the presence of butter. For two centuries the best bread, *pain de chapitre*, had been made from the firmest dough. It was literally the test of a master baker's craft, appearing as the *chef d'oeuvre* in the examination for admission to the guild. In Paris it was known as *pain de Gonesse*, in Caen, as *fouasse*. By 1761, when Malouin was writing, breads with a softer dough had come into favor.[17]

Malouin gives instructions for making three kinds of bread just for soup. The first, *pain à potage*, is a round loaf, made with the best flour, a sourdough starter supplemented further along with a little beer yeast, salt, and water. It is formed into loaves weighing as much as twelve pounds apiece, and each loaf is set in a basket for its final rising. It is baked thoroughly, emerging from the oven with a firm crust and a moderately moist crumb. Malouin warns against using too much yeast, which would spoil the flavor of the broth in which it steeped. *Pain à potage* was also used as an all-purpose household bread. The second variety, *pain à soupe*, can be just as large in diameter, but it is a flat loaf, all crust and no crumb, good only for putting into the broth. It has less flavor and is used chiefly in households where the

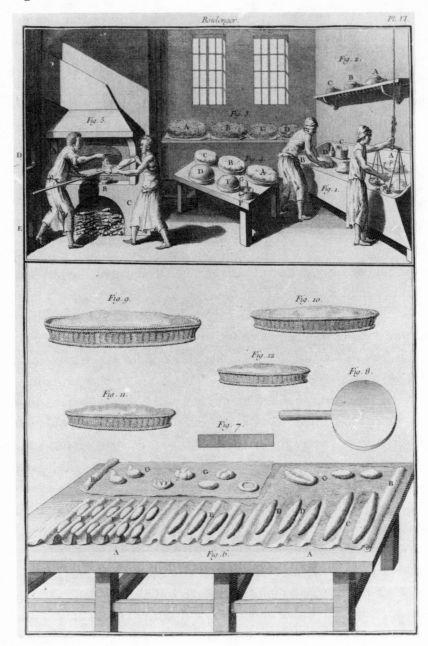

The bakery, engraving, from Paul Jacques Malouin, *Description des arts et métiers* (Paris, 1767). Above, at the left, bread is being put into the oven with a peel, the flat, long-handled wooden paddle. Below the windows loaves, ranging in weight from six to twelve pounds, rise in wicker baskets. At the right, bakers knead bread on the upper side of the lid of a large *pêtrin* or dough box in which the bread dough was put to rise, and another workman measures out flour on a balance scale. On the table in the middle of the room are *pains à soupe* (A–C) and *pains à potage* (D, E). On the work table rolls and small loaves are rising on a floured cloth; the ripples in the cloth serve as gentle supports. The baskets above the table contain dough that has just started to rise. (By permission of the Department of Special Collections, Iowa State University Library.)

servants receive a bread ration. Finally, soup-eaters have the option of taking their soup with rusks, or *croûtes à potage*. These are economically made from rolls that the baker had not sold on previous days. The crust is chipped off, and they are split horizontally; the crumb is then removed, and the rolls are set, concave side down, in a cooling oven to brown lightly and to dry, forming an early version of melba toast.[18]

CONFECTIONARY

In the confectioner's art as in the pastrycook's, the repertory grew from the Middle Ages on, but few preparations were dropped. Although medieval hashes disappeared, pies and wafers, marzipans, and fruit pastes continued and indeed increased in use and diversity. In the mid-eighteenth century *Les Soupers de la cour* contains a baker's dozen of marzipans, and Menon's *La Science du maître d'hôtel, confiseur* seventeen. The ancient mixture of ground almonds and sugar was enhanced with preserved fruit, either in pieces or puréed, and by a simple egg white and sugar glaze. Other variations substituted pistachios for almonds or used the basic mixture as a filling for a pie shell.

In the Middle Ages sugar was rare. Its position in the cookbooks is marginal: the Vatican manuscripts of the *Viandier* have two recipes for a confection called *tailliez* made by boiling figs, raisins, almond milk, and wafer crumbs into a thick paste.[19] In the *Ménagier de Paris* sweets are found among the "other little things which are not essential," but they are all made with honey.[20] Sugared almonds are mentioned in the menus that appear in the first printed *Viandier*, and among Pierre Gaudoul's borrowings from Platina there is that exceedingly sugar-rich *potage verseuse*.[21] But until the mid-sixteenth century the would-be confectioner was obliged to study with experienced individuals. A few recipes appear in the *Liure fort excellent de cuysine* (1555), notably for preserved cherries and for a pear gelatin, set with isinglass.[22] Isinglass is a flavorless gelatin made from the swim bladders of fish, especially sturgeon. After the sixteenth century it was seldom used in French cooking, though it continued in use in Germany and England. In seventeenth-century France it was largely replaced by grated, boiled staghorn (*corne de cerf*).

From the sixteenth century onward sugar was put to three principal uses: to sweeten dishes; in the preservation of fruit, flowers, and some vegetables; and decoratively, either as hand-formed or cast ornaments or as glazing. The

Liure fort excellent de cuysine gets double use from its slightly garbled cherry recipe: after cherries are cooked with a little white wine and their weight in sugar, they are drained and served as a part of the first course in a meal, while the syrup, perhaps reduced, is presented as a jelly.

In that same year of 1555 two more or less quacks, Michel de Nostradamus and Alexis of Piedmont, published the first French-language confectionary collections, which included examples of preserving and the manipulation of sugar. Sugar is mixed with water-softened gum tragacanth to make pastillage (a plastic dough that was put to many fantastic uses) and with almonds to make marzipan.[23] These two substances have been among the confectioner's principal resources ever since.

As the preparation of bouillon is to the kitchen, so sugar-boiling is to the *office*. As early as La Varenne's *Parfaict confitvrier* in 1667, there are descriptions of the various densities to which sugar syrup is to be boiled.[24] The best account is probably in Menon's *La Science du maître d'hôtel, confiseur* (1750); it opens the book, just as bouillon is the usual first recipe in an ordinary French cookbook. Menon's instructions are extraordinarily detailed: in the hundred Farenheit degrees between the boiling point of a sugar syrup and its turning to caramel he distinguishes thirteen stages.[25] Not until very recently have any modern cookbooks equaled this precision; a standard candy thermometer names only five stages.[26] Menon's stages are for the most part paired, as ours are. They go from *petit* and *grand lisse* (around 215 to 220° F.) to *petite* and *grande perlé* (around 220 to 222° F.) and then *petit* and *grand queue de cochon*; this pigtail forms in the middle and upper 220s. At about 228 to 230° F. a curious phenomenon appears: if one dips a pierced skimmer in the syrup and blows through it, little bubbles form briefly; this is known as the *soufflé* stage. The degrees beyond this match our modern categories, going from the thread stages in the lower 230° F. range as *petite* and *grande plume* (feather) to *petit* and *gros boulet* (soft and hard ball) between 235 and 265° F., and, finally, soft and hard crack from 270 to 310° F., after which caramelization begins. The home cook today, caught without a thermometer, usually dribbles the syrup into a bowl of cold water to test it; then and now a professional sugar-boiler would moisten thumb and forefinger in water, then plunge them rapidly into the boiling syrup to pull out a sample. I have seen it done but have never felt the desire to try it. The syrups produced by the careful work Menon describes were used for everything from fruit compotes to pulled sugar work, barley sugar, and other forms of caramel.

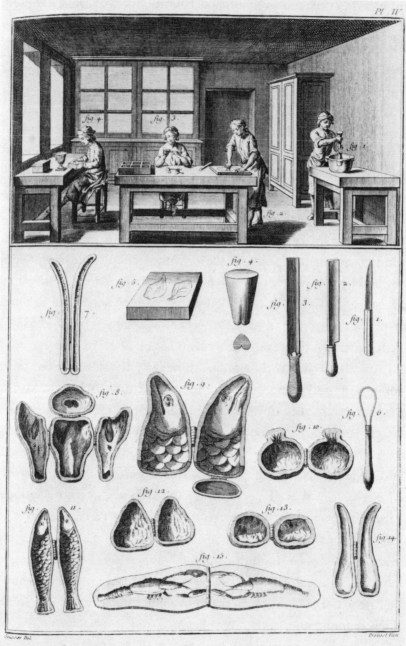

Confiseur, Pastillage et Moulles pour les Glaces.

Pastillage manufacture and molds for ices, engraving from *Encyclopédie: Recueil de planches* . . . (Paris, 1763–77). Above, workers make flowers from pastillage, or gum paste dough, a mixture of sugar and gum tragacanth. Below are cutters and a leaf mold for pastillage and a variety of molds for ices; many of these shapes, including the crayfish and the asparagus stalk, were still in use a century and more later. (By permission of the Houghton Library, Harvard University.)

Fruit was the confectioner's principal flavoring; it was dried, candied, and preserved in syrups or in brandy; it could be used to flavor syrups, to garnish marzipans, and, dipped in a light caramel glaze, to ornament the dessert table. Wild apple and cherry varieties little used today, many flowers, and even a few vegetables were used in sugar preparations. Even the core of mature lettuces was candied to make a highly regarded preserve called *gorge d'ange*, or angel's throat.[27]

CONFECTIONARY AND THE ARTS OF TABLE DECORATION

In the seventeenth and eighteenth centuries the sense of the topography of table setting was much stronger than it is today.[28] Strong vertical accents were as much a part of the decoration as the pattern in which plates and bowls and glasses were set out. These accents were to some extent supplied by silver and by flowers. Much remained, however, for the confectioner to provide. Since the sixteenth century, figures made of sugar had been an important part of the decorative and thematic scheme, as in the case of the previously described figures of Minerva in bas relief at the banquet for Elizabeth of Austria. By the early eighteenth century the designers of tabletops were consciously following the examples of landscape architects, constructing miniature landscapes down the middle of their tables.[29] The materials were sugar pastes, biscuit dough, wax, cardboard, silk chenille trimming, and colored sugar. The sugar paste and biscuit dough were transformed into classical deities on cardboard pedestals; they presided over parterres (the confectioner's term as well as the landscape architect's) whose wooden or cardboard edges were decorously concealed with silk trimmings. Sometimes the "gardens" were set out on mirrors to amplify the light. By the eighteenth century even in outdoor gardens leaves and flowers were sometimes replaced with colored sand, which was more easily arranged and kept in geometric patterns. The confectioners produced colored sugars similar to those found among the bakery supplies in a modern supermarket, which they called "sand," or *sable*. It is disconcerting, in the indexes of the confectioners' cookbooks, among the biscuits and jams, to find "sand, to color." This vogue lasted until the sugar figures were displaced, after midcentury, by the much more delicate productions of the porcelain manufacturers and, to a lesser extent, the silversmiths. The material changed, though the subject matter did not.

The second important element in the vertical arrangement of the table

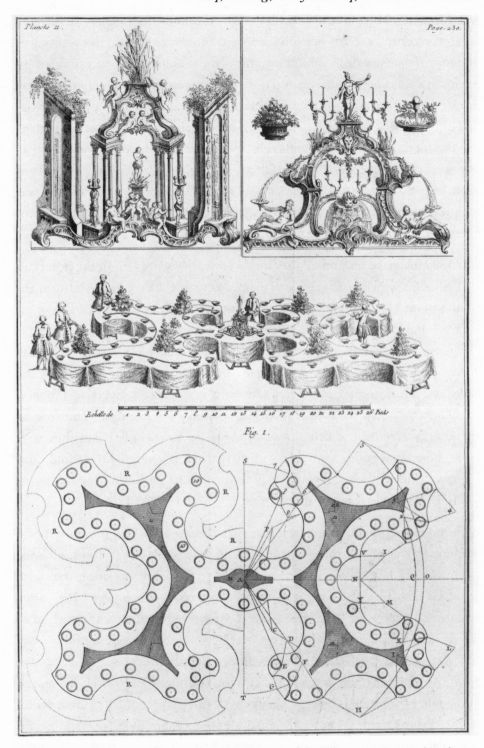

Plan and decorations for a table, engraving, from Joseph Gilliers, *Le Cannemeliste français* (Nancy, 1751). In the table diagram the spirit of geometry has run wild. The decorations in the top illustration could be made from sugar paste, porcelain, or silver. (By permission of the Houghton Library, Harvard University.)

was the pyramid of food. Nowadays flowers and candles generally provide whatever vertical accents our low-ceilinged rooms require. In the vast spaces of *ancien régime* interiors something more was needed and was provided by *service en pyramide*. It survives today in the *croquembouche*, in ceramic imitations of fruit, and occasionally in pyramids of real fruit, too often fixed on nail-studded wooden cones, which achieve reliability at the cost of damaging the food. In the seventeenth century a variety of methods of construction were current for many kinds of food—for example, a marinade of chickens with lemon slices and fried parsley was piled up *en pyramide*, and so was whipped cream stiffened with gum tragacanth, but fruit was used most often. Cherries, for example, were served thus:

> One must have pyramidal tin funnels, of various sizes, to fit the porcelain dishes on which you will place them. You put a cherry at the bottom for the point . . . on the second layer you put three, on the third, four or five, and thus to the end, according to the capacity of the mold, crisscrossing the stems toward the middle, which you fill up with some chopped worthless leaves, because your fruit will only be around the edges. To decorate these pyramids you may mix in layers of flowers, which will help to hold it in place, making, for example, one row of flowers after two or three rows of cherries. The whole being thus well arranged and solid, you put your dish at the opening of the mold, and having turned it over, you gently remove your mold, leaving the pyramid very well arranged and very tidy.[30]

At best, it was an unstable arrangement. Madame de Sévigné describes a dinner party at which the pyramid of fruit was made much too high and, "with twenty porcelains, was completely overturned at the door, the noise of which silenced the violins, oboes, and trumpets."[31] There were three ways to enhance stability. One method was to drizzle caramel over the surface of the fruit, though it cannot have been very convenient to eat anything from such a structure. Perhaps that was the idea; certainly the serving of a *croquembouche* nowadays is best accomplished with a hammer and chisel. Second, a dish could be inserted between every two or three layers of fruit; these dishes are always referred to as *pourcelaines*, though often silver, pewter, or tin "pourcelaines" were called for; they would have made for a quieter crash. Finally, the pyramid could be formed in a metal cone, as described above, and then water poured in and frozen. It would have become sloppy as it melted, but ice was so fashionable at that point that the mess might have been overlooked.[32] Despite the problems it presented, the pyramid remained in fashion at least from 1650 through the first quarter of the eighteenth century.

There were two basic types of table arrangement, the choice being determined by the proportions of the table. The first, for a long, narrow table, consisted of a central band of alternating features. The usual elements were candelabra and baskets of either fruit or flowers and sometimes both. The food was then ranged down the length of the table on either side. One of the earliest examples was seen in 1680 at the marriage of the prince de Conti to Mademoiselle de Blois, one of the illegitimate daughters of Louis XIV. The table was fifty-four feet long and only six and a half wide, and it had to accommodate 160 serving dishes at a time.

> The middle of it was ornamented in a wholly original manner, which had something elegant, magnificent, and supernatural about it, considering the season. There were nineteen openwork baskets, as many gilded as silver, which dominated all the length of the table. They were filled with anemones, hyacinths, Spanish jasmine, tulips, and orange leaves, and with little garlands of flowers crowning them above. There was nothing more natural, and seeing these baskets it was difficult to remember that it was the sixteenth of January.[33]

The other type of arrangement, better suited to a shorter, wider table, was formed around a central object, which could be flowers, fruit, confectionary, or metalwork; later in the eighteenth century the garden element tended to be larger and the dishes less crowded together. In this later period figures like garden statuary made of sugar or the newly developing porcelain were set in landscapes of imitation flower beds. Around this the food was disposed, as well as candlestands, stemmed goblets with ices or fruit, and often flowers. *Le Mercure Galant* commented on one such scene: "One had never seen so many flowers all at once. One would have thought each table was a formal garden, there was such an abundance of them there."[34]

When the table was arranged around a central object, that object had to be as fine as possible. The silver or silver-gilt *surtout* or centerpiece was the ideal, and it could be very ornate. An especially magnificent one was made for the maréchal comte de Daun by the celebrated silversmith Claude Ballin the younger, the nephew of the silversmith who produced Louis XIV's silver furniture for Versailles. It was the principal piece in a silver service of

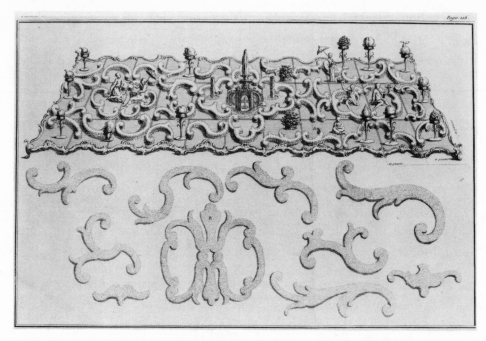

Design for centerpiece, engraving, from Joseph Gilliers, *Le Cannemeliste français* (Nancy, 1751). The principles of landscape architecture have been applied to table decoration. Only the incongruous scale of the pieces of fruit on their individual stands indicates that this is a tabletop and not a design for a real garden. (By permission of the Houghton Library, Harvard University.)

immense size and grandeur, including large soup tureens, olla-podrida basins, platters, candelabra, pepper pots, and specialized serving dishes. The *surtout* was made in the form of a rectangular temple, set slantwise on its base.

> The ingenious artist wished to represent a fête given by Comus, the god of feasts. His image is placed under a baldachino . . . , half reclining, his arms extended in a gesture and with an expression which indicates health, joy, contentment, which seems to invite one to the pleasures of the table. This baldachino is raised up on four arcades. Under the two larger ones one sees . . . the figures of Bacchus and Ceres, with their attributes. . . . At the base of the arches, four bacchantes, their torsos ending in consoles. . . . The center of the top of the baldachino is occupied by a kind of basket suitable for holding flowers, lemons, oranges, and other fruits in season.[35]

More commonly, an epergne rather than a primarily sculptural work would occupy such a central place. A less expensive version was made of gilded,

J. B. Oudry inv.   *J. Ouvrier Sculp.*

LE RAT DE VILLE ET LE RAT DES CHAMPS. Fable IX.

The City Rat and the Country Rat, engraving after J. B. Oudry from Jean de La Fontaine, *Fables* (Paris, 1755–59). This is a typical upper-class dining room, with a sumptuous marble buffet built against the wall and a silver centerpiece on the table. The remains of a once-symmetrical meal are still there, to the pleasure of the all-too-plentiful rats. (By permission of the Houghton Library, Harvard University.)

silvered, or painted basketwork. It formed a raised platform, with a lacy rim to hold fruit in place. On it in addition to fruit were set porcelain or tin dishes, according to the resources of the host. The tin dishes, also called "pourcelaines," Massialot assures us, will not be seen, because they can be masked with leaves or paper.[36] It was not even necessary to invest in these *machines*, as they were called. They could be made to order if one had special needs or ideas, but they could also be rented, in 1692, from "Sieur Coterot, at the entrance to the Faubourg Saint Antoine, the first on your right going out, at the sign of the eagle crowned with wicker. . . . He is supplied with all the newest and best of this kind of thing."[37] In a pinch, one could contrive a service with ordinary household silver, but it must not be skimpy.

The extreme to which the skilled technician could go with his fantasy is seen in an account of a traveler's experience at one Parisian table:

> About a fortnight ago, after dinner, at Madame de la Marck's (it being the birthday, I think, of the Count), with the dessert was brought in a very fine basket of (in appearance) large beautiful peaches; it was so contrived, however, that nobody offered to touch them till every body had done with the other fruit, and then a match was put to a little fuzee on one side of the basket, and the artificial peaches entertained the eye in a variety of explosions, as much as (had they been real) they could the palate of an epicure.[38]

At this point the extreme of food that does not taste of itself had been exceeded; it was a luxury only the affluent table could have enjoyed.

Frozen desserts were a favorite product of the *office*. Massialot's *Nouvelle instruction pour les confitures* gives directions for freezing mixtures in molds set in ice and salt. He uses creams thickened with rennet or curdled with lemon and also gives recipes for fruit-flavored waters which are frozen.[39] By the time Vincent La Chapelle was writing, he was able to include a greater variety of ices: coffee and chocolate ices, cream-based and custard-based ones, and water ices.[40] He uses Turk's head and melon molds. Similar recipes continued to be popular through the century, appearing in Menon's *La Science du maître d'hôtel, confiseur* and the *Dictionnaire portatif*.[41] Just how valued a luxury item ices were is indicated by their place in a meal given in August of 1728 to precede and celebrate the wedding of the duc de Durfort, eldest son of the duc de Lorges, to Mademoiselle de Portier, the daughter of the duc de Portier. The duc de Lorges borrowed the hôtel d'Evreux from its owner, and he arranged for the performance of a ballet, composed by Jean-Joseph Mouret. At ten o'clock at night, dinner was announced by

> le sieur Gondart, the aged and famous maître d'hôtel to the late premier président de Mesme, whom the duc de Lorges had charged with the arrangement of the banquet. There were twenty-five covers; . . . the magnificence of the service and of the silver was astonishing, and there was a double service of entrées and entremets; the best cooks of Paris surpassed themselves with new ragouts of an exquisite flavor, and the *officiers* imitated them in the sumptuousness and delicacy of the dessert. . . . But the impatience of the duc de Lorges to conduct the newly married to the church, and to see the last conclusion of an alliance which he had so long desired, prevented people from seeing it [the dessert], one of the most beautiful things and one of the most unusual in this superb banquet; it was a complete course of *sorbet glacé*, representing all kinds of fruit and in all flavors. They were not given time to serve them, the duke having asked his guests to abridge their meal. This course, which was entirely seasonable, because it was very hot, was abandoned to the crowd of people who had gathered to watch the fête, and which the guards had not been able to keep out.[42]

There were more than two thousand people in this crowd. The unstable situation ended on a cheerful note: the opera girls from the ballet, who had a private table in a room adjoining the grand salon, sang drinking songs for them; fireworks were set off in the garden, while the wedding guests finally saw the marriage performed at Saint Roch at two o'clock in the morning.

The production of these elaborately constructed entertainments demanded the most precise skills and substantial investments in specialized equipment. They also allowed the imagination full play. Nowhere are the links between the culinary arts and other facets of a culture's aesthetic style more clearly visible. In the eighteenth century, the confectioner in particular drew on the rococo decorative vocabulary of the landscape architect, the porcelain modeler, and the designer of interiors. Food was but one element of an integrated tabletop design. As we shall now see, both cooks and diners had views—sometimes conflicting—about the qualities of foods and the worth of cooks.

CHAPTER ELEVEN

Mid-Eighteenth-Century Trends and Controversies

S THE BAROQUE FESTIVAL had followed the Renaissance collation, so the rococo supper succeeded the festival. Whereas the archetypical seventeenth-century court meal was part of an elaborately orchestrated series of semipublic events, that of the eighteenth-century court was the *souper intime*. It was private, small scale, and studiedly informal, without inconographic theme or political message. It would be a mistake, though, to view the suppers of Louis XV, Madame de Pompadour, and their circle as either impromptu or simple. The guests were carefully selected; the sense of belonging to a chosen circle was very strong. As the diners at Louis XIV's court entertainments had rejoiced to be seen there by the spectators, so Louis XV's guests rejoiced to be seen passing through the door into the private apartments. Louis XIV had sat down to a table at which nearly all the other diners were women. At Louis XV's suppers servants were excluded so that men and women could share the delights of delicate food served with the finest porcelain and silver in an atmosphere of fashion and flirtation. After supper they could enjoy coffee prepared by the king himself, a beverage more intoxicating than any mere liqueur.[1]

The cultivation of an intimate atmosphere did not mean that cooking or menus became simpler. As the eighteenth century progressed, the division between the cuisines of large and small kitchens grew. Massialot's recipes and even many of La Chapelle's could be prepared in modest kitchens. Because their books remained in print in the 1740s, we may infer that the change that was taking place in the most opulent kitchens came more slowly to smaller ones. What is true of individual recipes is even more the case with entire menus. In general, a ratio of about two dishes per guest was followed in planning menus, and the planner could use his or her discretion as to whether these individual dishes were plain or fancy—whether, for example, to offer radishes or boned truffled quail as an hors d'oeuvre. Toward the later part of the century, the menus for elaborate meals included four courses prepared in the kitchen, in addition to the final course from the *office*. Doubling the required amount of cooking put the realization of such a meal beyond the reach of any but the wealthiest host. In addition, some recipes in the newest books, especially those of Menon, called for a large investment of both skilled labor and costly materials. The division, however, was not absolute. Simple foods still had a place on the grandest tables, and regional specialties—both ingredients and preparations—now appeared in menus elsewhere. *Garbure*, the Gascon pork and cabbage soup, was a great favorite. It often appeared with the olla-podrida as one of the two principal first-course offerings. Writers of cookbooks were at some pains to distinguish between bourgeois and aristocratic styles of cooking, though they also wanted as large a market as possible for their books. François Marin writes, in 1755, that "many bourgeois, wishing to imitate the great, exceed the limits of their position, covering their tables with dishes which cost a lot of money without doing them any honor, because to be successful the dishes must be dressed by a clever hand."[2] These individuals, he tells us, would be better off in health and pocketbook if they returned to the simplicity of the past. In the text of his book he repeatedly draws attention to recipes and methods suitable to the bourgeois table, and several recipes actually bear the designation "à la bourgeoise."[3] While the bourgeoisie were trying to eat like the nobility, among the latter there was a vogue for things bourgeois. Menon, whose *Nouveau traité de cuisine* represents the extreme of luxury, also wrote the *Cuisinière bourgeoise*, but he wrote it for the aristocracy, too.

La Nouvelle Cuisine AND GASTRONOMIC CONTROVERSY

The *haute cuisine* of mid-eighteenth-century Paris has some familiar aspects. Much has been said in recent years about our twentieth-century *nouvelle cuisine*, about the abandonment by "the best cooks of Paris" (and now in the provinces as well) of the heavy old sauces and elaborate dishes of past masters, and about the replacement of starchy liaisons by a judicious boiling down to concentrate flavors. Our jaded palates are to be surprised and refreshed by new combinations. Simplicity and purity reign—and of course it is all even more expensive than the old style was. Moreover, only initiates really understand the system. A similar "reform" movement took place in the 1740s. It was not identical to ours, though, for their *nouvelle cuisine* was much more labor-intensive, and individual dishes combined many more flavors.

The art of cookery underwent a marked change at that time, including an escalation of expense. Ironically, under the banner of simplification, more luxurious ingredients, more extravagant basic mixtures, and more elaborate combinations were used. Talk about the theory and practice of the art also increased. Cooks argued with each other; diners incorporated metaphors of kitchen and table into their conversation.

The midcentury crop of food writers was large, and their points of view were diverse, but they all agreed that the cumbersome cuisine of the past must go. They saw themselves as giants standing on the shoulders of dwarfs. Marin (the author of *Les Dons de Comus*), Menon (whose work spans both *haute cuisine* and bourgeois cooking), and the anonymous authors of the *Cuisinier gascon* and the *Soupers de la cour* were the rulers of this new empire.

In the kitchens and *offices* craftsmen were working at a new level of technical skill, and their self-esteem rose in proportion. La Varenne had written that "although his position in life did not make him capable of having a heroic heart, it nonetheless gives him enough true feeling not to forget his duty."[4] Audiger's *Maison reglée* was introduced by laudatory poems, and he wrote of the glory he enjoyed "from having had the honor many times of preparing and serving the food and drink of the most powerful of kings."[5] The author of *Soupers de la cour* says that he writes "for *officiers* of the kitchen who seriously appreciate their art and are ambitious to get ahead. They are the only ones whose approval I court, and I count for nothing certain performers of mediocre knowledge and yet more limited wit who, stupidly intoxicated by their pretended spirit, scorn works from which they could learn much."[6] In a calmer vein, Marin writes:

> But here is my idea [of a good cook]: he must know exactly the properties of everything he uses, so that he can correct or perfect the foods which nature presents to us raw. He should add to that a sound judgment, a sure taste, and a delicate palate, so that he can skillfully adjust both ingredients and proportions. . . . Let us add . . . the manual dexterity to work neatly . . . , and an assiduous attention to the master's taste, "whose palate should become his own."[7]

Elsewhere he writes that "one can recognize a good cook when he begins his work, but one knows him even better when he is all done."[8]

CONTROVERSY OVER THEORY

The first two editions of Marin's *Les Dons de Comus ou les délices de la table* (Paris, 1739 and 1740) contain an introductory essay discussing the history of cooking from man's earliest days. This unsigned introduction, said by Vicaire to be the work of two Jesuits, Fathers Pierre Brunoy and Guillaume Hyacinthe Bouvant, is a clear statement of how the advocates of *la nouvelle cuisine* perceived the contrast between it and the preceding style of cookery.[9] Beginning with the ancients and skipping quickly over the Middle Ages, they touch only lightly on the previous hundred years or so and then define the differences:

> For more than two centuries good food has been known in France, but . . . it has never been so delicate, . . . no one has ever before worked either so neatly or with such refined taste. People in the business, and those who pride themselves on having a good table, distinguish nowadays between the old style of cookery [*la cuisine ancienne*] and the modern style [*la cuisine moderne*]. The old style of cookery is that which the French made fashionable all over Europe, and which was generally practiced as recently as twenty years ago. The modern style of cookery, built on the foundations of the old style but with fewer encumbrances, less display, and as much variety, is simpler, neater, and perhaps even more expert. The old cookery was very complicated and extraordinarily detailed. Modern cookery is a kind of chemistry. The cook's science consists today of analyzing, digesting, and extracting the quintessence of foods, drawing out the light and nourishing juices, mingling and blending them together, so that nothing dominates and everything is perceived, producing the kind of union which painters give to their colors, and making them homogeneous, so that from their different flavors result only a fine and piquant taste, and, if I dare say it, a harmony of all the tastes joined together.[10]

This use of the language of the chemistry laboratory for the work of the kitchen reflects the rising status of the cook and perhaps contributed to that rise. The writer suggests that the cook can make a positive contribution to the diner's health; that, instead of the age-old idea that the cook and the doctor work in opposition, cookery should be wholesome.

> We have in France a number of noblemen who, for amusement, do not disdain to talk sometimes about cookery, and whose exquisite taste con-

The Cook, engraving by Hubert François Gravelot, from *Almanach de Loterie de l'Ecole Royale Militaire* (Amsterdam and Paris, 1759). The verse below reads: "New cooking every year, because every year tastes change; and every day there are new ragouts; and so you must be a chemist, Justine." Fortunately, her kitchen is equipped with a stove and appropriate saucepans. The fireplace continues in use, with a big cooking pot standing on a tripod over the glowing coals. (Courtesy of the Museum of Fine Arts, Boston, Sargent Collection.)

tributes much to mold excellent cooks. Since physical taste and spiritual taste depend equally on the structure of the fibers and the organs destined to operate their various sensations, the refinement of these two kinds of tastes proves assuredly the refinement of the organs to which they belong, and in consequence one can, it seems to me, go back from bodily taste to a very delicate principle, in which it has something in common with taste which is purely spiritual.[11]

The intellectual pretensions of this essay evoked a bantering reply from one Dessaleurs the elder, writing pseudonymously as "le pâtissier anglois."[12] According to this introduction, the pâtissier writes, cooks should not fail to use their methodical intelligence to perfect cookery by treating it, like other sciences, by the rules of geometry. Clearly, the pâtissier anglois is parodying the vogue for applying geometrical reason to all branches of human endeavor. Since Descartes's triumph, geometry had provided the paradigm for French thought. Some years earlier Fontenelle had recommended that the geometrical method should be applied to other subjects—to politics, morals, and criticism. "Even a manual on the art of public speaking would," he wrote, "other things being equal, be all the better for having been written by a geometrician."[13] The pâtissier anglois goes on to say that this geometric approach would surely lead to a more wholesome diet, ironically suggesting that the close link between mind and body be exploited for the education of children.

> Much precious time in their childhood is wasted, teaching them dead languages which they will not use; their memories are overloaded with mythology, history, and reading, which repel them. . . . To remedy this abuse, it is necessary, according to your principles, which I willingly embrace, . . . only to give to young people, for their whole education, whatever food and nourishment is suitable to the position for which they are destined. These foods would be measured out and seasoned by a clever cook, of consummate experience, who would know completely the thoughts produced in a soul by digesting a *potage à la Nivernoise*, a *sauce à la Chirac*, and similar dishes. In this way one would communicate unconsciously to young people the ideas, the knowledge, and even at the same time make them capable of using them in the occupations to which they are destined by birth or by their parents.[14]

For a fledgling courtier he recommends "whipped cream and calves' feet," to a young man of fashion, "linnets' heads, essence of may-bugs [*quintessence de hanneton*], and butterfly purée [*coulis de papillon*]," and to an aspiring lawyer "a great deal of mustard, verjuice, ginger, and things with a somewhat sharp or pungent flavor." He confesses, though, that it is harder to imagine a diet suitable "to give a child if you want to make a reasonable man or an upright citizen."[15] The pâtissier thus treats facetiously a conviction that sur-

vives in other guises today—the belief that one's diet, vegetarian, macro-
biotic, or what have you, has spiritual consequences. We have observed earlier the prevalence of theories relating diet to health and character in the
terms from late medieval biological science in the fifteenth, sixteenth, and
seventeenth centuries. And is not Brillat-Savarin best remembered for his
aphorism, "Tell me what you eat and I will tell you what you are?"

The pâtissier makes a revealing complaint against *la cuisine moderne*. Cooks
have become so clever, he says, so engrossed with making juices, extracts,
and quintessences and with blending flavors, that one can no longer recognize anything: "The great art of the new cookery is to give to fish the flavor
of meat, and to meat the flavor of fish, and to leave vegetables without any
flavor at all."[16] He compares this trend to the current literary taste for persi-
flage, which reduces all subjects and forms to a single level, so that all flavor
is lost, a condition equally unhealthy in cookery and in literature. At this
same time another literary man, Baron Melchior von Grimm, lamenting the
current vogue for publishing condensations of ideas, wrote in the converg-
ing language of kitchen and laboratory: "It looks as if we were out to quin-
tessentialize everything, to put everything through a sieve; we *must* get at
the quiddity, the rock-bottom of things."[17]

MID-EIGHTEENTH-CENTURY COOKBOOKS

Les Soupers de la cour is the most extensive work "for the best tables"
from this period, and its four volumes have long been esteemed by cooks
and collectors alike. Traditionally it has been ascribed to Menon, but its title
page and privilege name no author.[18] The collection clearly demonstrates the
breadth of the prerevolutionary culinary style. There are many recognizable
classic recipes and many that are lavish with materials and labor. Basic preparations are used fluently and subtly. Mechanical repetition has yielded to an
infinity of adjustments, as basic techniques are applied to ingredients with
differing properties. The recipes are a harvest of old and new, and nearly all
of them are French, except for pasta and for the English puddings that were
apparently introduced by La Chapelle and enjoyed favor in the second half
of the century. Among the items that hark back to the distant past are the
cheese pastries called *talemouses* and *échaudées* (a roll resembling a bagel), *sauce
Robert* (by 1750 efficiently made with some *coulis* and bouillon), and *sauce
poivrade*. Innovations are conspicuous, however. *Les Soupers* contains nearly

fifty ragouts, a vast array of sauces, and such delicate tidbits as quenelles, meringues, and various frozen desserts.

There are some novel presentations. For instance, foods themselves become containers for food. A pumpkin is hollowed out and its entire surface nicked with a knife; it is then covered with a meringue and browned in the oven. This conceit—a real pumpkin imitating a ceramic pumpkin imitating a real pumpkin—is then used as a container for pumpkin soup. Large crayfish shells are used in one recipe to conceal squabs in ragout, while in another the squabs nestle in artichoke bottoms, rather like Titania in the heart of a flower.[19]

The *Cuisinier gascon* (Amsterdam, 1740) is not Gascon (although it does contain a recipe for *garbure*), and there is some question as to whether the author was a *cuisinier*. The book opens with a fulsome dedication to the prince de Dombes—to whom it is sometimes attributed—"at whose side and under whose orders the author has had the honor to work in the kitchen a hundred times."[20] Was the prince so conceited that he dedicated his own book to himself?

This volume has enjoyed a certain notoriety because of the startling names of many of the recipes: green monkey sauce, eggs without malice, veal in the form of donkey droppings, chicken formed like bats, sky blue sauce.[21] The work, however, almost totally lacks organization; sweets tend to be placed toward the end of the book, but it concludes with a baker's dozen of soups. The recipes themselves are somewhat anticlimactic. Sky blue sauce is a cream sauce tinted green with herbs; the donkey droppings are veal birds; the unmalicious eggs are, although tasty, basically just creamed hard-boiled eggs. Many of the recipes are extremely vague: for example, of "calves' tails, glazed, and others" he writes:

> Take scalded calf tails, lard them [this is surely not worth the trouble] and cook them like stewing meat, or braise them; when they are cooked you glaze them; you can put spinach under them, or another vegetable, or you can use a little sauce according to your fancy. You can cook them without larding them, in the Italian manner, or in the Spanish manner, with basil, or grilled.[22]

This confusing advice is not very helpful to the practicing cook. The book is an undigested mixture, which seems to have been put together almost by chance, as if recipes from a variety of sources that had been scribbled onto scraps of paper were assembled almost randomly. The collection lacks stylistic uniformity, and the level of quality is extremely variable. There are detailed, professional-sounding recipes, including several coherent Italian dishes. Again, some of these recipes suggest that the compiler turned to the past for inspiration; other recipes are simple but appetizing. These could have been executed with little time and modest skill, perhaps by a gentleman who wanted to stand briefly by a stove without getting butter on his brocade—perhaps by the prince himself. In *filets à la Cabout*, mutton fillets are sautéed and sliced half an inch thick, then marinated in oil with chopped herbs, after which they are skewered and roasted on a spit. They are to be served with "a piquant sauce of balm and tarragon, highly seasoned."[23] Skewer cookery is a specialty. An especially complicated recipe involves cooking veal thus and then chilling it, still on the skewers; aspic is next molded around it, using special cylindrical molds that have a slot at the bottom for the skewer to pass through. This manner of presentation, *en attelet*, was to be a favorite of Carême's. Not all the recipes are to the modern taste—consider stuffed cow's teats, crumbed, fried in deep fat, and skewered. Nor would most of us enjoy the gratin of stuffed calves' eyes, also crumbed and fried, served up with a green sauce. He uses ground-up rabbit bones in a *coulis* and serves "chicken in bagpipes" by putting them into lambs' bladders, blown up by the cook.[24]

The cuisinier gascon uses the basic mixtures much less than do other eighteenth-century cooks, considering them a trifle old-fashioned: "I will not speak at all of *jus*, *coulis*, bouillon, essence, and all those old liaisons which are made; they are found in the book of Martialot [sic] in his old manuscripts [sic]."[25] Old though they may have been, this is the first time Massialot, if it is he, has been mentioned by name in another cookbook. Two basic mixtures appear here for the first time: a *chiffonnade*, printed or perhaps misprinted as *chifouade*, and a *macedoine*. The first occurs as a mixture of leaf and root vegetables "cut in fillets, as for a julienne" and used in a clear meat broth. The *macedoine à la Paysanne* is composed of peas, broad (fava) beans, green beans diced to the size of a pea, and carrot slices, the whole being cooked in butter.[26]

The Italian recipes include lasagna, ravioli, polpette, and gnocchi, the last being camouflaged as "nioc." The *Cuisinier gascon* also gives, as Italian, recipes for two varieties of what he calls "strouille," one sweet and the other savory.[27] They appear to be strudels, and I cannot explain their appearance

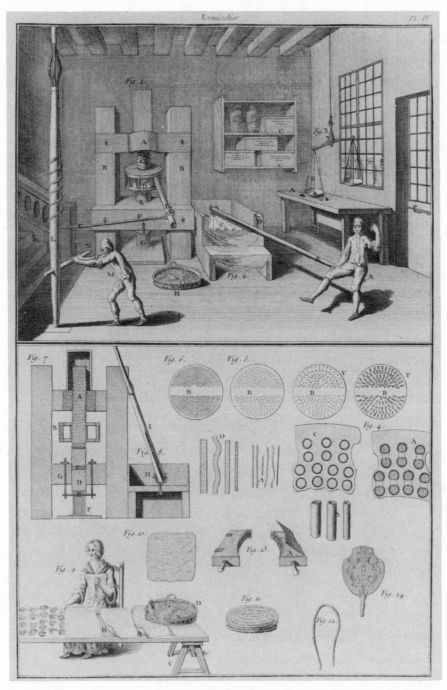

The manufacture of noodles, engraving from Paul Jacques Malouin, *Description des arts et métiers* (Paris, 1767). The man sitting on the long pole is bouncing up and down to knead the dough; on the left another workman is applying the force that turns the screw to extrude the pasta dough through one of the grids illustrated in the lower part of the plate. Flat, round, and tubular noodles of various sizes were produced. The fan (Figure 14) is used, Malouin tells us, to cool the pasta as it comes from the press. (By permission of the Department of Special Collections, Iowa State University Library.)

in Italian guise, save that Italian food of all sorts enjoyed a considerable vogue in mid-eighteenth-century France. Two years later La Chapelle included several Italian recipes in the fifth volume of *Le Cuisinier moderne*, which were intended to bring the work up-to-date.[28] Menon and Marin, too, give some attention to pasta, including soups garnished with it and oven-baked dishes. It was manufactured in France, in both flat and tubular form, though the pasta imported from Italy was the most highly regarded.[29]

The *Cuisinier gascon*'s more complicated recipes are sometimes merely frivolous. For example, roast chicken meat is sauced with the liquid pressed from the carcasses of partially roasted ducks, and elsewhere he calls for duck legs, saying that one can do whatever one wishes with the breasts.[30] An exceptionally picturesque dish is one in which poached eggs, under a sauce, are arranged alternately with crumbed, fried eggshells filled with braised larks, which are arranged with their heads sticking out of the shell.[31] Taken altogether, this uneven little volume is full of interest. If it had been more rigorously assembled, it would have been a better book; as it is it embodies the fleeting tastes of the fashion-intoxicated moment.

Marin ranks with Menon and above the compiler of the *Cuisinier gascon* among the chief cookbook writers of his day. Had he published no more than the 1739 and 1740 editions of *Les Dons de Comus ou les délices de la table*, we would know him only as the author of the first *abrégé de cuisine*, a handy little reference guide like those still used today—not recipe collections but prompt-books for maîtres d'hôtel and cooks.[32] The methodical nature of French cooking makes it uniquely suited to such treatment. But in the later editions Marin built upon this beginning; they are replete with well-structured and refined recipes, and they earn him a place among the preeminent cooks of the century.

In those first editions he describes his work as a summary of the modern cuisine, "a complete body of cookery." His sauce chapter is the keystone of the book. Until this time sauces had taken second place to the coarser, more robust *coulis* and *jus*. His selection is, he says, "a small part of the new sauces which I judged to be most suitable to give an idea of modern cookery."[33] His sauces are smoother in texture than earlier ones, depending for flavor and consistency upon the reduction of stocks. Although light in texture, they were expensive to make and still are. "It is true today, with all people of good taste, that the goodness of a meal—soups, hors d'oeuvres, entrées, entremets—is almost entirely dependent upon the substances of the stock which is the foundation of it." So for one quart of finished quintessence or *restaurant*, he uses four or five pounds of veal, a quarter of a pound of ham, and a boiling fowl, as well as onion, beef marrow, carrots, parsnips, and a fair amount of time and effort. An earlier cook could have used mutton as well. The resulting *restaurant* "should not be at all sharp or too strong, but soft, unctuous, and of a kind which will be useful to all sauces which usually contain these ingredients." He advises against the common practice of adding strongly flavored seasonings, concluding that "I am for the simplest method [!], and I believe that it is the best for taste and for health."[34] His consommé is an opulent broth, made from beef, veal, partridges, fowl, root vegetables, and spices, and the making of it "demands very close attention. It should be yellow as gold, soft, unctuous, and invigorating. It is used to give body to certain clear soups and to make little light sauces."[35] How he accomplishes this is demonstrated in what he calls a "sauce which can be used for a good many things."

> Put a spoonful of oil in a saucepan, one-half a *septier* [= one-half pound] quintessence, half a glass of champagne, an ordinary bouquet, three mushrooms, two shallots, and some parsley, all minced fine, a slice of ham, salt, and pepper. Boil everything together, letting it bubble five or six times; when you have tasted it, squeeze in a sour orange.[36]

La nouvelle cuisine, then as now, may be both fresh and refined, but it is neither simple nor cheap. This sauce is not based on a rich interplay of more elementary mixtures, and it is that which was to be one of the great and lasting contributions of nineteenth-century chefs. Marin's sauce is more in tune with our own day than with the era that flourished from Carême to Escoffier and beyond. The techniques were available, and were in use, but they had not assumed the importance that they would later.

The two- and three-volume editions of *Les Dons de Comus* are far more than a sequel to the first, though they were initially published as such. They are in fact the chief part of Marin's work. He writes very much as a practicing cook and one not above deceptions. He suggests, for example, that a *contrefilet* of beef, carved very thin across the grain, "when the guests have not seen it carved, can, if necessary, pass for fillet."[37] His occasional descriptions of techniques are some of the best from the period. He can ingeniously compose one of his sample menus primarily with the leftovers from the previous one. It is just as well, for he never stints with costly ingredients.

He neither strains for effect like the cuisinier gascon nor repeats himself mechanically like Vincent La Chapelle. Except for the obligatory "English"
puddings, masquerading as "poutinade," and some pasta, such as vermicelli
soup, his inventions stay within the French tradition, in which he exhibits
absolute confidence.

The *Traité historique et pratique de la cuisine. Ou le cuisinier instruit* (2 volumes, Paris, 1758) was the last of the notable prerevolutionary cookbooks,
but it probably supplies the best single introduction to eighteenth-century
French cookery. Along with a sizable collection of superior recipes it has
three special characteristics. First, it opens with a consolidated table of contents, with a pair of parallel vertical columns to represent the two volumes.
Cross-referencing is thus neatly handled. The table is also divided by recipe
type, so that, for example, all the basic mixtures can be found by looking in
a single place.[38] This is a considerable improvement over the other midcentury multivolume cookbooks, whose separate indexes for each volume make
recipe searches slow and clumsy. Second, the *Traité historique et pratique* is the
first French cookbook to use illustrations of how foods are to be presented
and, so far as I know, the only one before the Revolution. There are, however, only a few, and they are very crude.[39] The most striking are a pair of
rabbits, presented vis-à-vis, an imitation dolphin, and a galley. The rabbits
are skinned, right down to their eartips, cut off behind the shoulders, and
terminated with curling forcemeat tails; they are arranged facing each other
but slightly overlapped and are braised. At table they would have presented
an appearance fully as grotesque as anything imagined by a medieval cook.
The dolphin is more poetic but still basically forcemeat, hand-shaped according to the cook's inner vision. Most extravagant of all is a galley. Its hull
is made of forcemeat baked in a specially shaped container. When cooked
the meat is unmolded and filled with little birds in a ragout; they in turn are
hidden under planking made of veal. From each side of the ship project
skewers laden with sweetbreads, cockscombs, meaty bacon, and foies gras.
The mast is a larger skewer that flies a cockscomb pennant, and it is fes-
tooned with sausage-hung rigging—truly a caravel from the Land of Cock-
aigne! One is reminded of the extravagant headdresses worn by court ladies
at about the same time. The author concludes with a note of warning: the
person serving this production should be told how to go about it—to look
under the squares of veal to find the ragout, for example. The third very
good feature of this treatise is the way its author keeps interrupting himself

to make explanatory asides. The reader really can become a *cuisinier instruit*— a well-informed cook. One is reminded of the author of the *Ménagier de Paris*, sharing a rich store of information and a zeal for detail. As a result, this all-too-scarce work is a delight to read and even more useful than the Clermont translation-adaptation of *Soupers de la cour* in helping interpret *ancien régime* recipes. The author suggests variations in recipes and ways to use leftovers and to present standard fare; for example, some thirty-one sauces, ragouts, and garnishes for roast chicken are listed.[40] Best of all, there are many excellent definitions. For example, a *marinade* "is a sauce in which one puts things to soak when one wants to accentuate the flavor, and which one wishes to make more agreeable. There are two kinds of marinade, to wit, the marinade of vinegar or white wine with brandy, and the marinade of butter or oil. One puts into these marinades salt, pepper, clove, with parsley, scallions, and fines herbes, whole or chopped, according to what is needed."[41] He goes on to say that marinated foods are roasted, grilled, or fried and may be used either as independent dishes or as garnishes, and he tells the reader where to find particular recipes.

The recipes range from the simple to the very complicated. In general, practicality rules, but in some cases elaborately patterned arrangements of multicolored egg whites are used to decorate the sides of timbales, as was to be done more extensively in the following century.[42] Some of the recipes for large whole fish with extensive garnishes, such as the *carpe à la royale*, foreshadow Carême's constructions in the first decades of the next century.

Vicaire attributes the *Traité historique et pratique* to Menon, though without giving any reasons.[43] A comparison of it with works that bear Menon's name, such as *La Nouvelle cuisine*, *La Cuisinière bourgeoise*, and *La Science du maître d'hôtel, confiseur*, does not, to my mind, strengthen the claim. Sugar is clarified in the *Confiseur* by dissolving it in water and boiling it with a beaten egg white; the *Traité abrégé de la maniere de faire quelques confitures* contained in the *Traité historique* clarifies it with egg whites and yolks and with the crushed eggshells. The *Confiseur* describes the stages of boiling sugar in much greater detail than the *Traité abrégé*.[44] The author of the *Traité historique* writes in the preface, "I have by no means followed those recent writers on cookery, who in speaking of each ingredient point out and determine whether they are good or bad for health; that is only good for intimidating hypochondriacs [*malades imaginaires*], whose number is already too great. . . . I by no means claim to give lessons to those great *officiers* who have the honor of serving the tables of princes, who are better informed than I; I only want to share my experience with those who are novices in this profession, and who may long remain so for want of being instructed." This instruction Menon had given nearly twenty years before in his *Nouveau traité*. The successful author of the *Cuisinière bourgeoise* had allowed his name to appear on earlier books and would surely have done so again; there was no reason for him to keep his identity a secret.

Menon was the most prolific writer of cookbooks in eighteenth-century France. Nothing is known about his life, but although he may not have written all the cookbooks attributed to him, those works that are clearly his establish his right to be considered the most important culinary author of his age.[45] He wrote books for both large and small households. For the latter he wrote *La Cuisinière bourgeoise* (Paris, 1746), for the former, *La Science du maître d'hôtel, cuisinier*, *La Science du maître d'hôtel, confiseur*, which has been discussed in chapter 10, and *Nouveau traité de la cuisine*.[46]

The tradition of *haute cuisine* is well represented in Menon's *Nouveau traité de la cuisine. Avec de nouveaux desseins de tables et vingt-quartre menus; où l'on apprend ce que l'on doit servir suivant chaque saison, en gras, en maigre, et en pâtisserie; et très-utiles à toutes les personnes qui s'en mêlent, tant pour ordonner, que pour exécuter toutes sortes de nouveaux ragoûts, et des plus à la mode*. The author's style is sober and lucid, and his book is full of appetizing recipes. The *coulis* are rather old-fashioned; while his contemporaries were straining them (sometimes with a silk cloth to absorb every last drop of fat), he was still adding finely ground or pounded meats. The recipes are carefully thought out. His *ballon de dindon* is an example: a saucepan (doing temporary service as a mold) is lined with turkey skin, and the skin is lined with ground bacon and herbs, then filled with alternating layers of turkey, mushrooms, and ham, seasoned with herbs and garlic. The skin is then folded over the mixture and sewn up, and the whole thing is wrapped in a cloth. The resulting *ballon* is taken from the saucepan and set in a cooking pot that has been lined with pork fat and moistened with broth. It is cooked at a slow simmer. When done it is unswathed and presented with a band of cauliflower around it as a garnish.[47]

The mid-eighteenth-century French cook commanded a range of working methods that was unrivaled in Europe. This sense of mastery is expressed in an anecdote related by Marin:

Everything can be made acceptable if you know how to prepare it, and it is not yet twenty years since a famous caterer served to some gentlemen (for the lack of other meats) an old pair of water-buffalo leather gloves, shredded and stewed, with onions, mustard, and vinegar, which they found excellent as long as they did not know what they were eating.[48]

Marin has summed up the state of his art. The skilled cook could cook anything and cook it very well.

This skill was shared by female cooks, and in midcentury Menon, after publishing his treatise on the new cookery, addressed them, in *La Cuisinière bourgeoise* of 1746. It is the first French cookbook devoted exclusively to "la cuisine des femmes," or women's cooking, to use the current phrase. Cookbooks had been written for and even by women in sixteenth- and seventeenth-century England, Germany, and Holland, but France had lagged behind.[49] Can this have been the result of a lower level of female literacy, or does it reflect a different set of expectations of those women who were literate?

La Cuisinière bourgeoise—especially the expanded editions dating from 1752 onward—probably contains more good practical ideas for the modern cook than any other prerevolutionary cookbook. Menon writes that he has attempted to avoid expense, to simplify the methods, and to reduce to the levels of bourgeois kitchens that which does not seem to be reserved to opulent ones. "If appearance and taste lose something here, health gains, and the bourgeois garners the advantages of enjoying a diversity of foods at small expense and of avoiding the indispositions consequent upon an over-refined style of cooking [*une cuisine trop recherchée*]."[50] And he is indeed prepared to be careful about small things:

Everyone thinks he or she knows how to boil an egg in its shell. Many people in fact cook them too much or not enough. So that you cannot fail, when the water comes to a boil, put them in to boil for two minutes, rather less than more, take them off the fire and cover them for one minute to let them make their milk, and serve them in a napkin.[51]

If the cooking time seems short, remember that the eggs were already at room temperature when they went into the water and were smaller than ours.

L'ŒCONOME.

Quel prodige! une femme a des soins plus flateurs
Derobe un temps qu'elle donne au menage.
Ce tableau simple du vieux âge
Est pris dans la nature et non pas dans nos mœurs.

Tiré du Cabinet du Roy de Suède dessiné par Renn d'après le Tableau Original.

á Paris chéz J.Ph.Le Bas Graveur du Cabinet du Roy rue de la Harpe.

Chardin pinx.   *J.Ph. Le Bas sculp. An.1754.*

LŒconome, or The Housekeeper, engraving by Jacques Philippe Le Bas after J.B.S. Chardin (1754). Here we see a literate housekeeper working on her accounts, though a verse below states that this does not reflect contemporary custom. The compartmented basket is designed for carrying wine and liqueur bottles; the tall package in the lower left-hand corner contains a sugar loaf. (Courtesy of the Museum of Fine Arts, Boston, Babcock Bequest.)

Among the homely fare are *rôties*: slices of fried bread spread with a savory or sweet mixture and then baked. In one variation (an ancestor of the now ubiquitous *croque monsieur*), a loaf of bread is larded with strips of bacon, sliced, dipped in beaten egg, and fried. A sweet version consists of bread spread with almond-flavored pastry cream, covered with meringue, and baked until golden.[52]

Elaborate preliminary mixtures are kept to a minimum. A basic *coulis bourgeois* serves in a number of sauces, where a more elaborate cookbook would use several different kinds of *coulis*. Nonetheless, the cook was encouraged to take a well-thought-out, systematic view of her materials. Here is Menon's thorough introductory discussion of the leg of veal:

> The leg, which includes the round and the shank, is, so to speak, the soul of the kitchen, because from it is made: *jus* of veal; *restaurants* [rich broths]; *coulis bourgeois*, *coulis* of partridge, *coulis* of woodcock, and all kinds of sauces [which he enumerates], in addition to all kinds of little sauces in the new taste. It is used to give substance to several little braising mixtures and to make forcemeats, large and small pâtés, and many different kinds of entrées, such as sirloin served with all kinds of vegetables; veal birds; veal loaves; . . . grilled sirloin; sirloin cooked between two plates in the bourgeois style; sirloin à la Chantilly. The shank is given to the gouty and is also used to make meat jellies for the sick.[53]

How different this is from the *Cuisinier gascon*'s random observations!

"After meat," Menon writes, "nothing furnishes a greater diversity in cooking than eggs." Shirred eggs, eggs in browned butter, à la tripe (augmented with sautéed cucumber) are all present, as well as omelets and poached eggs. He adds some medical uses: to relieve rheumatism, an egg yolk is stirred into hot sugared water (*lait de poule*) and drunk at bedtime; the beaten white is applied to sore eyes; and the membrane from inside the shell is powdered and used on fever blisters.[54] Even the shell may be used, either as toothpaste or as a component in glue to mend china. Plainly, the cook in a bourgeois household was closely involved in the daily events of her employers' lives.

In the eighteenth-century view, the bourgeoisie was supposed to be satisfied with a diet suitable to its station in life. It was not, of course, content. Alain Girard has pointed out that it is "a cuisine of compromise, less costly" than *haute cuisine*, evoking ancestral simplicity to justify financial limitations.[55] It exceeded these limitations whenever possible. The aristocracy was not content to be restricted to its station either. In the preface to *La Cuisinière bourgeoise*, Menon writes that he has written it "at the request of a number of persons of distinction who have urged me to give it . . . to the public because it is to the taste of many great lords, especially those who care about their health." One nobleman who had a copy of *La Cuisinière bourgeoise* in his library alongside *Les Dons de Comus* (in the three-volume edition of 1758) and *Cuisine et office de santé* was the duc de Chaulnes.[56] The aristocracy's interest in bourgeois food was related to the idealized view it had of the bourgeois way of life in midcentury. Louis XV's *soupers intimes* were another manifestation of this feeling. Yet another was the collecting, by royalty and the aristocracy, of the paintings of domestic interiors and kitchen still lifes by Jean Baptiste Siméon Chardin, which illustrate the ambience of the well-ordered bourgeois household.[57]

Voltaire as Host and Diner

There were in practice few distinctly drawn social boundaries in the France of the *ancien régime*. Although in retrospect increasingly divergent tendencies toward the *haute cuisine* style and the bourgeois style can be identified in the history of fine cooking, it is difficult in practice to sort out one from the other. Voltaire, in his life as in his eating habits, reflected these ambiguities. Early in life he elected to add the aristocratic "de Voltaire" to his baptismal name of François Marie Arouet given him by his father, a notary. In his writings he was both an arbiter of taste for the nobility and a critic of its pretensions and privileges. The subversive character of his thought obliged him to live close to the Swiss border, where he could easily slip beyond the authority of the French government, and yet he was protected and subsidized by the highest court circles of France and was cosseted by the royalty and nobility of all Europe.

Voltaire loved to live well. He entertained lavishly, and his domestic arrangements at Les Délices were aristocratic in scale. But his was an aristocracy of taste, of the intellect, and of personal achievement, rather than of title and of inherited privilege. Perhaps, then, his tastes in dining can best be perceived as reflecting the refined tastes of the *haute bourgeoisie*.

Voltaire's vast correspondence contains many references to food and meals. In his early years he participated fully in the life of Parisian intellectual society—a life of suppers at which everyone talked at once and no one listened.

After one such dinner Voltaire wrote to one of his hosts: "Socrates gave lessons in bed, you give them at table."[58] They exchanged gifts of food to accompany the writings that were circulating so rapidly. In one case a wild boar arrived with a poem; another time a tragedy was accompanied by a deer.[59] One grateful friend joined to his thanks a dozen baskets of apricots, "the best we have been able to find here."[60] Voltaire thanks a correspondent: "His partridges and his ideas have been received—both are good."[61] One is reminded of how gifts of food were used in social exchanges in the sixteenth century.

When Voltaire grew rich he began to indulge his taste for hospitality; he hired good cooks. Among his acquaintances was Gaspard Grimod de La Reynière, the grandfather of the author of the *Almanachs des Gourmands*. Gaspard was a wealthy tax farmer, who sometimes acted as an intermediary for Voltaire's correspondence, receiving and transmitting under his own name books and letters that would have been opened and perhaps confiscated if they had traveled under Voltaire's.[62] He was famous for the excellence of his kitchens, both in his Paris residence and at his château, which was conveniently located on the road to Versailles. In 1745 Voltaire wrote him to ask if his cook might serve as assistant to Gaspard's for a few days. "It is not that I aspire to serve as good fare as you. But a cook gets rusty working for a sick man . . . and one must protect the fine arts."[63] Even when Voltaire was too ill to eat, he thought of his friends, and even after he left Paris he went to some trouble to employ good cooks.

He viewed his cooks, though, as a decidedly mixed blessing, repeatedly pairing them with doctors in his thoughts. His friend, the duc de Richelieu (Clouet's erstwhile employer), was known for serving superb and luxurious food, but Voltaire said that the duke's cook did him a lot of harm, that he had "passed through the hands of doctors, charlatans and cooks."[64] "Ah, my friend, how good fat hazel-hens are, but how hard they are to digest! My cook and my apothecary are killing me." The indigestion must have passed, for three weeks later he wrote that "a good cook is a fine doctor too."[65] In a letter to a Polish nobleman at the Prussian court in Berlin, who wanted a French or French-trained cook, he described what would be in store for an apprentice:

I am not surprised that you should want good cooks. You may send yours to me. But this is how the great art of *la nouvelle cuisine* is practiced, and these are its august laws: A young pupil puts himself under the direction of one of these illustrious poisoners who ruin families by giving them apoplexies, bloody fluxes, and malignant fevers in ragouts and hors d'oeuvres; the pupil pays his teacher, at least until he knows enough to be received as an assistant [in the kitchen of one of] our sybarites, and I would not presume that a Silesian would be so expert in our great art as to be raised to the dignity of kitchen assistant upon arriving in Paris.[66]

Voltaire used the contrast between the old and new styles of cooking as a metaphor to describe the relationship between his work and that of others. Over the decades his view of his place among the styles of cooking changed, just as it changed among writers and philosophers. In his early years he described himself as a practitioner of the *nouvelle cuisine*. As reactions to his ideas polarized he sometimes found it prudent to disavow his own writings. For example, his *Dîner du comte de Bovlainvilliers*, which was antireligious, met with much opposition, and in 1768 Voltaire was busy repudiating it: "I am by no means the cook who made this dinner. One cannot serve this kind of dish in Europe without someone saying that it is in my style. Some claim that this new cookery is excellent, that it may be health-giving, and especially that it may cure the vapors. Those who adhere to the old cuisine say that these new Martialo [Massialots] are poisoners. In any case, I by no means wish to pass for a public caterer."[67] Later he was to write about his play *Irène* as "a little supper which I prepared. . . . The news of this little party I was preparing became known to some cooks who prepared similar meals, more highly spiced than mine. This competition intimidated me, and I destined for you [his correspondent] another supper [*Agathocle*] of five courses. Perhaps the ranges [*fourneaux*] have overheated my head, and I will be obliged to renounce my trade of Martialo." Work on the play progressed slowly, and a few weeks later he was writing again that "your old cook, my dear angel, is very far from cooking you good fare. He is reduced to apothecaries, and very surprised to be alive still. Nonetheless he does not want to die without sending you the five pâtés which he promised you. . . . I don't know if they are of the old style of cookery or of the new. I cannot eat any of the new dishes that they have sent me from Paris, but my disgust by no means proves that I have succeeded better than the young cooks of the present time." Soon, in a mood of discouragement, he adds, "I had taken up my former trade of cook to console me; I am only too conscious upon thinking it over that I understand nothing of the new cookery, and the old is out of fashion." [68]

Voltaire would not have used cookery as a metaphor for his writing if the pleasures of the table had not been real to him. In 1754 he took up residence near Geneva, and over the years he owned a series of houses in the vicinity, devoting most of his attention to Les Délices and then to Ferney. He was wealthy, famous, and hospitable. His correspondence includes an enticing array of invitations. People came from all over Europe to visit him, and, if possible, to sit at his table. Scholars have observed that he spoke of his estates largely in terms of gardens. Similarly, his invitations hold out the inducement of local delicacies, such as, "Come and eat our trout and cream." He offers "a truffled turkey as tender as a squab and as fat as the bishop of Geneva." "A new tragedy and a trout are all we can give you here." As time passed the pleasure of receiving crowds of sightseeing travelers diminished, and in 1768 he wrote that he had retired from being "Europe's innkeeper." Nonetheless, up to the end of his life he continued to meet briefly, almost daily, with those who came to stare at him. The young James Boswell, making the Grand Tour, importuned Voltaire's niece, Madame Denis, in his own characteristic style, for an invitation to dinner with the sage and begged to be allowed to spend the night. "I shall not even refuse to sleep upon two chairs in the bedchamber of your maid. I saw her pass thro' the room where we sat before dinner." In the earlier years Voltaire's table was lavishly served, and at one point his household numbered thirty. One visitor left complaining of indigestion brought on by an excess of trout and cream served her— she might have added of greed in eating it. Even Voltaire wrote at one point that the grand dinners were killing him. After his niece came to live with him her indigestions are recorded, too. She was said to have had "the gift of furnishing houses and serving good fare in them." Voltaire scolded her repeatedly for overeating, with no apparent success, since by 1773 he was writing that she was "as fat as an abbess." Occasionally she rued her self-indulgence: "I love pleasure no more; the suppers are killing me." But soon thereafter Voltaire wrote that she "has regained all her vigor, and now takes her four daily meals." When a friend sent skate and codfish (ocean fish was a delicacy so far inland) Madame Denis hastened to eat both, "for fear they would spoil." The next year she was again found "gorging" on ocean fish and later feasting on a partridge pie which her uncle was too ill to eat. [69]

The problem of supplying these fast-emptying tables received Voltaire's close attention. He ordered casks of wine, bottles by the thousand, corks as many as three thousand at a time. Beaujolais was his favorite wine; on one occasion he topped off the casks with Burgundy, which has not, I think, been done in recent years. Coffee, sugar, and chocolate were ordered repeatedly. There were problems with adulteration—fava beans had been mixed in with the coffee in one shipment—and with pilferage in transit. The carters drank fifty bottles of Malaga from one order; Voltaire said he was glad that they would at least not drink the olive oil. Even at home there were depredations; he was obliged to order "cheap oil for the gardeners, who eat all the salads."[70]

When Candide spoke of cultivating his garden, he and Voltaire had more than just horticulture in mind, but in taking gardening as a metaphor Voltaire was evoking a real activity that was an important part of his own life. As soon as he established himself at Les Délices in 1755 he began to make a garden. He asked friends to send him lavender, he planted Egyptian onions, strawberries, and artichokes; his bankers sent gold, diamonds, and seeds— "but the seeds are the most precious." Misfortune visited the garden: the seeds did not always grow, and he could not get all the plants he wanted. Voltaire was a true gardener, though, and after disappointments he always began afresh the following spring. He badgered his friends for more seeds— even Frederick the Great sent them—and walls in the kitchen garden supported espaliered fruit trees. The gardener besieged him with demands and quarreled with the coachman over a load of sand. A poultry yard was established, and Voltaire attempted to increase its stock. Later he kept pheasants and turkeys and made an unsuccessful attempt to establish partridges. Eggs were sent, but the moss in which they were packed was disarranged by a customs inspector; nearly all were broken and the remainder did not hatch. Next he asked a friend to bring a male partridge with him when he came to visit: "The poor spinster you brought us is dying of *ennui* because she has no lover." Eventually he was able to enjoy fresh produce all the year around; he had learned that "the real secret to successful gardening is to spend a lot of money," and, he might have added, patience.[71]

How Voltaire viewed his domain can be seen in several of his letters. He deceptively called himself a hermit, and, paraphrasing La Fontaine, "a rat retired into his Gruyère cheese." He offered one prospective visitor "milk from our cows, honey from our bees, and strawberries from our gardens." His estate was a rural utopia. After he moved to Ferney, the emphasis of his

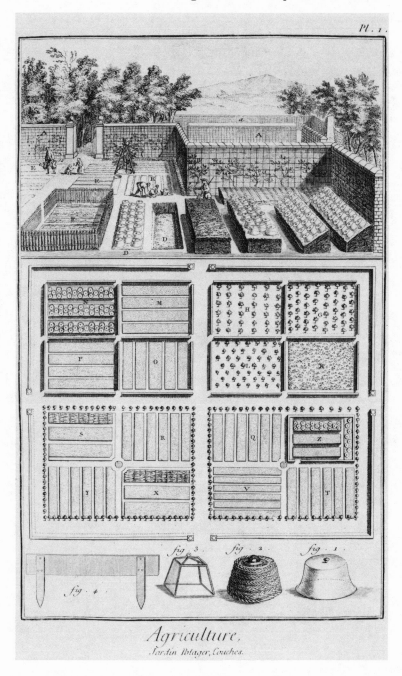

The kitchen garden and forcing beds, engraving, from *Encyclopédie: Recueil de planches . . .* (Paris, 1763–77). Above, the kitchen garden, built to receive the maximum warmth and light from the sun. The walls support espaliered fruit trees, and forcing beds are slanted south. Below, the *cloches*, made from leaded or blown glass and from straw, serve to protect plants set out early in the growing season. The plan shows plantings of fruit, vegetables, and orchard trees. Olivier de Serres and Bonnefons would have thought this beautifully articulated garden paradise, and Voltaire would have felt at home; there is even a melon bed. (By permission of the Houghton Library, Harvard University.)

LE RAT QUI S'EST RETIRÉ DU MONDE . Fable CXXVII.

J.B. Oudry inv.   *J. Ribaud sculp.*

The Rat Who Withdrew from Society, engraving by J. Ribaud after J. B. Oudry from Jean de
La Fontaine, *Fables* (Paris, 1755–59). A typical storage cellar, with typical rats. The wicker
cage is a variety of meat-safe; hung in a cool and airy place the meat will spoil less quickly
and is relatively safe from vermin. The basket probably contains eggs and the crock under
the shelf some sort of pickle. The housewife is regularly advised to inspect her stores frequently. (By permission of the Houghton Library, Harvard University.)

gardening changed. He did not cease to plant orchards or to beg his friends for roots and shoots and seeds, but he began to work to improve the lives of his tenants. In July of 1770 he wrote about how he had brought in settlers from around Geneva, building houses for them and encouraging the manufacture of watches. He was skeptical of foreign investment: "True riches are at home; they are in our work. I see that with my own eyes. My wheat feeds all my servants; my bad wine, which is by no means unwholesome, gives them drink; my silkworms give stockings; my bees supply excellent honey and wax; my hemp and flax supply linens. They call this life patriarchal, but no patriarch had such a farmstead as mine, and I doubt that Abraham's chickens were better than mine."[72]

When there were difficulties in getting flour for bread to supply the people of Ferney, he experimented with the use of potato starch in baking, and the results so pleased him that he wrote Parmentier to describe the "very savorous bread" obtained with equal parts of wheat and potato flour.[73] One is reminded of the books of Bonnefons, the *Jardinier françois* and *Les Delices de la campagne*, written more than a century before. The tradition of living well off one's own land was solidly rooted.

For all its continuities with the style of life of the seventeenth-century *haute bourgeoisie*, Voltaire's life on his estates exhibited changes as well. In his relations with the traditional aristocracy, the balance had shifted: it was they who sought him out because of his achievements as an individual; acquaintance with him conferred distinction; he established the standards of wit and elegance. Similarly, his relationship with the peasantry was different. Whereas, in the seventeenth century, actual agricultural practices had been beneath the notice of the proprietor and had been generally conservative, by the end of the eighteenth century, Voltaire assumed the role of the "gentleman farmer," interesting himself in the affairs of his peasantry and in the technological innovations of the day. In the seventeenth century the bourgeois household had used its control of land to assure itself of an adequate food supply in times of famine and to accumulate a surplus that could be sold to the less prosperous at an extortionate profit. Voltaire concerned himself with assuring and improving the material well-being of his dependents and with experiments in adopting the new agricultural techniques to tide them over during times of want. In these as in many other respects, Voltaire epitomized changing social and cultural conditions in France in the last years of the *ancien régime*.

CHAPTER TWELVE

The Late Eighteenth Century

N THE THREE AND A HALF DECADES between the publication of *Les Soupers de la cour* and the outbreak of the Revolution, cooks were virtually silent. Earlier cookbooks continued to be reprinted, sometimes with revisions, and a few volumes were published dealing with specialized fields. Why the cooks should have ceased to record new inventions is not clear; the ongoing reprinting of older works attests to the continued presence of buyers for cookbooks.[1] Instead, in this last generation of the *ancien régime*, the people who wrote about food and dining were philosophers, encyclopedists, and technicians.

Two aspects of late eighteenth-century French romantic antiquarianism bear on gastronomy: the neoclassical and the gothicizing. The neoclassicism is reflected in the attitudes of people writing about food who adopted the two extremes of ancient eating patterns for their own uses. At one pole is the farm-oriented simplicity of Virgil and Varro; at the other, the decadent, urban excesses of Petronius's Trimalchio. The Virgilian ideal was embraced by Jean-Jacques Rousseau and, to some extent, by the writers of the *Encyclopédie*; Trimalchio's by Grimod de La Reynière. Le Grand d'Aussy, who wrote the first history of the French kitchen and table, manifested the antiquarian spirit that looked to his own country's past times.

TREATISES ON GASTRONOMY

The revisions made of cookbooks consist largely of borrowings from earlier works by other authors. The later editions of the *Cuisinière bourgeoise*, for example, contain a recipe for *fricassée de poulets à la bourdois* which is taken from *Les Soupers de la cour*.[2] The recipe has been rephrased by someone who knows how to cook; a little detail has been added, and some unnecessary matter has been suppressed; the reader is referred elsewhere for further particulars. The added material in these late editions is very good but does not differ in nature or style from the earlier ones.

Two anonymous works mark this final stage: *Le Manuel des officiers de*

bouche of 1759 and *Le Dictionnaire portatif de cuisine* of 1762. Both volumes
are more systematically organized than any that had appeared before. The
Dictionnaire portatif contains definitions of ingredients and procedures, medical observations advising upon the circumstances in which foods are wholesome or harmful, lists of dishes according to their place in menus, and many
recipes. All this material is arranged alphabetically, the key words being
most often ingredients and preparations. The *Manuel* describes itself as a *vade
mecum* in which the reader "will find, abridged, and with enough information, all the procedures, all the mechanisms [*toute la marche, tout le mecha-
nisme*]" which are developed in greater detail in other works.[3] It opens with
an extensive introductory section giving clear, though not discursive, instructions for making some 86 basic preparations, before going on to give
more than 3,500 recipes in 550 pages. The volume concludes with a long
annotated index, which serves as a small dictionary.

Signs of the changes that have taken place over five centuries are to be
seen in the pages of the *Dictionnaire portatif*, which is described in its subtitle
as "a work equally useful to the most able heads [*chefs*] of *cuisine* and *office*,
and to [female] cooks who are only employed for bourgeois tables." Although very much a product of its time, the *Dictionnaire* addresses themes
of longstanding concern to writers and readers of cookbooks. The medical
advice can be traced back before that given by the doctors of Montpellier
who translated Platina's work to the fourteenth-century *Ménagier de Paris*.
As a sign of the anxious times, "medical observations have been added describing the properties of each ingredient, relative to health, and indicating
the dishes most appropriate to each temperament," thus approaching the
ideal that had been suggested facetiously by the cuisinier françois, who pre-
dicted the appearance of a book that listed diseases, from A to Z, and the
ragouts, from Z to A, which would cure them.[4] Some of the recipes are of
considerable antiquity, for example, recipes nearly five hundred years after
the earliest manuscript of the *Viandier* for blancmange made with milk, capon, almonds, sugar, and rosewater; pea purée with bacon; boar's head; and
marzipans.[5] Among the principal kitchen utensils, the mortar and pestle, the
sieve, and the big cooking pot on its adjustable hook over the fire are still
primary tools, though now there is likely to be a waist-high charcoal range
in the kitchen as well. The chef still wears his own pair of knives at his side,
and he still labors strenuously amid heat and steam.

What has changed since the late Middle Ages is the organization of the cook's work and the degree of respect accorded it. The kitchen work described in the *Dictionnaire portatif*, far more than individual dishes, reveals the achievement of these centuries. This difference is reflected in, for example, the recipe for *turbot au coulis d'écrevisses*. The turbot is cooked in a *braise*, which is a rich mixture of veal, bacon, root vegetables, and a bouquet garni, then thickened with a roux, and moistened with a bottle of white wine and some bouillon. It is served with a ragout of crayfish, which is itself thickened with a *coulis* of crayfish.[6] This series of processes (a modern-day computer programmer might call them subroutines) could have been executed without too much trouble in a large kitchen using the methods at every good cook's fingertips. The recording of the entire process would have been unwieldy, if generations of cooks had not learned to articulate and to rationalize their work so clearly. Moreover, recipes written in this system are ideally suited for transmission by a cook who could read to one who knew his or her craft but not his or her letters. The dishes elucidated are the result of much accumulated invention and experiment. Far more than new tools or new ingredients, what eighteenth-century cooks had that their medieval counterparts did not is this system built up by generations of men and women working in kitchens all over France, in the proud consciousness that they were the supreme masters of their craft.

Simultaneously with the appearance of these purely culinary reference works, the great *Encyclopédie* of Diderot and d'Alembert was being published. It included many articles on foods, as well as on the principles of nutrition, agriculture, and even the history of cooking. The principal author of the food-related articles was the chevalier de Jaucourt, a man with a vast supply of factual information and an exceptional capacity for work.[7] The *Encyclopédie*'s coverage of food topics is extremely uneven in extent and thoroughness. It treats in greatest detail food preparation done outside of the house: baking, sugar-cooking, pastrymaking, and the production of cheese. It describes in more detail the manufacture of cooking implements than their use.

The engravings illustrating equipment and craft methods are invaluable because they show in detail how workrooms were organized. They are not intended, however, to inform the craftsmen or entrepreneurs of the crafts. So far as I can see, except for the innumerable foldout table-setting plans, with their attendant menus, pictures in pre-nineteenth-century French cookbooks were not intended to show cooks how to carry out culinary processes.

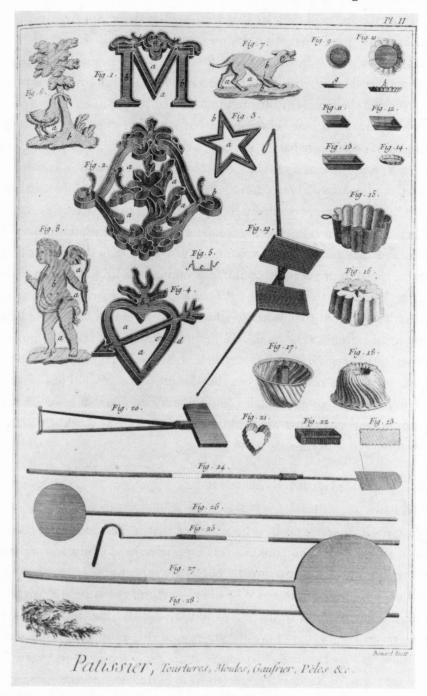

Palissier, Tourteres, Moules, Gaufrier, Pêles &c.

Equipment for the pastrycook, engraving, from *Encyclopédie: Recueil de planches* . . . (Paris, 1763–77). The very elaborate cutters are for marzipan; the small fluted pans are for *biscuits* and pastries. These plates, which were made to accompany the *Encyclopédie*, are addressed more to the general public with an interest in the arts and crafts than to practitioners of specific crafts; the emphasis is on tools and settings, not on instructing the observer. (By permission of the Houghton Library, Harvard University.)

The maître d'hôtel and educated general readers were apparently the intended audience for the few illustrations.[8] Similarly, in the *Encyclopédie*, the authors usually give information specific enough to be used in the kitchen only in articles dealing with food production, for example, with the raising of apricots and their subsequent preservation and preparation.

As Jean-Claude Bonnet has pointed out, Jaucourt conceived of the development of cooking as paralleling the development of language and social structure as a process of increasing complexity.[9] This was also to some extent Le Grand d'Aussy's view, though it is not one that can withstand much scrutiny by ethnographers. Precisely because food is a part of everyone's lives, it is available in every society for use as a carrier of meaning, as a social marker, and as a medium of exchange. Even a very modest gastronomic apparatus can support very complicated meanings. In Jaucourt's view, however, the elaborate banquets of the Romans (paralleling similar meals in his own day) represented the destructiveness of a cuisine that had carried elaboration to an extreme. The cook's sin lies in making food taste so good that the diner eats beyond his body's need. Pity the poor cook: the greater his skill, the greater his sin! The ragout thus becomes the symbol of poisonous temptation. Small wonder Voltaire could not decide whether his cook was a friend or an enemy or that the wickedness of cooks was so clearly seen by Rousseau.[10]

Rousseau and Grimod de La Reynière

If Voltaire was of two minds about the wholesomeness of fine cooking, Jean-Jacques Rousseau was not: he was sure that it was pernicious, and he was also sure that French cooking was especially bad. Children ought not be to brought up with a taste for it. "Let us not raise Emile so that he would die of hunger in other countries if he did not take a French cook everywhere with him in his suite, or so that he would say one day that they only know how to eat in France. . . . I would say myself that only the French do *not* know how to eat, because so specialized an art is required to make food eatable for them."[11] Rousseau preferred fresh ingredients of local origin, and he shared the general eighteenth-century passion for coffee (though it can hardly be called local). His preferred meal was impromptu and vegetarian: "If I am given milk, eggs, salad, cheese, brown bread, and ordinary wine I am sufficiently entertained."[12] It is certainly not a bad menu.

His writings about the diet of the young echo the humorous controversy that had taken place in the heyday of the vogue for *la nouvelle cuisine*, during the 1740s between the *Pâtissier anglois* and the *Cuisinier françois*, but Rousseau developed it seriously. Many of his attitudes chime with modern ones. We have, for example, assimilated his advice on feeding the young. From the moment the newborn child is put to its mother's breast, the food and the manner in which he gets it are a part of his formation. Rousseau states that "of our diverse sensations, taste gives those which generally affect us the most, [but it] has the least to say to the imagination, and is therefore not useful in a child's education." "Tender and voluptuous hearts, passionate and truly sensitive characters easily moved by the other senses, are indifferent enough to this one." [13] Rather puzzlingly, he goes on to say that smell is the sense associated with the imagination; apparently he had never noticed how closely it interacts with taste.

Rousseau begins by stipulating that the nursing mother's diet must be plain: "It is seasoning alone which makes [foods] unwholesome. Reform the rules of our cooking; have neither flour-thickening nor frying; butter, salt, and dairy products should never be put over the fire. Your vegetables boiled in water should not be seasoned until they arrive, hot, at the table." [14] The vegetarian diet is preferred because he considers it closer to the diet of man in a primitive state. Meat is not a suitable food for man; children naturally prefer dairy products, fruit, and pastry. Their natural taste should not be distorted to make them carnivores, "if not for the sake of their health, then for the sake of their characters. . . . Meat eaters are generally crueler and more ferocious than other men; this observation is from all places and from all times; English barbarism is known; Parsees, on the contrary, are the gentlest of men." [15] In a detailed examination of Rousseau's ideas about cooking and meals, Jean-Claude Bonnet points out that the philosopher's theoretical preference for a vegetarian diet was linked to his perception that the inequalities of French society enabled the rich to cannibalize the poor. [16]

Rousseau does not wish the diner to repudiate order but to replace the artificial conventions of society with nature's own superior order: "In the service of my table and in the decoration of my lodging I would wish to imitate with very simple ornament the variety of seasons, and to draw from each one all its delights without anticipating those which follow it. . . . The order of nature should not be troubled by wresting involuntary productions from it. . . . Nothing is more insipid than out-of-season fruit and vegetables. . . . If I had cherries when it was freezing and muskmelons in the depths of winter, with what pleasure would I taste them when my palate had no need to be moistened or cooled?"[17]

He considers a woman's household duties, too; his Sophie must have domestic skills. She is greedy but has her greed under control; her tooth is sweet and her taste fastidious. She "understands cooking the *office*" though her delicacy prevents her from performing mundane kitchen chores. Instead, "she serves as her mother's maître d'hôtel" and keeps the household accounts. Her greediness is brought under control when she learns that bonbons would spoil her teeth and that excessive eating would make her fat. Nonetheless, "she has kept the tastes proper for her sex; she likes dairy products and sweets; she likes pastries and entremets, but very little meat; she has never tasted either wine or strong liqueurs. Moreover, she eats very moderately."[18] In a word, her appetites, which might otherwise be dangerous to her innocence, are those of a child.

In contrast to Voltaire, the civilized country host, and to Rousseau, the rediscoverer of nature and spontaneity, Alexandre-Balthazar-Laurent Grimod de La Reynière was the thoroughgoing, calculating gourmand. Although the *Almanachs des gourmands*, for which he is now best known, did not start to appear until 1803, his gastronomic exploits began well before the Revolution.[19]

His grandfather, Gaspard, Voltaire's acquaintance, began his career as a pork butcher and went on to become a purveyor. During the Seven Years' War he supplied the celebrated table of the prince de Soubise. Gaspard was a notorious glutton. Upon his death in 1754, a diarist noted that "M. Grimod de La Reynière died a few days ago of indigestion. He had already had several very dangerous attacks, but he was so gluttonous that he was not able to control himself."[20] The parents of our Grimod were an ill-assorted couple, his mother being of higher rank than his father and exceedingly arrogant. His father was the administrator of postal services, through which he was growing immensely rich. Grimod was born in 1758, with deformed webbed hands. With the assistance of crude prostheses he learned to write and even to draw; the designs for the frontispieces of the *Almanachs des gourmands* are of his invention. He blamed his physical deformity on his mother and hated her for it, as he hated his father for what he felt to be a monstrous social position. Educated for a career in law, he showed an early interest in the theater. He wrote for and about it—he was for some years the drama critic of the *Journal de Neuchâtel*—and lived with a succession of actresses.

He achieved notoriety and at the same time a measure of revenge upon his parents with a remarkable supper he gave in February of 1783. The invitation was calculated to attract attention: it was in the form of a black-bordered invitation to a funeral and featured a picture of a catafalque surmounted with a crucifix. Besides specifying the time of arrival, it instructed the guest to bring neither dog nor servant. Grimod got his parents out of their *hôtel* for the night by telling them that he was going to put on a small display of fireworks in honor of the end of the American Revolution. The guests numbered sixteen, but there were spectators as well. He had distributed some three hundred tickets to people who were permitted to observe the spectacle from a balcony that ran around the dining room. Thus he turned the meal into a kind of bizarre theatrical performance, parodying the public dinners *au grand couvert* which were still taken by the royal family at Versailles. The intended audience was polite society in general. The room was draped in black; the table's centerpiece was a catafalque. One course consisted entirely of pork dishes. Grimod asked his guests if they liked them, and to their assurances that they did he replied that various of his relatives had supplied them, though in fact, by that time none of his family was in the pork trade. Another course featuring dishes prepared with oil was accompanied by a similar exchange. During these dialogues the spectators continued to pass along the balcony. Grimod's maternal uncle was among them; Grimod had him removed for not moving along fast enough. There is some question about how many courses were served; the accounts vary between nine and twenty. By three o'clock in the morning the guests had grown tired, but those attempting to leave found that the doors had been bolted. Seeking an escape via a back staircase, they found that their host had posted guards. Eventually, however, they were allowed to go home, bringing to an end a prime example of the dinner party as an act of aggression.[21]

This was surely one of the oddest meals of the late eighteenth century, but it was not unique. Grimod's parents obtained a *lettre de cachet* exiling him from Paris. Then his father died, and Grimod came into great wealth, which he promptly set about dissipating. He gave a second supper, even more morbid than the first. He arranged to have his own decease announced and then invited friends to a memorial service for himself. They arrived to find him alive and presiding over the table in another black-hung room adorned with a set of black velvet hangings, richly embroidered with representations of *charcuterie*. The table was set with knives and forks whose ivory handles were carved in the form of pigs.[22] Grimod, the would-be dramatist, thus made the dining room his stage, complete with elaborate props. His theater was macabre and sardonic, and his audiences were also his victims. He avenged himself upon the world for his own helplessness by making his guests helpless; and to his parents, for humiliations received, he returned yet more.

Beatrice C. Fink has found references in the meals imagined by the marquis de Sade to Trimalchio's feast in Petronius's *Satiricon*.[23] Grimod, too, may have intended to evoke that meal in the minds of those who heard about his supper. Trimalchio, the former slave, opened his feast with a silver skeleton seated at the table and ended it with a dirge; guests wishing to leave early were not allowed to do so.[24] The feast was a vulgar display of wealth, betraying Trimalchio's base origins. By casting himself in Trimalchio's role, Grimod reinforced the insult to his family.

LE GRAND D'AUSSY, THE FIRST HISTORIAN OF FRENCH COOKERY

The halt in the flow of new cookbooks did not mean that people had ceased to think about food, but their thought took the form of codification and recollection. It is entirely appropriate, therefore, that the first history of French cooking appeared at this time: Le Grand d'Aussy's *Histoire de la vie privée des françois*. He had intended to write a complete social history of the French, including accounts of the history of costume, domestic architecture, furniture, and amusements, but only the first three volumes, all dealing with food and the table, ever appeared. Unfortunately for the modern reader, he tells little about the cuisine of his own day, but in other respects it is a good piece of work and remorselessly thorough. He had begun work in collaboration with the marquis de Paulmy, the owner of a substantial library, who was already at work on a similar book. As others have since discovered, they had chosen too broad a field for the individual scholar to cover. The marquis set Le Grand to work on the lives of learned men of the sixteenth century, and out of these studies developed Le Grand's history of French food.[25] Brief accounts had appeared in the *Encyclopédie* and in *Les Dons de Comus*, but they are on a small scale.[26] Le Grand undertook "to trace . . . the chronological order of our different usages."[27] Unfortunately, he takes the reader through a very extensive quantity of material one ingredient at a time, always starting with the oldest information available. The effect is monotonous. His work is divided into four sections: foods drawn from the plant kingdom, the animal kingdom, prepared foods, and beverages. Most of the information he gives about his own century is related to commerce and technology. He describes the great mustard and vinegar firm of Maille and evidently was acquainted with its head.[28] The firm manufactured some sixty-five vinegars, including that darling of our modern *nouvelle cuisine*, raspberry vinegar. The varieties most sold in Paris in the late eighteenth century were vinegars flavored *à la ravigotte*, with tarragon, mixed flowers, elder-flowers, truffled, and with fines herbes. Le Grand describes threshers, a machine for extracting starch from potatoes, a horse-powered bread kneader, and improved methods of preserving foods for long periods of time. Ancient practices and modern improvements alike interested him, but the flavor of foods and the character of meals did not. Although the *Histoire* did not inaugurate a strong scholarly tradition in the study of French cookery, Le Grand d'Aussy deserves notice and respect in his effort to stake out and reconnoiter a new domain for the social historian.

Thus, in the decades before the Revolution a twofold assessment of cooking techniques took place—current practice was systematically described and past achievements were cataloged. At the same time chemists and agronomists had begun to improve the production and manufacture of ingredients. Meanwhile, as diners came to pride themselves on their discernment in matters of the table, gastronomy, with all its fine perceptions and foolish fads, was accepted as one of the facets of the Parisian kaleidoscope. One can sense that people were aware that even in this single area of human activity the rate at which change was taking place had begun to increase, that, as the verse in the plate on page 198 states, cooking changes every year:

> Tous les ans nouvelle cuisine,
> Car tous les ans changent les goûts;
> Et tous les jours nouveaux ragoûts:
> Soyez donc chimiste, Justine.

Conclusion

In the five hundred years before the outbreak of the Revolution, French cuisine and the attitudes of its patrons went through many changes. In the fourteenth and fifteenth centuries diners were less interested in the character or quality of the dishes served than in abundance and expense. Dishes that were exotic, representational, or allegorical were of most interest. Concerns about the wholesomeness of diet were expressed in spiritual terms; gluttony was a sin. But if the diner's concerns were physical he took advice from the school of Salerno, the theories of which go back to the ancient Greeks. The scanty and sometimes garbled recipe collections that have survived are ill-organized, and the individual recipes do not draw on a standardized terminology. Medieval cooking in France had much in common with medieval cooking elsewhere in Europe but little in common with that later developed in France.

Printed cookbooks came in the sixteenth century, giving first a wider distribution to medieval recipes and health theories and then information about new techniques in pastrymaking, confectionary, and preserving. Greek and Roman writings about food were published, but there were no new general cookbooks. Diners began to record their eating experiences, both in private journals and in published literary works. In the latter, foods and meals are used to delineate class, mood, and individual taste. During the regencies of Catherine de Medici, court festivals began to include collations featuring the newly popular fruit and sugar confectionary.

From the time of the publication of La Varenne's and Bonnefons's cookbooks in the 1650s, culinary trends can be followed in greater detail. These volumes inaugurated a tradition of two styles of cooking that developed side by side: from the larger kitchens, *haute cuisine*; from the small kitchens of the prosperous classes, *cuisine bourgeoise*. Never completely interchangeable or completely distinct, these two modes of cookery have competed fruitfully down to the present century. The volumes by La Varenne and Bonnefons are important not for the individual recipes they contain but for the way

231

these recipes are conceived. They use a repertory of infinitely adjustable basic mixtures, both liquid and solid, that can be combined with the many primary ingredients that come into the French kitchen. By organizing materials and work, the cook can produce great variety with no waste and can build up elaborate recipes with little or no recourse to the written word. At the same time, fine cooking gained a new public importance as meals became more prominent in court festivals under Louis XIV.

The eighteenth century saw an increasing divergence between the tables of the aristocracy and those of the merely prosperous. The craft of cooking, like many others, reached new heights. Refinement supplanted abundance. The characteristic meal was intimate and luxurious. Confectionary and pastry were the work of specialists, and cafés dispensed the new beverages and ices. Individual attitudes increasingly were expressed in terms of food preferences. The aristocrat ate dishes cooked *à la bourgeoise* to affect a taste for simplicity; Rousseau renounced meat to renounce violence; the bourgeoisie ate slightly dated aristocratic food as a way of displaying social aspirations. Cooks had become proud and enjoyed a freedom of movement resulting from the international prestige of French cooking. The language of written recipes had become sufficiently developed to allow rapid and clear communication. In the last decades of the century the publication of new cookbooks fell off. Manuals, dictionaries, and food-related articles in the *Encyclopédie* codified earlier material but introduced little that was new. At the same time the first attempts to write the history of French cooking were made, adding another dimension to the cooks' and diners' perceptions of their activities. A highly developed network of supply, centered in Paris, drew raw materials and finished preparations from all over France and the rest of the world. Similarly, those with a talent for cooking or a taste for fine food traveled to the metropolis to enjoy this concentration of opportunity.

Although the Revolution disrupted culinary and gastronomic institutions as it did the rest of French society, more survived than was lost. The guilds were abolished; aristocratic households, the center of *haute cuisine* until this time, were severely disrupted in many cases and destroyed in others. Some cooks went abroad, while others went to work for the newly important restaurants and the *notables* at the top of the reshaped social structure.

The idea of gastronomy, of a diner's devoting a substantial amount of care and attention to the planning and consumption of fine meals, which had been developing in the eighteenth century, survived to be embraced by a larger and more diverse clientele. A start had been made to work out a more scientific understanding of the composition of foods, the chemistry of cooking, and human nutritional needs and was further pursued in the nineteenth century. Food supplies from the colonies increased their proportional share of space on fine tables, and the specialty suppliers who had been trading since the end of the seventeenth century were joined by many more when the abolition of the guilds opened the door to outsiders. The publicity apparatus was greatly extended. Finally, in the kitchens, cooks continued to practice their craft. As in the eighteenth century, the cook's skill had been available to anyone who could afford to pay for it; during the Revolution and after there were ready employers. Home cooking went on uninterrupted—indeed, *La Cuisinière bourgeoise* remained in print through the Revolution and beyond. The continuity of French home cooking is as important as concurrent disruptions. The basic preparations, working methods, and classic recipes survived. After the Revolution some preparations moved down the social ladder, while new, elaborately constructed inventions enjoyed a great vogue. The basic methods of food preparation in French kitchens and the articulation of work remained constant. The *cuisiniers* and the *officiers d'office*, the specialist bakers and the pastrycooks continued to practice their trades, each drawing on a repertory of fundamental preparations, seasonal delicacies, and ways of combining and presenting ingredients. The particulars changed but the mental habits did not. Even the service of meals remained essentially the same. The spatially oriented *service à la française* was not displaced by the sequentially patterned *service à la russe* until after 1850.

With the nineteenth century it becomes possible to follow developments within regions and to follow the careers of individual cooks. The richness of the history of cooking from the Revolution to the demise of traditional *haute cuisine* after World War II has yet to be adequately studied. Only in the changed economic, social, and technological conditions of our own day can we observe the final moments of a cultural tradition that, in its essential features, survived for three hundred years.

Recipes

I offer here a small selection of recipes from some of the most important French cookbooks, in the hope of enticing readers to savor this segment of the past for themselves. Some adaptations have been necessary, but I have stayed as close to the originals as is possible for a cook in a modern American kitchen. I have included transcriptions of the French originals for two reasons: first, because the development of a culinary language is one of the threads in my narrative, and second, so that cooks can make their own adaptations if they disagree with mine. In using recipes for unfamiliar dishes, especially when those recipes contain few or no measurements and the ingredients are probably different from those in the past, there is a great deal of room for differences of opinion. It is my hope that as the richness of France's culinary past becomes known more people will try to cook old recipes. There are two legitimate approaches. One is to aim for strict authenticity, and the other is to look for forgotten combinations of flavors or forgotten techniques and presentations and to adapt them freely in a modern context. Either way is valid, so long as one knows which approach one is taking.

Old cookbooks can be used as portals to the past, through which we can savor the good fare of earlier days, with our senses of smell and taste giving the same sense of immediacy that being in old buildings, hearing period music, and seeing works of art can do for our bodies, our ears, and our eyes.

In recent years a number of people have made serious attempts to adapt recipes from the cookbooks of the past. Of those books that have used French recipes the most notable are Anne Willan's *Great Cooks and Their Recipes*, Robert Courtine and Céline Vence's *Les Grands maîtres de la cuisine française*, Jane Grigson's *Food with the Famous*, and Shirley King's *Dining with Marcel Proust*.

There are pitfalls for the adapter and translator of French recipes. The most notorious is *lard*, which must not be translated as lard, the rendered pork fat of the American kitchen. *Lard* is the unrendered fat meat of pork, which according to time, place, and intended use may or may not be streaked with muscle meat and may or may not be more or less heavily smoked or salted. In adapting recipes I have called for whatever variation I think most appropriate. The original recipes usually do not specify, because it was assumed to be obvious.

There is a problem, too, with mushrooms, though it is less serious. Our cultivated mushrooms are a variety of the field mushroom that was most commonly used in French cooking in the past. A wider range of other species was available, however. The most important of those we cannot get were morels and the boletinus mushrooms—*cèpes* in French, *steinpilzen* in German; although they can be bought dried and canned, neither is a substitute for the fresh variety. Because truffles have become prohibitively expensive, I have indicated them as optional. If one has the option, one should exercise it.

Measurements have been calculated from information in Armand Machabey's *La Métrologie dans les musées de province* and Bruno Kisch's *Scales and Weights*. The basic weight was the *livre de Paris* weighing about 490 grams. A *pinte* (980 grams) contained two *livres*, or *chopines*, or four *demi-septiers* (122.5 grams), or eight *poissons* (15 grams). Thus, two *poissons* equal in weight about one modern ounce. There are many regional variations, for which see Machabey. Let us be thankful that the cookbooks were written with a strong Parisian bias.

Recipes

Blanc mengier d'ung chappon pour ung malade

Cuisiez en yaue; broiez amandez grant foison, du broion du chappon; deffaitez de vostre boillon, passez parmy l'estamine, faitez boullir tant qu'il soit liant; pour taillier, versez en une escuelle; fillez demie douzene d'amandez pellez, et les asséez sur la moitié du bout de vostre escuelle; en l'autre moitié, de pepins de pomme de grenade et du succre.

From the Sion manuscript of the *Viandier*, Paul Aebischer, "Un manuscrit valaisian du 'Viandier' attribué à Taillevent," p. 95.

Blancmange of Capon for a Sick Person

2½ pounds breast meat of capon
2 quarts good chicken stock
I cup finely ground almonds
I teaspoon ginger (optional)

½ teaspoon cardamom (optional)
6 blanched almonds, slivered
pomegranate seeds
sugar

Poach the capon breasts in the chicken stock until they are cooked (about twenty minutes or a little more). Let cool. Cut up the meat and pass it through a food mill fitted with a fine grid. Beat in the ground almonds and, if desired, the spices. Dilute with as much of the cooking broth as is necessary to make the mixture agreeably moist but still rather stiff. Stick the slivered almonds into half of the top and the pomegranate seeds into the other half; sprinkle the second half with sugar.

I have suggested the use of spices because the author of the *Ménagier* calls for ginger and cardamom as spices for blancmange in his shopping list for a festivity. My choice of quantities is, of necessity, entirely arbitrary, except for the almonds. This recipe is one of that group of seven which first appears in the earliest manuscript of the *Viandier* and is still in circulation and was printed in the sixteenth century—so it is not only very ancient but must have had a long-lasting appeal.

Layt lardé

Prenez du lait et le mettez boullir sur le feu, et avoir moyeulx d'oeufz batuz, puis descendez le lait de dessus le feu, et le mettez sur ung pou de charbon, et fillez les oeufz dedans.

Et qui veult qu'il soit à chair, prenez lardons et les couppez en deux ou trois morceaulx, et gectez avec le lait boullir. Et qui veult qu'il soit à poisson, il n'y fault point mettre de lardons, mais gecter du vin et du verjus avant qu'on le descende, pour faire brosser, puis l'oster de dessus le feu et le mettez en une nappe blanche, et le laissier esgouter, et l'enveloper en ii ou en iii doubles de la nappe, et le pressourer tant qu'il soit dur comme foye de beuf; puis le mettre sur une table et le taillier par leesches comme de plainne paulme ou trois doys, et les boutonner de clou de girofle, puis les frire tant qu'ilz soient roussés; et les dressiez, et jectez du succre dessus.

Vatican manuscript of the *Viandier*, in Jérôme Pichon and Georges Vicaire, eds., *Le Viandier de Guillaume Tirel, dit Taillevent*, pp. 263–64.

Milk Made into Bacon

1 quart milk
either 4 egg yolks or ¼ cup
   white wine
¼ pound bacon cut in two or
   three slices (optional)

¼ cup butter
whole cloves
2 tablespoons sugar

Bring the milk to a boil and then remove from the heat. Immediately stir in the beaten egg yolks, or the wine, so that the milk curdles. If the milk does not curdle, heat it, while stirring, until it does. Have ready a sieve set over an ample basin and line the sieve with two or three layers of cheesecloth that have been previously dampened and then wrung out. Pour the milk mixture into the sieve, adding the bacon if desired. Let drain, folding the remaining cheesecloth over it; after about half an hour set a weight on top. The best way to contrive this is to set a cake pan or pie plate of suitable diameter on the cheesecloth and then set a two-pound weight on the pan (a can of something will do nicely or even a quart of water, suitably contained). Let stand for about four hours, until cool and firm.

Melt butter in a skillet, slice the *lait lardé*, and stick the pieces with cloves. Cook in the butter until the slices are lightly tinged with brown. Remove from the heat and serve with sugar sprinkled over them.

I prefer to omit the bacon. Use the wine for a sharper flavor; increase the quantity of egg yolks for a more opulent effect. The liquid that drains out of the curdled milk mixture may be used in making bread.

Tourtes Parmeriennes

Prenez chair de mouton ou de veau ou de porc, et la hachiez competemment; puis fault avoir de la poulaille, et faire boullir, et despecier par quartiers; et fault cuire ledit grain avant qu'il soit hachié, puis avoir poudre fine et l'en espicier très bien raisonnablement, et frire son grain en sain de lart, et, après, avoir de grans pastez descouvers, et qu'ilz soient plus hault dreciez de paste que autres pastez et de la grandeur de petitz platz, et faictz en manière de creneaulx, et qu'ilz soient fortz de paste affin qu'ilz puissent porter le grain; et, qui veult, on y met du pignolet et du roisin de Corinde meslez parmy le grain, et du succre esmié par dessus, et mettre en chascun pasté iii ou iiii quartiers de poullaille pour fichier les bannières de France et des seigneurs qui seront en la presence, et les dorer de saffren deffait pour estre plus beaulx. Et qui ne veult pas tant despendre de poullaille, ne fault que faire des pièces plates de porc ou du mouston rosty ou boully. Et quant ilz sont rempliz de leur grain, les fault dorer, par dessus le grain, d'un petit d'oeufz bastuz ensemble, moyeulx et aubuns, affin que le grain se tiengne plus ferme pour mettre les bannières dedans. Et convient avoir du fueil d'or ou d'argent ou du fueil d'estain pour les dorer avant les banières.

Vatican manuscript of the *Viandier*, in Jérôme Pichon and Georges Vicaire, eds., *Le Viandier de Guillaume Tirel, dit Taillevent*, pp. 261–62.

Chicken and Pork Pies

The filling must be prepared before the crust is begun because the pie must be assembled while the crust is still warm and then baked at once.

For the filling:

2 pounds boneless pork loin
1 pound boneless chicken
4 chicken drumsticks
about 3 cups water or meat broth
¼ cup lard

1 teaspoon spice powder (use the recipe from the *Liure fort excellent*)
salt
¼ cup pignola nuts (optional)
¼ cup currants (optional)

Cut the pork loin into slices about half an inch thick and place it in a saucepan with the chicken meat and the drumsticks. Add the water or meat broth, or a mixture of both, to cover. Cover the saucepan and simmer, removing each kind of meat as it becomes tender. Chop the pork and chicken (but not the meat on the drumsticks) rather fine.

Melt the lard in a skillet and brown the drumsticks lightly in it. Remove them and set aside. In the same lard brown the chopped chicken and pork. The flavor will be enriched if you take the time to cook and stir the meat until it has browned somewhat. Dust with the spice powder and, if you wish, salt, to suit your taste. If desired, add the pignola nuts and the currants. Taste again and proceed to the making of the crust.

There are no French medieval pie pastry recipes; I offer the following recipe as a plausible improvisation from more recent recipes.

For the crust:

6 tablespoons lard
1 cup + 2 tablespoons water
½ teaspoon salt
1½ cups fine whole wheat flour
2½ cups all-purpose flour
1 egg, beaten

2 tablespoons sugar
an 18″ length of waxed paper
string
½–1 cup rich meat stock (optional)
2 or 3 sheets of gold leaf (optional)

Preheat the oven to 300° F. Put the lard into a large saucepan with the water and bring to a boil. Remove from the heat. Add the salt to the whole wheat and all-purpose flours; gradually stir the hot liquid into them. As soon as it is cool enough to handle, knead briefly. Keep the pastry warm while you are forming the pie (in a covered bowl on top of the stove, for example). Roll out enough dough to make a circular base 5½ inches in diameter and about ¼ inch thick. Set it in the middle of a jelly-roll pan or other baking pan with sides to catch the overflow of liquid (though there should not be much because the filling is dry). Heap up a mound of the filling in the center of the base and place the chicken drumsticks, thick end down, at equal distances around the inner edge of the heap, on the crust. Reserve about one-third of the remaining pastry dough for the lid and turrets. Roll out the unreserved crust on the waxed paper in a long, narrow rectangle, about 4 inches wide and 16 inches long, to form the wall of the pie. With a small, sharp-pointed knife cut crenelations along one long edge, between ¼ and ½ inch deep, at regular intervals. Brush the outer edge of the base with a little beaten egg and do the same along the uncrenelated long side of the wall piece. Join the wall to the base, pressing the pieces firmly together. At this point it will be much easier if you can get someone to help you. If no one is available, the wall, which will want to collapse, can be kept up by propping large tin cans or wine bottles against the outside of it. Work quickly, spooning the filling into the pie (which will help stabilize the wall) and pressing the base and wall together. The drumsticks will help hold the wall in place. Brush the seam where the two ends of the wall join with more beaten egg. Fill the pie shell to within one inch of the crenelations, dust with sugar, and brush with a beaten egg. Roll out another 5½-inch circle to use as the lid. With a ½ inch pastry tube cut a hole in the center and cut semicircles out of the edge of the lid to accommodate the bones of the chicken drumsticks. Set the lid in place on top of the filling, inside the crenelated wall. With the remaining dough roll out strips long enough to wrap around each of the drumsticks, to form turrets. Brush the seams to help hold them together, as was done for the main structure. Check the crenelations to see that they have not been pushed out of shape during all the excitement.

Fold the waxed paper that was used for rolling out the dough twice, lengthwise, and wrap it around the pie, tying it at two levels with sturdy string to help the pie keep its shape as it bakes.

Set the pie in the center of a 300° F. oven for an hour and an quarter, then remove the paper band (cautiously) and bake for another half hour, or until the crust is firm. Remove from the oven and let cool on the baking sheet for half an hour, then set it on a wire rack until it is cool. Refrigerate.

Make banners to stick on the drumsticks, using either gold leaf or any other coloring materials you wish, if you prefer paper. Gold leaf is edible and may be applied directly to the pastry, using egg white as a binding agent. It will crack, however, as the egg white dries and therefore should be applied shortly before serving. To serve, cut the lid just inside the crenelations, lift it off, and spoon out the filling. If desired, the pie may be baked without a lid. For a moister filling add well-flavored (cold) meat stock after the pie has cooled.

Ipocras

Pour faire une pinte d'ypocras, il fault troys treseaux synamome fine et pares, ung treseau du mesche ou deux qui veult, demy treseau de girofle et graine, de sucre fin six onces; et mettés en pouldre, et la fault toute mettre en ung couleur avec le vin, et le pot dessoubz, et le passés tant qu'il soit coulé, et tant plus est passé et mieulx vault, mais que il ne soit esventé.

From the first printed edition of the *Viandier*, in Jérôme Pichon and Georges Vicaire, eds., *Le Viandier di Guillaume Tirel, dit Taillevent*, p. 98.

Hypocras

3 cups dry red wine

2 ounces fresh ginger, sliced and peeled

1 tablespoon whole cloves

2 ounces stick cinnamon

1 tablespoon cardamom

3⅓ cups granulated sugar

Put all the ingredients in a stainless steel, enamel, or earthenware pot to heat, without boiling, for about fifteen minutes, stirring to dissolve the sugar. Strain through a fine sieve, repeatedly if necessary, to remove all the spices. Let cool and serve at room temperature or slightly chilled.

This is a heavy, pungent, sweet drink, and the modern diner may wish to add a second bottle of wine. There is no point in using a good wine. Although the *Viandier* calls for powdered spices, I recommend whole ones because the powdered ones cloud the wine hopelessly. An alternative way of making this drink is to infuse the spices and sugar with one cup each of wine and water for fifteen minutes, without boiling, and after cooling and straining the mixture, to add it to the wine to suit one's taste. With congenial tasters to assist, this can be an agreeable if not a productive exercise.

Potaige appellé verseuse

Aies quatre roux d'oeufz bien frais, demye unce de cynamome, quatre unces de succre, du just d'orange quatre unces semblablement, deux unces d'eaue rose; mesle tout ensemble avec quelque cuillier, et réduis tout en ung corps et le fais cuyre, ainsi qu'est dict dessus au chapitre du just safranné ou jaune. Et, si veulx pareilement, y pourras adjouster ung peu de saffran pour donner couleur. Est viande merveilleusement saine, principalement en esté, et fort plaisante, nourrist bien et grandement, refraîche le foye et reprimist la colère.

From Pierre Gaudoul's borrowings of Platina's recipes for an edition of the *Viandier*, in Jérôme Pichon and Georges Vicaire, eds., *Le Viandier de Guillaume Tirel, dit Taillevent*, p. 108.

A Foamy Broth

4 fresh egg yolks

4 ounces sugar

2 ounces rosewater

½ ounce cinnamon

4 ounces orange juice, or 2 ounces each orange and lemon juice

the grated rind of one-half orange (optional)

½ teaspoon saffron (optional)

Mix all ingredients except saffron together with a spoon and reduce to a smooth mass. Cook, stirring constantly, over a low heat until the mixture thickens; remove from the heat and continue stirring for a few minutes, until it has cooled enough not to curdle. Add the saffron (infused first in a spoonful of water) if you wish more color. The original recipe states, "It is a marvelously healthy dish, especially in summer, very pleasant, and nourishes well, strengthens the liver, and suppresses bile."

I have suggested adding grated orange rind and using some lemon juice because in the sixteenth century intensely flavored, sour Seville oranges were usually used. This dish is more characteristic than agreeable; it is intensely sweet, and since measurements are given one may be reasonably sure that it was intended to be so. Sugar, the favorite sixteenth-century luxury food, was presumably even more luxurious in such abundance.

Potaige de chair

Ayes de la chair maigre et fais la bouillir: puis découpe icelle menuement, et la fais cuyre, de rechief, en ung aultre pot, au just gras, par demye heure, avec de la miette du pain gratusé, ung peu de poivre et de saffran; après que sera ung peu refroidie, auras des oeufz battus, du fromage gratusé, persil, marjoleine, mente, decouppez menuement, et ung peu de verjust, et mesleras tout ensemble, et puis le mettras dedans ton pot le remenant, tousjours doulcement avec ton cuillier. Semblablement, pourras faire des corées et polmons des gelines ou aultres oyseaulx.

From Pierre Gaudoul's borrowings from Platina for his edition of the *Viandier*, in Jérôme Pichon and Georges Vicaire, eds., *Le Viandier de Guillaume Tirel, dit Taillevent*, p. 110.

Meat Soup

2 pounds beef chuck, bottom of the round, or other lean meat	2 eggs, beaten
2 quarts water	¼ cup grated cheese (Parmesan, for example)
4 cups meat broth	1 tablespoon parsley, finely chopped
½ cup dry bread crumbs	
freshly ground black pepper, to taste	1 tablespoon marjoram, finely chopped
¼ teaspoon saffron	1 tablespoon mint, finely chopped

wine vinegar to taste (start with 2 or 3 teaspoons), or verjuice if available

Parboil the beef in water for ten minutes. Remove, discarding the water. Cut the meat into small pieces and put it in a clean cooking pot with the meat broth, bread crumbs, pepper, and saffron. Cook for thirty minutes. Let it cool a little and then stir in the eggs, grated cheese, parsley, marjoram, mint, and vinegar, stirring constantly.

The writer suggests that the same recipe may be used for the hearts and lungs of hens and other birds; I have not tried this. I would cook the meat until tender and would expect it to take substantially more than thirty minutes. This recipe, an authentic sixteenth-century Italian import, is very similar in character to medieval French recipes, with its pungent herbs and saffron, bread crumbs as a thickening, and verjuice or vinegar to accent the flavor.

Tartre de massapan

Prenes des amandes plumées bien nettes une livre, faites les piller fort dens un mortier de marbre avec demi livre de succre de Madere: et quand le tout sera tresbien pisté ensemble, vous y mettres un peu de l'eau rose, en les pillant, pour cause qu'elles ne rendent huylle: et quand elles seront tresbien pistées, vous en feres de petites tourteaulx, ou de petites tartelettes toutes rondes estendues dessus des oblies: et que soient primes: et pourres faire de petites quadratures . . . sus les dites oblies: et puis les feres cuire au four. Et quand elles seront demy cuites au four, vous aures du succre en pouldre, et le pasteres avec blancz d'oeufs, peu de suc des orenges: et feres qu'il sera fort liquide: et quand la tartre sera presque du tout cuite, vous la sortires du four, et avec une plume luy mettres par dessus de ce succre liquefié: et puis retourneres la tartre dens le four tant seulement pour prendre couleur: et quand sera cuite, la trouveres avoir un goust fort delectable et savoreux: car quand il y a du succre en plus grande quantité, la rend pasteuse, et fascheuse a manger, et en est moins delectable.

Michel de Nostradamus, *Excellent et moult utile opuscule à touts necessaire . . .* (1555)

Marzipan Tarts

For the marzipan:

> **2 cups blanched powdered
>   almonds**
> **¾ cup granulated sugar**
> **¼ cup rosewater**

For the crusts:

> **3 dozen sugar wafers, about 3 inches in diameter (see *petit mestier*,
>   p. 254)**

For the icing:

> **1 egg white**
> **2 tablespoons sugar**
> **the juice and grated rind of one-
>   half orange**

Using a food processor fitted with a steel blade (in place of the marble mortar and pestle), combine the almonds and sugar. With the motor running, slowly pour in as much of the rosewater as is needed to form a paste that holds together but is not sloppy. If the mixture is at all runny stir in additional powdered almonds.

Preheat the oven to 350° F. Spread each wafer with about 2 teaspoons of the marzipan to make a thin layer. It should be spread right up to the edge of the wafer. Smooth thoroughly with a flexible spatula, then use the spatula to mark the surface of the marizipan in a squared pattern. Set on an ungreased baking sheet and bake for four minutes.

Remove from the oven and brush the surface of the marzipan with the icing. Make the icing by beating the egg white in a bowl until it is just slightly foamy and then stirring in the sugar, the orange juice, and the rind.

Bake for another minute or two until the surface is dry. Cool on wire racks.

These tartlets may be frozen. If they are made with honey-sweetened wafers (*oublies*), they will be sweeter and very chewy.

Une paste de sucre

Pour faire vne paste de succre de laquelle on pourra faire toute sorte de fruit, et autre gentil-
lesse auec leur forme, comme plats, escuelles, verres, tasses et autres choses semblables des-
quelles on fournira vne table, et en la fin se pourra manger, chose delectable aux assistans.

Prens de la gomme dragant autant que tu voudras, et la mets destremper en eau rose, tant
qu'elle soit mollifiée. Et pour quatre onces de succre, prens en de la grosseur d'vne febue, ius
de limons plein l'escaille d'vne noix, et vn peu de glaire d'oeuf: mais il faut premier prendre
la gomme, et battre tant auec le pilon en vn mortier de marbre blanc ou bien d'erain, qu'elle
deuienne comme eau, puis y adiouste ledit ius auec la glaire d'oeuf, en incorporant le tout
ensemble. Ce fait, prens quatre onces de succre fin et blanc bien reduit en poudre, et le iette
petit à petit, tant que tout soit reduit en poudre, et le iette petit à petit, tant que tout soit
reduit en forme de paste. Tire-la puis apres du mortier, et la broye sus poudre de succre,
comme si ce fut farine, tant que tout soit reduit en paste mole, afinque tu le puisse tourner et
former à ton plaisir. Quand tu aura reduit la paste en ceste sorte, estans la et applanis auec le
rouleau en fueilles grosses ou menuës, ainsi que bon te semblera: et par ainsi en formeras aussi
telle chose que tu voudras, comme dessus est dit. De telles gentillesses pourras tu seruir à
table, te gardant bien de mettre quelque chose de chaud aupres. A la fin du banquet on pourra
tout manger, et rompre plats verres, tasses et toutes choses, car ceste paste est tres delicate et
sauoureuse. Si tu veux faire chose de plus grand gentillesse tu fera vn tourteau d'amandes
estampées auec du succre et eau rose, de la sorte que se font les mache-pains. Cecy mettras-tu
entre deux pastes de tels vaisseaux, ou fruits, ou autre chose que bon te semblera.

Alexis of Piedmont, *Les Secrets du rev. sr. Alexis piemontois* (1561), f.45v°.

A Dough of Sugar

To make a dough of sugar with which one may make all kinds of fruit and other
agreeable shapes, such as dishes, bowls, glasses, cups, and similar things with which
one may set a table, and at the end [of the meal] one can eat them, a delight for those
present.

1 teaspoon gum tragancanth, powdered	1 tablespoon lime juice
	1 egg white
1 teaspoon rosewater	
2 cups confectioners' sugar, measured after sifting (and perhaps more)	

Put the gum tragacanth and the rosewater in the bowl of an electric mixer (or a
marble mortar) and stir them together. Let stand at least two hours. Then add the
lime juice and the egg white and beat them in well; when the mixture is smooth,
which will take a while, gradually beat in about half of the sugar. Unless your mixer
is very powerful, the mixture will be too stiff by then to take any more sugar. Knead
in as much of the remaining sugar by hand as is necessary to make a firm dough
that is not sticky. Wrap thoroughly in plastic and let it cure overnight. Refrigeration
is not necessary.

To form shapes proceed as follows: To make a dish, roll out the dough on a surface dusted with sifted cornstarch. [This is an anachronism: amidon—wheat starch—would be more correct but is harder to get, and the substitution of corn-starch will not affect the flavor.] Roll the dough to the desired thickness; for a plate this would be about ⅛ inch. The shape is formed by draping the dough over a suitable form; either the outside or the inside of the form may be used. Measure the diameter of your chosen plate and cut a circle (or other relevant shape) somewhat larger. Flip the cut-out dough onto the rolling pin so it can be moved without distortion and then ease it onto or into the mold. Adjust it so that there are no wrinkles and trim the edges. There is no reason why the exposed side should not be decorated with impressed patterns. Set in a well-ventilated place that is dry and slightly warm for several days. Just how long it will take depends on the shape of the article, its thickness, and the weather. While the material is drying it is extremely fragile, and the temptation to handle it is great. Handling should be kept to a min-imum except to be sure that it is not sticking to its mold. The likelihood of sticking can be reduced by dusting the surface that will be placed against the mold with extra cornstarch or amidon.

When the object is dry it will be firm enough to set on the table and use as a container for light, dry foods, such as other *pastillage* work, biscuits, and nuts. The dough may be colored.

At the time when Alexis of Piedmont published this recipe people were begin-ning to use glazed earthenware on their tables in place of trenchers of bread, wood, or metal. The process of learning not to break this fragile new luxury must have made some diners anxious, and a luxury item that was supposed to be broken would have given a special feeling of delight. Even today I find that children are enchanted at finding plates they are *supposed* to break.

Menues espices

Prenes z iiij de Gingembre z iiii de canelle z ii de poyure rond z i de poyure long ij de noix de muscade z i de cloux de Giroffle z i de Graine de paradis z i de muscade z i de Garingal et i le tout mis en pouldre et passes par lesset.

Liure fort excellent de cuysine (1555), 27vº.

A Spice Mixture

7 tablespoons powdered ginger	5¾ tablespoons ground cinnamon
¼ cup ground pepper	[2 tablespoons long pepper*]
7¼ teaspoons grated nutmeg	4½ teaspoons ground cloves
5 teaspoons ground cardamom	2 tablespoons powdered galingale

Sift all the ingredient together and store in a cool place in a tightly covered container.

*Long pepper seems to be unobtainable; this is therefore a theoretical measure. Grains of paradise are almost as rare; I have substituted cardamom. Galingale can be bought in spice shops either as powder or as whole roots; it may also be found among the Indonesian bottled spices as *laos*.

An Herb Mixture

Prenes persil effueille deulx poignees mariolaine effueillee deux poignees et demye saulge demye poignee ysope autant sariette autant sarpollet Une poignee soulcye une poignee. Et quant cest pour faire farce aulcuns y mettent soulcye et peu de Baselicque. Elle seruent a tous potaiges et les fault faire seicher enuiron la sainct Jehan baptiste.

Liure fort excellent de cuysine (1555), ff. 28r°–v°.

An Herb Mixture

1 cup parsley	1¼ cups marjoram
¼ cup sage	¼ cup hyssop
¼ cup winter savory	½ cup pot marigold petals
¼ cup wild thyme	2 tablespoons basil (optional)

On or about 24 June pick the unsprayed herbs and pluck the leaves from the stems. Pluck the outer petals of the pot marigolds. A soft pastry brush is useful in dealing with the flower petals.

Dry the herbs in the sun or indoors fairly near a gentle fan. Measure, mix, and store in a tightly closed container in a cool, dark, dry place.

The "soulcye" in the original recipe is *Calendula officinalis*, the pot marigold. It served in the Middle Ages and even later as a cheap substitute for saffron, since it was (and is) easily grown in the home garden. Our common marigolds, *Tagetes patula* and *T. erecta*, were introduced into European gardens at the end of the sixteenth century from Mexico and are known, perversely, as French and African marigolds.

Paste de bugnolle ou friture

Prennez vne sopine de creme, et la faictes boulir en vne paelle auec vn peu de beurre, puis prennez blanche farine, et faictes la paste dedans la paelle sur le feu, qu'il soit bien meslé auec vne louse de bois, puis rompez quatre oeufs dedans, et le battez bien auec la louse, que les oeufs soient bien corrompus dedans la paste, puis prennez encor quatre oeufs et les battez de rechef tant que la paste soit molle comme vn papin espes, autant d'oeufs faut il mettre que la paste soit molle assez, puis prennez de beurre bien boully que le sel soit dehors, puis mettez le beurre sur le feu qu'il soit vn peu chaud, puis prennez de la paste auec vn cueiller d'argent aussi gros qu'vne gaille, et le iettez dedans le beurre, dixhuict ou vingt a la fois, et les retourne souuent auec vne escumette, et les laissez cuire tant que la paste se vient a fendre, et tirez le hors, et si vous voyez que la paste se retire, ils ne sont pas assez, remettez les encor dedans tant qu'il soit assez.

De ceste mesme paste.

Ayez vne speriche ou sering auec vn petit fer dedans, ayant deux ou trois troux, ou vn tout seul si voulez, et faictes passer la paste parmy, et les faictes cuire dedans le beurre comme les autres.

Autrement.

Prennez de ceste paste, et l'estendez sur vne planchette de boys la largeur d'vne main, l'espesseur d'vn petit doigt, et couppez auec vn couteau comme des lardons, et les faictes tomber dedans le beurre chaud, et faictes cuire comme les autres.

Autrement.

Prennez de ceste mesme paste pour vne liure pesante, prennez quatre onces de beurre fondu, quatre onces de succre en pouldre, et battez le bien tout ensemble, et prennez du papier qui soit bien engrassé de beurre, puis auec vne lousse prennez la paste, mettez la sur le papier comme petit pain, et succre par dessus, et le mettez cuire dedans le four, et seruez quatre ou cinque en vn plat.

Lancelot de Casteau, *Ovverture de cvisine* (1604), pp. 19–21.

A Fritter Dough

2 cups light cream
¼ cup butter
2 cups all-purpose flour

7 medium eggs
2 cups clarified butter

In a saucepan bring to a boil the cream and the butter. Add the flour, all at once, and stir the mixture vigorously over the heat. Beat together six of the eggs and then gradually beat them into the batter, as for a modern cream-puff pastry dough. If the mixture is too thick add some or all of the seventh egg (which has been beaten up first).

There are four ways of forming and cooking the dough. Three kinds of fritter may be formed. First, teaspoonful-sized irregular lumps of dough may be dipped out of the mixture; second, the dough may be rolled out to a thickness of ¼ to ½ inch and then cut into diamond shapes. Third, it may be put into a pastry bag and extruded through a nozzle having several small holes or one about ⅛ inch in diameter. All three of these shapes are then cooked in boiling clarified butter until a rich golden brown. The fourth way is to sweeten the dough with ¼ cup of sugar to a pound of dough. Lancelot also recommends adding more butter, but I found this to be more than my flour could absorb. This sweetened dough is then formed in little cakes with a spoon and baked on sheets of paper in the oven, at about 350° F.

The modern cook may wish to fry these cakes in a mixture of equal parts of oil and clarified butter, because the butter by itself foams up extravagantly, and its lower burning point requires very close attention. The final variation, of sweetened dough baked in the oven, is delicious served anachronistically with coffee. A dusting of powdered sugar is good on any of the versions, and one might wish to add cinnamon, nutmeg, or mace to the dough before cooking.

A Spice Mixture

Pichon and Vicaire, in their edition of the *Viandïer*, quote in modernized French a spice powder formula from the *Thrésor de santé* (1607): *Gingembre, quatre onces; canelle, trois onces et demie; poivre rond, une once et demie; poivre long, une once; muscade, deux onces; clous de girofle, une once ; graine de paradis, garingal, de chacun une once.*

7 tablespoons ginger	5 tablespoons cinnamon
4 tablespoons freshly ground pepper	[½ ounce long pepper★]
	4 nutmegs, grated
1 tablespoon + 1 teaspoon ground cloves	2 tablespoons galingale
5 teaspoons cardamom	

Mix all well together and store in a tightly closed container in a cool, dry, dark place.

Bouillon

La Maniere de faire le Boüillon pour la nourriture de tous les pots, soit des potages, entrées, ou entremets. Vous prendrez trumeaux derriere de simiere, peu de mouton, et quelques volailles, et suivant la quantité que vous voulez de boüillon voux mettrez de la viande à proportion, puis la ferez bien cuire avec un bouquet que vous serez avec persil, siboules et tin liez ensemble, et un peu de clou, et tenez toûjours de l'eau chaude pour remplir le pot; puis estant bien fait, vous le passerez dans une serviette pour vous en servir. Et pour la viande rostie, aprés en avoir tiré le jus, vous la mettrez boüillir avec un bouquet ainsi que dessus, faite la bien cuire, puis la passez pour mettre à vos entrées, ou au potages bruns.

François La Varenne, *Le Cvisinier françois* (1721), pp. 1–2.

Bouillon

4 pounds boneless chuck	2 pounds stewing lamb, bone in
a 5 or 6 pound boiling fowl	(mutton, if you can get it)

a bouquet made with 5 or 6 stalks of parsley, 3 or 4 scallions, 2 or 3 sprigs of thyme, and 2 cloves, all tied in a bundle with string.

Put the beef, chicken, and lamb (or mutton) in a pot; add cold water and bring slowly to a simmer, skimming off the foam as it rises. After the foam ceases to form, add the bouquet and continue to simmer for about four hours, or until all the meat is tender.

Strain all the liquid into a bowl and refrigerate. When it is cold lift off the solidified fat and use the bouillon as desired.

The proportions and quantities may be varied to suit particular needs. As La Varenne advises, if more water is needed, be sure it is hot. The meats will of course be good for many uses; remove them as they achieve tenderness and before they begin to fall apart.

★Again it must be noted that long pepper appears to be unobtainable. Unless you have some at hand it will be necessary to decide whether to substitute for it an additional quantity of black pepper or to omit it entirely. To my taste, the mixture already has ample black pepper.

Poulet d'Inde à la framboise farcy

*Apres qu'il est habillé levez en le brichet et tirez la chair, que vous hacherez avec graisse, et peu de chair de veau, que vous meslerez ensemble avec des jaunes d'oeufs et de pigeonneaux et le tout bien assaisonné, vous remplirez vostre poulet-d'Inde, avec sel, poivre, clou battu, et capres, puis le mettez à la broche, et le ferez tourner bien doucement, estant presque cuit tirez-le et **le** mettez dans une terrine avec de bon bouillon, champignons et un bouquet. Pour lier la sauce, prenez un peu de lard coupé, le faites passer par la poesle, lequel estant fondu vous tirerez, et y meslerez un peu de farine, que vous laisserez bien roussir et delayerez avec peu de bouillon et de vinaigre; la mettez ensuite dans vostre terrine avec jus de citron, et servez; si c'est en temps des framboises, vous y en mettrez une poignée par dessus.*

François La Varenne, *Le Cvisinier françois* (1654), p. 35.

Stuffed Turkey with Raspberries

a 12 to 13 pound turkey	2 quarts bouillon (see recipe,
4 squabs or 2 Cornish hens	p. 250)
¾ pound boneless lean veal	1½ pounds mushrooms
½ pound pork fat or bacon	bouquet garni
4 egg yolks	¼ cup diced bacon
2 teaspoons salt	¼ cup flour
1 teaspoon pepper	1 tablespoon wine vinegar
¼ teaspoon ground cloves	1 tablespoon lemon juice
3 tablespoons capers	1 pint fresh raspberries (optional)

Reaching under the skin of the turkey from both neck and tail ends, gently separate the skin from the meat with your hands. Use a sharp knife to cut it away from its attachment to the breastbone. Take care not to make any holes in the skin. (If they should appear, they may be sewn up with white buttonhole thread at a later stage.) Then, still using a sharp, pointed knife, cut the breast meat away from the bone; it will be necessary again to work from both ends. A certain amount of progress can be made by pulling the meat gently. Be especially careful in cutting away the tendons and muscle attached to the wings, where the skin is close to the working area. Set the meat aside to use in the forcemeat. Using heavy shears and great caution cut away the entire skeletal support of the breast—the breastbone, wishbone, and most of the ribs, leaving the spine, wings, and legs in place. Skin the Cornish hens or squabs and remove the meat from the bones; there should be about 1½ cups of meat, free from fat and sinew. Cut up the breast meat of the turkey into one-inch cubes. Cut the veal into similar chunks, taking extra care to remove any sinew or fiber. Cut the pork fat or bacon into one-inch cubes. Grind all these meats, in batches, in a food processor fitted with a steel blade, or in a meat grinder, or chop them by hand until they are the texture of hamburger, except for the fat, which should be almost creamy. Beat all these ingredients together well, adding the egg yolks, salt, pepper, cloves, and capers. Test a little of the forcemeat by cooking on both sides in a skillet with butter and adjust the seasoning if necessary.

Fill up the body cavity of the turkey with the forcemeat, shaping it symmetrically. This is the moment to sew up any holes that may have developed. Truss the bird with heavy string. If you are going to roast it on a spit, make as cylindrical a parcel as possible. Ordinary household rotisseries are neither strong enough nor large enough to accommodate a turkey. Modern turkeys are much rounder than their ancestors were and therefore less well suited to spit-roasting. I cannot give a precise time for spit-roasting, but it would take several hours. Alternatively, preheat the oven to 350° F. and roast the bird in it for about three and one-half hours. Then put it in a kettle, breast up, and add the bouillon, mushrooms, and bouquet garni. Simmer it gently until the interior of the bird registers 185° F. on a meat thermometer—about one hour. If you do not have a pot large enough to poach a turkey in, finish the process in the baking pan. Remove the bird from the roasting rack and set it directly on the pan. Pour the broth around it and add the mushrooms and the bouquet garni. Baste it every ten minutes. This will result in a more handsome appearance than poaching would.

To make the sauce, cook the diced bacon in a saucepan until all of its fat is rendered. Remove the crisp bits of bacon and use them for some other purpose. Add the flour to the fat and, stirring constantly, cook until it turns a tan color and has a pleasantly toasted smell. Strain the liquid out of the turkey pan; taste it to see that it is good and add one quart of it to the roux, stirring vigorously. Stir in the vinegar and lemon juice.

Serve the turkey on a carving board or platter, the sauce in a gravy boat, and the raspberries in a bowl. The bird is carved as if it had not been boned, cutting broad, thin slices from the breast. The berries should not be sweetened; their natural tartness complements the turkey. Unfortunately, like cranberries, they go badly with wine.

This recipe is taken from La Varenne's chapter of entrées that may be prepared in the country or when one is in the field with the army—in other words, when one wants simplified cookery.

Champignons à l'Olivier

Estans bien nettoyez, coupez les par quartiers, et les lavez dans plusieurs eaux l'un apres l'autre pour en oster la terre; Estans bien nets, mettez-les entre deux plats avec un oignon et du sel, puis sur le rechaut, afin qu'ils jetterez leur eau. Estans pressez entre deux asiettes, prenez du beurre bien frais, avec persil et siboule, et les fricassez; aprés celas mettez-les mitonner, et lors qu'ils seront bien cuits, vous y pouvez mettre de la cresme, ou du blancmanger, et servez.

François La Varenne, *Le Cvisinier françois* (1654), p. 121.

Mushrooms Olivier

4 cups mushrooms, washed and
   quartered
1 small onion
½ teaspoon salt
¼ cup cream or blancmange (optional; you may
   use the recipe p. 239)

3 tablespoons butter
2 tablespoons chopped parsley
2 tablespoons thinly sliced
   scallions

Put the mushrooms in a heavy skillet with the onion, salt, and 1 tablespoon butter. Cook slowly until the mushrooms have rendered their juice. Drain it off (reserving it for use in a broth or sauce), add the remaining butter, the parsley, and the scallions, and cook until the mushrooms and scallions have just begun to take on a little color. Add, if desired, the cream or blancmange. Serve hot.

Blancmange was used during the seventeenth century as a liaison. I would recommend the use of cream rather than blancmange, unless one wishes to emphasize the less familiar aspect of the dish. Scallions are used where we might use shallots.

Episse douce des pâtissiers

Prenez deux parties de gingembre, par exemple, deux onces, et une partie, c'est à dire, une once de poivre battu en poudre, mêlez les ensemble, ajoûtez-y de clou de girofle battu, de la muscade rapée bien menu, et de la canelle battuë, de chacun une once ou environ, pour une livre de poivre, plus ou moins, comme il vous plaira, et conservez toutes ces choses mêlées ensemble dans une boëte.

Remarquez qu'on peut garder separément quelque sorte d'episse dans des petites bourses de cuir, ou dans une boëte divisée en plusieurs tiroirs.

Remarquez aussi qu'il y a plusieurs personnes qui n'emploïent que du poivre seul au lieu des autres épisses; qui que l'épisse composée soit plus douce que le poivre seul.

Episse salée.

Faites secher du sel, puis vous le mettrez en poudre, et vous en mettrez autant pesant qu'il y aura d'épisse, gardez-la dans un lieu qui ne soit pas humide.

Le Pâtissier françois (1652).

Pastrycooks' Mild Spice Mixture

¾ cup ground ginger	10 tablespoons freshly ground
1½ teaspoons ground cloves	black pepper
1¾ teaspoons ground cinnamon	1 tablespoon grated nutmeg

Mix well together and store in a closed container. La Varenne observes that spices may be stored separately in little leather bags or in a box with several drawers. His cryptic remark about a pound of pepper probably refers to this mixture, in its original quantities, as supplying the equivalent in flavoring power of a pound of pepper. In some systems of measurement a pound was made of eight ounces. (See the introductory note on measurement.) As he also remarks, some cooks simply use pepper without additional spices, but the mixture produces a milder result and, I would add, a more interesting one.

Salted Spice

Dry some salt, beat it to a powder, and add an equal quantity by weight to the above mixture. Store it in a dry place.

Nowadays our salt comes out of its box dry and of a uniform consistency. These two recipes produce seasoning mixtures that would be appropriate for meat, poultry, or fish, served hot or cold; for cold dishes a larger quantity would be needed.

Concombres fricassées

Pour les fricasser, on les peut prendre à toutes âges, pourveu que les graines ne soient trop dures, et on les tranche de lépaisseur d'un écu blanc, puis on les poudre de sel, et on fricasse de l'oignon tranché par roëlles dans le boeure ou graisse, auparavant que de les mettre dans la poëlle, où on les assaisonnera d'épices, y donnant la pointe de vinaigre.

Nicolas de Bonnefons, *Les Delices de la campagne* (1679), p. 98.

Fricasseed Cucumbers

6 cups cucumber, sliced
½ teaspoon salt
2 tablespoons butter
2 yellow onions, sliced

¼ teaspoon mixed spices (see
  Bonnefons's recipe for a spice
  mixture, p. 255)
1 teaspoon vinegar

Slice the cucumbers about ⅛ inch thick, set in a colander, sprinkle with the salt, and allow to stand and drain for about thirty minutes.

Melt the butter in a large skillet and cook the onions until they have begun to take on a little color. Sprinkle the cucumber with the spices and the vinegar. Cook, stirring and turning them over so that they cook evenly. Serve hot.

Petit Mestier, et oublies

La composition de la paste se fait avec une livre de farine, une livre de sucre, deux oeufs, et une chopine deau; il faut fondre le sucre dans l'eau à froid, et délayer de la farine un peu ferme avec de l'eau sucrée, puys y mettre les oeufs, bien battre le tout y mélant le reste de l'eau petit à petit, aprés quoy vous y ajoûterez une once de bon boeure frais, qui ferez fondre avec un peu d'eau, et le verserez bien chaud dans vostre paste, mélant le tout bien promptement ensemble, vous en ferez essay dans vos fers, preparez comme pour le pain à chanter; si elle est trop foible, vous y ajoûterez la farine; et si trop forte l'eau pour les lever, il faut les rouler sous la paume de la main, en la retirant à vous avec promptitude, et les serrer seichement.

Les oublyes se fond de la mesme façon, reservé que pour épargner le sucre, on y employe de bon miel.

Nicolas de Bonnefons, *Les Delices de la campagne* (1679), p. 16.

Sugar and Honey Wafers

either 1¼ cups sugar, for *mestiers*
  or 1¼ cups honey, for *oublies*
1 cup water for the *mestiers*, ⅞
  cup for the *oublies*

2 cups unbleached all-purpose
  flour
1 large egg
2 tablespoons melted butter

Dissolve the sugar or honey in the water. Gradually beat most of it into the flour until the mixture is the consistency of very heavy cream. Add the egg, beating **till** very smooth. Add the melted butter and, if necessary, the remaining sweetened water.

Heat the wafer iron (see plate, page 223, figures 19 and 20) and brush it with cooking oil or with the fat rind of a piece of unsmoked bacon. Cook a sample wafer; if the batter is too thick to form a palatable wafer add a little water; if it is too thin to form a tidy one add a little flour. As soon as the wafer is cooked (it will be a golden tan), take it off the iron using a pointed knife or a fork, roll it into a cylinder, and set it on a rack to cool. Store in a dry place.

The wafers made with honey, the *oublies*, are an economy measure. They are chewier but taste agreeably of honey. Be especially careful not to cook them past the golden stage or they will turn dark very quickly and burn.

Wafer irons are available today from specialty kitchen equipment suppliers, in two forms. The simpler are designed just like their *ancien régime* ancestors, though they are likely to be made of cast aluminum. They are held over a burner on a kitchen range. The more elaborate, also aluminum, are electrically heated.

Doze des épices pour toutes sortes de pâtisseries et cuisine

Prenez trois quartrons de poivre, zingembre un quartron, cloud de girofle, muscade, et ca-nelle, de chacun une once; faut bien battre le tout, et le passer par le tamis delié, puis y ajoûter cinq livres de sel battu, et méler le tout ensemble; cette composition est bonne à toutes sortes d'assaisonnemens, sans en excepter aucun; et pour ceux qui n'aiment pas l'épice, il n'y en faut mettre que la moitié de ce que vous y mettriez, et recomponser l'assaisonnement d'encore autant de sel que vous y en aurés mis.

Nicolas de Bonnefons, *Les Delices de la campagne* (1679), p. 34.

Spice Mixture for All Kinds of Pastry and Cooking
   7 tablespoons + 2 teaspoons freshly ground black pepper
   3 tablespoons + 2 teaspoons ground ginger
   2 teaspoons ground cloves
   I nutmeg, grated
   2½ teaspoons cinnamon
   3 cups + 3 tablespoons salt

Mix everything well together. Bonnefons remarks extravagantly that "this com-position is good for all kinds of seasoning needs, without exception," and further, that in cooking for those who do not like spices one adds half again as much salt to the mixture. I have reduced the quantities substantially.

Pain de veau

Prenez de la roüelle de Veau, et coupez-la par tranches bien minces, que vous batrez avec le dos d'un coûteau. Vous en prendrez à proportion du plat que vous voulez faire. Aprés il faut

prendre d'autre Roüelle de Veau, et la bien hacher avec du lard blanchi, de la graisse blanchie,
du Jambon cuit, toute sorte de fines herbes, la chair d'un estomac de chapon et perdrix; un
peau de truffles hachées, et de champignons et mousserons aussi hachez; tout cela bien assai-
sonné, de toutes sortes de fines épices, et mêlé d'un peu de crême de lait. Il faut avoir une
casserole ronde, y arranger des bardes de lard, y mettre la moitié des tranches de veau battuës,
et ensuite la farce. Il faut achever de couvrir au-dessus de la même maniere que dessous, en
sorte que la farce soit bien enfermée. Ensuite mettez à la braise bien couvert, feu dessus et
dessous, et le faites bien cuire. On peu mettre dans la Farce une petite pointe d'ail. Il faut
servir chaudement, aïant bien degraissé, et dressé vôtre plat proprement et avec adresse.

On peu servir ce Pain de veau, aux pois et aux asperges, quand c'en est la saison.

François Massialot, *Le Cuisinier roïal et bourgeois* (1705), pp. 333–34.

Veal Loaf

1¼ **pounds thinly sliced veal scallops**
1 **pound bacon, sliced**
¼ **cup blanched bacon, diced**
¼ **cup beef suet, diced**
1¼ **pounds lean veal, ground**
½ **cup cooked Virginia ham, ground**
2 **tablespoons finely chopped herbs: parsley, thyme, chervil**
1 **cup raw chicken breast, diced, or a combination of chicken breast**
   and partridge (both raw)
1½ **cups diced mushrooms; ideally this should be a combination of**
   ordinary mushrooms, boletinus mushrooms, and truffles
1 **clove of garlic, finely chopped (optional)**
1 **teaspoon spice mixture (use La Varenne's or Bonnefons's)**
¼ **cup medium cream**

Trim all the nerves and sinews from the veal scallops. Using a cutlet bat or other heavy, broad-bladed knife, pound a series of parallel lines along one side of each cutlet, at a 45° angle to the grain of the meat, and then back along the same side, at right angles to the first set of lines. Turn each cutlet over and repeat the process. Then beat each cutlet with the flat side of the bat until it is thin; by now it will look like a worn-out piece of crocheted washcloth, but it will be tender.

Take a heavy, straight-sided ovenproof dish, measuring about 7 inches in diameter on the inside and at least 2 inches deep, and line it with the sliced bacon. To do this, place one end of each strip of bacon in the center of the pan and smooth it against the bottom of the pan toward the side and then up the side. Let the remainder hang over the outside temporarily. Then proceed to lay down the remaining bacon strips fanwise from the center, or from just outside the center (so that too large a hump of bacon does not build up there), barely overlapping the strips. When all the bacon is neatly in place, line it with the pounded veal scallops, reserving a piece to cover the center of the top. The veal used as lining will overhang the container; do not trim it off.

Prepare the farce by grinding together the blanched bacon and the suet. Then combine them (an electric mixer fitted with a dough hook is useful) thoroughly, adding the ground veal, ham, herbs, chicken breast (and optional partridge), mushrooms, garlic (also optional), spices, and cream. Sauté a spoonful of this forcemeat in a skillet with a little butter and taste to see if more seasoning is needed. Adjust if necessary. Fill the lined casserole with this mixture, folding the flaps of veal over it. Put the reserved slice of veal in the center to complete the enclosure and fold the strips of bacon over the veal, making a neat package.

Put a heavy lid over the loaf; what matters here is not that the contents be enclosed but that they be weighted down. Set the casserole in a pan with sides high enough to catch the liquid that may overflow. Bake in a 350° F. oven for about two hours, or until the internal temperature is about 180° F.

Remove from the oven and let stand for thirty minutes. Drain off the liquid and invert the loaf onto the center of a round serving dish. Surround it with a band of cooked peas or asparagus if either is in season. To serve cut cakelike wedges with a carving knife.

Jus de veau

Coupez une roüelle de Veau en trois, mettez-la dans un pot de terre, et le bouchez de telle sorte avec son couvercle et pâte, qu'il n'y ait point d'air. Vous le mettrez sur un peu de feu, environ deux heures de tems; et votre jus sera fait, pour vous en servir dans les choses où l'on marque qu'il est besoin d'en mettre, pour les rendre plus succulentes, et d'un meilleur goût.

Vous pouvez pratiquer la même choses pour le jus de Mouton et de Boeuf; ou bien voir ce qui a été dit au premier article des Coulis.

François Massialot, *Le Cuisinier roïal et bourgeois* (1705), p. 274.

Extract of Veal

1½ pounds boneless stewing veal cut into chunks
½ cup flour, with enough water stirred in to make a soft dough

Put the veal in a heavy cooking pot with a tight-fitting lid. Moisten the edges of the lid and pot with a little water, put the lid in place, and use the dough to seal the joint shut all the way around the vessel. Set it over a very low flame and cook it for two hours, counting from when a very quiet bubbling sound may be heard. If air escapes from the seal, lower the cooking temperature. Use a flame baffle if necessary. Strain off the *jus* when cooking is complete.

Refrigerate in a covered jar (lifting off the congealed fat) and use the *jus*, as Massialot says, to make your sauces and other concoctions more succulent and of a better flavor. This quantity of meat should yield about 1¼ cups of *jus*.

The leftover veal may be used in any well-seasoned recipe calling for cooked veal. Massialot says that beef and mutton are cooked similarly to yield *jus de boeuf* and *jus de mouton*, and there is no reason a modern cook should not make a *jus d'agneau*, even if lamb was considered insipid in the *ancien régime*.

Essence de jambon

Il faut avoir de petites tranches de Jambon crud, les battre bien, et les passez dans la casserole avec un peu de lard fondu: mettez-les sur un réchaut allumé, et aïant une cuillère à la main, faites-lui prendre couleur avec un peu de farine. Etant coloré, on y met du bon jus de Veau, un bouquet de ciboule et de fines herbes, du clou de girofle, une gousse d'ail, quelques tranches de citron, une poignée de champignons hachez, des truffes hachées, quelques croûtes de pain, et un filet de vinaigre. Lorsque tout cela est cuit, passez-le proprement par l'étamine, et mettez ce jus en lieu propre, sans qu'il boüille davantage: Il vous servira pour toute sorte de choses où il entre du Jambon.

François Massialot, *Cuisinier roïal et bourgeois* (1705), pp. 268–69.

Essence of Ham

½ pound lean meat from a Virginia ham, sliced thin
¼ cup fat rendered from a Virginia ham or from uncured pork
1 tablespoon flour
1 cup *jus de veau* (see recipe, p. 257)
a bouquet made with 3 scallions, a few sprigs of parsley, chervil, and
   thyme
2 whole cloves
1 clove of garlic
half a lemon, cut into slices
¼ cup mushrooms, sliced
2 tablespoons truffles, chopped (optional)
½ cup dry white bread crusts
1 or 2 teaspoons wine vinegar

Pound the ham slices with a cutlet bat to tenderize them. Cook them, stirring, in a saucepan with a little rendered pork fat or fat from the ham. Dust with the flour and continue to cook and stir until the mixture has become almost the color of cinnamon. Then moisten with the cup of *jus de veau* and add the bouquet, cloves, garlic, lemon slices, mushrooms, truffles, bread crusts, and vinegar. When everything is thoroughly cooked, pass the mixture through the fine blade of a food mill. This will take quite a while. Put the essence in a cold, clean place without boiling it any more. It will serve you for all kinds of dishes containing ham.

It is dense and intense, but a small spoonful will indeed contribute a lot of good flavor to a well-chosen dish.

Fromages glacés

Il faut prendre trois chopines de lait, et chopine de Crême; la mettre dans une poële sur le feu, avec du Sucre suffisamment, deux Zests de Citron coupez en rouelles; la laisser boüillir en la tournant, jusqu'à ce qu'elle commence à s'epaissir; ensuite la verser dans un plat d'argent: et lorsqu'elle commence à être froide, la verser dans le moule de fer blanc, et mettre le moule dans un baquet plein de glace; couvrir ledit moule dessus et dessous de glace, et prendre garde que l'eau n'entre point par la jointure du moule. Lorsqu'il est glacé; cela se connoît en appuyant le doigt dessus: il faut faire chauffer de l'eau dans une poële, y mettre le moule un moment pour détacher le Fromage; le dresser sur une Porcelaine, et le servir aussi tôt.

François Massialot, *Nouvelle instruction pour les confitures* (1717), pp. 283–84.

Iced Cheese

6 cups milk	the peel of 2 lemons
2 cups medium cream	the juice of 1 lemon
1 cup sugar	

Put the milk, cream, sugar, and lemon peel in a saucepan and stir until the sugar is dissolved. Heat nearly to boiling and then pour into a shallow metal pan. Stir in the lemon juice. The mixture will curdle. Freeze the mixture until it forms an icy slurry, then pour into a mold and freeze until firm (about two to three hours). Unmold and serve at once. Do not freeze overnight or it will be too hard. This makes a very crystalline ice; if a smoother one is desired the mixture should be beaten vigorously twice during the freezing process.

Autre fromage glacé

Prenez une chopine de Crême douce, foüettez-la bien, et délayez-la avec un petit Fromage caillé; mettez-y du Sucre raisonnablement, et un peu d'eau de Fleur d'Orange; passez le tout au travers d'un tamis: ensuite mettez-le dans un moule pour le faire glacer, comme celuy ci-dessus, et le servez de même. Vous pouvez diversifier le goût et la couleur, en y mettant selon les saisons, comme Fraises, Framboises, ou Fleurs d'Orange en feüilles, que vous mêlez avec vôtre Crême en la passant au tamis. La Fleur d'Orange ne passe point, mais y laisse son goût. En hiver on le fait cuire, comme le premier Fromage glacé, et on luy donne le goût de Canelle, de Chocolat, de Citron, ou d'Essence de Bergamotte.

François Massialot, *Nouvelle instruction pour les confitures* (1717), p. 284.

Iced Cheese, another way

6 ounces cream cheese
¾ cup sugar
Flavoring: either 1 teaspoon orange-flower water
　　　　　or　　12 ounces puréed strawberries
　　　　　or　　2 ounces unsweetened chocolate melted, with
　　　　　　　　⅛ teaspoon cinnamon
　　　　　　　　¼ cup additional sugar
2 cups medium cream, whipped

Beat the cream cheese until smooth and then beat in the sugar and the flavoring desired. Fold in the whipped cream and put the mixture in the freezer for an hour. Scrape the mixture off the sides of the container, beat vigorously, and return it to the freezer for another hour. Repeat. Pack into a mold and freeze for two hours. Unmold and serve.

The cinnamon is added to the chocolate variation because in Massialot's day it was customary to manufacture chocolate with cinnamon. Do not increase the quantity. This mixture is delicious unfrozen, too.

Pain aux champignons

Il faut tourner les champignons, les couper, et les faire cuire avec un peu d'eau, un pain de beurre de Vanvres, dont il en faut manier dans la farine, un bouquet. Quand ils sont cuits, y mettre un peu de sucre, une petite pincée de sel, & les lier avec des jaunes d'oeufs & de la crême. Vous prenez un grand croûton de pain, que vous passez dans du beurre. Quand il est passé & essuyé de son beurre, vous le mettez au fond du plat que vous devez servir, coupez le en six, sans qu'il soit dérangé, & dressez le ragoût de champignons dessus.

Menon, *Nouveau traité de la cuisine* (1739), 1:254.

Mushrooms on a Crouton

a 7-inch circle of French bread,
  1 inch thick
½ cup clarified butter
1½ pounds mushrooms
½ cup water
a bouquet garni composed of
  parsley, thyme, and bay leaf

2 tablespoons butter
2 tablespoons flour
1 teaspoon sugar
½ teaspoon salt
2 egg yolks
¼ cup heavy cream

Sauté the bread in the clarified butter, on both sides, until it is lightly browned. Cut into six neat wedges and arrange it in a serving dish; keep hot.

Cut the mushroom stems off at the base of the caps and set aside for some other use. Peel the caps and put them in a heavy saucepan with the water and the bouquet garni. Knead the butter and flour together to make a *beurre manié*; put it into the saucepan in pea-sized bits. Cook, covered, stirring occasionally, until the mushrooms are tender. Add the sugar and salt. Beat the egg yolks and cream together and stir into the mushroom mixture. Cook over very low heat, stirring continuously, until the sauce has thickened; take care that it does not boil. Spoon the mushrooms over the crouton and serve hot.

If served in a dish of suitable design this will resemble closely the faience *trompe l'oeil* dishes so dear to the eighteenth-century French heart.

Gâteau de Savoie

Prenez des oeufs selon la grandeur que vous voulez faire vôtre Gateau, mettez-les dans une des balances, et dans l'autre du sucre en poudre; aussi pesant d'oeufs que de sucre. Ensuite, ôtez de vôtre balance le sucre, et laissez la moitié des oeufs dans l'autre. Pesez ensuite, aussi pesant de farine que la moitié de vos oeufs. Puis, séparez les jaunes d'avec les blancs, et faites

*foüetter les blancs en nége le plus qu'il vous sera possible; étant foüettez, mettez-y les jaunes
et continuez de batre toûjours. Ensuite, mettez-y vôtre sucre; un moment après mettez-y
vôtre farine; ensuite, mettez-y de l'écorces de citron verd rapé, quelques feüilles de fleurs-
d'oranges pralinées et hâchées, si vous en avez. Ensuite, ayez un moule de fer blanc, ou
casserole, ou bonnet de Turquie beurré; vuidez-y vôtre Gâteau; jettez par-dessus quelques
filets d'amandes pralinées sans couleur, filets de pistaches de même, de l'écorces de citron confit,
hâché bien fin, et le faites cuire sur le champ au four; observez que vôtre four ne soit pas trop
chaud; et pour le faire cuire à propos, il y faut laisser une heure et demi de tems, selon la
grosseur de vôtre Gâteau. Etant cuit; tirez-le du moule; et s'il est d'une belle couleur, vous
le servirez de même, ou vous le glacerez avec une glache blanche, comme le Gâteau de mille
feüilles; ou bien vous le dorerez avec un peu de sirop, et le poudrerez de nonpareille. Ensuite,
dressez-le dans son plat, et le servez pour Entremets. Vous en pouvez faire d'aussi petits que
vous jugerez à propos dans des petits moules.*

Vincent La Chapelle, *Le Cuisinier moderne* (1742), 2:186–87.

Savoy Sponge Cake

4 eggs, separated   1 cup cake flour, sifted
½ cup granulated sugar   the grated rind of 1 lime
1 tablespoon chopped candied orange or other flowers (optional)
1 tablespoon candied slivered almonds
1 tablespoon candied slivered pistachios
1 tablespoon preserved lemon peel, chopped very fine

Preheat the oven to 325° F. Butter a tin mold, a straight-sided saucepan, or a
Turk's head mold (fluted, with a pipe in the center). Beat 4 egg whites until very
stiff and then beat in the 4 egg yolks, one at a time. Then gradually beat in the sugar
and immediately after that fold in the flour, the grated lime rind, and, if desired, the
candied flowers. Pour the batter into the prepared baking pan and sprinkle the top
with the nuts and peel. Bake at once. The cake is done when a skewer inserted into
the center comes out dry and when the cake just begins to draw away from the sides
of the mold.

Let stand ten minutes, then detach cake gently from the sides of the mold with
a slender, pointed knife. Unmold it onto a wire rack to cool. Serve, dusted with
confectioners' sugar, if you wish.

This recipe is unnerving to a modern cook: it goes against one's grain to beat
egg yolks into egg whites without even adding sugar first. Indeed, there is a resultant loss of volume. This is no modern cake; it has a coarser texture, an eggy flavor,
and is quite sweet. But it is palatable. Still-life paintings of the period show cakes
with an identical texture, which I find reassuring.

Boeuf en miroton

*Prenez du Boeuf de poitrine cuit dans la marmite, si vous en avez de la veille il sera aussi
bon, coupez-le par tranche fort mince, prenez le plat que vous devez servir, mettez dans le*

fonds deux cuillerées de Coulis, Persil, Ciboule, Capes, Anchois, une petite pointe d'Ail, le tout haché très-fin, Sel, gros Poivre, arrangez dessus vos morceaux de tranche de Boeuf, et les assaisonnez par-dessus, couvrez votre plat et le mettez bouillir doucement sur un fourneau pendant une demie heure, et servez à courte sauce.

Menon, *La Cuisinière bourgeoise* (1746), p. 41.

Boeuf en Miroton

Take some brisket of beef cooked in the stockpot; if you have some left over from the night before, that will do just as well. Slice it very thin. Take the fireproof dish you are going to use; put in the bottom two spoonfuls of *coulis* (see recipe, p. 264), some chopped parsley, scallions, capers, anchovies, a small clove of garlic, all chopped very fine, with some salt and pepper. Arrange over them your slices of beef and season them above as you did below; cover your dish and let it simmer gently on the stove for half an hour, then serve with just a little sauce.

Biscuits de chocolat

Mettez dans une terrine deux tablettes de chocolat rappé, avec une demie livre de sucre fin passé au tamis, quatre jaunes d'oeufs, battez le tout ensemble avec une espatule, ensuite vous y mettez huit blancs d'oeufs fouettés, que vous mêlez bien avec le sucre et le chocolat, vous avez un quarteron de farine un peu séchée au four que vous mettez dans un tamis, passez-la au travers dans la composition de biscuits, que vous remuez à mesure qu'elle tombe, pour la bien mêler avec; dressez vos biscuits dans des moules de papier, jettez un peu de sucre fin dessus en le faisant tomber légerement d'un tamis; mettez cuire dans un four doux.

Menon, *La Science du maître d'hôtel, confiseur* (1750), p. 408.

Small Cakes of Chocolate *Biscuit*

2 one-ounce tablets of semisweet chocolate, grated	8 egg whites, stiffly beaten
1 cup sugar	½ cup cake flour
4 egg yolks	2 tablespoons confectioners' sugar

Preheat the oven to 325° F. Beat the grated chocolate, sugar, and egg yolks in a bowl until thick and creamy. Fold in the stiffly beaten egg whites. Sift the flour over the mixture and fold it in gently. Set cupcake papers out on a cooky sheet and spoon a small amount of batter—not more than ¼ cup—into each one. Sift the confectioners' sugar over the batter. Bake at once, until the tops of the cakes are just firm. This should take fifteen or twenty minutes. Remove from the oven and cool on a wire rack.

By the mid-eighteenth century chocolate was less likely to be made with spices; if any were added they were still most likely to be cinnamon and black pepper. If this seems odd, consider that in this present century recipes are still circulating for chocolate cookies made with pepper. In baking these, if one uses silicone-coated cupcake papers, the task of extracting the cakes will be greatly simplified, though of course not so authentic.

Crême de fraises

Ayez une pinte de bonne crême que vous mettez dans une poële, avec un quarteron de sucre, faites-la boullir jusqu'à ce qu'elle soit réduite à moitié, voux prenez deux bonnes poignées de fraises épluchées & lavées; que vous pilez dans un mortier, délayez-les dans la crême; lorsqu'elle est à moitié froide, vous y délayez gros comme un pois de pressure, passez tout de suite votre crême dans une serviette, pour la mettre dans le compotier que vous devez servir, mettez ce compotier à l'étuve pour faire prendre la crême; lorsqu'elle sera prise, vous la mettez rafraîchir sur de la glace.

Menon, *La Science du maître d'hôtel, confiseur* (1750), pp. 46–47.

Strawberry Cream

½ cup sugar	1 pint ripe strawberries
4 cups medium cream	1 rennet tablet

Put the sugar and cream in a heavy saucepan and stir until the sugar is dissolved. Bring the cream slowly to a very gentle simmer and cook, stirring occasionally, until it has reduced to one-half its original volume. It will become thick and somewhat curdy and will have the color of old ivory. Put the strawberries through a food mill and stir the purée into the cream.

Let cool until it is exactly 98° F. Dissolve the rennet tablet in ½ teaspoon water, crushing it with the back of a spoon. Pour the cream into its serving dish, strain the dissolved rennet into it, stir immediately, and let stand at room temperature until it has set, which should take fifteen to thirty minutes. Cover and refrigerate for several hours or overnight.

The recipe for this rich confection says to line the serving dish with a cloth; it says nothing about removing it. I can imagine that the liquid is supposed to drain through the cloth, were it suspended in a colander or a pierced dish; on the other hand, if one omits this step the cream is still sumptuous. "Pinte" may look like pint, but in the eighteenth century it measured, in Paris, just under one quart.

Coulis général

Foncez une casserole de quelques tranches de jambon; un peu de lard et de la ruelle de veau suffisamment, suivant la quantité et la bonté du coulis que vous voulez faire; mettez dessus la viande deux carottes, un oignon piqué de deux clous de gérofle, un panais, un demi verre de bouillon sans être degraissé; faites suer sur un moyen feu jusqu'à ce que la viande ait rendu son jus, ensuite vous le poussez à plus grand feu jusqu'à ce qu'il se forme un beau caramel dessous la viande et autour de la casserole, ôtez tout ce qui est dans la casserole pour le mettre sur un plat, remettez le caramel sur le feu avec de la farine et du bon beurre, remuez toujours jusqu'à ce que la farine soit d'une belle couleur dorée sans le pousser à trop grand feu crainte

*que le coulis ne prenne un goût de roux: mouillez ensuite avec le bouillon de la piece de boeuf
& du jus jusqu'à ce qu'il soit d'une belle couleur; point trop clair ni trop lié, remettez y la
viande et faites bouillir à petit feu en le degraissant de tems en tems, jusqu'à ce qu'elle soit
cuite que vous la tirerez avec une écumoire: passez ensuite votre coulis dans une étamine sans
expression.*

Les Soupers de la cour (Paris), 1755, 1:72–73.

All-purpose Cullis

2 ounces bacon or streaky salt pork	**1 onion**
¼ pound Virginia ham, thinly sliced	**2 whole cloves**
	1 parsnip
½ pound lean veal scallops (or ground veal)	**1⅓ cups good bouillon**
	1 tablespoon butter
2 carrots	**1 tablespoon flour**
	1 tablespoon *jus* (see p. 257)

Melt the fat out of some bacon (it may be sliced or chopped) in a heavy saucepan
and then line the pan with the slices of ham and the veal. Put the carrots, onion
(stuck with the cloves), parsnip, and ⅓ cup of broth on the meat, and cover. Cook
over moderate heat until the meats and vegetables exude their juices. Then uncover
and raise the heat; cook and stir until a fine caramel-colored crust has formed on the
bottom and sides of the saucepan and its contents. Take it off the fire and set the
contents aside temporarily. Put the butter and flour in the saucepan and put it back
over the heat; cook and stir until the flour has taken on a rich golden color, but do
not push it too far over a great heat, for fear the cullis will develop a scorched flavor.
Then moisten it with 1 cup of bouillon and the *jus*; cook and stir until it is of a good
consistency (Menon says, helpfully, neither too thin nor too thick). "Return the
browned meats and vegetables to the saucepan and simmer over a gentle flame,
skimming off the fat from time to time, until it is cooked. Strain, without pressing
any of the solid matter through the sieve." This will produce a very small quantity
of a thick, meaty substance; more may be obtained by disregarding the author's
advice and squeezing the mixture through a purée sieve. The substantial amount of
remaining solids can be used as a sandwich spread, and people who like deviled ham
on the toast under their poached eggs will like this even better. It will keep for
several days in a covered container in the refrigerator.

Cullises were used to do two jobs at once—to thicken sauces and to intensify
their flavors. English cookbook writers routinely condemned them and routinely
included cullis recipes in their own books. The word "cullis" is typical of the way
the French language was dealt with by seventeenth- and eighteenth-century English
speakers.

Côtelettes d'agneau à la provençale

*Coupez des côtelettes d'agneau, et les appropriez; faites-les mariner avec un peu de bonne
huile, basilic en poudre, persil, ciboules, champignons hachés, sel, gros poivre; panez de mie*

de pain et faites grillier. Servez dessous une sauce de cette façon: Mettez dans une casserole un verre de vin de Champagne, autant de consommé, un pain de beurre manié avec un peu de mie de pain, échalottes, persil, ciboules, sel, gros poivre; faites bouillir et réduir au point d'un sauce, en servant mettez-y cinq ou six zestes, et le jus d'une orange.

Les Soupers de la cour (1755), 2:62.

Lamb Chops à la provençale

6 lamb chops from the rib
¼ cup olive oil
1 teaspoon dried basil
1 tablespoon parsley, chopped
1 tablespoon scallions, chopped
2 tablespoons mushrooms, chopped
¼ teaspoon salt
freshly ground black pepper
½ cup dry crumbs of French bread

½ cup Champagne (or other dry white wine)
½ cup consommé
1 tablespoon butter
2 tablespoons dry crumbs of French bread
1 tablespoon shallots, chopped
2 teaspoons parsley, chopped
1 teaspoon scallions, chopped
¼ teaspoon salt
freshly ground black pepper
1 orange

Trim all the fat you can from the chops and marinate them for half an hour in the olive oil, basil, 1 tablespoon parsley, 1 tablespoon scallions, mushrooms, salt, and pepper, turning them once. Without removing the marinading ingredients, coat the chops with the bread crumbs and broil them, not too close to the heat, for six to eight minutes on each side, or until the crumbs are nicely browned and the inside of the chops is pink.

Meanwhile make the sauce as follows: Cook the wine and consommé in a saucepan. Knead together the butter and the crumbs, 1 tablespoon shallots, 2 teaspoons parsley, 1 teaspoon scallions, salt, and pepper; add this mixture to the simmering liquid, stirring. Continue to simmer the sauce, stirring occasionally, until some of the liquid has evaporated and what remains has thickened somewhat. At the moment of serving add the finely chopped outer peel of ¼ of an orange and 2 or 3 tablespoons of orange juice—enough to flavor but not to overwhelm the sauce. Serve in a sauceboat with the chops.

Saumon aux fines herbes

Foncez le plat que vous devez servir avec du bon beurre, persil, ciboules, échalottes, une pointe d'ail, champignons, un peu de basilic, le tout haché très-fin, sel, gros poivre; arrangez dessus deux dardes de saumon frais; assaisonnez dessus comme dessous; pannez de mies de pain, et sur la mie de pain remettez-y des petits morceaux de beurre gros comme des pois, proche les uns des autres; faites cuire sur un petit feu et un couvercle de tourtière. La cuisson faite, penchez le plat pour en égoutter le beurre; servez dessous une sauce claire à l'Italienne, finie de bon goût.

Les Soupers de la cour (1755), 3:125–26.

Salmon with Fines Herbes

1 tablespoon parsley	¼ teaspoon salt
2 tablespoons scallions	coarsely ground black pepper to
1 tablespoon shallots	taste
1 clove garlic	2 salmon steaks, about 1 pound
2 tablespoons mushrooms	½ cup fine dry bread crumbs
2 teaspoons basil	2 tablespoons butter

Preheat the oven to 350° F. Butter a shallow ovenproof dish.

Chop together very fine the parsley, scallions, shallots, garlic, mushrooms, and basil. Add salt and pepper to taste. Scatter half of the mixture in the bottom of the baking dish and place the salmon steaks side by side on them. Put the other half of the chopped mixture on top. Crumb the tops generously with the bread crumbs and dot the surface with closely set dabs of butter.

Bake until the salmon is cooked through, which will take about half an hour. If the crumbs have not browned run the dish under the broiler momentarily.

Serve beneath a sauce petite claire à l'italienne. (See below.)

The crumb covering keeps the salmon moist and tender. "Darde," in the French text, appears to be a misprint for "darne." In the original recipe the pie lid set over the baking dish creates an ovenlike space; I have used an oven instead, believing that it makes for a crisper top.

Sauce petite italienne

Mettez dans une casserole une tranche de jambon, trois ou quatre champignons, deux ou trois échalottes, une demi-gousse d'ail, le quart d'une feuille de laurier, une bonne cuillerée d'huile; passez le tout ensemble sur un moyen feu, mouillez avec du consommé, un peu de coulis, un demi-verre de vin de Champagne, faites bouillir à petit feu pendant une demi-heure; dégraissez, passez au tamis.

Les Soupers de la cour (1755), 1:124.

A Little Italian Sauce

2 ounces well-flavored ham	1 tablespoon olive oil
3 or 4 mushrooms	⅔ cup consommé (or bouillon)
2 or 3 shallots	2 teaspoons coulis (see p. 263)
half a clove of garlic	⅓ cup Champagne (or other dry
a quarter of a bay leaf	white wine)

Put the ham, mushrooms, shallots, garlic, bay leaf, and oil in a saucepan and cook it, stirring, over medium heat until it has just begun to sizzle, then moisten it with some consommé (or good bouillon), the *coulis*, and the wine. Simmer, skimming off the fat, for half an hour. Strain and serve with the salmon.

Rôties soufflées

Pilez du blanc de volaille cuite à la broche avec moëlle de boeuf; Parmesan rapé, cinq jaunes d'oeufs, les blancs fouettés; dressez sur des mies de pain passées au beurre; unissez avec de l'oeuf; pannez moitié Parmesan et mies de pain; faites cuire au four; serves dessous un peu de consommé.

Les Soupers de la cour (1755), 4:32.

Croutons with Chicken Soufflé

> 8 ⅜-inch-thick slices of French bread, trimmed to 4 ½-inch ovals
> 6 tablespoons clarified butter
> 1½ cups roast chicken breast, ground
> ½ cup beef marrow, poached
> ½ cup Parmesan cheese, freshly grated
> 4 or 5 egg yolks, according to size
> 4 or 5 egg whites, also according to size, stiffly beaten
> I egg, beaten
> 2 tablespoons dry French bread crumbs
> 2 tablespoons Parmesan cheese, freshly grated
> 2 cups bouillon (see recipe, p. 269)

Preheat the oven to 350° F. Sauté the bread in the clarified butter until golden brown on one side. Beat together the chicken, marrow, half cup of Parmesan cheese, and egg yolks; gently stir in about one-quarter of the stiffly beaten egg whites and then fold in the remainder. Put the toasts on a lightly buttered baking sheet and spread them with the chicken mixture, heaping it up toward the middle. Brush the toasts with the beaten egg, using the brush to smooth the surface of the soufflé mixture. Dust with a mixture of 2 tablespoons each bread crumbs and Parmesan cheese. Bake until puffed and golden—about fifteen minutes. Serve at once, in a plate, with a small amount of rich bouillon.

This recipe appears in B. Clermont, *The Professed Cook* (1767), p. 439, where he changes the bouillon to "a good relishing Cullis-Sauce." I append it here as a good example of how eighteenth-century French recipes look when they are turned into English of the same period.

Rôties soufflées. Puffed or raised. *Soufflées*, blown.

Pound a Breast of a roasted Fowl, with some Beef-marrow, Parmesan-cheese, five Yolks of Eggs, and the Whites whipped to Frought; prepare it upon Pieces of Bread, cut like Toasts, and fried in Butter; rub them over with Yolks and whites of eggs; and garnish with Bread-crumbs and Parmesan-cheese mixed; bake in the Oven and serve a good relishing Cullis-Sauce under; you may make a Toast with Truffles, Mushrooms, or anything else.

Asperges en petits pois

Ayez des petites asperges; coupez tout le tendre comme des petits pois; étant bien lavées vous les faites faire deux ou trois bouillons à l'eau bouillante; égouttez et les passez sur le feu avec un bon morceau de beurre, un bouquet de persil, ciboules, un clou de girofle, un peu de sariette; mettez-y une pincée de farine; mouillez de bouillon, un peu de sucre et du sel; faites cuire et réduire à courte sauce; en finissant mettez-y une liaison de jaunes d'oeuf et de crême.

Les Soupers de la cour (1755), 4:173–74.

Asparagus Disguised as Peas

> 1 pound slender asparagus, weighed after the tough ends are cut off
> 3 tablespoons butter
> a bouquet of 3 or 4 sprigs of parsley, 2 scallions, trimmed, 1 whole
>   clove, and 3 or 4 sprigs winter savory, all tied with string
> 2 teaspoons flour   salt to taste
> ½ cup bouillon   2 egg yolks
> 1 teaspoon sugar   ¼ cup cream

Clean the asparagus and cut it into pea-sized lengths. Bring water to a boil and parboil them in it for one or two minutes, then drain. Melt the butter in a saucepan until it bubbles; add the asparagus and the bundle of herbs; sauté until half cooked, and then stir in the flour. Cook and stir for another minute or two, then add the bouillon, the sugar, and some salt. Cook and stir until the liquid has thickened and reduced slightly. Remove the mixture from the heat. Beat together the egg yolks and the cream; stir some of the asparagus mixture in it, and then pour the liaison into the saucepan; stir the mixture well together and heat but do not boil. Serve at once as a separate dish or as a garnish.

Bouillon ordinaire, ou mitonnage pour la base des potages et des sauces

Ce bouillon doit être fait avec toute l'attention possible. On prend la quantité de viande nécessaire. La meilleure est la tranche, le gîte et le trumeau. On y ajoûte une poule ou jaret de veau. Quand il est bien écumé, vous le salez légérement, et y mettez les racines convenables, comme navets, carottes, panais, oignons, cellery et poireaux, avec un clou de gerofle et une racine de persil. Ce bouillon ou mitonnage sert à faire cuire tout ce qui se met sur les potages, comme volailles, gibier, grosse viande, et toutes les garnitures ou légumes, excepté les choux, radix, gros navets et quelques autres légumes dont on fait le potage à part. Une partie de la bonté de tous les bouillons dépend de l'attention et du soin que l'on prend.

François Marin, Les Dons de Comus (1758), 1:2–3.

Everyday Bouillon

4 pounds round of beef
a 6-pound boiling fowl, trussed, or 4–5 pounds veal shanks
1 gallon cold water   1 stalk celery
2 onions   1 whole clove
3 leeks   salt to taste
1 parsley root or 6 parsley stems with leaves

Close attention must be paid in making this bouillon. Put the beef and the chicken or veal in a large stockpot with the gallon of cold water. Bring it slowly to a very gentle boil and simmer, skimming assiduously, until no more foam or sediment rises to the surface. Then add the vegetables, sticking the clove into the side of one of the onions. Simmer very gently, removing the fowl when it is tender. By the time the beef is done the bouillon will be, too; it should take about five hours.

Strain the broth and set it aside to chill. Lift the solidified fat off and discard it. The beef and chicken or veal can be used for a great variety of dishes. Salt to taste before using.

Marin observes that "this bouillon or simmering stock is used to cook everything which is put into soups, such as poultry, game, red meat, and so forth, and all the garnishes or vegetables, except for cabbages, root vegetables, and some other vegetables of which separate soups are made. Part of the goodness of all these bouillons depends on the attention given and care taken in making them." I would add that it is a delicious soup without further additions and, in providing cooked beef and veal or chicken, supplies the principal ingredients for other dishes.

Julienne pour toutes les saisons

Passez des pointes de cellery avec quelques zestes d'oseille, & de petites filets de laitüe: mouillez le tout avec de bon bouillon; puis empotez-le dans une marmite assez grande pour la quantité de potage que vous voulez faire; joignez-y deux carottes, deux panais, deux navets, un gros oignon piqué d'un clou. Faites bouillir le tout deux heures à petit feu, et que la marmite ne bouille que d'un côté, et faites ensuite mitonner. Il faut que ce potage soit parfumé, qu'il ait l'oeil clair et bien ambré. On y met des pois dans le tems, et autres ingrédiens suivant la saison.

François Marin, *Les Dons de Comus* (1758), 1:89–90.

A Julienne for All Seasons

½ cup celery tips, finely sliced   2 parsnips
1 cup lettuce, finely sliced   2 turnips
2 tablespoons butter   1 large onion
2 quarts bouillon (see above)   1 whole clove
2 carrots   1 cup sorrel, finely sliced

Cook the celery tips (leaves and stalk) and lettuce in 1 tablespoon of butter until wilted. Then put it in a heavy stockpot with the bouillon, carrots, parsnips, turnips, and the onion stuck with the clove. Simmer very gently for two hours. Marin, cooking over coals, says that the pot should boil on only one side. A few minutes before serving, cook the sorrel in the remaining tablespoon of butter until it is wilted and add it to the soup. Serve piping hot with hot French bread to sop in it.

Marin adds that various vegetables in season, such as green peas, may be added and that "this soup should be aromatic, clear, and of a fine amber hue." It is indeed.

Haricots verds en salade

Vos Haricots étant cuits, mettez-les à égouter, faites les sécher entre deux linges, fendez-les en deux, si bon vous semble, dans leur longueur; dressez-les dans le plat que vous devés servir; faites y autour un cordon de petites herbes hachées menues; sçavoir, cerfeuil, pimpre-nelle, estragon, civette et persil. On les assaisonne sur la table, d'huile et vinaigre, avec un peu de poivre concassée.

Quelques-un font de ces salades diverses armoiries, comme Croix de Chevalier, Croix de Malthe, Etoile, ou quelques autres desseins.

Traité historique et pratique de la cuisine. Ou le cuisinier instruit (1758), 2:489.

Green Bean Salad

1 pound green beans	**2 tablespoons parsley**
2 teaspoons burnet	**½ cup oil**
1 tablespoon chives	**2 tablespoons wine vinegar**
1 tablespoon chervil	**⅛ teaspoon coarsely ground black**
1 tablespoon tarragon	**pepper**

Slice the beans in two lengthwise if you wish and boil them in salted water. As soon as they are just tender, drain them and then dry them in a clean dish towel. Arrange them on their serving dish.

Chop all the herbs together very fine and arrange them in a band around the beans. Put the oil, vinegar, and pepper in a bowl and serve it with the beans; this dressing is put on the beans at the moment of serving.

The author remarks that "some people like to make various heraldic designs with this salad, such as a knight's cross, a Maltese cross, a star, or some other de-sign."

Oeufs à la Romaine

Faites un syrop avec du sucre et du vin blanc, cassés huit ou dix oeufs frais, (ce sont toujours les meilleurs à quelque sauce qu'on veuïlle les mettre,) assaisonnez-les d'une pincée de sel, de muscade, de six grains de coriandre & d'un peu de canelle, le tout mis en poudre; battés bien vos oeufs comme si vous vouliés faire une omelette; et les passés au travers d'une étamine, mettés votre syrop dans une casserole qui soit un peu platte, et dont le fond soit de la grandeur du plat dans lequel vous devés servir les oeufs, faites bouillir votre syrop avec un petit morceau d'excellent beurre, versez-y vos oeufs au travers d'une passoire, et vous verrés qu'ils cuiront dans le moment; retirez les ensuite, glacez-les, si bon vous semble, et servés.

Traité historique et pratique de la cuisine. Ou le cuisinier instruit (1758), 2:380.

Eggs in Wine Syrup

½ cup sugar
4 cups dry white wine
7 or 8 fresh eggs
½ teaspoon ground nutmeg

½ teaspoon ground cinnamon
½ teaspoon ground coriander
a pinch of salt
2 tablespoons butter

In a shallow heavy saucepan dissolve the sugar in the white wine and bring to a boil. Beat the eggs as if you were going to make an omelet, adding the spices and salt. Pass them through a strainer; this will assure that the spices have not formed little lumps and that the egg batter has no white streaks in it. Add the butter to the boiling syrup and pour the batter through the sieve into the boiling syrup. Turn down the heat so the eggs do not overcook; they will be set and therefore done in a minute or two.

Oranges de Portugal au caramel

Il faut prendre la chair des oranges, de celles dont vous avez ôté l'écorce pour mettre à l'eau-de-vie; vous les séparez en quatre, en prenant garde de percer la petite peau qui sépare les morceaux; vous avez un sucre cuit au caramel, que vous tenez chaudement sur un petit feu; mettez-y vos quartiers d'oranges un à un, et retournez-les avec une fourchette; en les retirant, vous mettez à chaque quartier un petit bâton pointu, pour les dresser sur un clayon; vous mettez les petits bâtons dans la maille du clayon, afin que le caramel puisse sécher en l'air.

Le Dictionnaire portatif de cuisine (1767), 2:101.

Oranges Glazed with Caramel

6 oranges
2 cups sugar
1 cup water

1 teaspoon wine vinegar
24 thin wood (or bamboo)
    skewers

Remove the outer peel from the oranges and reserve it for another use. Remove the inner peel (the bitter, white part) and discard it. Scrape away as much of the pith and fiber as you conveniently can, taking care not to pierce the membrane. If you do, dry the spot off with a paper towel. If the hole is large, do not attempt to glaze the piece of orange. Separate the oranges into quarters.

Make a caramel syrup by dissolving the sugar in the water with the vinegar. Stir before boiling; when the sugar is dissolved raise the heat until the mixture boils and then put a lid on the saucepan and simmer for five minutes. Remove the lid and cook the syrup until it has just begun to change color. Dip the orange quarters, one at a time, in the caramel syrup. Turn each quarter over with a fork and then lift it up and run a thin wooden skewer into one end. Hold it over the saucepan until the syrup has stopped running off.

Put a wire rack on top of a pan or bowl and put a one or two pound weight in the middle of it. When the finished orange quarter has finished dripping put the other end of the skewer through the rack and slant the skewer so that the weight of the orange at the end braces it. Thus the orange cools and dries. Do not put on a plate until immediately before serving. A very thin film of oil on the plate will prevent sticking. Serve within an hour or two of glazing.

Small oranges are better than large ones because the insides are juicy from being heated. As a modern variation, and for easy peeling, tangerines may be used. Those who are not expert with caramel may want to make two batches.

Epice fine propre pour l'assaisonnement de la pâtisserie et autres mets de la cuisine

Prenez une once de poivre long, une once de gingembre, une once de poivre ordinaire, une once de gérofle, une once de muscade, une once de macis, une once de canelle, une once de coriande, et cinq à six feuilles de laurier à sauce avec quelques brins de basilic qui soient bien secs; pilez bien toutes ces choses ensemble dans un mortier, et passez-les à travers d'un tamis; mettez ensuite cette Epice dans une bouteille que vous boucherez bien, afin que l'air ne puisse y entrer, et mettez la en un lieu sec.

. . . Elle vous servira non seulement pour la pâtisserie, mais aussi pour assaisonner toutes sortes de farces, tant en gras qu'en maigre; les gros lardons pour piquer toutes sortes de viandes, tant de boucherie que de volaille, et toutes sortes de ragoûts.

Lorsque vous voulez faire de l'Épice salée, il faut mettre une forte demie-once de cette Épice dans une demie-livre de sel bien pilé et passé à travers d'une passoire bien fine.

Pour la dose de cette assaisonnement, on voit à peu près ce que les choses demandent, le jugement en décide aisément, et un peu d'usage y rend les gens habiles. On peut cependent pour plus de sureté, se régler sur une forte demie once d'assaisonnement (compris le sel et les Epices) sur chaque livre de viande; j'entends pour ce qui se mange froid; mais pour ce qui se mange chaud, n'y mettez tout au plus que la moitié de cet assaisonnement qui est deux gros sur chacque livre. Vous agirez de même pour le maigre.

Traité historique et pratique de la cuisine. Ou le cuisinier instruit (1758), 2:241–42.

A Fine Spice Mixture for Seasoning Pastry and Other Dishes

[½ ounce long pepper if you can get it]

2 tablespoons + 2 teaspoons ginger

2 tablespoons + 1 teaspoon freshly ground black pepper

1 tablespoon + 1¼ teaspoon ground cloves

3½ whole nutmegs (about 4 tablespoons when grated)

3 tablespoons + 1 teaspoon mace

3 tablespoons ground coriander

2 or 3 bay leaves

2 teaspoons dried basil

The author's remarks are so useful that I will quote them in their entirety:
"It will be very useful to you not only for pastry, but also for seasoning all sorts

of ground meat mixtures, both for meat days and for fasts; [for seasoning] the big strips of pork for larding all kinds of meats, both red meats and poultry, and all kinds of ragouts.

"When you want to make salted spice you must put a good half-ounce of this spice in a half-pound of well-ground and sifted salt. [To experiment, try 2 tablespoons + 2 teaspoons of this mixture to 1 cup + 1 teaspoon of salt.]

"For the quantity of this spice to use, one must judge according to the circumstances; a little practice makes people handy. One may use, as a rule of thumb, a good half ounce of seasoning (*counting both the salt and the spices*) to each pound of meat; this is for things that are eaten cold; but for what is eaten hot, do not put in more than half as much of this seasoning, which is 2 *marcs* [or 2 teaspoons] per pound. You will do the same for fast-day foods."

This proportion of salted spice to meat is higher than we would use, but it is a tasty mixture.

Ragoût mêlé

Mettez dans une casserole des champignons coupés en quatre, des foies gras, deux ou trois culs d'artichaux cuits à moitié dans l'eau et coupés par morceaux, un bouquet persil, ciboules, une demi-gousse d'ail, un peu de beurre passez le tout sur le feu, mettez-y une pincée de farine, mouillez avec un demi-verre de vin blanc, un peu de coulis et du bouillon; faites cuire une demi heure, dégraissez, assaisonnez de sel, gros poivre. Si vous avez de petits oeufs, vous les faites bouillir un instant dans l'eau, ôtez-en la petite peau et les mettez dans le ragoût faire un bouillon; si vous n'en avez point de naturels, et que vous en vouliez faire qui en approchent, prenez deux jaunes d'oeufs durs, que vous pilez, et y mettez avec un jaune d'oeuf crud, une idée de sel fin; mettez-les sur une table farinée, roulez-les comme une petite saucisse, et les coupez en petits morceaux d'égale grandeur; roulez chaque morceau dans vos mains avec un peu de farine, pour les arrondir, et les mettez à mesure sur un plat fariné; lorsqu'ils seront tous faits, mettez-les un moment dans de l'eau bouillante; après qu'ils auront fait deux bouillons, retirez-les à l'eau fraîche, faites-les égoutter avant de les mettre dans le ragoût. Si vous voulez mettre ce ragoût au blanc, vous n'y mettrez point de coulis, avant que de servir, vous y mettrez une liaison de trois jaunes d'oeufs avec de la crème.

Menon, *La Cuisinière bourgeoise* (1790), 2:126.

A Mixed Ragout

4 chicken livers	2 or 3 artichoke bottoms
12 small mushrooms, quartered	2 tablespoons butter

4 stalks of parsley, the white part of 3 scallions, and a half a clove of garlic tied in a bundle

1½ teaspoons flour	2 teaspoons *coulis* (see p. 263)
¼ cup white wine	½ cup bouillon (see p. 269)
	salt and pepper to taste

some unlaid eggs or 2 hard-boiled egg yolks, 1 raw egg yolk, and ⅛ teaspoon salt; 2 tablespoons flour

Cut each chicken liver into three or four pieces. Half cook the artichoke bottoms in boiling water with a spoonful of vinegar. Cook the mushrooms, artichoke bottoms, and chicken livers in a saucepan with the butter and the bundle of herbs, stirring, for about five minutes. Sprinkle the flour over this mixture, stirring, and then add, still stirring, the wine, *coulis,* and bouillon. Cook for half an hour, degrease, and season to taste with salt and freshly ground black pepper.

Petits oeufs, or unlaid eggs, are found inside laying chickens; in Menon's recipe he recommends using them if they are available. They are slipped out of their still-soft shells into boiling water, to be poached, and are then added to the ragout for a brief final moment of cooking. Lacking these one makes a substitute as follows: The yolks of two hard-boiled eggs are put through a sieve and mixed with the yolk of one raw egg, then seasoned with a little salt. This mixture is formed into a little sausage (though if one adds the entire raw yolk the mixture will be too soft to form a sausage; the mixture may then be dropped from a teaspoon) by rolling it out on a floured surface. The imitation eggs are dusted with flour, and the excess is removed by rolling them gently, one or two at a time, in a sieve. Boil two cups of water in a small saucepan and drop the egg balls into it, a few at a time. As the flour becomes wet they will turn bright yellow. Poach them for about two minutes and then lift them out with a skimmer and put them in a bowl of cold water to wait until the moment before the ragout is served.

At serving time check the ragout's seasoning; heat it and add the egg balls, stirring them in gently. Cook for a minute and serve, either as a separate dish or as a garnish.

This is an economy version of the archetypical eighteenth-century ragout. A more sumptuous one would include truffles and cockscombs. Unlaid eggs were considered a delicacy. The egg balls included here add a startling note of color; their texture is smooth and slightly elastic. To the modern taste a chicken liver that has simmered for half an hour is tough and its flavor spoiled, but Menon is specific about the time. This is one of those cases where one must choose whether to satisfy one's curiosity about the past or one's desire for delicious food.

Notes

INTRODUCTION

1. Pierre Jean Baptiste Le Grand d'Aussy, *Histoire de la vie privée des françois depuis l'origine de la nation jusqu'a nos jours.*

2. Alfred Franklin, *La Vie privée d'autrefois.* See especially *L'Annonce et la réclame* (1887); *La Cuisine* (1888); *Les Repas* (1889); *Variétés gastronomiques* (1891); *Le Café, le thé et le chocolat* (1893); *La Vie de Paris sous la régence* (1897); *La Vie de Paris sous Louis XIV* (1898); *Variétés parisiennes* (1901).

3. Jérôme Pichon, ed., *Le Ménagier de Paris;* Jérôme Pichon and Georges Vicaire, eds., *Le Viandier de Guillaume Tirel, dit Taillevent.*

4. Louis Douët d'Arcq, "Traité de cuisine écrit vers 1306."

5. Bertrand Guégan, *Le Cuisinier français;* Raymond Oliver, *Gastronomy of France;* Anne Willan, *Great Cooks and Their Recipes from Taillevent to Escoffier.*

6. *Petits Propos Culinaires* (London: Prospect Books). Other periodicals that publish articles on culinary history include *L'Histoire,* with contributions by J. L. Flandrin, writing as "Platine"; *History Today,* with contributions from Maggie Black; *Natural History,* which has a regular monthly column by Raymond Sokolov; and a collection titled *Fading Feast* (New York: Farrar Straus and Giroux, 1981).

7. See, for example: Alfred Gottschalk, *Histoire de l'alimentation et de la gastronomie;* Georges Blond and Germaine Blond, *Histoire pittoresque de notre alimentation;* Jacques Bourgeat, *Les Plaisirs de la table en France des gaulois à nos jours;* Cécile Eluard-Valette, *Les Grandes heures de la cuisine française;* Christian Guy, *An Illustrated History of French Cuisine from Charlemagne to Charles de Gaulle.*

8. Cited but not endorsed in *Dictionnaire de l'Académie des Gastronomes,* 2:385.

9. Marcel Roethlisberger, *Claude Lorraine,* 1:3.

10. See, for example, Abel Lefranc, *La Vie quotidienne au temps de la Renaissance;* Jacques Levron, *La Vie quotidienne à la cour de Versailles au XVIIᵉ et XVIIIᵉ siècles;* Jean Robiquet, *La Vie quotidienne au temps de la Révolution;* and others.

11. Marc Bloch, "Les Aliments de l'ancienne France"; Lucien Febvre, "Aux origines de l'alimentation," p. 19; Febvre; "Pour la première enquête (1936), la parole est à Lucien Febvre," pp. 749–56.

12. Robert Forster and Orest Ranum, eds., *Food and Drink in History.*

13. Among the subjects of interest are essays on medieval cooking, no. 4, pp. 96–98; on *service à la française,* no. 20, pp. 90–92; and on medieval sauces, no. 35, pp. 87–89. Other contributors to the series include Pierre Goubert, Alain Girard, and Philip and Mary Hyman.

14. See, for example, Mary Douglas, "Deciphering a Meal"; Yvonne Verdier, "Pour une ethnologie culinaire"; Peter Farb and George Armelagos, *Consuming Passions.*

15. See Barbara L. Feret, *Gastronomical and Culinary Literature.*

16. Cookbooks were sparse in sixteenth-century France and again in the later part of the

eighteenth century; by contrast, the mid-seventeenth and mid-eighteenth centuries were periods of intense cookbook-publishing activity.

17. See also Suzanne Tardieu, *La Vie domestique dans le Mâconnais rural préindustriel.*

18. Elborg Forster and Robert Forster, eds., *European Diet from Pre-Industrial to Modern Times,* pp. 19–46.

19. Jean-Jacques Hémardinquer, "Les Graisses de cuisine en France."

20. Waverley Root, *The Food of France,* pp. 9–12.

21. Hémardinquer, "Graisses de cuisine," p. 271.

22. Jean-Jacques Hémardinquer, "Faut-il 'demythifier' le porc familial d'Ancien Régime?" Hémardinquer observes that the proprietorship of a pig required access to food for it. In oak-forested regions, where pigs could feed on acorns, the right of access was a carefully defended privilege not enjoyed by most peasants, whereas in farming country pigs competed with humans for food. With the introduction of the potato in the eighteenth century the competition became sharply defined. In times of prosperity potatoes were not needed as food for people, so they could be used to feed pigs. In bad times the potatoes went directly into human stomachs. In either case, their association with pigs and poverty did little to popularize potatoes among the affluent classes.

CHAPTER ONE

1. Olivier de La Marche, *Mémoires d'Olivier de La Marche, maître d'hôtel et capitaine des gardes de Charles le Témeraire,* 3:101–201.

2. Ibid., 3:180, 171, 200.

3. Léon de Laborde, *Les Ducs de Bourgogne,* vol. 2, pt. 2, pp. 199–309.

4. Otto Cartellieri, *The Court of Burgundy,* p. 159.

5. La Marche, *Mémoires,* 3:118–91.

6. John Paston, quoted in Cartellieri, *Court of Burgundy,* p. 163.

7. Laborde, *Les Ducs de Bourgogne,* vol. 2, pt. 2, p. 252; Louis Douët d'Arcq, *Nouveau recueil de comptes de l'argenterie des rois de France publiée pour la Société de l'histoire de France,* p. 61.

8. Louis Douët d'Arcq, *Comptes de l'argenterie des rois de France au XIVe siècle,* pp. 133–34.

9. "La Contenance de la table," quoted in Alfred Franklin, *La Vie privée d'autrefois: Les Repas,* p. 172.

10. For further information and a wealth of illustration see Charles Oman, *Medieval Silver Nefs.*

11. The sequence of the medieval meal is described in detail by Franklin, *La Vie privée d'autrefois: Les Repas,* pp. 7–107, and by La Marche, *Mémoires,* 4:13–58. For an excellent account of the English counterpart see Bridget Ann Henisch, *Fast and Feast,* pp. 190–236.

12. Franklin, *La Vie privée d'autrefois: Les Repas,* pp. 21–32.

13. Franklin, *La Vie privée d'autrefois: Les Repas,* pp. 151–287, includes a selection of etiquette books, spanning the twelfth through the eighteenth centuries; see chap. 2, n. 5, below.

14. Georgine E. Brereton and Janet M. Ferrier, eds., *Le Menagier de Paris,* p. 176.

15. This description is based on a fifteenth-century manuscript of "La Contenance de la table" in Franklin, *La Vie privée d'autrefois: Les Repas,* pp. 168–80. Other versions were printed in the late fifteenth and early sixteenth centuries; see Georges Vicaire, *Bibliographie gastronomique,* cols. 205–9, for editions; also, Anatole de Montaiglon, ed., *Recueil des poésies françoises des XVe et XVIe siècles, morales facétieuses, historiques, réunies et annotées,* 1:186–93.

16. Cartellieri, *Court of Burgundy,* p. 147.

17. La Marche, *Mémoires*, 3:134.

18. Ibid., 3:136–37, 195–96; Cartellieri, *Court of Burgundy*, pp. 167–72.

19. Johann Huizinga, *The Waning of the Middle Ages*, p. 250.

20. Laborde, *Ducs de Bourgogne*, vol. 2, pt. 2, p. 338.

21. See, for example, the calendar pages in *Heures a lusaige de Romme*; two sixteenth-century series of engravings of the months by Etienne Delaune and Virgil Solis, and Gravelot's and Cochin's *Iconologie par figures* (Paris, 1791).

22. Franklin, *La Vie privée d'autrefois: La Cuisine*, pp. 31–32.

23. F. Lichtenberger, ed., *Encyclopédie des sciences réligieuses*, s.v. "Carême"; *New Catholic Encyclopedia*, s.v. "Fast and Abstinence."

24. Guillaume Mollat, *Les Papes d'Avignon (1306–1378)*, p. 504.

25. Leo of Rozmital, *The Travels of Leo of Rozmital through Germany, Flanders, England, France, Spain, Portugal and Italy, 1465–1467*, p. 58 and n. 3.

26. The fast was less strictly observed in the later centuries; by the eighteenth century it was relatively easy to obtain dispensation, and meat and poultry were sold openly; see Franklin, *La Vie privée d'autrefois: Variétés gastronomiques*, pp. 160–63.

27. Robina Napier, ed., *A Noble Boke off Cookry*, p. 37; Hans Wiswe, "Ein mittelniederdeutsches Kochbuch des 15. Jahrhunderts," p. 52; François Massialot, *Le Cuisinier roïal et bourgeois* (1705), pp. 272–73; Vincent La Chapelle, *Le Cuisinier moderne* (1742), 4:193–94.

28. M. Edélestand Du Méril, ed., *Floire et Blanceflor, poèmes du XIIIᵉ siècle publiés d'aprés les manuscrits*, p. 120. There are no French recipes for blackbird pie in the cookery manuscripts, but there is one in the *Liure fort excellent de cuysine*, ff. 46vᵒ–47rᵒ (which may well date from an earlier century), and a medieval Italian recipe in Francesco Zambrini, ed., *Il libro della cucina del secolo XIV*, pp. 58–59.

29. Brereton and Ferrier, eds., *Menagier*, p. 258.

30. "Journal de la dépense du roi Jean en Angleterre," in Douët d'Arcq, *Comptes de l'argenterie*, pp. 193–284; the account includes (p. 245) a list of seeds ordered for the captive king's garden in London. It includes a wider variety of vegetables and herbs than either French or English cookbooks would lead us to expect.

31. Pichon, ed., *Ménagier*, 2:112, n. 2, and 219 and n. 2.

32. Theodora Fitzgibbon, *The Food of the Western World*, s.v. "cardamom," "galingale"; Frederic Rosengarten, Jr., *The Book of Spices*, p. 353; Philip Hyman and Mary Hyman, "Long Pepper."

33. Barbara K. Wheaton, "How to Cook a Peacock."

34. Saint Augustine, *The City of God*, in *Basic Writings of Saint Augustine*, 2:566.

35. Jérôme Pichon and Georges Vicaire, eds., *Le Viandier de Guillaume Tirel, dit Taillevent*, p. 230.

36. "Quailing before a Quail," p. 86.

37. Pichon and Vicaire, eds., *Viandier*, pp. 115–28.

38. Paul Aebischer, "Un manuscrit valaisian du 'Viandier' attribué à Taillevent." A facsimile of the manuscript appears in the reprint of Pichon and Vicaire's edition of the *Viandier* issued by Daniel Morcrette, pp. 227–52.

39. Günter Wiegelmann, *Alltags- und Festspeisen*, pp. 4–6.

40. Edmund O. von Lippmann, *Geschichte des Zuckers seit den ältesten Zeiten bis zum Beginn der Rübenzucker-Fabrikation*, pp. 283–84.

41. Joshua Prawer, *The Crusaders' Kingdom*, pp. 364–65.

42. Brereton and Ferrier, eds., *Menagier*, pp. 221–22; Napier, *Noble Boke*, p. 102; Ludovico Frati, ed., *Libro di cucina del secolo XIV*, p. 47; Wiswe, "Mittelniederdeutsches Kochbuch," pp. 41, 45.

43. A. J. Arberry, "A Baghdad Cookery Book, Translated from the Arabic."

44. Ibid., pp. 39–40, 44–45, 205; Claudia Roden, "Early Arab Cooking and Cookery Manuscripts." She includes two of her own recreations of recipes from the Baghdad cookbook.

45. Ibid., pp. 210–12.

46. Pichon and Vicaire, eds., *Viandier*, pp. viii–xxxi.

47. Ibid., pp. xxvii, xil–l.

48. Ibid., p. 232.

49. Ibid., pp. 213–76.

50. Ibid., pp. 261–62.

51. Ibid., pp. 260–61, 270, 265.

52. Ibid., pp. 272–73. The costume for the wild man is a coverall sewn thickly with strands of hemp, a formula that had proved disastrously flammable at the *bal des ardents* in 1393, when the costumes were ignited by a torch and four people died.

53. Vicaire, *Bibliographie*, col. 585. Much of the *Ménagier de Paris* was translated into English by Eileen Power, *The Goodman of Paris*. The translation is marred by an archaic prose style and by inaccuracies; "oie" means goose, not duck, and garlic comes in cloves, not sprigs; but it is the only English translation of any French cookbook from before the 1650s. In her *Medieval People*, Power devotes a chapter to the author and his bride.

54. Brereton and Ferrier, eds., *Menagier*, p. 1.

55. Vicaire, *Bibliographie*, cols. 227–30, 367, 527–31. Brereton and Ferrier, *Menagier*, pp. lv–lvi, discuss the vexing problem of the sources for this work, suggesting that some large compilation, now lost, supplied recipes to the *Viandier*, the *Ménagier*, and sixteenth-century printed cookbooks, or that the publishers used a copy of the *Ménagier de Paris*. Philip and Mary Hyman are at present making a study of sixteenth-century cookbooks that will help clarify which recipes from the Middle Ages appear in which printed cookbooks.

56. Brereton and Ferrier, eds., *Menagier*, p. 217.

57. Pichon and Vicaire, eds., *Viandier*, pp. 248–49.

58. Brereton and Ferrier, eds., *Menagier*, p. 226.

59. For illustrations of iron kitchen equipment from the Middle Ages through the nineteenth century see Henry René d'Allemagne, *Decorative Ironwork*, a reprint of the plates from the 1924 catalog of the Musée Le Secq des Tournelles in Rouen.

60. Pichon and Vicaire, eds., *Viandier*, p. 208.

61. Otto Wimmer, *Handbuch der Namen und Heiligen*, pp. 317–18.

62. Brereton and Ferrier, eds., *Menagier*, pp. 172, 277; Pichon and Vicaire, eds., *Viandier*, pp. 3, 37, 219.

63. Brereton and Ferrier, eds., *Menagier*, pp. 267–69.

CHAPTER TWO

1. The *Viandier* was first printed about 1490; in the 1540s and 1550s the *Grand cuisinier de toute cvisine*, the *Liure fort excellent de cuysine*, and others were published. Philip and Mary Hyman are now making a detailed study of these volumes, and their results will provide very welcome information. Georges Vicaire, *Bibliographie gastronomique*, cols. 816–28, 227–30, 367, 527–31, gives references to these volumes, but it is inaccurate and out of date.

2. According to Vicaire, *Bibliographie*, cols. 305–21, 511–13, 519–20, 548–51, the late eleventh-century *Regimen sanitatis salerni* was first printed in Rome about 1470, appeared in Paris in 1497, and was translated into French before 1500; the earliest editions whose place of origin is known was Montpellier. Other works on health include *La Nef de santé, auec le*

gouuernail du corps humain et la condenacion des bancquetz (Paris, ca. 1508), Vicaire, *Bibliographie*, cols. 618–22; Prosper Calanius, *Traicté excellent de l'entretenement de santé* (Paris, 1550), Vicaire, *Bibliographie*, cols. 140–41; Joseph du Chesne, *Le Povrtraict de la santé, ou est au vif représentée la Reigle vniuerselle et particulière de bien sainnement et longuement viure* (1605), Vicaire, *Bibliographie*, cols. 167–68; Nicolas Abraham, *Le Govvernement necessaire à chacvn povr vivre longuement en santé* (Paris, 1608), Vicaire, *Bibliographie*, col. 2; Louis Coronaro, *Hygiasticon* (Antwerp, 1613), translated as *Vray régime de vivre pour la conservation de la santé ivsques a vne extreme vieillesse* (Paris, 1624), Vicaire, *Bibliographie*, cols. 211–13; Philibert Gvybert, *Tovtes les oevvres charitables* (Paris, 1645), Vicaire, *Bibliographie*, cols. 432–34; Michel Bicais, *La Manière de régler la santé par ce qui nous environne, par ce que nous recevons et par les exercices ou par la gymnastique moderne* (1669), Vicaire, *Bibliographie*, cols. 92–93.

3. Apicius's cookbook was first printed in 1498 and was reprinted several times in the sixteenth century; see Vicaire, *Bibliographie*, cols. 28–31, and Barbara Flower and Elisabeth Rosenbaum, eds., *The Roman Cookery Book, a Critical Translation of "The Art of Cooking" by Apicius*, pp. 9–12. *The Diepnosophists* by Athenaeus was first published by the Aldine Press (Venice, 1514) and was translated into Latin and published by Isaac Casaubon at Heidelberg in 1599; see Vicaire, *Bibliographie*, cols. 50–51. See also Charles Burton Gulick, trans. and ed., *Athenaeus*, 1:xix. A collection of the works of the Latin agronomists was published earliest of all: *Rei rusticae scriptores; Marcus Priscus Cato; Marcus Terentius Varro; Lucius Junius Moderatus Columella; et Palladius Rutulius Aemilianus* (Venice, 1472).

4. Charles Estienne, *Proedivm rvsticvm* . . . (Paris, 1554), trans., with Jean Liébault as *L'Agricvlture et maison rvstique*, Vicaire, *Bibliographie*, cols. 343–46; Olivier de Serres, *Le Theatre d'agricvltvre et mesnage des champs*, Vicaire, *Bibliographie*, cols. 788–89; Nicolas de Bonnefons, *Le Jardinier françois qvi enseigne à cvltiver les arbres, les herbes potagères*, Vicaire, *Bibliographie*, cols. 461–63; Louis Liger, *Œconomie générale de la campagne, ov nouvelle maison rustique*, Vicaire, *Bibliographie*, cols. 520–23; Noël Chomel, *Dictionnaire œconomique contenant l'art de faire valoire les terres*, Vicaire, *Bibliographie*, cols. 172–73.

5. Michel de Nostradamus, *Excellent et moult utile opuscule*, Vicaire, *Bibliographie*, cols. 627–30; *Opera nuoua intitolata dificio de ricette* . . . (Venice, 1541), translated as *Le Bastiment de receptes* (Lyons, 1541), Vicaire, *Bibliographie*, cols. 71–73, 640–41; Alexis of Piedmont, *De Secreti* . . . (Venice, 1555), translated as *Les Secrets dv seigneur Alexis piemontois* (Antwerp, 1557). For etiquette books, Alfred Franklin, *La Vie privée d'autrefois: Les Repas*, pp. 168–287, extracts from the following works passages devoted to table manners: "La Contenance de la table," a fifteenth-century poem (see also Vicaire, *Bibliographie*, cols. 205–9); Jean Sulpice, *La Civilité*, first published in 1485, translated into French in 1545; excerpts from three translations of Erasmus's *De Civilitate morvm pverlivim* (Paris, 1530), Vicaire, *Bibliographie*, cols. 332–33, by Pierre Saliat in 1537, by C. Calviac in 1560, and by Claude Hardy in 1613; a poem published in Dijon in the seventeenth century; "Civilité puérile et morale, pour instruire les enfans à se bien comporter . . .," Vicaire, *Bibliographie*, cols. 757–58; Fleury Bourriquant, *Civilité honneste pour l'instruction des enfans* . . . (N.p., 1648); L.D.L.M., *La Civilité nouvelle* . . . (N.p., 1667); Antoine de Courtin, *Nouveau traité de la civilité qui se pratique en France parmi les honnestes gens; La Civilité puérile et honneste, dresée par un missionnaire* (N.p. 1747); Jean-Baptiste de La Salle, *Les Règles de la bienséance et de la civilité chrétienne* (N.p., 1782); Chemin-Dupontès, *La Civilité républicaine* . . . (Paris, 1798).

6. Elizabeth L. Eisenstein, *The Printing Press as an Agent of Change*, 1:399.

7. Jérôme Pichon and Georges Vicaire, eds., *Le Viandier de Guillaume Tirel, dit Taillevent*, pp. xl–xli. They describe the first edition as having been printed with "superb characters and a truly remarkable superabundance of misprints." For a detailed description of the editions known to them see pp. lii–lxviii.

8. Lucien Febvre and H.-J. Martin, *L'Apparition du livre*, pp. 221–22.

9. Eisenstein, *Printing Press*, 1:64–65.

10. Pichon and Vicaire, eds., *Viandier*, p. 45; Pierre Jean Baptiste Le Grand d'Aussy, *Histoire de la vie privée des françois*, 2:230–31. Modern writers using Le Grand's book uncritically repeat his error: it is a classic example of print perpetuating misinformation.

11. These seven recipes are for *bousac de lièvre, bouly lardé, poulaille farcy, cive d'oystres, chaudeau flament, blanc manger,* and *gournaulx et rougetz.*

12. Pichon and Vicaire, eds., *Viandier*, pp. 71–77.

13. Ibid., p. 98.

14. Ibid., pp. 105–11.

15. Ibid., p. 108.

16. Théodore Gobert, "Banquets officiels aux XVIᶜ et XVIIᶜ siècles à Liège," pp. 353–54. Gobert mistakenly describes the *Ovverture* as Lancelot's memoirs. See also Léon-E. Halken, "Lancelot de Casteau," pp. 409–17.

17. Halken, "Lancelot," p. 416.

18. Lancelot de Casteau, *Ovverture de cvisine*, pp. 147–53.

19. Ibid., pp. 149–51. There are recipes for ravioli, pp. 78–79; gnocchi, pp. 79–81; strips of pasta served with butter, Parmesan cheese, and cinnamon, described as *maquaron*, p. 81.

20. The most intriguing puzzle in the book is the menu for a second, relatively simple meal, which Lancelot describes as the banquet of the "enfans sans souci" [*innocenti?*] "such as Frans Floris, Michel Angelo, goldsmiths, painters, and several others, who wish to lodge at the Inn of the Cross." It is, in fact, scarcely a menu. The principal item in the first course is orange halves grilled with cinnamon sugar and butter, in the second a "potage" similar to zabaglione, and in the final course blancmange pies and candies—a sugar-laden meal. So far as I can determine, Frans Floris and Michelangelo never met; when the latter ordered food for one celebratory meal, at least, it consisted largely of meat, drink, and bread (*The Letters of Michelangelo*, 2:311–12; the meal celebrated the completion of one stage of building the base of the dome of Saint Peter's in 1552 and was supplied by an innkeeper). Floris and Lancelot may have been acquainted. Floris had studied painting in Liège with Lambert Lombard before going to Florence and Rome for further study, which included making drawings of the work of Michelangelo. By 1540 Floris was back in the Low Countries, and until his death in 1570 he lived and principally worked in Antwerp. His self-destructive attraction to food and drink was chronicled by Carel van Mander, *Dutch and Flemish Painters: Translation from the Schilderboeck.*

21. Casteau, *Ovverture*, p. 8.

22. Ibid., pp. 19–22, 28–32, 34–45.

23. Ibid., pp. 101–5, 87, 98–99, 105–7, 110, 115–16.

24. Ibid., p. 127.

25. Leonard N. Beck, "Praise is due Bartolomeo Platina: A Note on the Librarian-Author of the First Cookbook."

26. Vicaire, *Bibliographie*, cols. 687–98, 907–8.

27. Beck, "Praise," p. 242. The Library of Congress owns the manuscript which is discussed in Beck's very useful article.

28. The recipes were subsequently translated back into Italian by someone unfamiliar with the original collection. Beck (ibid., p. 250) points out that the translator turned the Latin recipes into Italian gibberish: Platina had translated *maccaroni Siciliani* and *biancomangiare* as *esicium frumentinum* and *cibarium album*, which the secondary translator turned into *exitio frumentino* and *leucofago*. Obviously, he was neither a cook nor a gastronome.

29. Jack C. Drummond and Anne Wilbraham, *The Englishman's Food*, pp. 67–69.

30. Bartolomeo Platina, *Platine en françoys tresutile et necessaire pour le corps humain qui traicte de hôneste volupte*, f. 6r°.

31. Ibid., ff. 9r° and v°.

32. Ibid., f. 12v°.

33. Ibid., f. 119r° and v°, 67v°.

34. Ibid., 78v° and 100v°.

35. Ibid., f. 175r°.

36. Ibid., ff. 85v°–86r°.

37. Jacques Pons, *Traité des melons ov il est parlé de leur nature, de leur culture, de leurs vertus et de leur usage*, pp. 12–23.

38. Ibid., pp. 24–30. Vicaire, *Bibliographie*, cols. 711–12, cites a poem, "Le Proces dv melon" (Paris, 1607), written to commemorate an attack of indigestion suffered by Henry IV caused by having eaten a melon.

39. Gui Patin, *Traité de la conservation de santé*, pp. 36–37.

40. François Rabelais, *Œuvres complètes*, p. 96. The poem about garum is "A Etienne Dolet," p. 969.

41. Ibid., pp. 174–75.

42. Lazare Sainéan, *L'Histoire naturelle et les branches connexes dans l'œuvre de Rabelais*, discusses in detail everything the author could learn about all the foods mentioned by Rabelais in his writings.

43. François Rabelais, *Gargantua and Pantagruel*, p. 571.

44. Ibid., p. 30.

45. Bartolomeo Scappi, *Opera di M. Bartolomeo Scappi*, ff. 86v°–87r°.

46. Grégoire Lozinski, ed., *La Bataille de caresme et de charnage*.

47. For onions: "Sermon ioyeulx de la vie saint ognon. Comment nabuzarden le maistre cuisinier le fist martrier. auec les miracles quil fait chascun iour," or, A merry sermon on the life of Saint Onion. How he was martyred by Nabuzarden, the master cook. With the miracles he does every day; Vicaire, *Bibliographie*, cols. 785–86. For cheese: Hélie Le Cordier, *Le Pont l'Evesque poëme dédié a Mademoiselle* (Paris, 1662), Vicaire, *Bibliographie*, cols. 509–10. For herring: *Sermon ioyeulx de monsieur sainct Haren* (N.p., n.d.), Vicaire, *Bibliographie*, cols. 786–87.

48. For the controversy, see chap. 11; for an example of the display of erudition, Muret, *Traité des festins*; as a point of departure for serious literary endeavor, see Voltaire, *Le Dîner du comte de Bovlainvilliers*.

49. Edmund O. von Lippmann, *Geschichte des Zuckers*, pp. 437–42.

50. On literacy see Natalie Zemon Davis, *Society and Culture in Early Modern France*, p. 210. For confectionary books, see n. 5 above and chap. 10.

51. The title and page references cited for Alexis [Ruscelli] of Piedmont are from the English translation (London, 1558). Michel de Nostradamus, *Excellent et moult utile opuscule à touts necessaire*, Vicaire, *Bibliographie*, cols. 627–30. It has been reprinted in part as *La Façon et maniere de faire toutes confitures liquides, tant en succre, miel, qu'en vin cuit*, p. 106. It has an informative preface by T. Coppel and Angèle Hahn, pp. 7–21.

52. Nostradamus, *Opuscule*, p. 106.

53. Alexis of Piedmont, *Les Secretes dv seigneur Alexis piemontois*, ff 45r° and v°.

54. Ibid., f. 47r°.

55. I was deceived into trying this recipe because it gives clear measurements. The *morselets* were unbelievably tough. Not only would no one eat them (not even I), but they jammed the garbage disposal.

CHAPTER THREE

1. Joycelyne G. Russell, *The Field of Cloth of Gold*, pp. 142–81.

2. Benvenuto Cellini, *The Autobiography of Benvenuto Cellini*, pp. 290–91, stated that the salt was used for the first time at a celebratory feast given by the artist for his friends after the king had approved the work but had not yet taken possession of it.

3. *Art Treasures from the Vienna Collections Lent by the Austrian Government*, p. 46.

4. Wallace K. Ferguson, *The Renaissance in Historical Thought*.

5. Mary Frances Kennedy Fisher's version of the story is by far the most entertaining: "Catherine's Lonesome Cooks," *The Art of Eating*, pp. 75–76. The classic version is found in Louis Eustache Ude, *The French Cook*, pp. xxxiii–xxxv: "A woman opened the gates of an enlightened age. . . . Accompanied by a troup of perfumers, painters, astrologers, poets, and cooks, she crosses the Alps [actually she came by sea, landing at Marseilles], and whilst Bullan planned the Tuileries, Berini recovered from oblivion those sauces which, for many ages, had been lost." I know nothing of Berini; sauces did not play a very important role on the sixteenth-century table. Ude goes on to say that she "dipped in a rich sauce the same hand that held the reins of the empire, and which Roussard compared to the rosy fingers of Aurora." She even, he tells us, planned the Saint Bartholomew's Day massacre at dinner, though he does not explain how this advanced the culinary art.

6. Jean Héritier, *Cathèrine de Medici*, pp. 58–126.

7. Michel de Montaigne, "On the Vanity of Words," in *The Complete Works of Montaigne*, pp. 222–23.

8. *Encyclopédie, ou dictionnaire raisonné des sciences, des arts et des métiers, par une société de gens de lettres*, vol. 4 (1754), s.v. "cuisine."

9. Nancy Lyman Roelker, trans. and ed., *The Paris of Henry of Navarre as Seen by Pierre de l'Estoile*, p. 37.

10. Roy Strong, *Splendor at Court*, pp. 19–56.

11. Frances A. Yates, *The Valois Tapestries*, pp. 51–101, gives a detailed account.

12. Marguerite de Valois, *Mémoires*, 10:403.

13. Yates, *Valois Tapestries*, pp. 56–57.

14. Strong, *Splendor at Court*, pp. 121–56; Yates, *Valois Tapestries*, p. 58.

15. Pierre Champion, *Cathèrine de Médicis présente à Charles IX son royaume*, pp. 19–20.

16. Héritier, *Cathèrine de Medici*, p. 238.

17. Paul Guérin, ed., *Registres des déliberations du bureau de la ville de Paris*, 6:311–15.

18. Strong, *Splendor at Court*, p. 144.

19. Guérin, ed., *Registres de la ville de Paris*, 6:313.

20. Ibid.

21. Ibid.

22. Ibid., pp. 314–15.

23. Thomas Artus, sieur d'Embry, *Description de l'Isle des Hermaphrodites*, pp. 60–61.

24. Ibid., p. 61.

25. Ibid., p. 98.

26. Lancelot de Casteau, *Ovvertvre de cvisine*, pp. 123–24.

27. Artus, *Description*, pp. 99–100.

28. Hans Wühr, *Altes Essgerät*, pp. 33–36.

29. W. A. Forbes, *Antiek Bestek*, p. 64.

30. Vicenzo Cervio, *Il Trinciante di M. Vicenzo Cervio, ampliato, et ridotto a perfettione dal cavallier reale Fusoritto di Narni trinciante dell'illust.ᵐᵒ et reuer.ᵐᵒ signor cardinal Farnese*, 4rᵒ–vᵒ.

31. Bartolomeo Scappi, *Opera di M. Bartolomeo Scappi*, unnumbered engraving.

32. Artus, *Description*, p. 103.

33. Ibid., p. 107.

34. Ibid.

35. Gilles de Gouberville, *Journal pour les années 1549, 1550, 1551, publié d'après le manuscrit original découvert dans le chartier de Saint-Pierre l'Eglise; Le Journal du sire de Gouberville publié sur la copie du manuscrit original faite par M. l'abbé Tollemer*, reprinted, with an informative introduction by Emmanuel Le Roy Ladurie, as *Un sire de Gouberville, gentilhomme campagnard au Cotentin de 1553 à 1562.* My references are to *Le Journal du sire de Gouberville* unless otherwise noted.

36. Gouberville, *Journal*, pp. 119, 187.

37. Ibid., pp. 279, 189.

38. Ibid., pp. 162, 163, 159, 306.

39. Ibid., pp. 292, 88, 273, 162, 292, 295.

40. Ibid., pp. 148, 322, 473, 543, 744.

41. Ibid., pp. 71, 161, 408.

42. For example, in Lent of 1553/4: ibid., pp. 73, 74, 77, 82.

43. Ibid., pp. 321, 648.

44. Ibid., 149, 65, 393, 69, 534, 620, 211.

45. Ibid., pp. 620–22, 791.

46. Ibid., p. 149.

47. Ibid., pp. 71, 827, 413, 491, 555.

48. Ibid., pp. 276–78.

49. Ibid., pp. 314, 68. For a description of a wedding in Britanny in recent times see Per Jakez Hélias, *The Horse of Pride.*

50. Gouberville, *Journal*, p. 491.

51. *Sire de Gouberville*, Introduction, pp. ix–x.

52. Gouberville, *Journal*, pp. 195, 151, 510, 715.

53. Ibid., pp. 476, 554, 721, 618.

54. Felix Platter, *Felix Platter: Tagebuchblätter aus dem Jugendleben eines deutschen Arztes des 16. Jahrhunderts*, p. 58. *Beloved Son Felix* is a somewhat condensed English translation.

55. Platter, *Tagebuchblätter*, pp. 62, 64, 67–68.

56. Ibid., pp. 75–76, 108–10.

57. Ibid., p. 68.

58. Ibid., p. 79.

59. Ibid., pp. 78–79, 84, 91, 138.

60. Ibid., p. 114. These fennel branches with sugar figures may have had a special significance. In the account of expenses for a banquet offered Catherine de Medici is a payment to an apothecary–spice merchant for six dozen nosegays of fennel, candied and adorned with pinks, roses, and stars, all coated with gilded sugar, shaped like trees, and planted in broad, deep dishes surrounded by sweetmeats ("Festin donné à la royne Catherine au logis épiscopal de l'évesché de Paris, le dix-neuviesme jour de juing 1549," in Felix Danjou and L. Cimber, eds., *Archives curieuses de l'histoire de France*, 1st ser., 3:421).

61. Platter, *Tagebuchblätter*, pp. 73–74.

62. Ibid., p. 145.

63. Montaigne, "Of the Power of the Imagination," *Works*, p. 74. There is a recipe for roast cat in Ruperto de Nola, *Libro de Guisados*, p. 231 and n. 250. Prosper Montagné and Alfred Gottschalk, eds., *Larousse Gastronomique*, s.v. "chat," contains an illustration comparing the leg bones of the cat and the rabbit.

64. Donald M. Frame, *Montaigne*, p. 202.

65. Montaigne, *Travel Journal*, in *Works*, pp. 876, 877, 904, 1002.

66. Ibid., pp. 877–78, 892. He found "such good flavor in the good inns, that the cuisines of the French nobility hardly seemed comparable; and there are few French noblemen that have dining rooms so well adorned" (p. 891).

67. Ibid., pp. 830, 940, 1023, 1037. He wrote, "Here [at Montmélian] I clearly felt the excellence of the Italian oils, for those over here gave me a stomach-ache, whereas the others never gave me an aftertaste."

68. Ibid., pp. 815–57.

69. Frame, *Montaigne*, p. 120.

70. Pierre de Ronsard, "La Salade," in *Œuvres complètes*, 15, pt. 2, pp. 76–84.

71. Olivier de Serres, *Théâtre d'agriculture et mesnage des champs* (1804–7), 2:24.

72. Ferdinand Hoefer, ed., *Nouvelle biographie générale depuis les temps les plus reculés jusqu'à nos jours*, s.v. "Serres."

73. De Serres, *Théâtre d'agriculture*, 1:21.

74. Ibid., pp. 22–23.

75. Ibid., 2:248–50.

76. Ibid., pp. 233–34, 334–37, 242–43, 245–46, 244–45, 262–63, 254–62.

77. Emmanuel Le Roy Ladurie, *Les Paysans de Languedoc*, 1:62–63.

78. De Serres, *Théâtre d'agriculture*, 1:22.

79. *Kalendrier et compost des bergers*, ff. 31r°–v°.

80. Jean Bodin, *Discours sur les causes de l'extreme cherté qui est aujourd'huy en France et sur les moyens d'y remédier*, pp. 425–57.

81. Ibid., p. 438.

82. Noël du Fail, *Œuvres facétieuses*, 2:162–63.

83. Pierre Belon, *L'Histoire de la nature des oyseaux*, p. 62.

84. Noël du Fail, *Contes d'Eutrapel*, quoted in Abel Lefranc, *La Vie quotidienne au temps de la Renaissance*, pp. 120–21.

85. De Serres, *Théâtre d'agriculture*, 1:22–23.

86. See, for example, the engravings of Dives and Lazarus in the *Heures a lusaige de Romme*, 56r°, and by Abraham Bosse.

87. Quoted in Roelker, *Paris of Henry of Navarre*, p. 278.

CHAPTER FOUR

1. For an exhaustive description of the places where foodstuffs were sold and an account of regulations, see Delamare, *Traité de la police*, vol. 2. He states that the quai de la Mégisserie "took the name of the Valley of Sorrows because of the large number of poultry and game, lambs, kids, and suckling pigs put to death here" (2:771). It was commonly called La Vallée.

2. René de Lespinasse, ed., *Histoire générale de Paris*, pp. 188–95.

3. Ibid., pp. 593–612; Alfred Franklin, *La Vie privée d'autrefois: La Vie de Paris sous Louis XIV*, pp. xii–xv; Franklin, *La Vie privée d'autrefois: Le Café, le thé et le chocolat*, pp. 192–212.

4. Delamare, *Traité*, 2:55–447.

5. Lespinasse, *Histoire*, p. 385.

6. Ibid., p. 377.

7. Ibid., p. 304.

8. Ibid.

9. Ibid., p. 342.

10. Jérôme Pichon, ed., *Le Ménagier de Paris*, 2:121–23.

11. Ibid., p. 116.

12. Jean Bodin, *Discours sur les causes de l'extreme cherté qui est aujourd'huy en France et sur les moyens d'y remédier*, p. 439. The categories of eating places were very loosely defined. Cotgrave, *Dictionarie*, says that a *rostisseur* is "a roster of meat; also a Cooke that sells, or dresses, none but rost-meat"; a *taverne* "is also (in some few places no better than) a victualling house"; and a *tavernier* is "a Vintner, Tauerne-keeper, Wine-drawer; also in some places a Victualler, of whom (as in our Tauernes of London) one may haue meat, and drink for his money." *Traîteur* does not appear.

13. Niccolò Tommaseo, ed. and trans., *Relations des ambassadeurs vénitiens sur les affaires de France au XVIe siècle*, 2:603.

14. Jacques Hillairet, *Connaissance de vieux Paris*, p. 213.

15. Nicolas de Blegny [Abraham du Pradel], *Le Livre commode contenant des addresses*, ed. Edouard Fournier, 2:318–20.

16. Ibid., 2:321.

17. Joachim-Christoph Nemeitz, *Séjour de Paris*, in Franklin, *La Vie privée d'autrefois: La Vie de Paris sous la Régence*, p. 15.

18. Louis Sébastien Mercier, *Tableau de Paris*, 1:131–32.

19. E. Littré, *Dictionnaire de la langue française*, s.v. "restaurant."

20. François Massialot, *Le Cuisinier roïal et bourgeois* (1705), pp. 378–79; it is designated as *potage sans eau* but is indexed also as *restaurant*. The *Cuisinier françois ov l'école des ragoûts*, pp. 34–37, also has two *restaurant* recipes, one of which calls for an alembic.

21. René Héron de Villefosse, *Histoire et géographie gourmandes de Paris*, pp. 111–12.

22. Ferdinand Hoefer, ed., *Nouvelle biographie générale*, s.v. "de Blegny."

23. De Blegny, *Livre*, 1:303.

24. Ibid., pp. 295–303.

25. Tobias Smollet, *Travels through France and Italy*, p. 54.

26. De Blegny, *Livre*, 1:296–99.

27. Georgine E. Brereton and Janet M. Ferrier, eds., *Le Menagier de Paris*, eds., p. 205.

28. Olivier de Serres, *Théâtre d'agriculture et mesnage des champs* (1804–7), 1:528–30.

29. Nicolas de Bonnefons, *Les Delices de la campagne* (1679), pp. 159–68.

30. Menon, *La Cuisinière bourgeoise* (1746), pp. 273–74; see also Louis Liger, *Œconomie générale de la campagne*, 1:338–39.

31. Nancy Lyman Roelker, *Queen of Navarre, Jeanne d'Albret, 1528–1572*, pp. 39–40. They or their progenitors probably came over or around the Pyrenees from Spanish Navarre into Navarre of which her father was then king.

32. "Festin donné à la royne Catherine au logis épiscopal de l'évesché de Paris, le dix-neuviesme jour de juing 1549," in Félix Danjou and L. Cimber, eds., *Archives curieuses de l'histoire de France*, 1st ser., 3:418.

33. Gilles de Gouberville, *Le Journal du sire de Gouberville publié sur la copie du manuscrit original faite par M. l'abbé Tollemer*, p. 541.

34. E. Rorschach, "Documents inédits sur le voyage du roi Charles IX à Toulouse," p. 45.

35. Charles Estienne and Jean Liébault, *L'Agricvltvre et maison rvstiqve*; English translation, *Maison Rustique, or The Covntrie Farme*, p. 116.

36. De Serres, *Théâtre d'agriculture*, 2:21–24.

37. Littré, *Dictionnaire*, s.v. "dindonné."

38. Lancelot de Casteau, *Ovverture de cvisine*, pp. 147, 150.

39. François Pierre de La Varenne, *Le Cvisinier françois*, (1654), p. 35.

40. Ibid., p. 144.

41. *Le Dictionnaire portatif de cuisine*, 1:214–22.

42. Robert Forster, *The House of Saulx-Tavanes*, p. 121.

43. See Redcliffe N. Salaman, *The History and Social Influence of the Potato*, pp. 1–187, for an account of the history of its development in pre-Columbian America and its introduction into Europe. For France see André J. Bourde, *Agronomie et agronomes en France au XVIIIᵉ siècle*, 2:637–43.

44. De Serres, *Théâtre d'agriculture*, 2:279.

45. Salaman, *History*, p. 116. Ironically, in parts of the Islamic world the potato has been called "the food of Satan" because of its European associations (Maxime Rodinson, *Encyclopedia of Islam*, 2:1067).

46. Joseph Michaud, *Biographie universelle ancienne et moderne*, s.v. "Parmentier."

47. *Encyclopédie, ou dictionnaire raisonné des sciences, des arts et des métiers, par une société de gens de lettres*, s.v. "pomme de terre."

48. Martin Lister, *Voyage de Lister à Paris en MDCXCVIII*, p. 137.

49. Pierre Jean Baptiste Le Grand d'Aussy, *Histoire de la vie privée des françois*, 1:143–45.

50. Salaman, *History*, pp. 133–34.

51. Le Grand d'Aussy, *Histoire*, 1:148.

52. Salaman, *History*, pp. 126–41.

53. Ibid., p. 160; Carl Ortwin Sauer, *Agricultural Origins and Dispersals*, p. 126.

54. Lawrence Kaplan, "New World Beans," pp. 43–44, 46, 48–49; J. Smartt, "Evolution of American *Phaseolus* Beans under Domestication."

55. Charles B. Heiser, *Seed to Civilization*, p. 122.

56. De Serres, *Théâtre d'agriculture*, 2:4.

57. Randle Cotgrave, *A Dictionarie of the French and English Tongues*, s.v. "Faseols."

58. Emmanuel Le Roy Ladurie, *Les Paysans de Languedoc*, 1:72.

59. *Le Cuisinier françois ov l'ecole des ragouts*, pp. 133–34.

60. *Encyclopédie*, s.v. "Haricot." D. A. Lincoln, *Mrs. Lincoln's Boston Cook Book*, p. 250, writes of baked beans: "They afford a nutritious and cheap food for people who labor in the open air."

61. Bonnefons, *Le Delices de la campagne* (1654), p. 124; *Le Jardinier françois* (1683), pp. 222–23.

62. François Massialot, *Nouvelle instruction pour les confitures, les liqueurs, et les fruits* (1717), p. 450.

63. Liger, *Œconomie générale de la campagne*, 2:46–51, 121, 126.

64. Vincent La Chapelle, *Le Cuisinier moderne* (1742), 4:171; *Les Soupers de la cour*, 3:24–25.

65. Menon, *La Cuisinière bourgeoise* (1746), p. 210.

66. Günter Schiedlausky, *Tee, Kaffee, Schokolade*, pp. 7–8. For further information see Wolf Mueller, *Bibliographie des Kaffee, des Kakao der Schokolade des Tee und deren Surrogate bis zum Jahr 1900*.

67. Franklin, *La Vie privée d'autrefois: Le Café, le thé et le chocolat*, pp. 157–58.

68. Ibid., pp. 162–64, 166–67.

69. Massialot, *Le Cuisinier roïal et bourgeois* (1705), pp. 285–86. He writes that widgeon "is a sea bird closely resembling ducks, but nonetheless we place it among the fish, and serve it on fast-days because it is cold-blooded" (p. 284).

70. Menon, *La Science du maître d'hôtel, confiseur*, pp. 406–7. Brillat-Savarin thought the practice of using leftover chocolate as a starter for the next batch was a lost secret. He had learned it, fifty years before writing the *Physiologie du goût*, from Madame d'Aretrel, superior of the convent of the Visitation in Belley. She recommended letting it stand overnight in an earthenware coffeepot. "The night's rest concentrates it and gives it a velvety texture which

makes it much better. The Good Lord cannot take offence at this little refinement, for He is Himself all excellence" (Alfred Charles Frédéric Fayot, ed., *Les Classiques de la table*, p. 50). If the original mixture was made with egg yolk the overnight repose would also give any bacteria present a running start.

71. Massialot, *Nouvelle instruction* (1717), pp. 185–86, 205–6.

72. La Chapelle, *Cuisinier moderne* (1742), 5:226–27.

73. Menon, *La Science du maître d'hôtel, confiseur*, pp. 407–12.

74. Franklin, *La Vie privée d'autrefois: Le Café, le thé et le chocolat*, pp. 116–24; Schiedlausky, *Tee, Kaffee, Schokolade*, p. 67.

75. Samuel Pepys, *The Diary of Samuel Pepys*, 1:253.

76. Franklin, *La Vie privée d'autrefois: Le Café, le thé et le chocolat*, p. 130.

77. Ibid., pp. 125–26.

78. Massialot, *Nouvelle instruction* (1692), pp. 270–72.

79. La Chapelle, *Cuisinier moderne* (1742), 3:259–60.

80. N. Audiger, *La Maison réglée et l'art de diriger la maison d'un grand seigneur et autres, tant à la ville qu'à la campagne*, p. 262.

81. Jules Michelet wrote in *La Régence* (Paris, 1879) of "coffee, the sobering beverage, a mighty nutrient of the brain, unlike spiritous liquors, increases purity and clarity; coffee, which clears the imagination of fogs and heavy vapours, which illumines the reality of things with the white light of truth; anti-erotic coffee, which at length substitutes stimulation of the mind for stimulation of the sexual faculties!" (quoted in Heinrich Eduard Jacob, *The Saga of Coffee*, p. 193).

82. Jean Leclant, "Coffee and Cafés in Paris, 1644–1693," pp. 86–97, gives a thorough description of the introduction of coffee into Parisian life.

83. Ibid., p. 87.

84. Franklin, *La Vie privée d'autrefois: Le Café, le thé et le chocolat*, pp. 33–38; Leclant, "Coffee and Cafés," pp. 87–88. For further information on the early history of coffee see C. Van Arendonk and K. N. Chaudhuri, "Ḳahwa," *The Encyclopedia of Islam*, 4:449–55.

85. Leclant, "Coffee and Cafés," pp. 89–91.

86. De Serres, *Théâtre d'agriculture*, 2:25.

87. Hoefer, ed., *Nouvelle biographie générale*, s.v. "Clieu ou Declieu."

88. As a beverage, Massialot, *Nouvelle instruction* (1692), pp. 268–69; as an ice, *Les Soupers de la cour*, 4:304; as a junket, La Chapelle, *Cuisinier moderne* (1742), 3:260–61. The first recipe for coffee as a beverage is probably the one in Philippe Sylvestre Dufour, *Traitez nouveau et curieux du café, du thé, et du chocolat*, pp. 54–58. "So as not to be burned, one must not put one's tongue in the cup, but hold the edge [of the cup] between the tongue and the lower lip, and the upper one, pressing so little that they do not quite meet, and then take little sips" (ibid., p. 58).

89. *Les Soupers de la cour*, 4:238.

90. Nicolas de Blegny, *Le Bon usage du thé, du caffé et du chocolat*, pp. 152–54, 160, 181–85.

CHAPTER FIVE

1. The term "bourgeois" was used in a variety of senses both in the *ancien régime* and subsequently, giving rise to an extensive scholarly debate over whether the nineteenth-century usage, designating a social class defined primarily in economic terms, can be applied to an earlier stage of French society. See Roland Mousnier, "Problèmes de méthode dans l'étude des structures sociales des XVIᶜ, XVIIᶜ et XVIIIᶜ siècles," in his *La Plume, la faucille et le marteau*, pp. 12–26; Mousnier, J.-P. Labatut, and Y. Durand, *Problèmes de stratification sociale*,

pp. 9–24; Robert Mandrou, *Classes et luttes de classes en France au début du XVIIe siècle*; Régine Robin, *La Société française en 1789*, pp. 15–58. Pierre Goubert illustrates and discusses many of the meanings of the term in *L'Ancien régime*, vol. 1: *La Société*, pp. 217–41. I use the term to indicate nonnoble people of property, living primarily in towns—those Goubert (p. 221) calls "the bourgeoisie as a style of living, an enduring type of person living off his income from investments." Both François Massialot, in *Le Cuisinier roïal et bourgeois*, and Menon, in *Le Cuisinière bourgeoise*, speak of the bourgeois kitchen as simple in style and limited in possibilities, but where special occasions required special efforts, indicating that for them the term designated a style of life and social position beneath that of the nobility. The distinction was, in fact, not always clear, especially in matters of the table.

2. N. Audiger, *La Maison reglée et l'art de diriger la maison d'un grand seigneur et autres, tant à la ville qu'à la campagne*, in Alfred Franklin, *La Vie privée d'autrefois: La Vie de Paris sous Louis XIV*, pp. 3–203; present references are to the latter edition.

3. Ibid., pp. 110–11.

4. Ibid., p. 113.

5. Ibid.

6. Robert Wheaton, research based on marriage contracts, 1640 and 1647, Series 3E, Archives Départementales de la Gironde (personal communication).

7. Audiger, *Maison reglée*, p. 107.

8. The housekeeper's work supplemented or even replaced that of the maître d'hôtel in some houses of moderate size (ibid., pp. 104–7). Like him she may have risen from being a cook to a supervisory position. She did a great deal of counting and dispensing, kept the keys, set the table (because she was responsible for the silver and linen), and sometimes supervised preserving and distillation. Housekeepers in large establishments in France in the seventeenth and eighteenth centuries do not seem to have been as prominent as in similar English households.

9. Ibid., p. 108.

10. Reprinted by Franklin, *La Vie privée: La Vie de Paris sous Louis XIV*, pp. 344–56.

11. G. Schafer, "Historical Facts Concerning the Production and Use of Soap," pp. 2014–24; "Development of Soap Boiling," pp. 2025–30.

12. Franklin, *La Vie privée: La Vie de Paris sous Louis XIV*, p. 356.

13. A study of the incidence of thefts of foodstuffs in eighteenth-century Paris shows that most prosecutions were for food stolen outside of kitchens and that most people convicted were not domestics. The sentences were often severe. See Arlette Farge, *Délinquance et criminalité*.

14. Menon, *La Cuisinière bourgeoise* (1746), p. 301.

15. Lois Banner, "Why Women Have Not Been Great Chefs."

16. Jean-Pierre Babelon, *Demeures parisiennes sous Henri IV et Louis XIII*, p. 96; Antoine Furetière, *Dictionnaire universelle, contenant tous les mots françois tant vieux que modernes, et les termes de toutes les sciences et des arts*, s.v. "potager."

17. Audiger, *Maison reglée*, pp. 11–12.

18. Jean Anthèlme Brillat-Savarin, *Physiologie du goût ou méditations de gastronomie transcendante*, p. 19.

19. Pierre Couperie, "Les Marchés de pourvoierie."

20. François Massialot, *Le Nouveau cuisinier royale et bourgeois* (1712), 1:2–10.

21. Audiger, *Maison reglée*, pp. 53–54.

22. Ibid., p. 55.

23. Ibid., p. 52.

24. The final portion of *La Maison reglée* is devoted to his work.

25. Randle Cotgrave, *A Dictionarie of the French and English Tongues*, defines "dessert" as "the last course, or service at table; of fruits, comfets, sweet meats, etc." From the end of the sixteenth century it was also served separately as a collation, usually in the evening.

26. L.S.R., *L'Art de bien traiter*, pp. 65–70.

27. Ibid., pp. 69–70.

28. Claude Fleury, *Les Devoirs de maitres et des domestiques* (Paris, 1688), reprinted in Franklin, *La Vie privée d'autrefois: La Vie de Paris sous Louis XV*, p. 308.

29. L.S.R., *L'Art de bien traiter*, p. 70.

30. Le Sieur Crespin, *L'Œconomie ou le vray advis povr se faire bien servir*, pp. 14–16.

31. Duc de Luynes, *Mémoires du duc de Luynes sur la cour de Louis XV (1735–1758)*, 2:260.

32. Ibid., 4:152, 9:4.

33. Marie de Rabutin Chantal, marquise de Sévigné, *Lettres*, 1:747–48.

CHAPTER SIX

1. Carl Joachim Friedrich, *The Age of the Baroque, 1610–1660*, pp. 113–17.

2. Paul Hazard, *The European Mind, 1680–1715*, pp. 131–32.

3. Elizabeth L. Eisenstein, *The Printing Press as an Agent of Change*, 1:272–74.

4. Alain Girard, "Le Triomphe de la Cuisinière bourgeoise."

5. François Pierre de La Varenne, *Le Cvisinier françois* (1651), dedication.

6. Ibid., pp. 1–2.

7. Ibid., pp. 134–35.

8. Ibid., p. 321.

9. Ibid., pp. 24, 57–58.

10. Ibid., p. 39.

11. Ibid., p. 108.

12. Ibid., p. 121.

13. Ibid., p. 8.

14. Ibid., p. 127.

15. Ibid., pp. 132–33.

16. For an abundance of reproductions see Michel Faré, *La Nature morte en France*; Michel Faré, *Le Grand siècle de la nature morte en France*; and Michel and Fabrice Faré, *La Vie silencieuse en France*.

17. La Varenne, *Cvisinier françois* (1651), pp. 200, 202.

18. Ibid., p. 284.

19. It appeared as late as 1726 at Rouen and at Troyes in 1738; see Alfred Morin, *Catalogue descriptif de la Bibliothèque bleue de Troyes (almanachs exclus)*, pp. 89–91; Bonnefons's *Jardinier françois* enjoyed the same distinction (ibid., pp. 274–76).

20. It was plagiarized, paraphrased, and rearranged as the *Traité de confiture ou le nouveau et parfait confiturier*.

21. The attribution of the *Pâtissier françois* to La Varenne was made by Vicaire. His reasoning was, first, that the *Pâtissier* was bound with La Varenne's *Confiturier* and with the *Cvisinier méthodiqve* (later called *Le Cuisinier françois ov l'ecole des ragouts*, which Vicaire attributes to La Varenne because editions from 1685 onward do bear his name), and second, that the great Elzevier press in Amsterdam published an edition of the *Pâtissier* and is said to have published an edition of the *Cvisinier*. Can Vicaire have read them thoughtfully? In *Great Cooks and Their Recipes from Taillevent to Escoffier*, Anne Willan argues that it is not by La Varenne, first,

because "the profession of the *pâtissier* was completely separate [from the *cuisinier*]" and, second, because she finds it "hard to believe that two years after writing the *Cuisinier françois*, the same author could turn out a second book so different in style and content." This second volume bears no dedication. Both include many recipes for the same kinds of pies and tourtes, so trade specialization alone cannot support the argument for separate authorship. The matter of differing styles is more serious and more plausible. The recipes in the *Pâtissier* are much more detailed about quantities, timing, and procedures than any in the *Cvisinier*. Recipes that appear in both books differ in ways that suggest the hands of two different cooks. For example, the proportions of fat to flour in the puff pastry recipes are different. The *Pâtissier* is not arranged for use by a busy cook, as is the *Cvisinier*. Rather, there are sections on various types of pastry cooking and then, at the end, a series of egg recipes. There is a discrepancy in the presentation of omelets. In the *Cvisinier* La Varenne consistently folds his into squares; the author of the *Pâtissier* usually serves them either flat or rolled, occasionally splitting the ends of the rolled ones, turning them outward to make a star shape and to display the filling.

22. *Le Pâtissier françois* (Paris, 1653), reprinted in *Le Cuisinier françois ov l'ecole des ragouts*, p. 311.

23. See Marc Venard, *Bourgeois et paysans au XVIIe siècle*.

24. Nicolas de Bonnefons, *Le Jardinier françois* (1651), pp. 373–74.

25. Bonnefons, *Le Jardinier françois* (1683), pp. 240, 270–76.

26. Nicolas de Bonnefons, *Les Delices de la campagne* (1679), pp. 127–28.

27. Bonnefons, *Jardinier* (1683), pp. 78–79. English and American gardens boasted a good variety as well; see Peter Wynne, *Apples*; Ann Leighton, *Early American Gardens "For Meate or Medicine,"* and *American Gardens in the Eighteenth Century "For Use or For Delight."*

28. Bonnefons, *Jardinier* (1683), Epistre aux dames. Randle Cotgrave, *A Dictionarie of the French and English Tongues*, defines "friand" as "a sweet-lips, picke-morsell, curious feeder, lickourous companion, daintie-mouthed fellow; an eat-well, slap-sauce, lick-dish."

29. Bonnefons, *Jardinier* (1683), Epistre aux dames.

30. Bonnefons, *Delices* (1679), Epistre aux dames.

31. Ibid., pp. 159–68.

32. Ibid., pp. 170–75.

33. André J. Bourde, *Agronomie et agronomes en France au XVIIIe siècle*, pp. 80–103.

34. Georges Vicaire, *Bibliographie gastronomique*, cols. 502–3, ascribes the *Cvisinier méthodiqve* to La Varenne. The edition published in Lyons as *Le Cvisinier françois ov l'ecole des ragouts* (1662) bears La Varenne's name on the title page, but the quality of the recipes is so much lower and the working methods are so much less advanced than those in the original *Cvisinier françois* that it is hard to believe they are the work of the same person. This Lyons volume contains, in addition to the texts of the *Cvisinier méthodiqve* and the *Pâtissier françois*, the *Confiturier françois* and a confused little treatise called *La Maniere de plier toutes sorte de linge de table, et en faire toutes sortes de figures.* Delightful as ornamentally folded table linen may be, the lack of illustrations and vagueness of the directions make it impossible to realize from it the promised "two chickens in a pie," "dog's head in a collar," or "suckling pig." Like their modern counterparts, these napkins often concealed the diner's roll. My references to the *Cvisinier méthodiqve* are in its disguise as *Le Cuisinier françois ov l'ecole des ragouts* (Lyons, 1695), because it is the only edition available to me.

35. *Le Cvisinier méthodiqve* reprinted as *Le Cuisinier françois ov l'ecole des ragouts*, pp. 55–56.

36. Ibid., p. 13.

37. Pierre de Lune, *Le Cvisinier ov il est traitté de la véritable méthode pour apprester toutes sortes de viandes, gibbier, volatiles, poissons tant de mer que d'eau douce.*

38. *Cvisinier méthodiqve*, pp. 7–9.

CHAPTER SEVEN

1. "Semirestricted," because any respectably dressed person could come to the palace to watch the king when he dined in public (W. H. Lewis, *The Splendid Century*, p. 50).

2. For example, in 1674 the king held a festival to celebrate the conquest of the Franche Comté, but there are no references in the program of the festival to any events in that campaign. See André Félibien, *Les Divertissemens de Versailles donnez par le roy à toute sa cour au retour de la conqueste de la Franche Comte en lannée M. DC. LXXIV.* John B. Wolf, *Louis XIV*, p. 352, says that the king used his fêtes "to mask his intentions in high politics."

3. Wolf, *Louis XIV*, pp. 187–90.

4. Molière, *Œuvres complètes*, 1:861, 864, n. 13.

5. Jean de La Fontaine, *Lettre à M. de Maucroix*, in *Œuvres diverses*, 7:522–27.

6. André Félibien, *Les Plaisirs de l'Isle enchantée.*

7. Ibid., p. 4.

8. Ibid., p. 8.

9. Ibid., pp. 15–16.

10. Ibid., p. 20.

11. Ibid., p. 43.

12. Wolf, *Louis XIV*, p. 351.

13. Félibien, *Divertissemens*, pp. 8–9.

14. André Félibien, *Relation de la feste de Versailles de 18 juillet mil six cens soixant-huit*, p. 7.

15. Félibien, *Divertissemens*, p. 20.

16. Félibien, *Relation*, p. 9.

17. Alfred Franklin, *La Vie privée d'autrefois: La Cuisine*, pp. 175–80.

18. Alfred Franklin, *La Vie privée d'autrefois: Variétés gastronomiques*, pp. 192–93.

19. Franklin, *La Vie privée d'autrefois: La Cuisine*, p. 179.

20. Elisabeth Charlotte Orléans, *Correspondance complète de Madame, duchesse d'Orléans, née Princesse Palatine, mère du Régent*, 2:37.

21. Louis de Rouvroy, duc de Saint-Simon, *Mémoires de duc de Saint-Simon*, ed. Truc, 6:879–81.

22. Orléans, *Correspondance*, 2:322–23.

23. Ibid., 2:171–72.

24. N. Audiger, *La Maison reglée et l'art de diriger la maison d'un grand seigneur et autres, tant à la ville qu'à la campagne*, pp. 132–36.

25. *Le Mercure Galant*, June 1679, pp. 144–57.

26. Louis Sébastien Mercier, *Le Tableau de Paris*, 10:125.

27. François Massialot, *Le Cuisinier roïal et bourgeois* (1705), pp. 110–11.

28. Françoise d'Aubigné, marquise de Maintenon, *Correspondance de Madame de Maintenon*, 3:52.

29. Henri Brocher, *Le Rang et l'etiquette sous l'ancien régime*, p. 28.

30. *Service à la russe*, in simplified form, is the style of service practiced today, in which dishes are passed in sequence around the table for the diners to serve themselves or to be served from. Large items, such as roasts, are presented and then taken to a side table for carving. Antonin Carême observed the practice when he was at the court of Alexander I in 1818; he admired it but considered it unsuitable for French cuisine. In the mid-nineteenth century Urbain Dubois spent some years in Russia as chef to Prince Orloff. Upon his return to France after 1870 he helped popularize *service à la russe*, which was then taken up with enthusiasm.

31. Modern purists tell us that *hors d'oeuvre* is always written in the singular; in the sev-

enteenth and eighteenth centuries the plural form was often though not invariably used; Vincent La Chapelle writes one *hors d'oeuvre*, two *hors d'oeuvres*, and so on.

32. Nicolas de Bonnefons, *Les Delices de la campagne* (1654), p. 375.

33. "Remove" has remained the English word for such dishes into the twentieth century, although by the end of the nineteenth it had come to refer to a separate course.

34. For illustrations see Kathryn C. Buhler and John Meredith Graham, *The Campbell Museum Collection.*

35. Antoine de Courtin, *Nouveau traité de la civilité qui se pratique en France parmi les honnestes gens,* in Alfred Franklin, *La Vie privée d'autrefois: Les Repas,* p. 234.

36. Ibid., p. 231.

37. *Le Mercure Galant,* January 1680, pp. 60–61, 80.

38. Ibid., October 1677, p. 271.

39. Ibid., February 1680, p. 211.

40. Ibid., October 1677, pp. 222–23.

41. Ibid., pp. 227–29.

42. Ibid., pp. 229–30.

43. Auguste Jal, *Dictionnaire critique de biographie,* s.v. "Watel."

44. Marie de Rabutin Chantal, marquise de Sévigné, *Lettres,* 1:232–36. Jean Moura and Paul Louvet, *La Vie de Vatel,* is hampered by the almost total lack of substantive information about him. Letters exist in which he orders salmon, but even his first name is uncertain (it may have been François); he may have been a Fleming named Watel. The authors attempt to fill the gaps with descriptions of what they think their subject was thinking. Nothing specific is known about his contribution to the arts of the table.

45. Jean Hérault de Gourville, *Mémoires,* 2:39: "The first thing I did was to tell them to put him on a wagon and take him to the parish [church?] half a league away to bury him, and I found that the seafood was just arriving."

46. Antonin Carême, "Aphorismes, pensées et maximes," p. 367.

47. *Le Mercure Galant,* January 1677, p. 75.

48. Ibid., July 1677, p. 285.

49. Ibid., November 1691, p. 194.

50. Ibid., January 1705, p. 353.

51. Ibid., February 1705, p. 279.

CHAPTER EIGHT

1. Among the provincial and foreign editions of *Le Cvisinier françois* are the following: Rouen, 1689 and 1700; Troyes, ca. 1723 and 1738, Brussels, 1698 and 1712; Amsterdam, 1712; The Hague, 1721. In Italy it appeared as *Il Cvoco francese* in Bologna in 1682 and 1693; in Venice in 1696, 1703, 1715, 1728, and 1783; and in Bassano in 1787, 1802, and 1805. It appeared in England as *The French Cook* in 1653, 1654, and 1673. See Georges Vicaire, *Bibliographie gastronomique,* cols. 495–501; Lord Westbury, *Handlist of Italian Cookery Books,* pp. 130–31; Arnold Whitaker Oxford, *English Cookery Books to 1850,* pp. 23–24. See also Alain Girard, "Le Triomphe de 'la cuisinière bourgeoise,'" pp. 497–508.

2. Pierre de Lune, *Le Cvisinier ov il est traitté de la véritable méthode pour apprester toutes sortes de viandes, gibbier, volatiles, poissons,* pp. 77–80, 133.

3. *L'Eschole parfaite des officiers de bouche* (Paris, 1708), p. 284. The other editions include 1662, 1666, 1676, 1680, 1708, 1715, 1716, 1729, 1737, and the last in 1742. It was translated into English by Giles Rose as *A Perfect School of Instructions for the Officers of the Mouth . . .* (London, 1682).

4. L.S.R., *L'Art de bien traiter, divisé en trois parties.* Vicaire discusses the possible author, *Bibliographie*, cols. 43–44, 891; the name traditionally given is Le Sieur Robert, of whom nothing is known; Vicaire quotes Pichon as proposing a Sieur Rolland, who is known to have been working in and around the court at approximately this time. Elizabeth David, "Death in the Glass," plausibly suggests that the book is by two writers, one "a pamphleteer castigating, in somewhat intemperate language, the social fads and follies of the age; the other a serious, genteel arranger," what she calls a "*House and Garden* entertaining supplement."

5. L.S.R., *L'Art de bien traiter*, pp. 1, 5–7.

6. Ibid., p. 21.

7. Ibid., pp. 320–25.

8. After the first edition, from 1693 onward, the spelling of *roïal* changed to *royal*. The last edition appeared in 1751; see Vicaire, *Bibliographie*, cols. 573–76.

9. François Massialot, *Le Cuisinier roïal et bourgeois* (1705), preface. The text of this edition is close to that of the first.

10. Ibid., pp. 3–48.

11. The phrase or similar ones occur in *Le Mercure de France*, August 1728, p. 1895; a letter of the earl of Chesterfield, Philip Dormer Stanhope, *The Letters of Philip Dormer Stanhope, Fourth Earl of Chesterfield*, 6:2949; Edmond Jean François Barbier, *Chronique de la régence et du règne de Louis XV, 1718–1763*, 4:395; *Mémoires du duc de Luynes sur la cour de Louis XV (1735–1758)*, 4:152.

12. Barbier, *Chronique*, 4:395.

13. Randle Cotgrave, *A Dictionarie of the French and English Tongues*, defines "porte-chappe" as "a feast-furnisher; one that hires out all manner of naperie and vessel, and all other prouision whatsoever (except victuals) fit for the setting out of a feast."

14. A magnificent table alone would not bring social acceptance. Money and power were far more important, but fine and abundant fare helped bring desirable company to the host's table.

15. Massialot, *Cuisinier roïal et bourgeois* (1705), pp. 24–25.

16. Ibid., pp. 291–93.

17. Ibid., p. 311.

18. Ibid., pp. 203–8.

19. Ibid., p. 181.

20. Ibid., pp. 268–69.

21. Ibid., pp. 176, 225–26.

22. Ibid., pp. 254–55, 327–28, 173.

23. François Massialot, *Le Nouveau cuisinier royal et bourgeois* (1712), 2:272–96.

24. Massialot, *Le Cuisinier roïal et bourgeois* (1691), pp. 28–29; *Nouveau cuisinier royal et bourgeois* (1712) 1:16–19.

25. Massialot, *Cuisinier roïal et bourgeois* (1705), pp. 89–90; *Le Nouveau cuisinier royal et bourgeois* (1734), 1:94–95.

26. Philip Hyman and Mary Hyman, "La Chapelle and Massialot."

27. Vincent La Chapelle, *Le Cuisinier moderne* (1742), 4:Avertissement, and 5:330–46.

28. Elisabeth Charlotte Orléans, *Correspondance complète de Madame, duchesse d'Orléans, née princesse Palatine, mère du régent*, 1:349.

29. Louis de Rouvroy, duc de Saint-Simon, *Mémoires du duc de Saint-Simon*, ed. Chéruel and Regnier, 12:441–42.

30. A painting by Eugène Lamie, dating from 1854, *Supper with the Regent*, in the Wallace Collection, London, fully evokes the nineteenth-century view of the regent's supper parties as occasions of disorder in an elegant setting.

31. Warren Hamilton Lewis, *The Scandalous Regent*, p. 98.

32. La Chapelle, *Cuisinier moderne* (1742), 5:68–69.

33. See also Mary Frances Kennedy Fisher's an-aphrodisiac meal, which is a triumph of subversive menumaking, *An Alphabet for Gourmets*, reprinted in *The Art of Eating*, pp. 711–12.

34. Giacomo Casanova, chevalier de Seingalt, *History of My Life*, 4:39.

CHAPTER NINE

1. J. Jean Hecht, *Continental and Colonial Servants in Eighteenth Century England*, pp. 9–11.

2. Günter Wiegelmann, *Alltags- und Festspeisen*, pp. 28–29, 43–44.

3. Tomasius, *Nachahmung*, cited by Wiegelmann, *Alltags- und Festspeisen*, p. 43.

4. For lists of household staffs see Eduard Vehse, *Geschichte der deutsche Höfe seit der Reformation*, 2:232, 4:34, 227, 18:120, 19:23, 28:271, 33:115.

5. Giacomo Casanova, chevalier de Seingalt, *History of My Life*, 10:56, 303. Frederick II wrote a poem to Noël.

6. Vehse, *Geschichte*, 4:34–35.

7. Ibid., pp. 197–205.

8. W. S. Lewis et al., eds., *The Yale Edition of Horace Walpole's Correspondence*, 19:356.

9. Marcus Cheke, *Cardinal de Bernis*, p. 233.

10. Hecht, *Continental and Colonial Servants*, pp. 1–10.

11. William Harrison, *The Description of England*, p. 126.

12. Samuel Pepys, *The Diary of Samuel Pepys*, 1:269.

13. Ibid., 2:29, 4:95, 189.

14. Ian Nairn and Nikolaus Pevsner, *Surrey*, p. 140. According to Vehse, *Geschichte*, 23:209, the duke owned one of prerevolutionary Europe's five solid gold dinner services.

15. Stanhope, *Letters*, no. 792.

16. Ibid., no. 1843.

17. Philip Dormer Stanhope, *Characters*, p. 44.

18. Mary Wortley Montagu, *The Letters and Works of Lady Mary Wortley Montagu*, 1:256.

19. Romney Sedgwick, "The Duke of Newcastle's Cook," pp. 308–16.

20. Ibid., p. 212.

21. Ibid., pp. 212–13.

22. William Verral, *A Complete System of Cookery, in which is set forth a Variety of Genuine Receipts, collected from several Years Experience under the celebrated Mr. de St. Clouet*. The work has been reprinted as *The Cook's Paradise*; my page references are to this latter edition.

23. Ibid., pp. 28–29. The *Shorter Oxford English Dictionary* defines "pope's eye" as "the lymphatic gland surrounded with fat at the middle of a leg of mutton."

24. Thomas Gray, the poet, owned the copy of Verral's book from which the reprint was prepared, and its editor, Mégroz, has included Gray's notes, p. 133, which include an "index of such receipts as are continually referred to, and necessary in preparing all the rest, or several of them," including bouillon, gravy, "cullis," forcemeat, salpicon, braise, liaison, and hot marinade.

25. Ibid., pp. 88–89.

26. Lewis et al., eds., *Walpole Correspondence*, 17:485, n. 9.

27. Marshall Belle Isle was the grandson of Louis XIV's minister Fouquet, of Vaux-le-Vicomte.

28. Improvisational spelling is an enduring characteristic of cookbooks, sometimes be-

coming so erratic as to suggest that the author is writing in dialect. Verral's *Complete System of Cookery* and both the English and French versions of La Chapelle's *Cuisinier moderne* are examples. This defect is not surprising in view of the low level of literacy among eighteenth-century artisans. Most information was passed along by the spoken, not the written, word. Where French cooks were assisted by Germans, Englishmen, Dutchmen, and other itinerant cooks, conversation in the kitchen (to say nothing of the clash of egos) must have resembled that among members of an opera company today.

29. Stanhope, *Letters*, Appendix 1, no. 2.

30. Ibid., no. 735.

31. Vincent La Chapelle, *Le Cuisinier moderne*, 1:59–60.

32. Among the English recipes is a pudding—potin, he calls it—made with red currants wrapped in pastry and boiled in a cloth (ibid., 2:156). There are Dutch recipes throughout the book, but the fifth volume, which was added for the 1742 edition, contains the most.

33. Ibid., 1:84–87; Casanova, *History*, 9:34.

34. La Chapelle, *Cuisinier moderne* (1742), 5:257. There is a *ragoût indien* in the 1712 edition of Massialot's *Nouveau cuisinier royale et bourgeois*, 3:124, but it contains no *piment enragé* and resembles none of La Chapelle's three Indian recipes.

35. Philip Hyman and Mary Hyman, "La Chapelle and Massialot."

36. La Chapelle, *Cuisinier moderne* (1742), 4:88–93.

37. Ibid., 3:182–84.

38. Ibid., pp. 54–55. Philip Hyman and Mary Hyman, "Vincent La Chapelle," quote Carême and Guégan as attributing to La Chapelle the credit for simplifying French cuisine. In their view it was this simplification—and of course the ever-invoked refinement—that made La Chapelle a modern cook.

39. La Chapelle, *Cuisinier moderne* (1742), 2:252–53.

40. Ibid., 1:252–54.

41. Ibid., 4:Avertissement de l'auteur, pour cette seconde édition; 5:331–46. The Hymans, "La Chapelle and Massialot," point out that La Chapelle accused Massiaiot of recipe-stealing, but they cannot find such an accusation in Massialot's writings. Neither can I; perhaps it was made orally or in a lost or unrecognized broadside.

42. La Chapelle, *Cuisinier moderne* (1742), 5:42.

CHAPTER TEN

1. Georgine E. Brereton and Janet M. Ferrier, eds., *Le Menagier de Paris*, p. 254.

2. Ibid., p. 245.

3. Jérôme Pichon and Georges Vicaire, eds., *Le Viandier de Guillaume Tirel, dit Taillevent*, pp. 76–77.

4. *Le Pâtissier françois*, reprinted in *Le Cuisinier françois ov l'ecole des ragouts*, p. 270; Nicolas de Bonnefons, *Les Delices de la campagne* (1679), p. 30.

5. *Le Liure fort excellent de cuysine*, f. 47r°.

6. Ibid., 57v°; Randle Cotgrave, *A Dictionarie of the French and English Tongues*, s.v. "brides à veaux"; P. Dorveaux, "'Brides à veaux.'"

7. Lancelot de Casteau, *Ovverture de cvisine*, pp. 34–35, 66–67, 21–22.

8. Ibid., pp. 78–80, 19–20.

9. *Le Pâtissier françois*, reprinted in *Le Cuisinier françois ov l'ecole des ragouts*, to which edition the present page references are made, pp. 181–83; Armand Machabey, *Le Métrologie dans les musées de province et sa contribution à l'histoire des poids et mesures en France depuis le treizième siècle*.

10. *Pâtissier*, pp. 326–27.

11. Nicolas de Bonnefons, *Les Delices de la campagne* (1679), p. 30.

12. Ibid., pp. 18–19.

13. François Massialot, *Nouvelle instruction pour les confitures, les liqueurs, et les fruits* (1717), pp. 210–11.

14. Vincent La Chapelle, *Le Cuisinier moderne qui apprend à donner toutes sortes de repas, en gras et en maigre, d'une manière plus délicate que ce qui en été écrit jusqu'à présent* (1742), 2:101–2.

15. Bonnefons, *Delices* (1679), pp. 2, 3, 11, 13–14.

16. Nicolas de Blegny, *Le Livre commode contenant les adresses de la ville de Paris et le tresor des almanachs pour l'année bissextile 1692*, ed. Fournier, 2:304–8, quotation on p. 209.

17. Paul Jacques Malouin, *Description des arts et métiers faites ou approuvées par messieurs de l'Académie Royale des Sciences*, pp. 212, 216–71.

18. Ibid., pp. 218–21.

19. Pichon and Vicaire, eds., *Viandier*, p. 232.

20. Brereton and Ferrier, eds., *Menagier*, pp. 267–70.

21. Pichon and Vicaire, eds., *Viandier*, p. 108.

22. *Liure fort excellent de cuysine*, ff. 3r°, 37r°.

23. Alexis of Piedmont, *Les Secrets dv seignevr Alexis piemontois*; editions in French were published from 1557 to 1691; the Italian original was still being reprinted in the late eighteenth century; see Lord Westbury, *Handlist of Italian Cookery Books*, p. 8. Michel de Nostredamus, *Excellent et moult utile opuscule à touts necessaire, qui desirent auoir cognoissance de plusieurs exquises receptes, diuisé en deux parties*; the culinary part has been reprinted as *La Façon et maniere de faire toutes confitures liquides, tant en succre, miel, qu'en vin cuit*, from which page references here are taken. For pastillage, see Alexis of Piedmont, *Secrets*, f. 45v°; for marzipan, Nostradamus, *Opuscule* (1962), pp. 114–16.

24. François La Varenne, *Le Parfaict confitvrier qvi enseigne a bien faire toutes sortes de confitures tant seiches que liquides de compostes, de fruicts, de sallades, de dragées, breuvages délicieux et autres délicatesses de bouche* (1667); reprinted as *Le Confiturier françois, où est enseigné la manière de faire toutes sortes de confitures dragées, liqueurs, et breuvages agréables. Ensemble la manière de plier le linge de table et en faire toutes sortes de figures* (Troyes, n.d.); this was in turn reprinted in *Le Cuisinier françois ov l'ecole des ragouts* (1695), pp. 381–83.

25. Menon, *La Science du maître d'hôtel, confiseur* (1750), pp. 4–8. The work was reprinted in 1760, 1768, 1777, and 1788.

26. Gaston Lenôtre, *Lenôtre's Ice Creams and Candies*, pp. 204–5, 207.

27. La Varenne, *Confiturier* (1695), p. 420; Nicolas de Bonnefons, *Le Jardinier françois* (1683), p. 285.

28. Georgiana Reynolds Smith, *Table Decoration Yesterday, Today, and Tomorrow*, surveys the subject from the point of view of a flower arranger; the volume is extensively illustrated.

29. Menon, *La Science du maître d'hôtel, confiseur*, facing pp. 1, 338.

30. Massialot, *Nouvelle instruction* (1692), pp. 336–37.

31. Marie de Rabutin Chantal, marquise de Sévigné, *Lettres*, 1:351.

32. Massialot, *Nouvelle instruction* (1717), pp. 247–48, 437, 298–300.

33. *Le Mercure Galant*, January 1680, pt. 2, pp. 59–80, quotation on pp. 66–67.

34. Ibid., July 1679, p. 85.

35. *Le Mercure de France*, May 1726, pp. 990–93, quotation on pp. 991–92.

36. Massialot, *Nouvelle instruction* (1692), p. 437.

37. Ibid., p. 442; in the edition of 1704, p. 478, he has been replaced by one Sieur Delavarenne.

38. Philip Thicknesse, *Observations on the Customs and Manners of the French Nation, in a*

Series of Letters, in which That Nation is vindicated from the Misrepresentations of some Late Writers, pp. 152–53.

39. Massialot, *Nouvelle instruction* (1717), pp. 299, 283–84. For the early history of ice creams, ices, and molds see the following articles in *Petits Propos Culinaires*: Elizabeth David, "Hunt the Ice Cream," 1:8–13; "Fromages Glacés and Iced Creams," 2:23–35; The Editors, "Waist-Deep in Ice Cream," 2:36; Elizabeth David, "The Harvest of Cold Months," 3:9–16; W. S. Stallings, Jr., "Ice Cream and Water Ices in 17th and 18th Century England," Supplement to Issue 3; Elizabeth David, "Savour of Ice and of Roses," 8:7–18. This last article has little to do with France but contains a delicious description of the festivities accompanying the marriage of a French princess to the heir of the Grand Duke of Tuscany in 1661, at which frozen sweets were prominent.

40. La Chapelle, *Cuisinier moderne* (1742), 5:220–31.

41. Menon, *La Science du maître d'hôtel, confiseur,* pp. 165–73; *Le Dictionnaire portatif de cuisine,* pp. 102–3, 158–62, 284, 294–95, and throughout.

42. *Le Mercure de France,* August 1728, pp. 1893–96.

CHAPTER ELEVEN

1. The prince de Croï, quoted by Nancy Mitford, *Madame de Pompadour,* p. 109.

2. François Marin, *Les Dons de Comus, ou l'art de la cuisine réduit en pratique* (1750), 3:469–70.

3. Ibid., *sauce Robert à la Bourgeoise,* 1:133; grilled tripe, 1:170; veal, 1:242; stuffed veal breast, 1:246; *fricandeaux,* 1:271; braised mutton tongues, 1:309; *hachis de mouton,* 1:354; sirloin of beef, 1:540.

4. François de La Varenne, *Le Cvisinier françois* (1651), preface.

5. N. Audiger, *La Maison réglée,* madrigal. The poems at the beginning of the book were omitted by Alfred Franklin in his reprint of Audiger's work in *La Vie privée d'autrefois: La Vie de Paris sous Louix XIV.*

6. *Les Soupers de la cour,* 1:v.

7. Marin, *Les Dons de Comus, ou l'art de la cuisine réduit en pratique* (1758) 1:xxiii–xxiv.

8. Ibid., pp. 82–83.

9. Georges Vicaire, *Bibliographie gastronomique,* col. 285.

10. François Marin, *Les Dons de Comus ov les délices de la table* (1740), pp. xii–xiv.

11. Ibid., p. xvii.

12. *Lettre d'un pâtissier anglois au nouveau cuisinier françois,* reprinted in Marin, *Les Dons de Comus* (1740). Vicaire, *Bibliographie,* col. 518, identifies the author. The author of the avertissement in the 1740 edition of the *Dons de Comus* suggests that "the cuisinier and the pâtissier must have been able to borrow the pen of some man of letters, whom they fed well upon the condition of adopting his work and publishing it under their names" (p. 222). It would not have been a unique occurrence. The page references in this chapter are to the texts of the pamphlets as reprinted in the 1740 edition of *Les Dons de Comus.*

13. Preface to *Histoire de l'Académie royale des sciences depuis le règlement fait en 1699,* quoted by Paul Hazard, *The European Mind, 1680–1715,* p. 132.

14. *Lettre d'un pâtissier anglois,* reprinted in *Les Dons de Comus* (1740), pp. 225–27.

15. Ibid., pp. 228–29. The idea persists; see Laura J. Stevens and Rosemary B. Stoner, *How to Improve Your Child's Behavior through Diet* (Garden City: Doubleday, 1979).

16. Ibid., p. 232.

17. Baron Grimm, *Correspondance littéraire,* 2:187–88, quoted by Paul Hazard, *European Thought in the Eighteenth Century,* p. 200.

18. B. Clermont, *The Professed Cook*, p. 200, states that the *Fricassee de Poulets à la Bourdois* is "after the name of the Author Bourdois," but I fear he is speaking only of this one recipe (which does appear in *Les Soupers de la cour*, 2:118), though this turn of phrase is used nowhere else by Clermont.

19. *Soupers de la cour*, 1:117–18, 204–5, 222–23.

20. *Le Cuisinier gascon*, épitre.

21. Ibid., pp. 9–10, 45–46, 79–80, 64, 71–72.

22. Ibid., p. 11.

23. Ibid., pp. 88–89.

24. Ibid., pp. 153, 8, 26–27, 128–29.

25. Ibid., p. 133.

26. Ibid., pp. 180–81, 139–40, 144.

27. Ibid., pp. 44–45, 172–73.

28. Vincent La Chapelle, *Le Cuisinier moderne* (1742), 5:4–10.

29. Paul Jacques Malouin, *Description des arts et métiers faites ou approuvées par messieurs de l'Académie Royale des Sciences*, pp. 101–110.

30. *Cuisinier gascon*, pp. 90, 21. La Chapelle, *Cuisinier moderne* (1742), 3:54, calls for fifty duck or goose tongues to make a single small dish.

31. *Cuisinier gascon*, pp. 91–92.

32. The edition of 1740 has a shorter introduction than the first edition, of 1739, but it includes the *Lettre d'un pâtissier anglois* and a reply, the *Apologie des modernes ou réponse du cuisinier françois*. In 1742 the expanded edition of *Les Dons de Comus* appeared in three volumes, with a different preface and without the pamphlet materials, as *Suite des dons de Comus ou l'art de la cuisine réduite en pratique*. All these editions were published in Paris. The *Suite* was reprinted in 1750 and again in 1758 and 1775 as *Les Dons de Comus ou l'art de la cuisine réduit en pratique*. Is that clear?

33. *Dons de Comus* (1740), pp. 158–59.

34. Ibid., pp. 129–30.

35. Ibid. (1758), 1:7.

36. Ibid. (1740), pp. 140–41.

37. Ibid. (1758), 1:383.

38. *Traité historique et pratique de la cuisine ou le cuisinier instruit, de la connoissance des animaux, tant volatiles, que terrestres, aquatiques et amphibie*, 1:xxvi–xcvi.

39. Ibid., 1:207, 466, 467, 2:31, 32, 35, 150, 383–87.

40. Ibid., 1:242.

41. Ibid., 2:422.

42. Ibid., 2:403–5.

43. Vicaire, *Bibliographie*, col. 592.

44. *Traité*, 1:Abrégé, 2–6; Menon, *La Science du maître d'hôtel, confiseur*, pp. 2–8.

45. Menon is named as author in the *privilèges* but not on the title pages of the two-volume *Nouveau traité de la cuisine* (1739); *La Nouvelle cuisine* (1742, as a third volume of the *Nouveau traité*); *La Cuisinière bourgeoise* (1746); *La Science du maître d'hôtel, cuisinier* (1749); and *La Science du maître d'hôtel, confiseur* (1750). All of these are listed in a publisher's catalog in the *Confiseur*, where they are attributed to him. Two other works are traditionally attributed to him, for less convincing reasons. They are the *Cuisine et office de santé* (1758) and *Les Soupers de la cour* (1755); the latter is discussed above. The author of the *Cuisine et office de santé* recommends the *Cuisinière bourgeoise* and the *Soupers de la cour* to those who like good food (whence, I believe, the attribution of that work to Menon), but (I do not think the attributor was reading carefully) who care neither about their health nor their pocketbook—hardly an endorsement,

much less a claim of authorship. The culinary style of the *Cuisine et office de santé* is very different from the other works attributed to Menon, containing, for example, only five sauce recipes, three of which have water as their principal liquid.

46. *Nouveau traité* and *La Nouvelle cuisine* were published as a three-volume set in 1751 but do not appear to have enjoyed a long-lived popularity. The two *Maîtres d'hôtel* did better, the *Cuisinier* having editions in 1768, 1776, and 1789, and the *Confiseur* in 1760, 1768, 1777, and 1788.

47. Menon, *Nouveau traité de la cuisine*, 1:173–74.

48. Marin, *Les Dons de Comus* (1758), 1:167.

49. Among English cookbooks addressed to women up to 1746 are *The Treasurie of Commodious conceites, and hidden secrets. Commonly called the Good Huswives Closet of provision for the health of her household* (London, 1573); Thomas Dawson, *The Good Huswifes Iewell* (London, 1587); John Partridge, *The Widdowes Treasure* (London, 1595). Cookbooks by women include Hanna Wolley, *The Ladies Directory* (London, 1661), *The Cooks Guide* (London, 1664), and *The Queen-Like Closet* (London, 1670); and Mrs. *Mary Eales's Receipts* (London, 1718). In 1747 the first edition of Hannah Glasse's *Art of Cookery Made Plain and Easy* appeared. In Germany, Anna Weckerin's *Köstlich new Kochbüch von allerhand Speisen* appeared in 1608; Wolfgang and Susanna Maria Endter's *Der aus Parnasso ehemals entlauffenen vortrefflichen Kochin. . . . Kochkunst beflissenen Frauen zu Nurnberg* (1691); the *Wohl-unterwiesenen köchinn zufälliger Confect-Tisch* (Brunswick, 1692). Annie van t'Veer, *Oud-hollands kookboek* (Utrecht: Prisma, 1966), pp. 180–81, cites a Netherlandish *Koochboec, oft familieren Keuckenboeck, . . . voor alle Jouffrouwen* (Louvain, 1612), and *De Volmaakte Hollandse Keuken-Meid* (Amsterdam, 1746). Like the *Cuisinière bourgeoise*, also of 1746, and Glasse's *Art of Cookery*, which appeared the next year, this volume enjoyed repeated printings.

50. Menon, *La Cuisinière bourgeoise* (1790), 1:iii; this edition contains everything that is in the enlarged text of 1759, as well as some additional recipes, which are marked with an asterisk.

51. Ibid. (1746), p. 259.

52. Ibid. (1790), 1:128–31.

53. Ibid. (1746), pp. 74–75.

54. Ibid., pp. 255–57.

55. Alain Girard, "Le Triomphe de la cuisinière bourgeoise," p. 515.

56. *Catalogue des livres manuscrits et imprimées . . . de la bibliothèque de M. le duc de Chaulnes.* His books on diet and cookery, listed in the category "histoire naturelle de l'homme," include books on vegetarian diet and the school of Salerno, as well as two editions of Scappi's *Opera.* The *Cuisine et office de santé* is described as being by Menon (items 908–18).

57. Pierre Rosenberg, *Chardin, 1699–1779*, pp. 73–76.

58. Voltaire, *Correspondence and Related Documents*, 1:42.

59. Ibid., 2:269, 6:166–67.

60. Ibid., 7:425–26.

61. Ibid., 31:76.

62. Gustave Desnoiresterres, *Grimod de La Reynière et son groupe*, pp. 7–8.

63. Ibid., p. 8.

64. Voltaire, *Correspondence*, 12:254.

65. Ibid., 18:384, 426.

66. Ibid., 9:205.

67. Ibid., 33:64–65. Joyce Toomre has pointed out, in her paper "A Literary Feast," given at the Victorian Society Symposium in Philadelphia, September 1981, that Henry Fielding, writing in the preface to *Tom Jones* (London, 1749), states that "an author should consider

himself as the master of a public ordinary or tavern" and describes the character of the novel in culinary terms.

68. Voltaire, *Correspondence*, 44:229, 293–94, 329–30.

69. Ibid., 21:182, 19:330, 20:420, 33:181, 28:260, 19:298, 82, 17:398, 18:64, 40:47, 34:334, 42:137, 44:114, 45:133, 177–78.

70. Ibid., 17:357, 18:22, 24:110, 16:28–29, 15:105, 21:162, 17:196.

71. Ibid. 16:59, 39:20–22, 360, 17:243, 16:55, 34:27, 43:38, 20:202, 263, 34:17, 27:77.

72. Ibid., 24:236, 30:303, 36:337–38.

73. Ibid., 41:388.

CHAPTER TWELVE

1. Among the cookbooks and confectionaries in print between 1760 and 1789 were Menon, *La Science du maître d'hôtel cuisinier*, with editions in 1768, 1776, and 1789; his *Science du maître d'hôtel, confiseur*, with editions in 1760, 1776, 1777, and 1788; his *Cuisinière bourgeoise*, with Paris editions in 1767, 1769, 1778, 1788, and 1789, Brussels editions in 1764, 1767, 1774, 1775, 1777, and 1790, and editions published in Lyons in 1783 and in Liège in 1788. Massialot's *Nouvelle instruction pour les confitures* appeared as *Le Confiturier royal ou nouvelle instruction pour les confitures* in 1776 and again in 1791, and Marin's three-volume *Dons de Comus* in 1775; and the last edition of *Les Soupers de la cour*, reduced to three volumes from four, appeared in 1778.

2. Menon, *La Cuisinière bourgeoise* (1790), 1:142; *Soupers de la cour*, 2:118–19.

3. *Le Manuel des officiers de bouche*, introduction.

4. *Apologie des modernes, ou réponse du cuisinier françois auteur des dons de Comus au patissier anglois*, reprinted in François Marin, *Les Dons de Comus* (1740), pp. 281–82.

5. *Le Dictionnaire portatif de cuisine*, 1:83–84, 2:202–3, 300, 14–18.

6. Ibid., 2:358.

7. Joseph Michaud, *Biographie universelle ancienne et moderne*, s.v. "Jaucourt."

8. The single exception is in the *Traité historique et pratique de la cuisine. Ou le cuisinier instruit*; see chap. 11, n. 39.

9. Jean-Claude Bonnet, "Le Réseau culinaire dans l'Encyclopédie."

10. Ibid., pp. 905–7. When Jaucourt turned from the conflicting demands of nutrition and gastronomy to the techniques of cooking and confectionary, he took up, as Bonnet has shown, an entirely new vocabulary, one that had been developed during the preceding century by the technicians.

11. Jean-Jacques Rousseau, *Emile*, p. 409.

12. Jean-Jacques Rousseau, *Confessions*, p. 72.

13. Rousseau, *Emile*, p. 409.

14. Ibid., p. 416.

15. Ibid., p. 411.

16. Jean-Claude Bonnet, "Le Système du repas et de la cuisine chez Rousseau."

17. Rousseau, *Emile*, pp. 279–80.

18. Ibid., p. 749.

19. Gustave Desnoiresterres, *Grimod de La Reynière et son groupe*.

20. Edmond Jean François Barbier, *Chronique de la régence et du règne de Louis XV, 1718–1763*, 6:7.

21. Desnoiresterres, *Grimod de La Reynière*, pp. 73–95.

22. Ferdinand Hoefer, ed., *Nouvelle biographie générale*, s.v. "Grimod de La Reynière."

23. Beatrice C. Fink, "The Banquet as Phenomenon or Structure in Selected Eighteenth-century French Novels."

24. Petronius, *Satiricon*, trans. Michael Heseltine, Loeb Classical Library, pp. 39–141.

25. Hoefer, ed., *Nouvelle biographie générale*, s.v. "Le Grand d'Aussy."

26. Oddly enough, the *Traité historique* contains virtually no history, except for a brief remark on the origin of turkeys (1:260–61) and similar asides; it is *historié*, that is, it contains illustrative figures.

27. Pierre Jean Baptiste Le Grand d'Aussy, *Histoire de la vie privée des françois* (1815), 1:10.

28. Ibid., 2:160–63.

Bibliography

Adams, William Howard. *The French Garden, 1500–1800.* World Landscape and Architecture Series. New York: George Brazillier, 1979.

Aebischer, Paul. "Un manuscrit valaisian du 'Viandier' attribué à Taillevent." *Vallesia* 8 (1953):73–100.

Aignan. *Le Prestre médecin, ou discours physique sur l'établissement de la médecine, avec un traité du caffé et du the en France, selon le système d'Hippocrate.* Paris, 1696.

Allemagne, Henry René d'. *Decorative Ironwork: A Pictorial Treasury.* Translated by Vera K. Ostia. New York: Dover Publications, 1968.

Almanach parisien, en faveur des étrangers: Contenant, par ordre alphabétique, l'indication de tout ce qui est nécessaire et utile à sçavoir pour un etranger: Ce qui comprent le logement, la nourriture, l'habillement, les voitures . . . Paris, n.d.

Apologie des modernes, ou réponse du cuisinier françois auteur des dons de Comus au patissier anglois. N.p., n.d. Reprint. In François Marin, *Les Dons de Comus,* pp. 257–302. Paris, 1740.

Arberry, A. J. "A Baghdad Cookery Book, Translated from the Arabic." *Islamic Culture* 13 (1939):21–47, 189–214.

Aron, Jean-Paul. *The Art of Eating in France: Manners and Menus in the Nineteenth Century.* Translated by Nina Rootes. New York: Harper and Row, 1975.

———. "Biologie et alimentation au XVIIIᵉ siècle et au début du XIXᵉ siècle." *Annales: Economies, Sociétés, Civilisations* 16 (1961):971–77.

———. *Le Mangeur du XIXᵉ siècle.* Paris: Editions Robert Laffont, 1973.

Artus, Thomas, sieur d'Embry. *Description de l'Isle des Hermaphrodites . . . pour servir du supplement au journal de Henri III.* Cologne, 1724.

Audiger, N. *La Maison reglée et l'art de diriger la maison d'un grand seigneur et autres, tant à la ville qu'à la campagne . . . avec la veritable methode de faire toutes sortes d'essences d'eaux et de liqueurs, fortes et rafraîssantes à la mode d'Italie.* Paris, 1692. Reprint. In Alfred Franklin, *La Vie privée d'autrefois: La Vie de Paris sous Louis XIV, tenue de maison et domesticité,* pp. 1–203. Paris, 1898.

Saint Augustine. *The City of God.* In *Basic Writings of Saint Augustine,* ed. Whitney J. Oates. New York: Random House, 1948.

Austin, Thomas, ed. *Two Fifteenth-century Cookery-Books, Harleian MS. 279 (ab. 1430), and Harl. MS. 4016 (ab. 1450), with Extracts from Ashmole MS. 1439, Laud MS. 533, and Douce MS. 55.* Early English Text Society, old ser. 91. London: Oxford University Press for the Early English Text Society, 1888. Reprint. London: Oxford University Press for the Early English Text Society, 1964.

Axford, Lavonne B. *English Language Cookbooks, 1600–1973.* Detroit: Gale Research, 1976.

Babeau, Albert. *Les Artisans et les domestiques d'autrefois.* 2d ed. Paris, 1886.

Babelon, Jean-Pierre. *Demeures parisiennes sous Henry IV et Louis XIII.* Paris: Le Temps, 1965.

Banner, Lois. "Why Women Have Not Been Great Chefs." *South Atlantic Quarterly* 72 (1973):198–212.

Barbier, Edmond Jean François. *Chronique de la régence et du règne de Louis XV, 1718–1763.* 8 vols. Paris, 1866.

Barra, M. P. *L'Usage de la glace, de la neige, et dv froid.* Lyons, 1675.

Barthes, Roland. "Pour une psycho-sociologie de l'alimentation contemporaine." *Annales: Economies, Sociétés, Civilisations* 16 (1961):977–86.

Le Bastiment de receptes, nouuelement traduict de italien en langue françoyse. Lyons, 1541.

Baudrillart, H. *Histoire du luxe privé et public de l'antiquité jusqu'à nos jours.* Vol. 3: *Le Moyen Age et la Renaissance.* Paris, 1880.

Baurain, Georges. "Le Cabaret Guillot à Amiens au temps de Rabelais." *Revue des Etudes Rabelaisiennes* 10 (1912):75–103.

Béarn, Pierre. *Grimod de La Reynière.* Vie des hommes illustres 58. Paris: Gallimard, 1930.

Beck, Leonard N. "Praise is due Bartolomeo Platina: A Note on the Librarian-Author of the First Cookbook." *Quarterly Journal of the Library of Congress* 32 (1975):238–53.

Belon, Pierre. *L'Histoire de la nature des oyseaux, avec levrs descriptions, et naïfs portraicts retirez dv natvrel: Escrite en sept livres.* Paris, 1555.

Benítez, Ana M. de. *Cocina Prehispánica: Pre-hispanic Cooking.* Translated by Mary Williams de Varela. Mexico City: Editiones Euroamericanas Klaus Thiele, 1974.

Bernard, R.-J. "L'Alimentation paysanne en Gévaudan au XVIIIe siècle." *Annales: Economies, Sociétés, Civilisations* 24 (1969):1449–67.

Berthod, le sieur. *La Ville de Paris en vers bvrlesqves.* Paris, 1652.

Bicais, Michel. *La Manière de régler la santé par ce qui nous environne, par ce que nous recevons et par les exercices ou par la gymnastique moderne.* Aix, 1669.

Bitting, Katherine Golden. *Gastronomic Bibliography.* San Francisco: Privately published, 1939. Reprint. Ann Arbor: Gryphon Books, 1971.

Blegny, Nicolas de. *Le Bon usage du thé, du caffé et du chocolat . . .* Paris, 1687.

———. [Abraham du Pradel]. *Le Livre commode contenant les adresses de la ville de Paris et le tresor des almanachs pour l'année bissextile 1692 . . .* Paris, 1692. Reprint. Edited by Edouard Fournier. 2 vols. Paris, 1878.

Bloch, Marc. "Les Aliments de l'ancienne France." *Encyclopédie française,* 14:40–43.

Blond, Georges, and Blond, Germaine. *Histoire pittoresque de notre alimentation.* Paris: Arthème Fayard, 1960.

Bodin, Jean. *Discours sur les causes de l'extreme cherté qui est aujourd'huy en France et sur les moyens d'y remédier.* Paris, 1574. Reprint. In Felix Danjou and L. Cimber, eds., *Archives curieuses de l'histoire de France,* 1st ser., vol. 6, pp. 425–57. Paris, 1835.

Boileau, Etienne. *Réglemens sur les arts et métiers de Paris, rédigés au XIIIe siècle, et connus sous le nom du livre des métiers d'Etienne Boileau.* Edited by G. B. Depping. Collection des documents inédits sur l'histoire de France, 1st ser. Paris, 1837.

Bonnefons, Nicolas de. *Les Delices de la campagne. Suitte du jardinier françois ov est enseigné a preparer pour l'vsage de la vie tout ce qui croist sur la terre, et dans les eaux. Dédié avx dames mesnageres.* Paris, 1654; also Paris, 1679, 1682.

———. *Les Delices de la campagne, suite du jardinier françois, ov est enseigné à preparer pour l'usages de la vie, tout ce qui croist sur la terre, et dans les eaux, dedié aux dames ménageres.* 2d ed. Amsterdam, 1655.

———. *Le Jardinier françois, qvi enseigne à cvltiver les arbres, les herbes potagères. Auec la manière de conseruer les fruicts, et faire toutes sortes de confitures, conserues et massepans, dedié aux dames.* Paris, 1651.

———. *Le Jardinier françois, ˜qui enseigne à cultiver les arbres, et herbes potageres; avec la maniere de conserver les fruicts, et faire toute sorte de confitures, conserves et massepains: Ensemble des maladies des arbres, et leurs remedes, dedié avx dames.* Lyons, 1683.

Bonnet, Jean-Claude. "Le Réseau culinaire dans l'Encyclopédie." *Annales: Economies, Sociétés, Civilisations* 31 (1976):891–914. Translated by Elborg Forster as "The Culinary System in the *Encyclopédie*," in *Food and Drink in History: Selections from the Annales, vol.* 5, edited by Robert Forster and Orest Ranum, pp. 139–65. Baltimore: Johns Hopkins University Press, 1979.

———. "Le Système du repas et de la cuisine chez Rousseau." *Poétique* 6, no. 22 (1975):244–67.

Boucaud, Philippe, and Frégnac, Claude. *Les Etains: Des origines au début du XIXe siècle.* Fribourg: Office du Livre, 1978.

Bourde, André J. *Agronomie et agronomes en France au XVIIIe siècle.* Les Hommes et la terre, vol. 13. Paris: S.E.V.P.E.N., 1967.

Bourgeat, Jacques. *Les Plaisirs de la table en France des gaulois à nos jours.* Paris: Hachette, 1963.

Brantôme, Pierre de Bourdeille, sieur de. *Œuvres complètes.* Edited by Ludovic Lalanne. 10 vols. Paris, 1881.

Braudel, Fernand. "Histoire de la vie matérielle. Bulletin n° 2. Alimentation et catégories d'histoire." *Annales: Economies, Sociétés, Civilisations* 16 (1961):723–28.

———. *La Méditerrannée et le monde méditerranéen à l'époque de Philippe II.* Paris, 1949.

Brereton, Georgine E. "La Source des additions du Pierre Gaudoul au *Viandier de Taillevent.*" *Bibliothèque d'Humanisme et Renaissance: Travaux et Document* 16 (1954):208.

———, and Ferrier, Janet M., eds. *Le Menagier de Paris.* Oxford: Clarendon Press, 1981.

Brillat-Savarin, Jean Anthèlme. *Physiologie du goût ou méditations du gastronomie transcendante.* Reprint. In *Les Classiques de la table, à l'usage des praticiens et des gens de monde*, edited by Alfred Charles Frédéric Fayot, pp. 1–146. Paris, 1843.

Brocher, Henri. *Le Rang et l'etiquette sous l'ancien régime.* Paris: Félix Alcan, 1934.

Buchon, Marianne. "Etude sur deux traités latins d'art culinaire." *Positions des thèses soutenues par les élèves de la promotion de 1950 pour obtenir le diplôme d'archiviste paléographe.* Paris: Ecole des Chartes, 1950.

Buhler, Kathryn C., and Graham, John Meredith. *The Campbell Museum Collection.* 2d ed. Camden, N.J., 1972.

Carême, Antonin. "Aphorismes, pensées et maximes." In *Les Classiques de la table, à l'usage des praticiens et des gens de monde*, edited by Alfred Charles Frédéric Fayot, pp. 363–70. Paris, 1843.

Cartellieri, Otto. *The Court of Burgundy: Studies in the History of Civilization.* New York: Haskell House, 1970.

Casanova, Giacomo, chevalier de Seingalt. *History of My Life.* Translated by Willard R. Trask. 12 vols. New York: Harcourt Brace Jovanovich, 1966–71.

Casteau, Lancelot de. *Ovverture de cvisine, par Maistre Lancelot de Casteau, montois, en son temps maistre cuisinier de trois princes de Liege; premierement à monsieur Robert de Berghe, conte de VValhain, Euesque de Liege; secondement à monsieur Gerard de Groisbeek, cardinal et euesque de Liege; tiercement à noble et puissant prince Ernest, duc de Bauiere, archeuesque de Cologne, electeur, et evesque de Liege, etc.* Liège, 1604.

Castelot, André. *L'Histoire à table: "Si la cuisine m'était contée . . . "* Paris, n.d.

Catalogue des livres manuscrits et imprimées . . . de la bibliothèque de M. le duc de Chaulnes. Paris, 1770.

Cellini, Benvenuto. *The Autobiography of Benvenuto Cellini.* Translated by George Bull. Harmondsworth: Penguin, 1956.

Cervio, Vicenzo. *Il Trinciante di M. Vicenzo Cervio, ampliato, et ridotto a perfettione dal cavallier reale Fusoritto da Narni trinciante dell'illust.^mo et reuer.^mo signor cardinal Farnese.* Venice, 1581.

Champion, Pierre. *Catherine de Médicis présente à Charles IX son royaume: 1564–1566.* Paris: Bernard Grasset, 1937.

Cheke, Marcus. *Cardinal de Bernis.* London: Cassel, 1958.

Chesne, Joseph du, sieur de la Violette. *Le Povrtraict de la santé, où est au vif représentée la Reigle vniuerselle et particulière de bien sainement et longuement viure*. Paris, 1605.

Chomel, Noël. *Dictionnaire œconomique contenant l'art de faire valoire les terres*. 2 vols. Paris, 1709.

Christine de Pisan. *Le Livre des fais et bonnes meurs du sage roi Charles V*. Edited by S. Solente. 2 vols. Paris, 1936–41.

Clark, Priscilla P. "Thoughts for Food, I: French Cuisine and French Culture." *French Review* 49 (1975):32–41.

———. "Thoughts for Food II: Culinary Culture in Contemporary France." *French Review* 49 (1975):198–205.

Clermont, B. *The Professed Cook: or the Modern Art of Cookery, Pastry, and Confectionary made Plain and Easy*. 2d ed. London, 1769.

Cotgrave, Randle. *A Dictionarie of the French and English Tongues*. London, 1611. Reprint. Introduction by William S. Woods. Columbia, S.C.: University of South Carolina Press, 1968.

Couperie, Pierre. "Les Marchés de pourvoierie: Viandes et poissons chez les grands au XVIIᵉ siècle." In *Pour une histoire de l'alimentation*, edited by Jean-Jacques Hémardinquer, pp. 241–53. Cahiers des Annales 28. Paris: Armand Colin, 1970.

———. "Régimes alimentaires dans la France du XVIIᵉ siècle." *Annales: Economies, Sociétés, Civilisations* 18 (1963):1133–41.

Courtin, Antoine de. *Nouveau traité de la civilité qui se pratique en France parmi les honnestes gens*. Paris, 1695. Extracts reprinted in Alfred Franklin, *La Vie privée d'autrefois: Les Repas*, pp. 225–42. Paris, 1889.

Courtine, Robert J., and Vence, Céline. *Les Grands maîtres de la cuisine française du Moyen Age à Alexandre Dumas, les meilleures recettes de cinq siècles de tradition gastronomique recueillies et adaptées par Céline Vence et Robert Courtine*. Paris: Bordas, 1972. Translated and adapted by Philip Hyman and Mary Hyman. *The Grand Masters of French Cuisine: Five Centuries of Great Cooking*. New York: G. P. Putnam's Sons, 1978.

Crespin, le sieur. *L'Œconomie ou le vray advis povr se faire bien servir*. Paris, 1641.

Cuisine et office de santé, propre à ceux qui vivent avec œconomie et régime. Paris, 1758.

Le Cuisinier gascon. Amsterdam, 1740.

Le Cvisinier méthodiqve, où est enseigné la manière d'apprester toute sorte de viandes, poissons, legumes, salades et autres curiositez, vtile à toute sorte de personnes. Paris, 1691. Reprint: *Le Cuisinier françois, ov l'ecole des ragouts. Ou est enseigné la maniere d'apprêter toute sorte de viandes, de faire toute sorte de pâtisseries, et de confitures*. 12th ed. Lyons, 1695.

Cussy, marquis de. "L'art culinaire." In *Les Classiques de la table, à l'usage des praticiens et des gens du monde*, edited by Alfred Charles Frédéric Fayot, pp. 249–83. Paris, 1843.

Danjou, Félix, and Cimber, L., eds. *Archives curieuses de l'histoire de France*. 27 vols. Paris, 1834–40.

David, Elizabeth. "Death in the Glass." *Petits Propos Culinaires* 4 (1980):73–74.

———. *English Bread and Yeast Cookery*. Introduction and notes for the American cook by Karen Hess. New York: Viking Press, 1980.

———. "Fromages Glacés and Iced Creams." *Petits Propos Culinaires* 2 (1979):23–35.

———. "The Harvest of Cold Months." *Petits Propos Culinaires* 3 (1979):9–16.

———. "Hunt the Ice Cream." *Petits Propos Culinaires* 1 (1979):8–13.

———. "A Midsummer Night's Dream." *Petits Propos Culinaires* 5 (1980):59–62.

———. "Savor of Ice and of Roses." *Petits Propos Culinaires* 8 (1981):7–18.

Davis, Natalie Zemon. *Society and Culture in Early Modern France*. Stanford: Stanford University Press, 1975.

Deerr, Noel. *The History of Sugar*. 2 vols. London: Chapman and Hall, 1949.

Defourneaux, Marcelin. *La Vie quotidienne au temps de Jeanne d'Arc*. Paris: Hachette, 1952.

Delamare. *Traité de la police, ou l'on trouvera l'histoire de son etablissement, les fonctions et les prerogatives de ses magistrats; toutes les lois et tous les reglements qui la concernent*. 2d ed. 4 vols. Paris, 1722.

Desnoiresterres, Gustave. *Grimod de La Reynière et son groupe, d'après de documents entièrements inédits*. Paris, 1877.

Dictionnaire de l'Académie des Gastronomes. 2 vols. Paris: Editions Prisma, 1962.

Le Dictionnaire portatif de cuisine, d'office et de distillation, contenant la manière de préparer toutes sortes de viandes, de volailles, de gibier, de poissons, de légumes, de fruits, etc., la façon de faire toutes sortes de gellées, de pâtes, de pastilles, de gâteaux, de tourtes, de pâtés, vermichel, macaronis, etc., et de composer toutes sortes de liqueurs, de ratafias, de syrops, de glaces, d'essences, etc. Ouvrage également utile au chefs d'office et de cuisine les plus habiles, et aux cuisinieres qui ne sont employées que pour des tables bourgeoises. On y a joint des observations médicinales qui font connoître la propriété de chaque aliment, relativement à la santé, et qui indiquent les mets les plus convenables à chaque tempérament. Paris, 1767.

Dorveaux, P. "'Brides à veaux': Notes pour le commentaire." *Revue des Etudes Rabelaisiennes* 10 (1912):421–25.

Douët d'Arcq, Louis. *Comptes de l'argenterie des rois de France au XIVe siècle, publiés pour la Société de l'histoire de France d'après des manuscrits originaux*. Paris, 1851.

———. *Comptes de l'hôtel des rois de France au XIVe et XVe siècles*. Paris, 1865.

———. *Nouveau recueil de comptes de l'argenterie des rois de France publiées pour la Société de l'histoire de France*. Paris, 1874.

———. "Traité de cuisine écrit vers 1306." *Bibliothèque de l'Ecole des Chartes*, 5th ser., 1 (1860):216–44.

Douglas, Mary. "Culture: Structure of Gastronomy." In *Russell Sage Foundation: The Future and the Past: Essays on Programs and the Annual Report, 1976–1977*, pp. 55–81. N.p., n.d.

————. "Deciphering a Meal." *Daedalus: Journal of the American Academy of Arts and Sciences*, Winter 1972, pp. 61–81.

Drummond, Jack C., and Wilbraham, Anne. *The Englishman's Food: A History of Five Centuries of English Diet*. 2d ed. Revised by Dorothy Hollingsworth. London: Jonathan Cape, 1957.

Dufour, Philippe Sylvestre. *Traitez nouveaux et curieux du café, du thé, et du chocolat* . . . Lyons, 1685.

Dumas, Alexandre. *Grand dictionnaire de cuisine*. Paris, 1873.

Edélstand du Méril, M. *Floire et Blanceflor, poèmes du XIIIᵉ siècle publiés d'aprés les manuscrits*. Paris, 1856.

Eisenstein, Elizabeth L. *The Printing Press as an Agent of Change: Communications and Cultural Transformations in Early-Modern Europe*. 2 vols. Cambridge: Cambridge University Press, 1979.

Eluard-Valette, Cécile. *Les Grandes heures de la cuisine française*. Paris: Les Libraires Associés, 1964.

Encyclopédie française 14: La civilisation quotidienne, sect. E., "se mieux nourrir." Paris: Larousse, for the Société Nouvelle de l'Encyclopédie Française, n.d.

Encyclopédie, ou dictionnaire raisonné des sciences, des arts et des métiers, par une société de gens de lettres. Mis en ordre et publié par m. Diderot. et quant à la partie mathématique, par m. d'Alembert. 17 vols. Paris and Neufchatel, 1751–77.

————. *Supplément à l'Encyclopédie*. 4 vols. Amsterdam, 1776–77.

————. *Recueil de planches, sur les sciences, les arts libéraux, et les arts méchaniques, avec leur explication*. 11 vols. Paris, 1763–77.

————. *Suite du Recueil de planches*. Paris, 1777.

————. *Table analytique et raisonnée des matieres contenues dans les xxxiii volumes in-folio du Dictionnaire des sciences, des arts et des métiers, et dans son Supplément*. 2 vols. Paris, 1780.

————. Reprint. *Encyclopédie ou Dictionnaire raisonné des sciences, des arts et des métiers (mis en ordre et publié par Diderot, quant à la partie mathématique, par d'Alembert)*. 35 vols. Stuttgart–Bad Cannstatt: Frommann, 1966.

L'Eschole parfaite des officiers de bouche; contenant la vray maistre-d'hostel, le grand escuyer-tranchant, le sommelier royal, le confiturier royal, le cuisinier royal, et le patissier royal. Paris, 1662.

L'Escole parfaite des officiers de bouche, contenant la vray maistre d'hostel, le grand escuyer-tranchant, le sommelier royal, le confiturier royal, le cuisinier royal, et le patissier royal. Paris, 1708.

Estienne, Charles, and Liébault, Jean. *L'Agricvlture et maison rvstiqve*. Paris, 1564. ["Charles Stevens and John Liebavlt"]. *Maison rustique, or, The Covntrey Farme*. Translated by Richard Svrflet. London, 1600.

l'Estoile, Pierre de. *Mémoires-journaux de Pierre de l'Estoile*. Edited by G. Brunet et al. 12 vols. Paris, 1875–96.

Fail, Noël du. *Œuvres facétieuses*. Edited by J. Asséezat. 2 vols. Paris, 1874.

Farb, Peter, and Armelagos, George. *Consuming Passions: The Anthropology of Eating*. Boston: Houghton Mifflin, 1980.

Faré, Michel. *Le Grand siècle de nature morte en France: Le XVIIe siècle*. Fribourg: Office du Livre, 1974.

————. *La Nature morte en France; son histoire et son évolution du XVIIe au XXe siècle*. 2 vols. Geneva: Cailler, 1962.

————, and Faré, Fabrice. *La Vie silencieuse en France: La Nature morte au XVIIIe siècle*. Fribourg: Office du Livre, 1976.

Farge, Arlette. *Délinquance et criminalité: Le Vol d'aliments à Paris au XVIIIe siècle*. Civilisations et mentalités. Paris: Librarie Plon, 1974.

Fayot, Alfred Charles Frédéric, ed. *Les Classiques de la table, à l'usage des praticiens et des gens du monde. Beau volume de 550 pages, avec les portraits, gravés au burin, par nos premiers artistes, de M. le prince de Talleyrand, M. Grimod de la Reynière, Berchoux, marquis de Cussy, Colnet, feu le docteur Marcel Gaubert, Carême, Appert, etc.* Paris, 1843.

Febvre, Lucien. "Aux origines de l'alimentation: La Part du folklore." *Annales: Economies, Sociétés, Civilisations* 3 (1941):19.

————. "Pour la première enquête (1936), la parole est à Lucien Febvre." *Annales: Economies, Sociétés, Civilisations* 16 (1961):749–56.

————, and Martin, H.-J. *L'Apparition du livre*. Paris: Michel, 1958.

Félibien, André. *Les Divertissemens de Versailles donnez par le roy a toute sa cour au retour de la conqueste de la Franche Comté en l'année M. DC. LXXIV.* Paris, 1676.

————. *Les Plaisirs de l'Isle enchantée; covrse de bagve, collation ornée de machines; comédie meslée de danse et de musique, ballet du palais d'Alcine, feu d'artifice: et autres festes galantes et magnifiques; faites par le roy à Versailles, le 7 may 1664, et continuées plusieurs autres iours.* Paris, 1664.

————. *Relation de la feste de Versailles de 18 juillet mil six cens soixant-huit.* Paris, 1679.

Feret, Barbara L. *Gastronomical and Culinary Literature: A Survey and Analysis of Historically-Oriented Collections in the U.S.A.* Methuen, N.J.: Scarecrow Press, 1979.

Ferguson, Wallace K. *The Renaissance in Historical Thought: Five Centuries of Interpretation*. Boston: Houghton Mifflin, 1948.

Filho, Antonio Gomes. *Um Tratado da cozinha portuguesa do seculo XV*. Dicionario de la lingue portuguese, textos e vocabularios, 2. N.p.: Instituto Nacional do Livro, Ministerios da Educacao e Cultura, 1963.

Fink, Beatrice C. "The Banquet as Phenomenon or Structure in Selected Eighteenth-Century French Novels." *Studies on Voltaire and the Eighteenth Century* 152 (1976): 729–40.

————. "Food as Object, Activity and Symbol in Sade." *Romanic Review* 65 (1974):96–102.

Fisher, Mary Frances Kennedy. *The Art of Eating*. New York: World Publishing, 1954.

Fitzgibbon, Theodora. *The Food of the Western World: An Encyclopedia of Food from North America and Europe*. New York: Quadrangle/New York Times, 1976.

Flandrin, J.-L. [Platine]. "Gastronomie historique: L'Ancienne service à la française." *L'Histoire* 20 (1980): 90–92.

Fleury, Claude. *Les Devoirs des maitres et des domestiques*. Paris. 1688. Reprint. In Alfred Franklin, *La Vie privée d'autrefois: La Vie de Paris sous Louis XIV*, pp. 205–329. Paris, 1898.

Flower, Barbara, and Rosenbaum, Elisabeth, eds. *The Roman Cookery Book, a Critical Translation of "The Art of Cooking" by Apicius*. London: Peter Nevill, 1958.

Forbes, W. A. *Antiek Bestek: Korte Ontwikkelingsgeschiedenis van Mes, Lepel en Vork*. Bussum: C. A. J. Van Dishoeck, 1969.

Forster, Elborg, and Forster, Robert, eds. *European Diet from Pre-Industrial to Modern Times*. New York: Harper Torchbooks, 1975.

Forster, Robert. *The House of Saulx-Tavanes: Versailles and Burgundy, 1700–1830*. Baltimore: Johns Hopkins University Press, 1971.

————, and Ranum, Orest, eds. *Food and Drink in History: Selections from the Annales: Economies, Sociétés, Civilisations, vol. 5*. Translated by Elborg Forster and Patricia M. Ranum. Baltimore: Johns Hopkins University Press, 1979.

Frame, Donald M. *Montaigne: A Biography*. New York: Harcourt, Brace and World, 1965.

Franklin, Alfred. *La Vie privée d'autrefois. Arts et métiers, modes, moeurs, usages de parisiens du XIIe au XVIIIe siècle d'aprés des documents originaux et inédits. La Cuisine*, 1888; *Les Repas*, 1889; *Variétés gastronomiques*, 1891; *Le Café, le thé et le chocolat*, 1893; *La Vie de Paris sous la régence* 1897; *La Vie de Paris sous Louis XIV*, 1898; *L'Annonce et la réclame. Les Cris de Paris*, 1887; *Variétés parisiennes*, 1901.

Frati, Ludovico, ed. *Libro di cucina del secolo XIV*. Livorno, 1899.

Frere, Catherine Frances, ed. *A Proper Newe Booke of Cokerye*. Cambridge: W. Heffer and Sons, 1913.

Friedrich, Carl Joachim. *The Age of the Baroque, 1610–1660*. New York: Harper, 1952.

Furet, François, and Ozouf, Jacques. *Lire et écrire: L'Alphabétisation des français de Calvin à Jules Ferry*. Paris: Les Editions de Minuit, 1977.

Furetière, Antoine. *Dictionnaire universelle, contenant tous les mots françois tant vieux que modernes, et les termes de toutes les sciences et des arts . . .* 3 vols. The Hague, 1690.

Gilliers, Joseph. *Le Cannameliste français ou nouvelle instruction pour ceux qui desirent d'apprendre l'office, rédigé et orné de dictionnaire, contenant les noms, les descriptions, les usages, les choix et les principes de tout ce qui se pratique dans l'office, l'explication de tous les termes dont on se sert; avec la maniere de dessiner et de former toutes sortes de contours de tables et de dormants. Enrichi de planches en taille douce.* Nancy, 1751.

Girard, Alain. "Le Triomphe de la cuisinière bourgeoise. Livres culinaires, cuisine et société en France aux XVIIᵉ et XVIIIᵉ siècles." *Revue d'Histoire Moderne et Contemporaine* 24 (1977):497–523.

Gobert, Théodore. "Banquets officiels aux XVIᵉ et XVIIᵉ siècles à Liège." *Bulletin de l'Institut Archéologique Liègeois* 37 (1907):337–60.

Gottschalk, Alfred. *Histoire de l'alimentation et de la gastronomie.* 2 vols. Paris: Hippocrate, 1948.

Goubert, Pierre. *L'Ancien régime.* Vol. 1: *La Société.* 2d ed. Paris: Armand Colin, 1969.

Gouberville, Gilles de. *Le Journal du sire de Gouberville publié sur la copie du manuscrit original faite par M. l'abbé Tollemer.* Edited by Eugène de Robillard de Beaurepaire. Mémoires de la Société des Antiquaires de Normandie, ser. 4, vol. 1. Caen, 1892. Reprint, with an introduction by Emmanuel Le Roy Ladurie. *Un sire de Gouberville, gentilhomme au Cotentin de 1553 à 1562 . . .* Maison des Sciences de l'Homme 10. Paris: Mouton, n.d.

―――. *Journal pour les années 1549, 1550, 1551, publié d'après le manuscrit original découvert dans le chartier de Saint-Pierre l'Eglise.* Société des Antiquaires de Normandie, ser. 4, vol. 2. Caen, 1895.

Gourville, Jean Hérault de. *Mémoires.* Edited by Léon Lecestre. 2 vols. Paris, 1894–95.

Grewe, Rudolf, ed. *Libre de sent sovi (receptari de cuina).* Els nostres clàssics: Obres completes dels escriptors catalans medievals, coll. A, vol 115. Barcelona: Editorial Barcino, 1979.

Grouchy, victomte de. "Comtes de maison du cardinal de Richelieu, des ducs de Nemours et de Candalle, du cardinal Mazarin, du roi Louis XIV, de mesdemoiselles d'Orléans, de la duchesse de Bourgogne et de la reine Marie Leczinska." *Bulletin de la Société de l'Histoire de Paris et de l'Ile-de-France* 19 (1902):38–60.

Guégan, Bertrand. *Le Cuisinier français.* Paris: Emile Paule frères, 1934.

―――. *La Fleur de la cuisine française.* 2 vols. Paris: Editions de la Sirène, 1920–21.

Guérin, Paul, ed. *Registres des déliberations du bureau de la ville de Paris.* Vol. 6. Paris, 1892.

Guerrini, Olindo. *Frammento di un libro di cucina del sec. XIV, edito nel di delle nozzi Carducci-Gnaccarini.* Bologna, 1887.

Gulick, Charles Burton, trans. and ed. *Athenaeus: The Diepnosophists.* Loeb Classical Library. 7 vols. Cambridge, Mass.: Harvard University Press, 1927–44.

Guy, Christian. *An Illustrated History of French Cuisine from Charlemagne to Charles de Gaulle.* Translated by Elisabeth Abbott. New York: Orion Press, 1962.

Hajek, Hans. *Daz bůch von gůter spize aus der Würzburg-Münchener Handschrift.* Text des späten Mittelalters, 8. Berlin: Erich Schmidt, 1958.

Halken, Léon-E. "Lancelot de Casteau." *La Vie Wallonne* 44 (1970):409–17.

Harrison, William. *The Description of England*. Edited by Georges Edelen. Folger Documents of Tudor and Stuart Civilization. Ithaca: Cornell University Press for the Folger Shakespeare Library, 1968.

Hazard, Paul. *The European Mind, 1680–1715*. Translated by J. Lewis May. New York, 1963.

———. *European Thought in the Eighteenth Century*. Translated by J. Lewis May. New Haven: Yale University Press, 1954.

Hecht, J. Jean. *Continental and Colonial Servants in Eighteenth Century England*. Smith College Studies in History, vol. 40. Northampton, Mass.: Department of History, Smith College, 1954.

Heiser, Charles B. *Seed to Civilization: The Story of Man's Food*. San Francisco: W. H. Freeman, 1973.

Hélias, Per Jakez. *The Horse of Pride*. New Haven: Yale University Press, 1979.

Hémardinquer, Jean-Jacques. "Essai de cartes des graisses de cuisine en France." *Annales: Economies, Sociétés, Civilisations* 16 (1961):747–49.

———. "Faut-il 'demythifier' le porc familial d'Ancien Régime?" *Annales: Economies, Sociétés, Civilisations* 25 (1970):1745–66. Translated by Patricia M. Ranum as "The Family Pig of the Ancien Régime," in *Food and Drink in History: Selections from the Annales, vol. 5*, edited by Robert Forster and Orest Ranum, pp. 50–72. Baltimore: Johns Hopkins University Press, 1979.

———. "Les Graisses de cuisine en France: Essais de cartes." *Annales: Economies, Sociétés, Civilisations* 16 (1961):749–71.

———, ed. *Pour une histoire de l'alimentation*. Cahiers des Annales 28. Paris: Armand Colin, 1970.

Henisch, Bridget Ann. *Fast and Feast: Food in Medieval Society*. University Park, Pa.: Pennsylvania State University Press, 1976.

Héritier, Jean. *Cathèrine de Medici*. Paris: Fayard, 1940.

Héron de Villefosse, René. *Histoire et géographie gourmandes de Paris*. Paris: Les Editions de Paris, 1956.

Hess, John L., and Hess, Karen. *The Taste of America*. New York: Grossman, 1977.

Heures a lusaige de Romme. Paris, 1497.

Hillairet, Jacques. *Connaissance de vieux Paris: Rive gauche et les îles*. Paris: Gonthier, 1954.

Hoefer, Ferdinand, ed. *Nouvelle biographie générale depuis les temps les plus reculés jusqu'à nos jours*. Paris, 1859–70.

Huizinga, Johann. *The Waning of the Middle Ages*. New York: Anchor Books, 1954.

Hyman, Philip, and Hyman, Mary. "La Chapelle and Massialot: An 18th Century Feud." *Petits Propos Culinaires* 2 (1979):44–54.

———. "Long Pepper: A Short History." *Petits Propos Culinaires* 6 (1980):50–52.

———. "Vincent La Chapelle." *Petits Propos Culinaires* 8 (1981):35–40.

Jacob, Heinrich Eduard. *The Saga of Coffee: The Biography of an Economic Product.*

Translated by Eden Paul and Cedar Paul. London: George Allen and Unwin, n.d.

————. *Six Thousand Years of Bread*. Garden City: Doubleday, 1944.

Jal, Auguste. *Dictionnaire critique de biographie*. 2d ed. 2 vols. Paris, 1872.

Kalendrier et compost des bergers. Paris, 1490.

Kaplan, Lawrence. "New World Beans." *Horticulture*, October 1980, pp. 43–44, 46, 48–49.

Kisch, Bruno. *Scales and Weights: A Historical Outline*. New Haven: Yale University Press, 1965.

Laborde, Léon de. *Les Ducs de Bourgogne*. 2 vols. Paris, 1851.

Labrousse, Ernest; Léon, Pierre; Goubert, Pierre; et al. *Histoire économique et sociale de la France*. Vol. 2: *Des derniers temps de l'âge seigneurial aux préludes de l'âge industriel (1660–1789)*. Paris: Presses Universitaires de France, 1970.

La Chapelle, Vincent. *Le Cuisinier moderne qui apprend à donner à manger toutes sortes de repas, en gras et en maigre, d'une maniere plus délicate que ce qui en a été écrit jusqu'à présent*. 4 vols. The Hague, 1735. 2d ed., 5 vols. 1742.

————. *The Modern Cook*. 2 vols. London, 1733.

La Fontaine, Jean de. *Œuvres diverses*. Edited by Pierre Clarac. Bibliothèque de la Pléiade 62. 7 vols. Paris: Gallimard, 1942.

La Marche, Olivier de. *Mémoires d'Olivier de La Marche, maître d'hôtel et capitaine des gardes de Charles de Témeraire*. Edited by Henri Beaune and J. d'Arbaumont. 4 vols. Paris, 1885.

La Varenne, François Pierre de. *Le Cvisinier francois enseignant la maniere de bien apprester et assaisonner toutes sortes de viandes grasses et maigres, legumes, patisseries, et autres mets qui se servent tant sur les tables des grands que des particuliers*. Paris, 1651, 1654.

————. *Le Parfaict confitvrier qvi enseigne a bien faire toutes sortes de confitures tant seiches que liquides de compostes, de fruicts, de sallades, de dragées, breuvages délicieux et autres délicatesses de bouche*. Paris, 1667.

————. *Le Vray cuisinier françoys enseignant la maniere de bien apprester et assaisonner toutes sortes de viandes, grasses et maigres, légumes et pâtisseries en perfection, etc. Augmenté d'un nouveau confiturier, qui apprend à bien faire toutes sortes de confitures, tant sêches que liquides, des compotes de fruits, des dragées, bruvages delicieux, et autres delicatesses de bouche . . .* The Hague, 1721.

Lebault, Armand. *La Table et le repas à travers les siècles, histoire de l'alimentation, du mobilier à l'usage des repas, du cérémonial et des divertissements de table chez les peuples anciens et les français précédée d'une étude sur les moeurs gastronomiques primitives et sur le rôle du repas dans la civilisation*. Paris: Lucien Laveur, 1910.

Leclant, Jean. "Le Café et les cafés à Paris (1644–1693)." *Annales: Economies, Sociétés, Civilisations* 6 (1951):1–14. Translated by Patricia M. Ranum as "Coffee and Cafés in Paris, 1644–1693" in *Food and Drink in History: Selections from the Annales: Économies, Sociétés, Civilisations, vol. 5*, edited by Robert Forster and

Orest Ranum, pp. 86–97. Baltimore: Johns Hopkins University Press, 1979.

Lefranc, Abel. *La Vie quotidienne au temps de la Renaissance.* Paris: Hachette, 1938.

Le Grand d'Aussy, Pierre Jean Baptiste. *Histoire de la vie privée des françois depuis l'origine de la nation jusqu'a nos jours . . .* 3 vols. Paris, 1782. 2d ed., rev. and ed. Jean Baptiste Bonaventure de Roquefort. 3 vols. Paris, 1815.

Leighton, Ann. *American Gardens in the Eighteenth Century "For Use or For Delight."* Boston: Houghton Mifflin, 1976.

———. *Early American Gardens "For Meate or Medicine."* Boston: Houghton Mifflin, 1970.

Lenôtre, Gaston. *Lenôtre's Ice Creams and Candies.* Edited and translated by Philip Hyman and Mary Hyman. N.p.: Barron's, 1979.

Le Roy Ladurie, Emmanuel. *Les Paysans de Languedoc.* Bibliothèque générale de l'Ecole Pratique des Hautes Etudes. Paris: S.E.V.P.E.N., 1966.

Lespinasse, René de, ed. *Histoire générale de Paris: Les Métiers et corporations de la ville de Paris.* Vol. 1: *XIVᵉ–XVIIIᵉ siècles: Ordonnances générales: Métiers de l'alimentation.* Paris, 1886.

Lettre d'un pâtissier anglois au nouveau cuisinier françois. N.p., n.d. Reprint. In François Marin, *Les Dons de Comus,* pp. 221–56. Paris, 1740.

Lévi-Strauss, Claude. "The Culinary Triangle." *Partisan Review* 33 (1966):586–95.

Levron, Jacques. *La Vie quotidienne à la cour de Versailles au XVIIᵉ et XVIIIᵉ siècles.* Paris: Hachette, 1965.

Lewis, William Hamilton. *The Scandalous Regent: A Life of Philippe, Duc d'Orléans, 1674–1723, and of His Family.* New York: Harcourt, Brace and World, 1961.

———. *The Splendid Century: Life in the France of Louis XIV.* Garden City, N.Y.: Doubleday Anchor Books, 1957.

Lewis, W. S., et al., eds. *The Yale Edition of Horace Walpole's Correspondence.* 39 vols. New Haven: Yale University Press, 1937–74.

Lichtenberger, F., ed. *Encyclopédie des sciences réligieuses.* Paris, 1877.

Liger, Louis. *Œconomie générale de la campagne, ov nouvelle maison rustique.* 2 vols. Paris, 1700.

Lincoln, D. A. *Mrs. Lincoln's Boston Cook Book.* Boston, 1891.

Lippmann, Edmund O. von. *Geschichte des Zuckers seit den ältesten Zeiten bis zum Beginn der Rübenzucker-Fabrikation.* Berlin: Julius Springer, 1929.

Lister, Martin. *Voyage de Lister à Paris en MDCXCVIII.* Translated by the Société des Bibliophiles français. Paris, 1873.

Littré, Emile. *Dictionnaire de la langue française.* 54 vols. Paris, 1881–83.

Liure fort excellent de cuysine tresutile et proffitable contenant en soy la maniere dhabiller toutes viandes . . . Lyons, 1555.

Lozinski, Grégoire, ed. *La Bataille de caresme et de charnage.* Bibliothèque de l'Ecole des Hautes Etudes, fasc. 262. Paris: Libraire ancienne Honoré Champion, 1933.

Lune, Pierre de. *Le Cvisinier ov il est traitté de la véritable méthode pour apprester toutes sortes de viandes, gibbier, volatiles poissons tant de mer que d'eau douce. Suiuant les* *quatre saisons de l'année. Ensemble la manière de faire toutes sortes de patisseries,* *tant froides que chaudes, en perfection.* Paris, 1656.

―――. *Le Novveav et parfait maistre d'hostel royal, enseignant la maniere de couurir les* *tables dans les ordinaires et festins . . .* Paris, 1662.

Luynes, duc de. *Mémoires du duc de Luynes sur la cour de Louis XV (1735–1758).* Edited by L. Dussieux and E. Soulié. 17 vols. Paris, 1860–61.

Machabey, Armand. *La Métrologie dans les musées de province et sa contribution à l'histoire des poids et mesures en France depuis le treizième siècle.* Les Conférences du Palais de la Découverte, Ser. D: Histoire. Paris: Edition de la Revue de métrologie pratique et légale, 1962.

Magne, Emile. *La Vie quotidienne sous Louis XIII.* Paris: Hachette, 1942.

Maintenon, Françoise d'Aubigné, marquise de. *Correspondance de Madame de Maintenon.* Edited by M. Langlois. 5 vols. Paris, 1933–39.

Malouin, Paul Jacques. *Description des arts et métiers faites ou approuvés par messieurs de l'Académie Royale des Sciences. Avec figures en taille douce. Description et détails des arts du meunier, du vermicelier et du boulenger; avec une histoire abrégé de la boulengerie et un dictionnaire de ces arts.* Paris, 1767.

La Maltôte des cuisinières, ou la manière de bien ferrer la mule. Dialogue entre une vieille cuisinière et une jeune servante. Paris, n.d. Reprint. In Alfred Franklin, *La Vie privée d'autrefois: La Vie à Paris sous Louis XIV,* pp. 344–56. Paris, 1898.

Mander, Carel van. *Dutch and Flemish Painters: Translation from the Schilderboeck.* Translated and edited by Constant Van de Wall. New York: McFarlane, Warde, McFarlane, 1936.

Mandrou, Robert. *Classes et luttes de classes en France au début du XVII* *siècle.* Messina: d'Anna, 1965.

Le Manuel des officiers de bouche, ou le precis de tous les apprêts que l'on peut faire des alimens pour servir toutes les tables, depuis celles des grands seigneurs jusqu'à celles des bourgeois, suivant l'ordre des saisons et des services: Ouvrage très-utile aux maîtres pour ordonner des repas, et aux artistes pour les exécuter. Paris, 1759.

Marin, François. *Les Dons de Comus ou les délices de la table. Ouvrage non seulement utile aux officiers de bouche pour ce qui concerne leur art, mais principalement à l'usage des personnes qui sont curieuses de sçavoir donner à manger, et d'être servies délicatement, tant en gras qu'en maigre, suivant les saisons et dans le goût le plus nouveau.* Paris, 1739.

―――. *Les Dons de Comus, ov les délices de la table. Ouvrage non-seulement utile aux officiers de bouche pour ce qui concerne art, mais principalement à l'usage des personnes qui sont curieuses de sçavoir donner à manger, et d'être servies délicatement, tant en gras qu'en maigre, suivant les saisons, et dans le gout le plus nouveau.* Paris, 1740.

―――. *Suite des dons de Comus ou l'art de la cuisine réduit en pratique.* 3 vols. Paris, 1742.

————. *Les Dons de Comus ou l'art de la cuisine réduit en pratique.* Rev. ed. 3 vols. Paris, 1750.

————. *Les Dons de Comus, ou l'art de la cuisine, réduit en pratique, nouvelle edition.* 3 vols. Paris, 1758.

Massialot, François. *Le Cuisinier roïal et bourgeois: Qui apprend a ordonner toutes sorte de repas en gras et en maigre, et la meilleure maniere des ragoûts les plus delicats et les plus à la mode. Ouvrage tres-utile dans les familles, et singulierement necessaire à tous maîtres d'hôtels, et ecuïeres de cuisine.* Paris, 1691.

————. *Le Cuisinier roïal et bourgeois qui apprend a ordonner toute sorte de repas en gras et en maigre, et la meilleure maniere des ragoûts les plus delicats et les plus à la mode.* Rev. ed. Paris, 1705.

————. *Le Nouveau cuisinier royal et bourgeois; qui apprend à ordonner toute sorte de repas en gras et en maigre, et la meilleure maniere des ragoûts les plus delicats et les plus à la mode; et toutes sortes de pâtisseries: avec des nouveaux desseins de tables.* 2 vols. Paris, 1712, 1734.

————. *Le Nouveau cuisinier royal et bourgeois; qui apprend à ordonner toute sorte de repas en gras et en maigre, et la meilleure maniere des ragoûts les plus delicats et les plus à la mode; et toutes sortes de pâtisserie: Avec des nouveaux desseins de tables . . . Augmenté de nouveaux ragoûts par le sieur Vincent de la Chapelle.* 3 vols. Paris, 1748–50.

————. *Nouvelle instruction pour les confitures; les liqueurs, et les fruits. Avec la maniere de bien ordonner un dessert, et tout le reste qui est du devoir des maîtres d'hôtels, sommeliers, confiseurs, et autres officiers de bouche. Suite du Cuisinier roïal et bourgeois.* Paris, 1692.

————. *Nouvelle instruction pour les confitures, les liqueurs, et les fruits: où l'on apprend à confire toute sortes de fruits, tants secs que liquides; et divers ouvrages de sucre qui sont du fait des officiers et confiseurs, avec la maniere de bien ordoner un fruit. Suite du nouveau cuisinier royal et bourgeois.* Rev. ed. Paris, 1717.

Menon. *La Cuisinière bourgeoise.* Paris, 1746. Rev. ed. Paris, 1756. 2 vols. Brussels, 1790.

————. *Nouveau traité de la cuisine. Avec de nouveaux desseins de tables et vingt-quatre menus; où l'on apprend ce que l'on doit servir suivant chaque saison, en gras, en maigre, et en pâtisserie; et très-utiles à toutes les personnes qui s'en mêlent, tant pour ordonner, que pour exécuter toutes sortes de nouveaux ragoûts, et des plus à la mode.* 2 vols. Paris, 1739.

————. *La Nouvelle cuisine avec de nouveaux menus pour chaque saison de l'année, qui explique la façon de travailler toutes sortes de mets, qui se servent aujourd'hui, en gras et en maigre; très utile aux personnes qui veulent diversifier une table par des ragoûts nouveaux. Pour servir de continuation au nouveau traité de la cuisine.* Paris, 1742.

————. *La Science du maître d'hôtel, confiseur. A l'usage des officiers, avec des observations sur la connoissance et les propriétés des fruits. Enrichie de desseins en décora-*

tions et parterres pour les desserts. Suite du maître d'hôtel cuisinier. Paris, 1750.

—————. *La Science du maître d'hôtel cuisinier avec des observations sur la connoissance et propriétés des alimens.* Paris, 1749.

Mercier, Louis Sébastien. *Le Tableau de Paris.* Rev. ed. 12 vols. Paris, 1783–89.

Le Mercure de France. 1725–29.

Le Mercure Galant. 1672–1705.

Michaud, Joseph. *Biographie universelle ancienne et moderne.* Rev. ed. Paris, n.d.

Michelangelo. *The Letters of Michelangelo.* Translated and edited by E. H. Ramsden. 2 vols. London: Peter Owen, 1963.

Michelant, Henri Victor, ed. *"Le Livre des mestiers." Dialogues français-flamands composés au XIVe siècle par un maître d'école de la ville de Bruges.* Paris, 1875.

Mitford, Nancy. *Madame de Pompadour.* New York: Harper and Row, 1968.

Molière, Jean-Baptiste Poquelin. *Œuvres complètes.* Edited by Maurice Rat. Vol. 1. Bibliothèque de la Pléiade. Paris, 1956.

Mollat, Guillaume. *Les Papes d'Avignon (1306–1378).* 10th ed. Paris: Letouzey et Ané, n.d.

Montagné, Prosper, and Gottschalk, Alfred. eds. *Larousse gastronomique.* Paris: Larousse, 1938.

Montaiglon, Anatole de, ed. *Recueil des poésies françoises des XVe et XVIe siècles, morales facétieuses, historiques, réunies et et annotées.* 13 vols. Paris, 1855–73.

Montaigne, Michel de. *The Complete Works of Montaigne: Essays: Travel Journal: Letters.* Translated by Donald M. Frame. Stanford: Stanford University Press, 1957.

Morin, Alfred. *Catalogue descriptif de la Bibliothèque bleue de Troyes (almanachs exclus).* Histoire et civilisation du livre 7. Geneva: Droz, 1974.

Moura, Jean, and Louvet, Paul. *La Vie de Vatel.* Vies des hommes illustres 34. Paris: Gallimard, 1929.

Mortimer, Ruth, comp. *Harvard College Library, Department of Printing and Graphic Arts: Catalogue of Books and Manuscripts, Part I: French 16th Century Books.* 2 vols. Cambridge, Mass.: Harvard University Press, The Belknap Press, 1964.

Mousnier, Roland. *La Plume, la faucille et le marteau: Institutions et sociétés en France du Moyen Age à la Revolution.* Collection Hier. Paris: Presses Universitaires de France, 1965.

—————, Labatut, J.-P., and Durand, Y. *Problèmes de stratification sociale: Deux cahiers de la noblesse.* Publications de la Faculté des Lettres et Sciences Humaines de Paris, Série "Textes et documents," vol. 9. Paris: Presses Universitaires de France, 1965.

Mueller, Wolf. *Bibliographie des Kaffee, des Kakao der Schokolade des Tee und deren Surrogate bis zum Jahre 1900.* Bibliotheca Bibliographica 20. Vienna: Walter Krieg, 1960.

Mulon, Marianne. "Les Premières recettes médiévales." In Jean-Jacques Hémardinquer, ed., *Pour une histoire de l'alimentation*, pp. 236–40. Paris: Armand Colin, 1970.

Muret. *Traité des festins*. Paris, 1682.

Nairn, Ian, and Pevsner, Nikolaus. *Surrey*. The Buildings of England, 21. Harmondsworth: Penguin, 1962.

Napier, Robina, ed. *A Noble Boke off Cookry*. London, 1892.

Nemeitz, Joachim-Christoph. *Séjour de Paris, c'est à dire, instructions fidéles pour les voiageurs de condition . . . à Paris*. 2 vols. Leiden, 1727. Reprint. In Alfred Franklin, *La Vie privée d'autrefois: La Vie de Paris sous la régence*. Paris, 1897.

New Catholic Encyclopedia. New York: McGraw-Hill, 1967.

Nicolardot, Louis. *Histoire de la table: Curiosités gastronomiques de tous les temps et de tous les pays*. Paris, 1868.

Nola, Ruperto de. *Libro de Guisados*. Edited by Dionisio Pérez. Los Clásicos olvidados 9. Madrid: Nueva Biblioteca de Autores Espagñoles, 1929.

Nostradamus, Michel de. *Excellent et moult utile opuscule à touts necessaire, qui desirent auoir cognoissance de plusieurs exquises receptes, diuisé en deux parties . . .* Lyons, 1555. Reprint, in part, in *La Façon et maniere de faire toutes confitures liquides, tant en succre, miel, qu'en vin cuit*. Preface by T. Coppel and Angèle Hahn. Paris: Fernand Hazan, 1962.

Oliver, Raymond. *Gastronomy of France*. Translated by Claude Durrell. N.p.: The Wine and Food Society, World Publishing, 1967.

Oman, Charles. *Medieval Silver Nefs*. Victoria and Albert Museum Monograph no. 15. London: Her Majesty's Stationery Office, 1963.

Orléans, Elisabeth Charlotte. *Correspondance complète de Madame, duchesse d'Orléans, née princesse Palatine, mère du régent*. Translated and edited by M. G. Brunet. 2 vols. Paris, n.d.

Oxford, Arnold Whitaker. *English Cookery Books to 1850*. London: Oxford University Press, 1913. Reprint. London: Holland Press, 1977.

Patin, Gui. *Traité de la conservation de santé par vn bon régime et legitime vsage des choses requises pour bien et sainement viure*. 2d ed. Paris, 1632.

Le Pâtissier françois. Où est enseigné la manière de faire toute sorte de pastisserie, tres-utile à toute sorte de personnes. Ensemble le moyen d'aprester toutes sortes d'oeufs pour les jours maigres et autres, en plus de soixantes façons. Paris, 1653, 1664. Reprint in *Le Cuisinier françois ov l'ecole des ragouts. Ou est enseigné la maniere d'apprêter toute sorte de viandes, de faire toutes sorte de pâtisseries, et de confitures*, pp. 167–372. 12th ed. Lyons, 1695.

Pepys, Samuel. *The Diary of Samuel Pepys*. Transcribed and edited by Robert Latham, William Matthews, et al. 8 vols. Berkeley and Los Angeles: University of California Press, 1970–74.

Pichon, Jérôme, ed. *Le Ménagier de Paris, traité de morale et d'économie domestique composé vers 1393, par un bourgeois parisien*. 2 vols. Paris, 1846. Reprint. Geneva: Slatkine Reprints, n.d.

————, and Vicaire, Georges, eds. *Le Viandier de Guillaume Tirel, dit Taillevent.* Paris, 1892. Reprint. Luzarches, France: Daniel Morcrette, n.d.

Piedmont, Alexis of. [Sometimes identified as Girolamo Ruscelli.] *Les Secrets dv seigneur Alexis piemontois.* Paris, 1561.

Platina, Bartolomeo. *Platine en françoys tresutile et necessaire pour le corps humain qui traicte de hôneste volupte . . .* Translated by Didier Christol. Lyons, 1505.

Platter, Felix. *Beloved Son Felix: The Journal of Felix Platter, a Medical Student in Montpellier in the Sixteenth Century.* Translated by Séan Jennett. London: Frederick Muller, n.d.

————. *Felix Platter: Tagebuchblätter aus dem Jugendleben eines deutschen Arztes des 16. Jahrhunderts.* Edited by Horst Kohl. Voigtländers Quellenbücher 59. Leipzig: R. Voigtländer, n.d.

Pons, Jacques. *Sommaire traitté des melons contenant la nature et l'usage d'iceux, avec les commodités et incommodités qui en reviennent.* Lyons, 1583. Rev. ed. *Traité des melon ov il est parlé de leur nature, de leur culture, de leurs vertus et de leur usage . . .* Lyons, 1680.

Power, Eileen. *The Goodman of Paris.* New York: Harcourt, Brace, 1928.

————. *Medieval People.* Garden City: Doubleday, 1956.

Prawer, Joshua. *The Crusaders' Kingdom: European Colonialism in the Middle Ages.* New York: Praeger, 1972.

"Quailing before a Quail." *Scientific American* 242 (January 1980):86.

L.S.R. *L'Art de bien traiter, divisé en trois parties. Ouvrage nouveau, curieux et fort galant, utile à toutes personnes et conditions . . .* Paris, 1674.

Rabelais, François. *Gargantua and Pantagruel.* Translated by J. M. Cohen. Harmondsworth: Penguin, 1955.

————. *Œuvres complètes.* Edited by Guy Demerson. Paris: Editions Seuil, 1973.

Robin, Régine. *La Société française en 1789: Semur-en-Auxois.* Civilisations et mentalités. Paris: Plon, 1970.

Robiquet, Jean. *La Vie quotidienne au temps de la Revolution.* Paris: Hachette, 1938.

Roden, Claudia. "Early Arab Cooking and Cookery Manuscripts." *Petits Propos Culinaires* 6 (1980):16–27.

Rodinson, Maxime. *Encyclopedia of Islam,* s.v. "Ghidha."

————. "Recherches sur les documents arabes relatifs à la cuisine." *Revue des Etudes Islamiques,* 1949, pp. 95–165.

Roelker, Nancy Lyman, trans. and ed. *The Paris of Henry of Navarre as Seen by Pierre de l'Estoile: Selections from his Mémoires-Journaux.* Cambridge, Mass.: Harvard University Press, 1958.

————. *Queen of Navarre, Jeanne d'Albret, 1528–1572.* Cambridge, Mass.: Harvard University Press, 1968.

Roethlisberger, Marcel. *Claude Lorraine: The Drawings.* 2 vols. Berkeley and Los Angeles: University of California Press, 1968.

Ronsard, Pierre de. *Œuvres complètes*. Edited by Paul Laumonier. 20 vols. Société des textes français modernes. Paris: Marcel Didier, 1921–75.

Root, Waverley. *The Food of France*. New York: Alfred A. Knopf, 1958.

Rorschach, E. "Documents inédits sur le voyage du roi Charles IX à Toulouse." *Mémoires de l'Académie des Sciences . . . de Toulouse*, 9th ser., vol. 7 (1895):45.

Rosenberg, Pierre. *Chardin, 1699–1779*. N.p.: Indiana University Press for the Cleveland Museum of Art, 1979.

Rosengarten, Frederic, Jr. *The Book of Spices*. Wynnewood, Pa.: Livingston, 1969.

Rousseau, Jean-Jacques. *Œuvres complètes*. Edited by Bernard Gagnebin, Marcel Raymond, et al. Bibliothèque de la Pléiade. Paris: Gallimard, 1959–65.

Rouvroy, Louis de, duc de Saint-Simon. *Mémoires de duc de Saint-Simon*. Edited by Gonzague Truc, Bibliothèque de la Pléiade. 7 vols. Paris: Gallimard, 1947–66.

———. *Mémoires du duc de Saint-Simon*. Edited by Chéruel and Regnier. 20 vols. Paris, Hachette, 1923.

Rozin, Elisabeth. *The Flavor-Principle Cookbook*. New York: Hawthorne Books, 1973.

Rozmital, Leo of. *The Travels of Leo of Rozmital through Germany, Flanders, England, France, Spain, Portugal and Italy, 1465–1467*. Edited and translated by Malcolm Letts. Hakluyt Society, ser. 2, vol. 208. Cambridge: For the Hakluyt Society, 1957.

Rumpolt, Marx. *Ein new Kochbuch*. Frankfurt, 1581.

Russell, Joycelyne G. *The Field of Cloth of Gold: Men and Manners in 1520*. London: Routledge and Kegan Paul, 1969.

Sainéan, Lazare. *L'Histoire naturelle et les branches connexes dans l'oeuvre de Rabelais*. Paris: Edouard Champion, 1921.

Salaman, Redcliffe N. *The History and Social Influence of the Potato*. London: Cambridge University Press, 1949.

Sauer, Carl Ortwin. *Agricultural Origins and Dispersals: The Domestication of Animals and Foodstuffs*. 2d ed. Cambridge, Mass.: MIT Press, n.d.

Scappi, Bartolomeo. *Opera di M. Bartolomeo Scappi, cvoco secreto di papa Pio Qvinto divisa in sei libri . . .* Venice, 1570.

Schafer, G. "Historical Facts Concerning the Production and Use of Soap" and "Development of Soap Boiling." *Ciba Review* 56 (1947):2014–30.

Schapira, Joel, Schapira, David, and Schapira, Karl. *The Book of Coffee and Tea: A Guide to the Appreciation of Fine Coffees, Teas, and Herbal Beverages*. New York: St. Martin's Press, 1975.

Schiedlausky, Günter. *Tee, Kaffee, Schokolade, ihr Eintritt in die europäische Gesellschaft*. Bibliothek des Germanischen National-Museums 17. Munich: Prestel, 1967.

Schmidt, Paul. "As If a Cookbook Had Anything to Do with Writing." *Prose* 8 (1974):179–203.

Schumacher-Voelker, Uta. "German Cookery Books, 1485–1800." *Petits Propos Culinaires* 6 (1980):34–46.

———. "Reprints of Old German Cookery Books." *Petits Propos Culinaires* 7 (1981):47–55.

Sedgwick, Romney. "The Duke of Newcastle's Cook." *History Today* 5 (1955):308–16.

Serres, Olivier de. *Le Theatre d'agricvltvre et mesnage des champs*. Paris, 1600. Rev. ed. *Théâtre d'agriculture et mesnage des champs, d'Olivier de Serres, Seigneur du Pradel; dans lequel est représenté tout ce qui est nécessaire pour bien dresser, gouverner, enrichir et embellir la maison rustique*. Edited by La Société d'Agriculture du départment de la Seine. 2 vols. Paris, 1804–7.

Sévigné, Marie de Rabutin Chantal, marquise de. *Lettres*. Edited by Emile Gérard-Gailly. 3 vols. Bibliothèque de la Pléiade. Paris: Gallimard, 1953.

Simon, André. *André L. Simon's Guide to Good Food and Wines: A Concise Encyclopaedia of Gastronomy Complete and Unabridged*. London: Collins, 1960.

———. *Bibliotheca Gastronomica. A Catalogue of Books and Documents on Gastronomy*. London: The Wine and Food Society, 1953. Reprint. London: Holland Press, 1978.

Smartt, J. "Evolution of American *Phaseolus* Beans under Domestication." In Peter J. Ucko and G. W. Dimbleby, eds., *The Domestication and Exploitation of Plants and Animals: Proceedings of a Meeting of the Research Seminar in Archaeology and Related Subjects Held at the Institute of Archaeology, London University*, pp. 451–63. London: Gerald Duckworth, 1969.

Smith, Georgiana Reynolds. *Table Decoration Yesterday, Today, and Tomorrow*. Rutland, Vt.: Charles E. Tuttle, 1968.

Smith, Page, and Daniel, Charles. *The Chicken Book*. Boston: Little, Brown, 1975.

Smollet, Tobias. *Travels through France and Italy*. London: John Lehmann, 1949.

Les Soupers de la cour, ou l'art de travailler toutes sortes d'alimens, pour servir les meilleurs tables, suivant les quatre saisons. 4 vols. Paris, 1755.

Stallings, W. S., Jr. "Ice Cream and Water Ices in 17th and 18th Century England." *Petits Propos Culinaires* 3 (1979), Supplement.

Stanhope, Philip Dormer, *Characters*, London, 1777.

———. *The Letters of Philip Dormer Stanhope, Fourth Earl of Chesterfield*. Edited by Bonamy Dobrée. 6 vols. London: Eyre and Spottiswoode, 1932.

Strong, Roy. *Splendor at Court: Renaissance Spectacle and the Theater of Power*. Boston: Houghton Mifflin, 1973.

Sulpice, Jean. *La Civilité, imitée en français par Guillaume Durand en 1545*. Reprint. In Alfred Franklin, *La Vie privée d'autrefois: Les Repas*, pp. 180–87. Paris, 1889.

Tardieu, Suzanne. *La Vie domestique dans le Mâconnais rural préindustriel*. Université de Paris, Travaux et Mémoires de l'Institut d'Ethnologie 69. Paris: Institut d'Ethnologie, Musée de l'Homme, 1964.

Thicknesse, Philip. *Observations on the Customs and Manners of the French Nation, in a Series of Letters, in which That Nation is vindicated from the Misrepresentations of some Late Writers.* London, 1766.

Thion, Camille. *La Principauté et le Diocèse de Liège sous Robert de Berghes (1557–1564).* Bibliothèque de la Faculté de Philosophie et Lettres de l'Université de Liège, fasc 31. Liège: H. Vaillant-Carmanne, 1922.

Tommaseo, Niccolò, ed. and trans. *Relations des ambassadeurs vénitiens sur les affaires de France au XVIe siècle.* 2 vols. Paris, 1838.

Traité de confiture ou le nouveau et parfait confiturier. Paris, 1689.

Traité historique et pratique de la cuisine. Ou le cuisinier instruit, de la connoissance des animaux, tant volatiles, que terrestres, aquatiques et amphibie; de la façon, de préparer les divers alimens, et de les servir. Suivi d'un petit abrégé. Sur la maniere de faire les confitures liquides et autres desserts de toute espéce. Ouvrage très-utile, non-seulement pour les maîtres d'hôtel et officiers de cuisine; mais encore pour toutes les communautés religieuses, les grandes familles, et tous ceux qui veulent donner à manger honnêtement. 2 vols. Paris, 1758.

Treichlinger, W. M. *Kleine Kaffee-Visite. Geschichte-Anekdoten-Rezepte.* Zurich: Sanssouci, 1960.

Ucko, Peter J., and Dimbleby, G. W., eds. *The Domestication and Exploitation of Plants and Animals: Proceedings of a Meeting of the Research Seminar in Archaeology and Related Subjects Held at the Institute of Archaeology, London University.* London: Gerald Duckworth, 1969.

Ude, Louis Eustache. *The French Cook: A System of Fashionable and Economical Cookery, Adapted to the Use of English Families.* 10th ed. London, 1829.

Valois, Marguerite de. *Mémoires.* In *Nouvelle collection des mémoires pour servir à l'histoire de France,* edited by Joseph Michaud and Jean Joseph François Poujoulat, vol. 10. Paris, 1838.

Vehse, Eduard. *Geschichte des deutsche Höfe seit der Reformation.* 48 vols. Hamburg, 1851–56.

Venard, Marc. *Bourgeois et paysans au XVIIe siècle; recherche sur le rôle des bourgeois parisiens dans la vie agricole au Sud de Paris au XVIIe siècle.* Paris: S.E.V.P.E.N., 1957.

Vence, Céline, and Courtine, Robert J. *Les Grands maîtres de la cuisine française: Du Moyen Age à Alexandre Dumas, les meilleures recettes de cinq siècles du tradition gastronomique.* Paris: Bordas, 1972. Edited and translated by Philip Hyman and Mary Hyman. *The Grand Masters of French Cuisine: Five Centuries of Great Cooking.* New York: G. P. Putnam's Sons, 1978.

Verdier, Yvonne. "Pour une ethnologie culinaire." *L'Homme: Revue Française d'Anthropologie* 9 (1969):49–57.

Verdot, C. *Historiographie de la table, ou abrégé historique, philosophique, anecdotique et littéraire des substances alimentaires et des objets qui leurs sont relatifs.* Paris, 1833.

Verral, William. *A Complete System of Cookery, in which is set forth a Variety of genuine Receipts, collected from several Years Experience under the celebrated Mr. de St. Clouet*. London, 1759. Reprint with introduction and appendices by R. L. Mégroz and notes by Thomas Gray, as *The Cook's Paradise*. London: Sylvan Press, 1948.

Vicaire, Georges. *Bibliographie gastronomique*. Paris, 1890. Reprint, with an introduction by André L. Simon. London: Derek Verschoyle Academic and Bibliographical Publications, 1954.

Villefosse, René Héron de. *Histoire et géographie gourmandes de Paris*. Paris: Les Editions de Paris, 1956.

Voltaire, François Marie Arouet, called. *Correspondence and Related Documents*. Definitive ed. Edited by Theodore Besterman. 45 vols. Geneva, 1968.

——. *Le Dîner du comte de Bovlainvilliers*. N.p., 1767.

Westbury, Lord. *Handlist of Italian Cookery Books*. Biblioteca de bibliografia italiana 42. Florence: Leo S. Olschki, 1963.

Wheaton, Barbara K. "How to Cook a Peacock." *Harvard Magazine* 82 (1979):63–65.

Wiegelmann, Günter. *Alltags- und Festspeisen: Wandel und gegenwärtige Stellung*. Marburg: Elwert Verlag, 1967.

Wiley, W. L. *The Gentleman of Renaissance France*. Cambridge, Mass.: Harvard University Press, 1954.

Willan, Anne. *Great Cooks and Their Recipes from Taillevent to Escoffier*. New York: McGraw-Hill, 1977.

Wilson, C. Anne. *Food and Drink in Britain*. Harmondsworth: Penguin, 1976.

——. "The French Connection: Part I." *Petits Propos Culinaires* 2 (1979):10–17.

——. "The French Connection: Part II." *Petits Propos Culinaires* 4 (1980):8–20.

——. "The Saracen Connection: Arab Cuisine and the Mediaeval West: Part I." *Petits Propos Culinaires* 7 (1981):13–22.

——. "The Saracen Connection: Arab Cuisine and the Mediaeval West: Part II." *Petits Propos Culinaires* 8 (1981):19–27.

Wimmer, Otto. *Handbuch der Namen und Heiligen*. Munich, 1959.

Wiswe, Hans. "Ein mittelniederdeutsches Kochbuch des 15. Jahrhunderts." *Braunschweigisches Jahrbuch* 37 (1956):19–55.

——. *Kulturgeschichte der Kochkunst: Kochbücher und Rezepte aus zwei Jahrtausenden mit einem lexikalischen Anhang zur Fachsprache von Eva Hepp*. Munich: Heinz Moos, n.d.

Wolf, John B. *Louis XIV*. London: Panther Books, 1970.

Wortley Montagu, Mary. *The Letters and Works of Lady Mary Wortley Montagu*. Edited by Lord Wharncliffe and W. Moy Thomas. 2 vols. London, 1893.

Wühr, Hans. *Altes Essgerät: Löffel—Messer—Gabel*. Wohnkunst und Hausrat: Einst und jetzt 36. Darmstadt: Franz Schneekluth, 1961.

Wynne, Peter. *Apples*. New York: Hawthorne Books, 1975.

Yates, Frances A. *The Valois Tapestries*. 2d ed. London: Routledge and Kegan Paul, 1975.

Zambrini, Francesco, ed. *Il Libro della cucina del secolo XIV*. Bologna, 1863.

Index

The italicized page references are to the illustrations.

Cook's Index